DOCKWORKER
POWER

THE WORKING CLASS IN AMERICAN HISTORY

Editorial Advisors
James R. Barrett, Julie Greene, William P. Jones,
Alice Kessler-Harris, and Nelson Lichtenstein

A list of books in the series appears at the end of this book.

DOCKWORKER POWER

RACE AND ACTIVISM
IN DURBAN AND THE
SAN FRANCISCO BAY AREA

PETER COLE

UNIVERSITY OF ILLINOIS PRESS
Urbana, Chicago, and Springfield

Publication supported by a grant from the Howard D.
and Marjorie I. Brooks Fund for Progressive Thought.

Library of Congress Cataloging-in-Publication Data
Names: Cole, Peter, 1969– author.
Title: Dockworker power : race and activism in Durban
    and the San Francisco Bay area / Peter Cole.
Other titles: Working class in American history.
Description: Urbana : University of Illinois Press, 2018. |
    Series: The working class in American history | Includes
    bibliographical references and index.
Identifiers: LCCN 2018033487 | ISBN 9780252042072 (hardcover :
    alk. paper) | ISBN 9780252083761 (pbk. : alk. paper)
Subjects: LCSH: Stevedores —Labor unions —California —San
    Francisco —History. | Stevedores —South Africa —Durban
    —History. | Stevedores —Political activity —California —San
    Francisco —History. | Stevedores —Political activity —South
    Africa —Durban —History. | Labor unions —California —San
    Francisco —History. | Civil rights movements —California —
    San Francisco —History. | Anti-apartheid movements —South
    Africa —Durban —History.
Classification: LCC HD8039.L82 U65123 2018 | DDC 331.761387164
    —dc23
LC record available at https://lccn.loc.gov/2018033487
ISBN 9780252050824 (e-book)

*I dedicate this book to all workers on the waterfront,
particularly those who shared their stories,
over the past decade, with me.*

Contents

Illustrations

Maps

Figures

Acknowledgments

Despite the name on the cover, my book—like most others—has been a collective endeavor. At the risk of forgetting someone, I want to thank some who helped make this book possible.

I confess I felt a little uneasy, at first, diving into writing South African history, as I am not formally trained in the field and, therefore, was mindful of being an interloper or worse. Nevertheless, a vast array of South Africans and South Africanists welcomed and assisted me. After spending many months in the "rainbow country" over the past decade, I have come to love South Africa, and I remain inspired by its history of struggle for freedom, equality, and justice. Having already spent a great deal of time in the San Francisco Bay Area, I felt no such hesitation researching there; in fact, my fascination with the Bay Area has only grown over time though the ravages of gentrification have pushed nearly all my friends out of San Francisco over to the East Bay, which ain't cheap either!

Historians love archivists and librarians, and I am no different. In South Africa, thanks to Nellie Somers, Mwelela Cele, and others at the Killie Campbell Africana Library in Durban; Gabriele Mohale, Michele Pickover, and others at the Historical Papers of the University of the Witwatersrand; Clive Kirkwood and others at the University of Cape Town Libraries Special Collections; Yolanda Meyer at the Transnet Heritage Library in Johannesburg; the librarians at the Don Africana Central Reference Library in Durban; and staff members at the National Archives in both Pretoria and Durban. The community of scholars who study or work in South Africa deeply impresses me. Shout-outs to Peter Alexander, Gabeba Baderoon,

Rita Barnard, Terry Barnes, Omar Basha, Patrick Bond, Keith Breckenridge and Cath Burns, Ralph Callebert, Marcelle Dawson, Ashwin Desai, Bernard Dubbeld, Sarah Duff, Kate Evans, Tyler Fleming, Bill Freund, Jon Hyslop, Bridget Kenny, Vukile Khumalo, Peter Limb, Arianna Lissoni, Ian Macqueen, Brij Maharaj, Laura Mitchell, Sean and Barbara Morrow, Kathy Oberdeck, Neil Roos, Srila Roy, Shaun Ruggunan, Luke Sinwell, Jabulani Sithole, Goolam Vahed, Natasha Vally, Lucien van der Walt and Nicole Ulrich, and Leslie Witz. Karl von Holdt, Eddie Webster, and others in the Society, Work and Development Institute (SWOP) at Wits—now an institutional home for me—were most supportive. Patrick Bond, Brij Maharaj, and others also welcomed me at the University of KwaZulu-Natal's Centre for Civil Society. Jane Barrett formerly of the South African Transport and Allied Workers Union (SATAWU), who introduced me to SATAWU members and others, both in "Joburg" and Durban, was of tremendous assistance. Dear friends I've made along the way include Claire Ceruti, Kenichi Serino, and Botsang Mmope in Johannesburg and Soweto; Tony Botto and his family in Athlone (thanks to Henry Trotter's connection); Glen Thompson, who took me surfing in Muizenberg; and in Durban—where I love me some veg curry bunnies—Lauren and Walter Shapiro, along with Nellie and her family.

I also am deeply fortunate to have a large community in the United States who supported me. Again, my heartfelt thanks to folks in the San Francisco Bay Area and beyond: Robin Walker, Gene Vrana, Craig Merilees, Roy San Filippo, Peter Olney, and others at the ILWU Library and Archives at its international headquarters; Catherine Powell, Tanya Hollis, and others at San Francisco State University's Labor Archives and Research Center; Gina Bardi at the San Francisco Maritime National Historical Park Research Center; Claude Marks at the Freedom Archives; Chris Root and Richard Knight of African Activist Archive; Esmeralda Kale at the Melville J. Herskovits Library of African Studies at Northwestern University; and Chris Carlsson and LisaRuth Elliott, who operate Shaping San Francisco/FoundSF and even provide local labor history tours by bike! Activists, friends, and scholars in the Bay Area include Alex and Harriet Bagwell, Sean Burns, Mat Callahan, Bob Cherny, Stacy Cole (no relation!), Lincoln Cushing, Jason Ferreira, Segie Govender, Archie Green, Gifford Hartman, Jack Heyman, Toby Higbie, Marcus Holder, Robert Irminger, Howard and Isis Keylor, Richard Mead, Brian McWilliams, Mike Miller, Herb Mills, Bill Proctor, Stacey Rodgers, "the other" Clarence Thomas, Jack Thorpe and Sharon Virtue, Walter Turner, and Steve Zeltzer. Matt Freedman and Kyra Millich hosted me numerous times, as did Jimmy and Mary Jo Rice. Thanks also to other Bay Area friends who tolerated my rambling on about ILWU Local 10, including those in Salon Soleil off and on the playa in Black Rock City. I must single out the generosity and knowledge of Harvey Schwartz, who, more than anyone, assisted me. Beyond the Bay, scholars across North America have offered me assistance, including John Beck, Martha Biondi, Connor Casey, Leon Fink, Erik Gellman, Jim Gregory, Rick Halpern, Alex Lichtenstein, Peter Limb, Prexy Nesbitt, Marcus Rediker, Jim Barrett, Katherine Turk, and the anonymous reviewers of my book manuscript.

I wish to thank my colleagues at Western Illinois University and friends too numerous to mention who make life in Macomb so pleasurable. WIU librarians John Stierman and Bill Thompson, and those in Interlibrary Loan, provided endless assistance.

I want to express another heap of thanks to those who allowed me to interview them (some named above) but especially acknowledge those who since have passed away. To those who wish to interview anyone, ever, don't delay! To George Cobbs, Carol Cuénod (Schwartz), Archie Green, Herb Mills, Leo Robinson, Don Watson, Cleophas Williams, and "Captain Josh" Josiah Williams . . . presente!

My friends and family often do not know what the hell I'm talking about, but they love and support me nevertheless. My cousin Philip keeps me honest, as do my brother, David, and mother, Barbara. Finally, not only does my partner, Wendy Pearlman, support and believe in me, she helped me figure out how to shoehorn all the different topics I want to discuss inside a single book! For that and much more, my thanks and love.

I would like to thank the journals that published earlier versions of some of this material.

- Portions of chapters 4 and 5 first appeared in "The Tip of the Spear: How Longshore Workers in the San Francisco Bay Area Survived the Container Revolution," *Employee Responsibilities and Rights Journal* 25, no. 3 (2013): 201–216.
- An earlier version of chapter 6 appeared as "No Justice, No Ships Get Loaded: Political Boycotts on the Durban and San Francisco Bay Waterfronts," *International Review of Social History* 58, no. 2 (2013): 185–217. Portions of the chapter also appeared in "An Injury to One Is an Injury to All: San Francisco Longshore Workers and the Fight against Apartheid," *Journal of Civil and Human Rights* 1, no. 2 (2015): 158–181, and "Hooks Down! Anti-Apartheid Activism and Solidarity Among Maritime Unions in Australia and the United States," co-authored with Peter Limb, *Labor History* 58, no. 3 (2017): 303–326.

DOCKWORKER
POWER

INTRODUCTION

The shipping industry has a feature that should
never be underestimated—the economic power of the
longshoremen is fantastic compared to most workers,
the amount of economic leverage they have.

—Louis Goldblatt, interview

Dockworkers have power. Integral to shipping, the world's first global industry, and hence instrumental to the rise of capitalism, these so-called unskilled workers amassed—through collective action, ideological commitment, and sheer force of will—a surprising amount of power. As any other human beings would, they have used their leverage to improve their own lot. This book, however, focuses on how they deployed their power on behalf of a vast array of other social movements, particularly to advance racial equality and freedom in their own unions, cities, and nations as well as beyond their shores. In the San Francisco Bay Area, Local 10 of the International Longshore and Warehouse Union (ILWU) turned itself from a nearly all-white union in the 1930s into one that fully integrated its own ranks and, thirty years later, became majority black. Bay Area dockworkers also actively participated in the local and national civil-rights movement. As with the handful of unions and other institutions fiercely committed to racial equality, many leftists led and belonged to ILWU Local 10. Durban's all-black dockworkers, by contrast, did not have the right to organize a union, nor did they even imagine an integrated workforce. From the 1940s into the early 1970s, however, through their considerable efforts—especially downing tools (South African, and British, slang for work stoppages)—they proved among the most important forces in Durban that fought apartheid. Moreover, they periodically wielded their power in solidarity with social movements in other nations. Hence, in these great port cities, radical dockworkers—very much leftists—played catalytic roles in some of the world's greatest social movements since World War II, particularly the US civil-rights movement and the South African anti-apartheid movement. How dockworkers in Durban and the San Francisco Bay Area each fought for racial equality in their home countries as well as abroad constitute two of this book's three main themes.

Since employers could not use one of their most reliable tactics to weaken workers—dividing and conquering via racial divisions—they resorted to another time-tested strategy, introducing a new technology. The ILWU became the first waterfront union in the world to negotiate the transition to container shipping, in which the manual loading and offloading of cargo was replaced by massive cranes moving large, standardized containers, thereby drastically reducing the amount of time and number of workers needed to process a ship's cargo. Its leaders chose to negotiate rather than resist and, though the union survived, it had far fewer (if far better-paid) members. Containers particularly devastated dockworkers in ports where they had less power, in Durban as elsewhere, especially in the short run, though in both the Bay Area and Durban they managed to hold on to their unions. From the 1960s into the 1980s, containerization expanded trade by orders of magnitude, dramatically increased productivity, sent the number of dockworkers plummeting, increased employers' profits, and weakened dockworkers' unions. The work culture profoundly changed, but dockworkers' historical memory, commitment to one another, and willingness to engage in collective action did not. Building on their legacies of militancy and solidarity—and still occupying a logistical choke point of one of the world's key industries—they restored some of their power and unions while earning themselves higher wages. Further, despite being fewer in number, dockworkers continued acting on behalf of others, near and far, who suffered from oppression. The book's third main theme, then, is the way Bay Area and Durban dockworkers grappled with containerization, one of the most revolutionary if overlooked technological changes in the twentieth century. Important in its own right, examining how dockworkers persevered in the face of a game-changing technology remains relevant in light of the fact that technology continues to remake the nature of work in nearly every industry the world over. Examining containerization also is something of a corrective for a widely held view of technology—as destroyer of worker power and unions—that, admittedly, is all too often true but need not be.

To understand these matters, I compare Durban and the San Francisco Bay Area, ports vital to their cities, regions, countries, and oceans. Examining port cities is instructive for historians of all interests, but especially for those interested in global history. As Frederick Cooper noted, "Ports are not simply specific instances of a general phenomenon; they are connected to one another. Whatever the spatial fixity of a port, the reason for its existence was its links with other specific locations"—quite often in other nations and other parts of the world. In Durban and the Bay Area, shipping has dominated the local and regional economies for domestic and global trade while being central to their identities to this very day. California historian Kevin Starr wrote that San Francisco "functioned as the most notable urban center west of Chicago and east of Hong Kong" in the second half of the nineteenth century. San Francisco and the entire metropolitan region, generally called the Bay Area, remained the dominant one on the US West Coast and entire West until the last few decades of the twentieth century, when the city of Los Angeles and southern California's combined megaport of Los Angeles–Long Beach supplanted it. The Bay Area, however, remains quite important to the cultural, economic, political, and social affairs of the United States. Similarly, Durban was and still is South Africa's leading port. As Jonathan Hyslop declared, "Durban went from being a very marginal British colonial settlement to becoming the greatest port of southern Africa and one of the biggest in the southern hemisphere." With its harbor as the base, Durban became a major manufacturing hub and population center, though Johannesburg and Cape Town remain larger and more influential.

Comparing the history of dockworkers in two great ports in two nations follows Saskia Sassen in her influential work *The Global City*, connecting the local and the global while somewhat decentering nation-states as a topic. As mighty ports, Durban and San Francisco were "global cities" if not possessing the capital or gravitas of a London, New York, or Tokyo, à la Sassen. And though often overlooked, dockworkers were central to shipping and thus to their cities. They were, as Alice Mah highlighted in *Port Cities and Global Legacies*, the "iconic symbols of urban identity within port cities. In many ways, the history of the waterfront represents the backbone of historic port city identities and mythologies." The ports played foundational roles in Durban and San Francisco.[1]

Investigating the history of maritime labor is fascinating but also necessary, for dockworkers and sailors possessed the power to interrupt trade and, hence, the economy itself—locally, nationally, and globally. German philosopher Peter Sloterdijk opined, "With every ship that is launched, capital begins the movement which characterizes the spatial 'revolution' of the Modern Age"; but those ships also created (maritime) workers. The word that describes workers' most powerful weapon, to stop work or "strike," emerged from the sea. Historians Peter Linebaugh and Marcus Rediker described how, in 1768, sailors "struck (i.e., took down) the sails of their vessels, crippling the commerce of the empire's leading city [London] and adding the strike to the armory of resistance." While some recent commentators write of the "frictionless flows" of goods and capital, nothing could be further from the truth. As sociologist Deborah Cowen contended, ports are "where one can expose the seam of the supposedly seamless flows of global capital," for just as "rogue" waves can upend massive container ships, dockworkers can stop loading or unloading cargo, as the epigraph from ILWU leader Lou Goldblatt highlights at the start of this introduction. Dockworker power is understood the world over, as the general manager supervising Durban dockworkers explained in 1975: "Two factors predominate in Port working all over the world: 1. The necessity to turn around a ship in the shortest possible time and 2. The vulnerability of a Port when its Work-force withholds its labour." While these ideas also apply to other forms of transport (wagons, railroads, trucks, and so on), the very emergence and growing domination of capitalism depended on shipping. Simply put, without the circulation of goods by sea, the capitalism that Adam Smith and Karl Marx so thoughtfully analyzed would not have emerged. Michel Foucault understood this reality, too: "the boat has . . . been for our civilization, from the sixteenth [or even fifteenth] century until the present, the great instrument of economic development." Alas, as Alice Mah wrote, "many scholars have underestimated the *continuing significance* of material support trade [shipping] to global capitalism." Indeed, Rose George titled her popular book on the shipping industry *Ninety Percent of Everything*, emphasizing her argument that "the clothes on your back, gas in your car, and food on your plate" are transported by sea.[2]

Containerization, now an intermodal system of logistics or supply chains that includes rail and road, is among the most significant symbols and components of global capital even though the people most directly affected by it, dockworkers and sailors, are hidden. The philosopher-filmmakers Allan Sekula and Noël Burch rightly declared in *Forgotten Space*, "the sea remains the crucial space of globalization. Nowhere else is the disorientation, violence, and alienation of contemporary capitalism more manifest, but this truth is not self-evident, and must be approached as a puzzle, or mystery, a problem to be solved." Even they, however, fell into the trap, in that other parts of their ominous film, ironically, make dockworkers invisible. Mah clarified this point by returning to place: "While the story of containerization is often neglected in accounts of globalization and deindustrialization, it has been central to accounts of port cities." Durban and the San Francisco Bay Area have much in common with other port cities, such as Liverpool, whose Capital of Culture website declared, "Port cities do not always feel loved or understood by their countrymen, they have an identity with each other rather than with their domestic neighbours." While agreeing with Mah and the Liverpudlian website, this book centers on waterfront workers, just as their cities' original neighborhoods—as in every other port—orbited their harbors.[3]

This project compares the history of two sets of waterfront workers—their militant struggles against racism, experiences with containerization, and solidarity with freedom struggles elsewhere—to draw out common and distinctive themes. In many nations and on every continent, dockworkers have proven among the most likely workers to strike and unionize. Their history of militancy—be it in

Hamburg or Mombasa, Sydney or Valparaiso—is remarkable and depends on the collective nature of their work, their strategic location in the global economy, and their cosmopolitan nature. Many scholars have investigated dockworkers because of their militancy and radicalism, the most significant scholarship resulting in a publication titled *Dock Workers: International Explorations in Comparative Labour History, 1790–1970*, spearheaded by the International Institute of Social History and with contributions by several dozen historians. In its introduction, Sam Davies and Klaus Weinhauer argued that "this important occupational group" should be "considered in a comparative fashion on an international scale." Sadly, comparative labor history generally, and of dockworkers in particular, remains a rarity. Two of the only examples are Colin Davis's book on London and New York City and historian Jordi Ibarz's extensive 2016 unpublished survey of two hundred historical studies—written in English, French, Portuguese, and Spanish—which revealed the great many gaps in the field. In addition to other shortcomings Ibarz identified, *Dockworker Power* helps correct the following: (1) almost all histories of dockworkers focus on a single port, (2) few studies exist on African ports, with Durban being an exception, (3) few comparative studies exist, (4) no comparison of North-South ports exists, (5) few studies examine both the casual and decasualized eras of a port, (6) almost no port or dock labor studies combine the traditional and container eras, and (7) and few studies examine dockworkers in the container era, period. Indeed, the editors of *Dock Workers*, the mandatory starting point for all subsequent studies, consciously ended their project with the advent of containerization, as did Davis. There has been virtually no work by historians on how containerization transformed the labor of dockworkers or their unions. Further, Hyslop recently noted that "in the extraordinary development in recent decades of global and transnational history, on the one hand, and of new kinds of critical imperial history, on the other, ships and harbours have remained somewhat out of sight." *Dockworker Power* examines these understudied topics and others by crossing scholarly boundaries rarely breached, including global North-South and industrialized-developing country divides.[4]

This book describes, analyzes, and compares how dockworkers built on a distinctive occupational subculture and used their strategic position in what Anna Tsing named "supply chain capitalism" to improve their own conditions and contribute to domestic and global social movements. Dockworkers in both ports have proud, strong, long-standing, and self-consciously militant traditions of organizing and unionism. Numerous strikes in both ports affected their respective cities and even their nations. Both waterfront workforces were heavily (San Francisco) or entirely (Durban) black. Both sets of dockworkers had left-wing union traditions and undertook actions that were not simply pragmatic and self-interested. For instance, as Bruce Nelson wrote in his classic *Workers on the Waterfront*, when

San Francisco longshoremen helped create the ILWU, they participated in "a long overdue festive upheaval, a search for more humane and just patterns of work relations, and the flowering of an insurgent consciousness." The Bay Area's union and informal organizing of Durban dockworkers proved quite important in their respective labor and antiracist movements, which were often interconnected. Their embrace of direct-action tactics proved effective in an industry predicated on the mantra "the ship must sail on time." The power of dockworkers, predictably, rankled employers, whose embrace of containerization must be understood as a desire to both increase productivity and break worker control.[5]

The emergence of containers as a new technology in the global economy's most important industry revolutionized waterfront work and, indeed, the world. For millennia, the job of loading and unloading cargo from ships had changed little, primarily relying on the backbreaking manual labor of gangs of men to do the heavy lifting, literally. Generally, workers were hired on a "casual" basis, meaning for a specific shift or ship and with no certainty about when or whether another job would come. The end of the casual hiring system—decasualization—arrived in the Bay Area and Durban waterfronts prior to containers, though sometimes the two emerged together. In 1934, in the aftermath of their Big Strike in San Francisco and all West Coast ports, the resurgent union decasualized work via a union-controlled dispatch hall. By contrast, in 1959 employers decasualized the Durban waterfront to disempower dockworkers, who repeatedly had stopped work even though strikes were illegal for black workers—a legal loophole that allowed these casual (black) laborers to exert power despite apartheid. Worker power motivated both shifts, but San Francisco dockworkers saw decasualization as benefiting them and so initiated the change, whereas Durban employers initiated decasualization because they believed it would weaken dockworkers. During the 1960s in San Francisco (and along the entire West Coast), the hiring hall provided the ILWU with some leverage in responding to containerization. This technological system represented an entirely new method of working cargo, in which twenty- and forty-foot metal boxes, or containers, loaded often far from the waterfront, were moved off and onto ships using huge dockside cranes. Over time, huge ships transported ever larger numbers of containers. The very nature of dock work, shipping, and the global economy irrevocably changed.[6]

Dockworkers' experiences with containers shared much with those of workers in other industries affected by technological change worldwide. Time and again in the nineteenth and twentieth centuries, new technologies vitiated unions or undermined worker militancy and power. Particularly in heavy industries like coal mining or steel manufacturing, new technologies allowed employers to pay workers less, reduce benefits, and break once-mighty unions. Of course, awareness of this reality is neither novel nor recent. Capitalism's best-known critic, Karl Marx, wrote in 1857, "The appropriation of living labor by capital is directly expressed in machinery. It is a scientifically based analysis, together with the application of mechanical laws that enables the machine to carry out the work formerly done by the worker himself. . . . hence we have the struggle of the worker against machinery. What used to be the activity of the living worker has become that of the machine." Thus far, the twenty-first century appears no different. For instance, a 2013 article in the *New York Times* laid out just how near we are to a future in which robots do increasingly more of the factory work that humans have done for the past few centuries.[7]

Generally, and unsurprisingly, workers quickly realized the high stakes presented by new technologies. As early as the 1810s, English workers in the world's first modern manufacturing industry, textiles, demonstrated their fear of and opposition to job-destroying technologies by sabotaging machine looms—what the prominent historian Eric Hobsbawm called "collective bargaining by riot." Their actions gave rise to the term *Luddite*, which has since been invoked whenever a human expresses suspicion or fear of a new technology, but one's view of Luddites often depends upon one's class position. Employers claim workers "can't stop the march of progress" by resisting new technologies, but many others—and it should be noted that the working class remains larger than the middle and upper classes—have been far more sympathetic to those whose work and lives are threatened. Another great English historian, E. P. Thompson, cautioned against painting Luddism "as a blind opposition to machinery," arguing, rather, "What was at issue was the 'freedom' of the capitalist to destroy the customs of the trade" by means including "new machinery." To give but one example of containerization's huge impacts, in New York City, the busiest US port for 150 years, 35,000 dockworkers moved 13.2 million tons of (precontainerization) cargo in 1954, but in 1995 a mere 3,700 moved 44.9 million tons, an incredible 3,118 percent increase in cargo handled per worker.[8]

Though the entire nature of waterfront work changed irreversibly, little research has been conducted about containers' effects on labor. For example, *Dock Workers*, the most comprehensive global history of this trade, consciously ended its study prior to containerization. Labor and business historians, regardless of the cities or nations they study, largely have abdicated study of the matter to the occasional economist, sociologist, geographer, or popular writer. Perhaps more surprising, few maritime (labor) historians have examined this epochal shift's impacts. This study starts to fill this yawning gap. What also makes the ILWU Local 10 case so interesting was that this union was the *first* to negotiate containerization; their 1960 contract gained these dockworkers a "share of the machine" and protected current members' jobs at a time when San Francisco was the greatest port on the US West Coast *and* the first to see rapid containerization. Durban ports received containers much later, which is not surprising when one considers South Africa's relative place in the global economy. The experience of dockworkers in Durban is typical of ports with nonunion or weaker workforces, but that case must also be discussed in the context of apartheid in the late 1970s.[9]

Similarly, historians and other scholars of technology have undertaken few studies of containerization and none on its impacts on dockworkers, a topic that straddles the nexus of technology and labor. In a recent review, Jonathan Coppersmith explained the efficacy of comparison, "for the history of technology, comparative approaches offer very tempting fruit. The history of the automobile [e.g.] looks very different in Europe than the United States (not to mention the variations within Europe)." He continued, "Looking at the evolution of a technology across societies as well as across time can reveal far more than just looking at one country or region." Despite his statements' seeming logic, one of the most impactful technologies of the past few generations (containers) largely remains untouched. Although perhaps obvious, Coppersmith offered one explanation, "Comparative history is particularly hard to do well, especially for one person. You are studying different environments with different cultures." Yet Kate Brown, author of a recent, award-winning comparative history of technology, discussed why it is nevertheless vital: "My larger point is that by staying in boundaries, within carefully compartmentalized national histories, it is easy to miss very big stories that are right there, in plain site [*sic*]." The dockworkers' experiences with containers seems now ever-present and important, yet no historian has sufficiently analyzed the impacts of the ILWU's historic agreement with employers—the first dockside union in the world to negotiate containers. It should go without saying that no scholar has compared the San Francisco experience with another port, let alone one in another part of the world, including Africa's greatest one.[10]

Indeed, by comparing the similarities and differences of dockworkers, their efforts, and their organizations' experiences, we can learn more about both groups, what is unique about each group and nation, and what might be more universal. George Fredrickson, among the greatest comparative historians, rhetorically asked, "How is one to know if a process or development is really the unique product of a special constellation of forces and influences within a given society unless one has actually compared it with analogous cases elsewhere? To the extent that historians persist in looking for causes or explanations for the phenomenon they describe and are not simply content to be mere chroniclers or storytellers, they must perforce develop comparative perspectives."

This book seeks to discern, among many other issues: how these cities shape their workers and vice versa; how the processes of industrialization and urbanization interact and evolve, simultaneously shaped by movements from below and the nation-state and corporations from above; how race relations develop among groups, in cities, and across nations and the globe; how worker activity (for example, strikes and unionism) relates to antiracist struggles citywide, nationally, and transnationally; how dockworkers were uniquely situated to play pivotal roles in each city's labor and other social movements; and what Durban can teach about the San Francisco Bay Area and vice versa. For one, the history of dockworkers in Durban shows Americanists that worker movements simply cannot be ignored, especially as the legendary 1973 Durban strikes (triggered, in part, by a 1972 dock strike) played such a crucial role in the reemergence of the struggle against apartheid in the 1970s. By contrast, the bold antiracist efforts of the ILWU largely remain outside discussions of Bay Area and US-wide histories of the civil-rights movement, though the ILWU and its members in Local 10 fought long and hard for racial equality. Thus, one of this book's primary objectives, on the US side, is to increase awareness of the vital ILWU contributions to the Bay Area's and the nation's social movement history. Following Fredrickson, this comparative history very much strives to "be of equal interest to specialists on all of the societies examined."[11]

South Africa and the United States have much in common, though this fact may not seem obvious. US Senator Robert F. Kennedy gave perhaps the most concise and thoughtful explanation during a University of Cape Town speech in 1966:

> I came here because of my deep interest and affection for a land settled by the Dutch in the mid-seventeenth century, then taken over by the British, and at last independent; a land in which the native inhabitants were at first subdued, but relations with whom remain a problem to this day; a land which defined itself on a hostile frontier; a land which has tamed rich natural resources through the energetic application of modern technology; a land which once imported slaves, and now must struggle to wipe out the last traces of that former bondage. I refer, of course, to the United States of America.

Alongside Kennedy's cogent analysis exists a rich tradition among historians, social scientists, literary critics, and others who compare South Africa and the United States; hence, this book need not rehash that topic. For many SA-US scholars, the attraction is based upon the ways each society has grappled with diversity and seen powerful social movements emerge to combat racial inequality. Both countries are divided by systems of racial oppression and yet both have overcome the worst of those systems while also inspiring the world with promises of freedom and equality. Still, many differences between the two exist: (post-)industrial versus developing economy; African Americans and immigrants who possessed citizenship rights versus the formal denial of rights for the African (black) majority until 1994; the existence of formal unions in the United States in contrast with the legal denial of such worker rights for blacks; and, perhaps most significant, that African Americans always have been a distinct (albeit important) minority of the total

US population but blacks of numerous ethnic groups (along with "coloreds" and Indians) make up the vast majority of South Africans. Historians must accommodate these and other divergent aspects of this comparison; fortunately, these differences are not insurmountable.[12]

This book also employs transnational methods and self-consciously belongs to the field of global labor history. Although framing histories within national boundaries is understandable and useful, many subjects benefit from being repositioned in a comparative, transnational, or global fashion. Ian Tyrrell described transnational history simply as "the movement of peoples, ideas, technologies and institutions across national boundaries." As a matter of course, those interested in the maritime world have engaged in this method for generations prior to the formal designation of transnationalism, because we see oceans as highways rather than barriers. Scholars such as Shel Stromquist and Leon Fink demonstrated the merits of transnational labor history on both land and sea. Marcel van der Linden, most notably, championed global labor history—which "focuses on transnational and even the transcontinental study of labour relations and workers' social movements in the widest sense of the word." He warned historians not to fall into the trap of imagining any nation's history "as a *self-contained process*" and argued that the history of the world's working classes should not exclusively be "interpreted according to North-Atlantic [and Eurocentric] schemes." Decolonization across the postwar world also necessitates a global approach in that Pan-Africanism, labor internationalism, and (labor) migration continue to flow across transnational and transcontinental imagined communities. Finally, I would underline van der Linden's observation about "the strongly intensified contacts between historians of different countries and continents" also contributed to the comparative, transnational, and global viewpoints. In using these approaches, *Dockworker Power* reframes familiar topics by considering cross-border linkages, activities, and processes that "methodological nationalism" obscures.[13]

This book rests upon the assumption that both South Africa and the United States practiced racial capitalism and that the varied, deep intersections of class and race in these two nations cannot and should not be decoupled. In both societies, capitalism's emergence and evolution depended on and were inextricably bound to white supremacy. In South Africa, scholars who advanced this idea, according to Alex Lichtenstein, "linked the rise of segregation and formalized state racism to the 'mineral revolution' of the late 19th century, the penetration of Southern Africa by British capital and imperialism and the accompanying growth of the migrant labor system." South African historians Martin Legassick and Harold Wolpe, among others, contended that apartheid built on this edifice in which racial segregation and migratory labor policies simultaneously aided capitalism and white supremacy or, in Legassick's words, "apartheid and capitalism were two sides of the same bloody coin." Political scientist Cedric J Robinson was the first US scholar to apply this concept to the United States. In his path-breaking book *Black Marxism*, he wrote, "The development, organization, and expansion of capitalist society pursued essentially racial directions," in other words the economic system rested upon racism and racial violence as ordering principles. Considering this book's focus on South Africa and the United States, it is appropriate that, as Robin Kelley recently wrote, "during a sabbatical year in England, Robinson encountered intellectuals who used the phrase 'racial capitalism' to refer to South Africa's economy under apartheid. He [Robinson] developed it from a description of a *specific* system to a way of understanding the *general* history of modern capitalism."[14]

The application of racial capitalism in the United States continues to gain credence thanks to a raft of excellent recent scholarship, especially on slavery's centrality to the rise of industrialization. Edward Baptist argued in his prize-winning book *The Half Has Never Been Told: Slavery and the Making of American Capitalism*, "the expansion of American capitalism [was built] on the backs of enslaved human beings." For instance, slaveholders turned black slaves into financial investments, just as bonds were bought and sold throughout the Western world from New York City to London. Similarly, Sven Beckert's *Empire of Cotton* provides an authoritative account of how cotton launched the Industrial Revolution in the United States and Europe. Textile manufacturing, after all, was capitalism's first manufacturing industry with cotton its raw material. Cotton, primarily grown by millions of African slaves in the US South and processed by millworkers from Massachusetts to England and continental Europe, provided immense profits for financiers, industrialists, and slaveholders on both sides of the Atlantic. So, too, in the twentieth century as Thomas Sugrue noted, "Detroit's postwar urban crisis emerged as the consequence of two of the most important, interrelated, and unresolved problems in American history: that capitalism generates economic inequality and that African Americans have disproportionately borne the impact of that inequality."[15]

The concept of racial capitalism is also linked to the classic and sometimes vexing race-class debate, as though one identity, if either, could matter more. I follow Dave Roediger, who named W. E. B. DuBois as his primary influence, "at least in the US, the most pressing task for historians of race and class is not to draw precise lines separating race and class but to draw lines connecting race and class." The same applies, as Rob Lambert wrote, to "the South African formulation as racial capitalism." To Lambert and others of similar mind, South African "political unionism collapses the [race-class] divide, and provides the basis for new forms of struggle and transformation." Hence, this book presumes that race and class always are twinned and intends to keep these matters conjoined. Just as capitalism helped make white supremacy, the other half of the equation is that "rainbow coalitions of the oppressed," to use Robin Blackburn's phrase, simultaneously fought racial and economic oppression. Dockworkers on the Durban and San Francisco Bay waterfronts belonged to and sought to overhaul societies built on racial capitalism. Even their short-term economic demands had political ramifications, and they integrated race matters into their organizations and goals, which is not surprising in light of their demographics and the fact that race has proven a central fault line in both societies.[16]

Chapter 1 provides necessary historical background and context for the rest of the book. Some material will be familiar to many, but which material is familiar will likely vary from reader to reader. I hope this book's readership will include some people more knowledgeable about San Francisco and the United States while others will know Durban and South Africa far better. Other readers will know about containerization and maritime history but not labor, racial, or other social-justice movements. Some readers will bring their expertise on the civil rights, anti-apartheid, or other black movements to this text. Accordingly, and on the basis of my experiences presenting research in public and in writing, chapter 1 provides background information on the histories of these port cities, including their cultural, demographic, economic, maritime, and political history; race relations; dock work and dockworkers; and labor organizing in these ports. Chapters 2 and 3 examine how and why dockworkers in Durban and the San Francisco Bay Area fought for racial equality, locally and nationally, which also had the effect of empowering themselves, their unions, and related social justice movements. Worker power proved important in the political push for racial equality, but workplace gains also were central to their projects; no less a figure than Dr. Martin Luther King Jr. once quipped, "What good does it do to be able to eat at a lunch counter if you can't buy a hamburger?" Chapter 2 explores the origins of ILWU Local 10 and how its nearly all-white membership committed itself to racial integration and then set about accomplishing it. There were, and are, few organizations in the United States as successful at diversifying and integrating their ranks. Once achieving this goal, Local 10 fought to increase the number of blacks in other ILWU locals, the Bay Area's maritime industry, local governments, and area businesses. In Durban, dockworkers agitated repeatedly in the 1940s and 1950s, using their casual status to maximum benefit. In so doing, they demonstrated that blacks had power, particularly on the job, and were willing and able to use it. Their work stoppages must be understood as central to the fight against apartheid—and, more broadly, African liberation struggles—just as employers and government officials viewed them. Dockworkers demonstrated their savvy by exploiting other opportunities, like wartime labor shortages. Ultimately, employers and local government officials, who shared common interests and fully understood the implications of black dockworker power, overhauled the entire hiring system in 1959 to reassert control and racial capitalism.[17]

Chapter 3 continues examining how dockworkers contributed to labor and other social movements in their respective cities. In the Bay Area during the 1960s and 1970s, longshoremen used their considerable power to advocate and agitate for a vast array of causes, though this book primarily focuses on struggles for ethnic and racial equality. Local 10 played a central role in the Bay Area civil-rights movement and provided support to the national movement, so much so that Dr. King traveled to San Francisco to learn from these longshoremen and receive an honorary membership in their union (like Paul Robeson before him). Similarly, Durban dockworkers' power on the job and ability to organize, despite multifarious legal and workplace obstacles, resulted in their stopping work in 1969, threatening to do so in 1971, and striking again in late 1972. That these actions occurred in the aftermath of massive efforts to shut down all anti-apartheid opposition is impressive, indeed shocking. In a time when almost no domestic opposition to apartheid remained, often referred to as the "quiet decade," Durban dockworkers demonstrated that blacks still possessed power in at least one venue—the workplace. The Durban Strikes of 1973 justifiably command an important place in the history of the struggle, but far too few historians and other people appreciate that Durban dockworkers helped inspire and educate African and Indian workers in Durban who laid down their tools in 1973. After reading these two chapters, the centrality of (black) dockworker power in the fight for equality in both societies should be apparent.

Chapters 4 and 5 shift the focus to explore one of the truly revolutionary technological changes in the post–World War II era, containerization, and how it affected those who moved cargo on and off ships. Though of tremendous import to global history, this topic remains somewhat invisible. In analyzing containers, I also tackle the interrelated matter of how workers were hired, traditionally done "casually." In doing so, the focus will be on power, as in who has it, how they got it, and how it was contested. Chapter 4 describes how Local 10 and the ILWU, in the 1930s, successfully ended casual hiring in San Francisco and instituted a union-run hiring hall to the chagrin of employers. Bay Area longshoremen became the "lords of the docks" for the next generation until employers successfully introduced containers to reset the power dynamic. In 1960, the ILWU became the world's first union to negotiate this process and the union, thus, is essential to understand. The ILWU leadership, particularly President Harry Bridges, chose to protect the current generation of members, none of whom was fired despite the drastic changes coming. Essentially, Bridges traded job protection and a "share of the machine," that is, a small part of the predicted profit, in exchange for not resisting. In Durban, the year prior, employers decasualized the waterfront to do something similar: reassert control over a powerful, well-organized (albeit informally) workforce. Durban did not experience containers for nearly twenty more years because employers and the state appeared content with the incredibly cheap labor provided by defanged black dockworkers.

Chapter 5 discusses the ongoing implications of containers for Bay Area longshoremen when employers introduced further changes to consolidate their resurgent power. When the union's leadership proved unwilling or unable to challenge employer authority, a massive rank-and-file rebellion, in the Bay Area and across the West Coast, resulted in the longest strike in US dock labor history, in 1971–72. This strike—which still rubs nerves in the union and has almost entirely escaped scholarly attention—failed to alter containerization and confirmed that employers ultimately had reassumed control. Truly, the ILWU never has been the same even though it remains a proud, progressive union that is relatively strong and militant. In Durban, employers and the state proved quite slow to transition to containerization, officially launching only in 1977. Containers were introduced, though, at a pivotal time in the struggle against apartheid, just a year after the Soweto student uprising. Although many black workers, after the Durban strikes, had begun organizing in the mid-late 1970s, dockworkers no longer remained in the struggle's front ranks. Instead, the late 1970s and early 1980s witnessed the evisceration of dockworker power as half of them were "retrenched" (laid off) as a result of containers and an inability to contest them. If not as central to the global capitalist project, South Africa's largest port, a major one in the southern hemisphere, is an excellent one to examine and compare with the Bay Area's, particularly in the differences between a workforce capable of negotiating from a position of strength and one with little power.

Chapter 6, while also comparative, examines a transnational topic, namely, how dockworkers in both the Bay Area and Durban engaged in activism on behalf of black and working-class struggles against authoritarian regimes in other countries. On multiple occasions, these two sets of dockworkers—as in other ports—boycotted cargo or ships from nations engaged in repressive policies. The main cases are when Local 10 rank-and-file activists refused to unload cargo from South Africa to protest apartheid, most dramatically for eleven days in 1984, and when Durban's union dockworkers, in 2008, refused to unload weapons intended for neighboring Zimbabwe, whose leader used his substantial military and police powers to destroy the electoral opposition. In both cases, primarily black dockworkers boycotted cargo in solidarity with black freedom struggles in other countries. The engagement of these people in transnational political actions also belonged to a black internationalist agenda, also known as Pan-Africanism. Their actions were similarly part of a working-class or labor internationalism, acting as part and on behalf of working-class struggles for democracy and power in other lands. Indeed,

Local 10 arguably contributed more to the US anti-apartheid movement than any other union did. Similarly, Durban dockworkers, and their union, demonstrated a commitment to democracy and working-class power across southern Africa. Dockworkers in both ports demonstrated a robust sense of working-class and black internationalism, believing they had the right and responsibility to act in solidarity with democratic struggles in other nations.

In the twenty-first century, as a result of containers, personal computers, the Internet, and other technological changes, the world has drastically changed. It may not be physically smaller, but humans are more connected culturally, economically, politically, and socially. For centuries, historians—myself included—mostly engaged in histories of specific nation-states largely in isolation from other nations. Globalization, with its many meanings, has prompted historians and other scholars to break away more and more from nation-focused studies. Nations, of course, still matter, but history never has been contained within individual nations. People, ideas, and goods always have moved around. Hence, this book seeks to engage with the increasingly interconnected world of (historical) scholarship and conversation happening across political boundaries. By comparing dockworkers' contributions to struggles for racial equality and democracy, the effects of containerization upon them (so vital to global trade), and their efforts to project power transnationally, I hope readers will learn about two great port cities as well as dockworker power.

CONTEXT

Great port cities are noted for being different, they have their own
particular identities, their own notions of: independence, freedom,
dissent, and cosmopolitanism. Their own perceptions of work,
justice, politics, and culture.

—Liverpool Capital of Culture 2008 (website)

Port cities matter, a lot. They are places where peoples, ideas, information, and commodities come together, are exchanged, and become transformed. They exert an outsized influence on economies, cultures, and imaginations. They are enthralling and fun. They are cosmopolitan, that is, places where diverse people and cultures converge, clash, and interact. They are global in that their inhabitants connect to people in and from faraway lands. Some might say port cities are translocal in that they are interconnected—as cities—and their identities are not entirely due to national allegiances. These descriptions apply to port cities on the Swahili Coast of East Africa, encircling the South China Sea, and countless other ports across the literal seven seas. Accordingly, dockworkers stood at the center of not only economic matters but also political and social ones in Durban and San Francisco that, in turn, shaped their respective nations.[1]

This chapter introduces two port cities on opposite sides of the globe. It starts with brief histories of Durban and the San Francisco Bay Area, highlighting the centrality of the maritime industry in both. Ethnic and racial demographics of the cities and workforces then are discussed. The chapter proceeds to the nature of dock labor generally and on these waterfronts along with, briefly, housing. Scholarship on dockworkers has firmly established that they share much in the work performed and, crucially, in its collective nature. Finally, efforts by Durban dockers (as they are known there) and Bay Area dockworkers to organize themselves via strikes, unions, and other methods is explored. Though the Introduction covered comparative methods, this chapter more fully establishes how much these two ports share.

A Brief History of Durban

Durban—South Africa's greatest port city—is located on the country's east coast, on the Indian Ocean, with a unique mix of residents. Curiously, Durban has an enormous Indian population and people regularly assert it has the largest Indian community outside South Asia. Some people call it the most English of South African cities because, demographically and culturally, it is more Anglo than Afrikaner. The city also has many African residents, particularly Zulus (the isiZulu term for Zulu people is amaZulu) who also are the largest African ethnic group in South Africa; in this book, the terms *African* and *black* will be used interchangeably. Since 2000, the city officially is eThekwini, the isiZulu name, though Durban remains the most commonly used term and is the one used throughout this book. The eThekwini municipality incorporates a huge metropolitan area that, in the United States, would encompass both the city and its suburbs, in other words, it is comparable to the San Francisco Bay Area. Many South Africans consider Durban a distant third to the larger, better known cities of Johannesburg and Cape Town. In South African history, Durban perhaps is best known for the Durban Strikes of 1973. Its subtropical climate and oceanside location translate into a climate considered lovely in the winter but quite hot and humid in the summer. Most important for this study, since the early twentieth century Durban has been the busiest port in South Africa and the entire African continent. Maritime economist Trevor Jones wrote, "the original establishment and subsequent development of the port is the reason why a diverse community and economy has located itself around the shores of the Bay of Natal; without Durban harbour this Bay would resemble many of the other picturesque but ultimately irrelevant tidal lagoons that proliferate on the KwaZulu-Natal coast."[2]

Humans likely first visited Durban and its well-protected harbor during the Stone Age, more than fifty thousand years ago. The first peoples to settle there probably are the ancestors of various Bantu-speaking peoples who migrated to the southernmost tip of Africa relatively recently, one to two thousand years ago, and who practiced a combination of farming and herding. Among these peoples, Zulus now are the best known and most numerous, though, before the nineteenth century, none of the Bantu-speaking peoples lived in large societies.[3]

European imperialism drastically altered the course of southern Africa. The first Europeans in the area, the Portuguese, arrived by sea. A volume of the Natal Regional Survey noted, "It was on Christmas Day, 1497, that Vasco da Gama, sailing northward from Mossel Bay, sighted land on the Pondoland coast near the Umzimvubu River and named it 'Terra Natalia' in commemoration of Christ's natal day. It was this stretch of coastline, therefore, that rightly earned the name of Natal." (See map 1.) A few days later, da Gama anchored in what first was named Port Natal

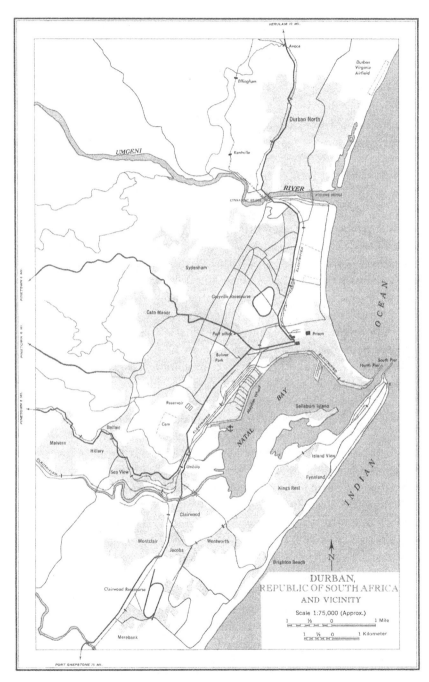

Map 1. Durban, South Africa. U.S. Army Map Service, Corps of Engineers. Durban. Edition 2-AMS. Scale 1:250,000. South Africa (Republic of South Africa) 1:250,000, Sheet SH 36–5. Washington, DC: Army Map Service, 1964.

and later Durban. In the words of the wonderfully curated South African History Online, despite the arrival of the Portuguese, "local residents continued to lead happy, productive lives, planting grain, herding cattle, paying *lobola* [bridewealth], engaging in the occasional squabble with some neighbouring clan, and eventually joining the great spiritual body of ancestors. In the larger scheme of world affairs, Natal continued to do what it has always done best: slumber." Dutch, English, and Portuguese ships continued sailing past Durban and only as a result of a series of shipwrecks did some Europeans establish a tiny presence in the late seventeenth century.[4]

The British found Durban the "best available" Indian Ocean port on the southeast coast of Africa; the city's "official" birthdate is cited as 1823. They placed a trading post on Durban Bay (Port Natal), for it offered the best natural harbor on the eastern coast of Africa, south of Portuguese-controlled Lourenço Marques (also called Delagoa Bay and, now, Maputo) in Mozambique. These Europeans primarily wanted to trade with native peoples, particularly Zulus, for elephant ivory. In this era, the Zulus emerged as the dominant African group and still, nearly two centuries later, represent the largest black population in the city. Led by the famous King Shaka, the Zulus incorporated many smaller chiefdoms principally by creating a powerful army that subjugated anyone unwilling to accept Shaka's rule. The small British settlement at Durban maintained close ties with the powerful leaders of Zululand (or KwaZulu in isiZulu). In 1843, Great Britain established a larger colony in the region, also named Natal; from 1910, Natal became the name of the province that, in 1994, became KwaZulu-Natal. In the mid-nineteenth century, thousands of English "settled" in Durban and its environs among the more numerous Africans and smattering of Afrikaners (descendants of Dutch settlers from the Cape Colony in the western part of South Africa). Theophilus Shepstone, son of an English missionary who grew up in the eastern frontier of the Cape Colony that the British had seized from the Dutch in the early 1800s, was tasked with controlling the African population. The most important British official in Natal, Shepstone created key methods, often called indirect rule, which the British later applied, worldwide, to many of its colonies.[5]

Durban may be best known for its conspicuously large Indian population, a product of administrative policies of the British Empire, Zulus' unwillingness to work in the sugarcane fields, Shepstone's supposed unwillingness to push them, the subtropical climate, and British consumer tastes. That is, English colonists wanted to create sugar plantations but needed cheap labor to do so prosperously. Africans had neither the experience growing sugar nor the desire to undertake the brutal labor required; moreover, the Zulus remained sufficiently independent into the mid-nineteenth century that they successfully refused to perform this brutal work. Hence, colonists turned to another part of the British Empire, India, with its huge impoverished population, and "imported" nearly one hundred fifty thousand Indians to Natal in the late nineteenth and early twentieth centuries. Of course, this group was not monolithic and consisted of a Hindu majority and a significant number of Muslims, along with Buddhists, Christians, and others. In a few decades, the Indian population surpassed that of the Anglo in Durban. From the late nineteenth century onward, then, the three largest ethnic groups in Durban have been Indians, Zulus, and Anglos along with other African peoples and some Afrikaners.[6]

The port has been integral to Durban's identity and economy since its settlement by the British, though Africans had lived in the vicinity for centuries prior. As mentioned, the initial purpose for English settlement was trade but, by the late nineteenth century, sugar became Natal's primary export, along with gold mined in the interior city of Johannesburg, which railroads connected to Durban in the 1890s. As historian Ralph Callebert wrote, "By 1910, Durban handled almost forty per cent of the country's imports by volume and more than three-quarters of its exports." Prior to World War I, Durban had become the country's largest port, surpassing Cape Town, and has remained so. In the twentieth century, Durban also developed a large manufacturing economy, particularly textiles and petrochemicals. The tip of the northern peninsula, enclosing the narrow mouth to the harbor, is referred to as "the Point" and is located next to the central business district. The Point was the center of Durban's shipping industry from its inception. As in many port cities, the old port area has declined as massive cranes needed to move modern shipping containers came to dominate the industry; though within the city limits, the vast majority of harbor traffic now happens along its southern portion. Jones succinctly noted that Durban established "itself as the major general cargo port of the African continent, the container hub port of the western Indian Ocean and in most respects the dominant port of the southern hemisphere." In the 2010s, local and national business and political leaders are pushing for a massive expansion of the port in south Durban, at the site of the old airport, to maintain this position and keep up with the demand to handle ever-larger ships and an increasing volume of container trade.[7]

Although the nature and methods of working ships changed over time, the composition of the workforce—Zulu men—has not. In the mid-nineteenth century, Zulu men first were hired to perform the heavy manual labor required to load and unload cargo. A history of the port by the University of Natal Economics Department noted, without irony, "The first settlers were carried on the backs of Bantu [Africans] to the shore. Passengers arriving in later years still had to be landed by baskets from steamers into tugs." Whether unloading humans or loading sugar, manual work was "casual" in nature, called *togt* in Durban (the practice is discussed further below). In Durban, whites, generally Englishmen, entirely dominated management and ownership of firms in the industry, often called stevedoring. Though huge numbers of Indians came to make up a large percentage of the Durban working class, few worked on the docks and none on ships, as David Hemson explained: "The allocation of labour by sector tended to take a racially specific form." Thus, Indians dominated some sorts of work, Africans others, with working-class whites holding the most "skilled" and best-paid positions. Zulus have worked almost all the manual dock jobs up until today. Some dockers belonged to other African ethnic groups, particularly amaPondos, who speak isiXhosa but form a separate ethnic group; Pondos hail from a coastal portion of the eastern Cape (formerly known as the Transkei) also called Pondoland.[8]

   Durban docker housing is one example of an interesting and crucial difference in racial politics between South Africa and the United States that requires further background. In 1910, the Union of South Africa was created when the British "granted" independence to some of its southern African colonies. One should not consider this event true decolonization because the rights of four-fifths of the people—Africans, Indians, and coloreds (people of mixed-race ancestry)—had precious few legal rights. At that time, the white minority government enacted brutal white supremacist policies that, among other effects, ensured that cities remained white-dominated; even to this day, blacks remain underrepresented in cities. Whites (who also referred to themselves as Europeans) created a system that allowed blacks to migrate to cities only if they had white employers, a classic example of South African–style racial capitalism. In the language of the Native (Urban Areas) Act of 1923, blacks had the right to be in cities only if "ministering to the white man's needs." With the institution of formal apartheid, upon the National Party's 1948 electoral victory, more and harsher state policies further restricted black migration to and in cities. The Group Areas Act of 1950, a central pillar of apartheid, restricted Africans (along with Indians and coloreds) to racially homogeneous "townships," satellite cities sometimes many miles from the actual, white-only cities. As a result, tens of thousands of people in Durban—and many more nationwide—were forcibly moved to homogeneous places in the 1950s and 1960s. In Durban, Africans townships included Umlazi and KwaMashu and Chatsworth was the largest Indian township.[9]
   Dockers lived in single-sex apartment buildings called hostels that typically were awful but atypically located right at the port, next to the city's central business district. Because of their centrality to the city economy, it should come as no surprise that "One of the first groups [of African workers] to be catered for [with housing in the city] was the dock workers for whom barracks were erected in the Point area in 1903." Some stevedoring companies built their own hostels, as did the city, with its Bell Street *Togt* Barracks that, together, housed upwards of five

thousand dockers. Barracks were strictly segregated by race: African *togt* laborers lived at Ordinance Road, Bell Street, and Dalton Road, and Indians (in various trades) lived in other hostels in the center city: Magazine, Greyville, and Railway. Employers created and municipal leaders endorsed these hostels, predating apartheid, in the hopes of maximizing efficiency and reducing worker power.

Charles Van Onselen, in his classic work on southern Rhodesian miners, labeled hostels "a college of colonialism . . . the unique and powerful social, political and economic cutting-edge." Writing about the early twentieth century, Hemson elaborated: "Most of Durban's African labour was housed in single-sex compounds or hostels under close supervision. Such conditions were intended to deny family life to African workers." White elites sought to limit the number of Africans in cities to keep the cities white with the added benefit of justifying lower wages to (male) dockers on the grounds that "their" women and children lived elsewhere, in rural areas, and supposedly could support themselves; that is, the costs of social reproduction were placed upon the already poor and oppressed African peoples. Some hostels housed more than a thousand men, with twenty or more men commonly sharing a single room, creating disgusting and unsanitary conditions, as well as precluding privacy. In 1942, a South African government commission described Bell Street, the largest docker barrack, as "over-crowded, dirty, and quite unfit for the purpose for which it was being used." Generally, accommodations and some food were provided free to dockers, a major benefit to typically destitute rural blacks, who migrated to the city desperate for work. Hostels remained the norm for dockers until the end of apartheid. The poor conditions also had the unintended, if predictable, consequence of creating another shared grievance and, hence, stronger collective identity among dockers.[10]

Crucially—and in contrast to other African and Indian workers increasingly pushed out of the city—docker hostels remained at the Point, in the heart of the city, despite the Group Areas Act. In this respect, Durban hostels at the Point differed from, say, those of miners in Johannesburg and throughout the Rand's goldfields. Simply put, the nature of the shipping industry and "logic" of global capitalism dictated that workers be ready to work anytime, day or night, because "the ship must sail on time." Durban also was unusual in that portions of the KwaZulu "homeland" (also called Zululand) literally bordered the city; by contrast, blacks who migrated to work in Johannesburg and Cape Town came from "homelands" generally hundreds of miles away. Just outside Durban, the black townships of Umlazi and KwaMashu bordered Zululand. This geographic reality meant that dockers who lived in city hostels could visit their (rural) homes in Zululand more easily than migrant workers elsewhere in South Africa, who generally returned home only for a month, around Christmas, each year. Nevertheless, poverty ensured that, despite their relative closeness, Durban dockers did not return home frequently.

All hostel dwellers had regular interactions with coworkers outside the job, resulting—often—in closer ties. Yet the hostels proved a double-edged sword for organizing efforts, as legendary labor and anti-apartheid activist Billy Nair recalled: "Because of the compound system it was especially easy for the Durban authorities to identify and target striking workers and to deport not just the 'ringleaders' but also whole work groups, or gangs, back to their rural area." Nevertheless, David Hemson convincingly claimed that "the evidence tends to contradict those who would argue that compounds are total institutions and make impossible collective action among African workers." Indeed, as van Onselen wrote, although African workers lived in oppressive compounds where the "police, spies, censorship and the *sjambok*" (Afrikaans for a leather whip) were ever-present, they found other ways to resist, namely "in the nooks and crannies of the day-to-day work situation," as well as off the job. The role of hostels in the history of urban and race relations is important in South Africa's larger history, including the fight against apartheid.[11]

A Brief History of the San Francisco Bay Area

The city of San Francisco and its larger metropolitan area, especially Berkeley and Oakland in the "East Bay," have a legendary if skewed place in the collective memory of the United States.[12] Highly cosmopolitan, diverse, and "open" to people of many sorts; stronghold of the counterculture (the hippies) and other social movements of the 1960s and 1970s; commanding an outsized role in the history of sexual radicals and others rejecting heteronormative lifestyles. These and other traits define San Francisco for better or worse—more likely better *and* worse—and can be traced to the fact that it originated as a port city.[13]

Like ports around the world, the movement of people, ideas, and goods resulted in a highly diverse city, demographically and culturally. The first peoples to make their home in what now is San Francisco were the indigenous Ohlones and Coast Miwoks, dozens of small tribes with distinct languages that lived in the area for ten thousand years or more. Much more recently, in 1776, San Francisco (Saint Francis in English) was founded by the Spanish as one of the northernmost outposts of its massive western hemispheric empire. The Spanish military established a fortress, or *presidio*, and were accompanied by Franciscan friars, who established a mission near the Presidio to convert the indigenous people to Catholicism; to this day, Mission Dolores church anchors a well-known neighborhood called the Mission District. When Mexico declared independence from Spain in 1821, the region that today is the state of California was one portion of a larger province the Spanish called Las Californias. John C. Frémont, who led US geographical and military expeditions in 1844–46, confirmed US interest in Alta (or upper) California. Subsequently, excited Anglo settlers wanted to seize California in the same way that Anglo-Americans in Texas earlier had, and so in 1846 unilaterally proclaimed the California Republic during this Bear Flag Revolt. The same year, the United States declared war against Mexico and soundly defeated it. The Treaty of Guadalupe Hidalgo (1848) transferred Alta California, including San Francisco, to the victorious United States. By 1850, only a relatively few indigenous and Spanish people remained in the Bay Area.[14]

Simply put, San Francisco is the city it is because its harbor is the best deep, protected one on the Pacific coast of North America. As had the Ohlones and Spanish, Americans came to San Francisco because of this harbor and its location. Undeniably, its most famous structure is the Golden Gate Bridge (completed in 1937), but most do not know that this name derives from the natural feature beneath it, the Golden Gate Strait; a ship passing through the Golden Gate (heading west to east) arrived in a huge, deep harbor well protected from the much harsher weather along the coast. In 1846, while exploring the still-Mexican province of California, Frémont named the narrow, milewide strait between two peninsulas that connects the Pacific Ocean to the San Francisco Bay by invoking Byzantine history: "To this Gate I gave the name of 'Chrysopylae' or 'Golden Gate' for the same reasons that the harbor of Byzantium was called Chrysoceras, or Golden Horn." It also, according to Frémont's report to Congress, "is a golden gate to trade with the Orient." The city, located on the peninsula south of the strait, acknowledges the role of the sea—and shipping—in its 1859 seal with a steamship in the middle and a sailor with an anchor at his feet.[15]

San Francisco possessed another crucial geographic advantage, its proximity to gold. San Francisco was the closest port to the Sierra Nevada, where the discovery of gold set off a historic frenzy in 1849 and the 1850s, just as a similar discovery at Johannesburg, nicknamed the City of Gold, did in 1886. Almost overnight, "49ers" who participated in the gold rush made San Francisco the largest city in the American West. Though few prospectors became rich, many who made San Francisco their home got rich from those searching for gold. The other human on the San Francisco seal is a miner, for the mining industry proved to be the other essential ingredient in the city's explosive population and economic growth, much as Durban grew, in part, because it shipped Johannesburg's gold to Britain and the world. The nexus of mining, shipping (commercial and naval), and newspapers emerged after the Civil War to make San Francisco into what geographer Grey Brechin labeled an "imperial city." San Francisco–based mining companies and mine owners subsequently developed the region's financial industry to tap into more capital for mining and invest mining profits into ranching, water, energy, transportation (railroads, shipping, and shipbuilding for transport and warfare), and real estate. The Hearst family was the best known; the father, George, became fabulously wealthy in mining. His son, William Randolph Hearst, built a

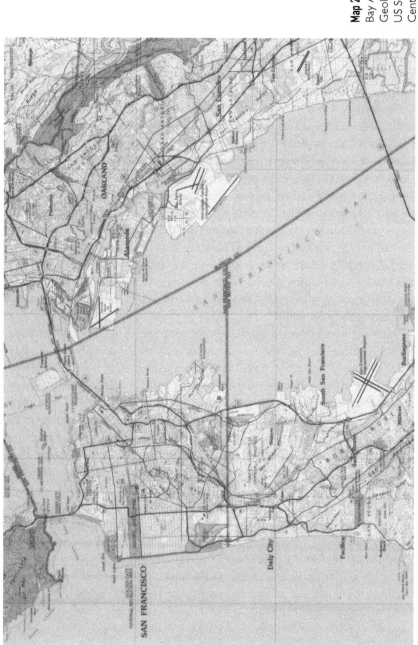

Map 2. San Francisco Bay Area. US Geological Survey and US Soil Conservation Center, 1978.

vast fortune upon a newspaper empire, starting with the *San Francisco Examiner* that George gave his son in 1887. The excellence of the city's harbor and proximity to gold, explain its meteoric rise after the US acquisition of the city and region.[16]

The 1914 opening of the Panama Canal further secured San Francisco's dominance in the western United States, tied it more closely to markets in the eastern United States, and—crucially—secured the city's status as the US gateway to the Pacific. The canal drastically cut the sailing time between the West Coast and New York City (East Coast). Shortly after the United States annexed Hawaii, it started to seek dominance over Latin America, took control of the Philippines (after defeating Spain in its 1898 war), and sought more trade and investment in Asia, especially China. The magnates of San Francisco sought to dominate the entire Pacific basin and, in the process, brought great wealth to their city and region. The population grew accordingly. San Francisco arguably remained the preeminent (if not most populous) western city until Los Angeles surpassed it in the 1970s. The San Francisco Bay Area remains the second most important metropolitan region in the US West, and shipping remains an important industry.[17]

The demographics of San Francisco and the larger Bay Area both reflect and defy US norms. When the United States took ownership of California, the population of San Francisco was quite small, perhaps a thousand people. The discovery of gold in the foothills of the Sierra Nevada and ensuing gold rush triggered a population boom in San Francisco, the gateway city, skyrocketing to perhaps thirty thousand in 1850. On the eve of the Civil War in 1860, more than fifty-six thousand lived there, the nation's fifteenth-largest city. San Francisco remained the largest city in the West for another sixty years.

The population was primarily European American. Some native *Californios* who accepted US citizenship under the Treaty of Guadalupe Hidalgo remained, though they suffered massive discrimination. Other Latinos attracted by the gold rush also lived in the city. Like other US cities, San Francisco saw a huge influx of Irish and German immigrants in the mid-nineteenth century. Similarly, in the late nineteenth century, a large and diverse group of Europeans settled in the city, especially Italians and Scandinavians, but also French, Greeks, Russians, Spanish, and others. North Beach, close to the port and downtown, became majority immigrant with a particularly Italian flair that continues, albeit far less so, today.[18]

San Francisco is well known for its Chinatown neighborhood. Its Chinese population, the country's first large Asian community, experienced virulent prejudice. Many of them arrived in the 1850s and 1860s—mostly poor men, that is, little different from most immigrants. The first waves arrived to work in railroad construction, though many ended up working in mining. The Chinese, however, experienced truly horrific persecution, legal and extralegal, driven particularly by working-class white men fearing job competition, though anti-Chinese sentiment involved cultural racism far more severe than "simple" xenophobia. Throughout the nineteenth and early twentieth centuries, in San Francisco, other California towns, and across the West, Chinese immigrants periodically suffered from lynchings, mob violence, and forced removals. Ultimately, the US Congress passed an unprecedented law, the Chinese Exclusion Act of 1882. In short, working-class white Californians led the assault against Chinese people—overwhelmingly working-class, too—choosing to put race and self-interest above class unity. When it emerged in the 1930s, the ILWU had to tackle such racism.[19]

Because of prejudice and these other factors, San Francisco became overwhelmingly white by the late nineteenth century. One result, ironically, of the lack of Chinese, Mexicans, and African Americans in San Francisco was a labor movement that, in part as a result of its homogeneity, became quite strong. San Francisco's working class and its labor movement even elected two mayors running on the Union Labor Party, who belonged to unions and were quite progressive (aside from their racist blind spot). By the 1930s, of the 635,000 people in San Francisco, 95 percent were white and fewer than 1 percent African Americans. Among the 20 percent of foreign-born San Franciscans, in that era, Italians and Germans were the most numerous, with fewer than five thousand Mexicans.[20]

Smaller and less well known, Oakland's development benefited from its proximity to San Francisco, emerging as the leading city in the East Bay. Founded in 1852, Oakland quickly became a transportation hub, just six miles east across the bay from San Francisco, which suffered from being on the northern tip of a long, narrow peninsula. A bridge, the San Francisco–Oakland Bay Bridge, was not opened until 1936. Hence, Oakland—not San Francisco—became the western terminus of the first (in 1869) and subsequent transcontinental rail lines. It developed its own port and shipbuilding operations, both important to the city though less so than in the mid- to late twentieth century. It became a manufacturing center especially for automobiles, earning the nickname "Detroit of the West." Oakland also benefited from being just south of Berkeley, location of the now world-famous flagship campus of the University of California. In 1930, Oakland had almost 285,000 residents—as in San Francisco, only 3 percent of whom were African American. World War II transformed the city, as shipbuilding and canning exploded, resulting in nearly one hundred thousand new residents between 1940 and 1945.[21]

World War II unleashed dramatic demographic changes in San Francisco and the entire Bay Area, as across the nation (and in Durban and South Africa), by sparking a mass internal migration to industrial cities for war-related jobs. For African Americans, this historic movement away from the racially segregated South is called the Great Migration, with World War II sparking the second wave of it. More than one hundred twenty thousand African Americans arrived in the

Bay Area during and after the war. The African American population of San Francisco exploded by 650 percent during the war years and nearly doubled again in the 1950s. Similarly, the percentage of blacks in Oakland quadrupled during World War II. African American population growth continued so that by 1970 African Americans made up 13 percent of San Franciscans and about 35 percent of Oaklanders.[22]

As in the case of Chinese and Mexican American populations in Western cities, pervasive residential segregation of African Americans occurred on both sides of the bay. In pre–World War II San Francisco, African Americans were so numerically insignificant that they did not seem to suffer nearly as much prejudice as the much larger Chinese population, nor did they live in a single neighborhood. The war-induced population explosion, however, accompanied by a housing shortage (felt nationwide), deepened residential segregation based upon race. Federal New Deal programs, created during the 1930s, promoted racial exclusivity (adding to restrictive covenants on literally millions of property deeds), along with racist practices in banking, construction, and real estate, resulted in hypersegregation in San Francisco and Oakland. San Francisco blacks increasingly became ghettoized in the Western Addition (also called the Fillmore) and Bayview–Hunter's Point; in parts of the former, called Nihonmachi or Japanese town, a lot of vacant housing existed after the forced removal of Japanese and Japanese Americans to internment camps in 1942. Similarly, much of West and North Oakland (and South Berkeley) became heavily—in some cases, entirely—black enclaves. As *Planning History of Oakland* pointedly noted, "In 1940, 60 percent of the city's black population lived in West Oakland. In 1950, 80 percent of the black population lived in the same area (despite this population quintupling in size)." Simply to name the Fillmore, Bayview-Hunter's Point, North Oakland, or West Oakland was to suggest African American neighborhoods. In the words of Paul Cobb, an African American from Oakland and civil-rights activist in the 1960s, West Oakland was an "urban plantation," but historian Donna Murch invoked another of its nicknames, "Baby Harlem." Later, in 1965, the Black Panther Party for Self-Defense was founded in Oakland, spawned by the city's troubled race relations.[23]

The ethnic, gender, and racial demographics of San Francisco's longshore workers historically followed the norms of the city's workforce: almost entirely white (albeit quite ethnically diverse) and entirely male. Sidney Roger, a labor journalist connected to the ILWU for forty years, recalled that "The waterfront was a United Nations, you know." Historian Robert Cherny reported that San Francisco longshoremen, in the early 1930s, were literally 99 percent white: 10 percent native-born whites of native-born parents, 27 percent white of foreign-born parents, and 62 percent European immigrants, 45 percent of whom were Irish, 12 percent Scandinavians, 11 percent German, 9 percent British, 8 percent Serbs and Croats, and a smattering of Finns, Italians, East European Jews, Portuguese, Puerto Ricans, Greeks, and French Canadians. The workforce also was entirely male and remained so for decades to come (discussed below). However, the combination of a wartime labor shortage and the political ideologies of many in the ILWU quickly transformed the San Francisco waterfront into the single most attractive workplace for southern black men.[24]

Dock Work on the Durban and San Francisco Waterfronts

Because of their importance to global capitalism—as well as their propensity to strike, unionize, and take solidarity actions—dockworkers have received considerable attention from historians and other scholars. Charles Barnes, author of the first serious analysis of US dockworkers, painted a vivid picture of the New York waterfront in 1915 that is applicable to most others:

> In and out among rolling and swinging boxes, bales, heavy iron rails, one moment stepping aside to avoid a collision with a truck, another dodging to escape a descending draft, bustle slouchily or push ahead with eager alertness the cosmopolitan denizens of the waterfront. Here a tall, stalwart blond from Germany or the Scandinavian peninsula, there a brawny son of Ireland, here a stocky Polack, there a quick, wiry Italian, tug together at some refractory bale, forgetful of the accumulated animosities of their respective races, under the influence of a new world of commerce which knows nothing of racial resentment or governmental tyranny, back and forth, within and yet without, moves the Negro, still under the ban of his half freedom, doing as he may the simpler work of trucking on the pier. Such is the picture, rough but representative, that one sees the length of the waterfront as the ship comes in.[25]

Barnes highlights, intentionally or not, the workforce's diversity but also the many and frenzied challenges of waterfront work in ports around the world.

Traditional or conventional dock work involved very hard manual labor, much danger, irregular work, and low pay. Mr. Khanye, a Zulu dockworker, described Durban: "There are lots of things pressing down on the workers at the docks. The work is heavy and very dangerous. The pay is low. Foreman [sic] swear at workers and treat them badly. And after a long day's work the men can't go home to rest. Their families live far away in the countryside. So the workers go back to the compounds. The compounds are not like home. The beds are hard. There are no children playing. There are no women. And the food is bad." Except for the housing, Khanye could be describing San Francisco. The essence of this work inspired jazz pianist Clarence Williams, an African American who lived in the port city of New Orleans, to write "Longshoreman's Blues."[26]

Dockworkers were renowned for the great strength needed to handle the heavy and varied commodities that they lifted, loaded, assembled into slings and onto pallets, carried, pushed, and unloaded.[27] Dockworkers in Durban described themselves using the isiZulu word *onyathi* or *inyathi*, literally meaning buffalo, intended to signal their strength as well as the collective nature of their labor.[28] In the United States, they also boasted of their hard and risky work; Barnes wrote, "it is a matter of pride with the longshoreman that he should not show fear nor evade necessary danger." Such pride was understandable, in that they hauled five-hundred-pound sacks of coffee or sugar. They even carried such loads up steep ladders from the holds of ships rolling on the edge of a stormy sea, during a rainstorm, or at night. One Durban dockworker, Ram, described his labor in the 1940s: "Most of the work was done by hand. The workers had some tools but not much. Say like this box landed here now and its [sic] heavy—about 20 or 30 tons. They used to have special jacks. The jacks lifted the box up a bit. And then the workers put some wood underneath it. And then they dragged it." Wet hides might have been the most awful cargo worked in both ports. Reg Theriault vividly described unloading them in San Francisco: "Hides came from the hide house folded into a bundle with the hair in and slimy side out, sort of loosely tied together with a string. Frequently they were crawling with maggots. To protect the hide from the maggots a scoop of manure from the steer was shoved onto the center of the skin before it was folded and tied. On the voyage overseas the maggots ate the manure and not the hides. It saved the leather, but it did not make the hides much fun to pick up." Experienced dockworkers possessed many skills, but nevertheless the work required brute strength and a strong stomach.[29]

Dock work ranked among the world's most dangerous occupations, with injuries incredibly common and deaths a possibility on every shift. During "Hitler's War," as editor Tina Sideris named it, Durban (and Bay Area) dockworkers loaded bombs onto ships; Mr. Ngcobo recalled, "We were very scared of them because they could explode." He had good reason to fear for, in 1944, 320 US Navy sailors (including 202 African American dockworkers) were killed in a controversial explosion while loading ammunition at Port Chicago, north of Oakland. Khanye in Durban lamented, "the conditions were very poor. . . . people got injured. They broke legs and arms." So, too, in San Francisco, where Harry Bridges, the legendary ILWU leader, recalled, "I broke my foot in '29 working in the hold. I was standing there on a pile and we let a load go out, and my foot got jammed between two cases that came together. I worked for a couple days with it—couldn't afford to lay off, you see? But it swelled up so high that I couldn't work down there, so the boss put me on the deck." In 1934, testimony before the (US) National Longshoremen's Board reported that a quarter of workers were injured the previous year and an eighth suffered accidents that forced them to take at least a week off work. Charles Barnes concluded, "It is probable that there is no other heavy physical work which is accompanied with so much overtime and such long stretches of toil without interruption. Even steel mills do not require the extreme length of working hours found on the piers." Accordingly, he warned, "danger of bodily injury [is] ever present."[30]

Dock work also was quite irregular (or "casual," though the term is insulting), causing many to struggle to "make ends meet." Work varied greatly from season to season because of the inherently erratic nature of both the weather and economic conditions. A dockworker might unload a ship and, then, not work for another week, month, or longer. Mr. Nzuza noted in Durban, "Sometimes we couldn't get work. On some days there were no ships for us to work. And when there was no work we even had to sell our clothes to buy food." In 1936, the San Francisco union local published "The Maritime Crisis," describing conditions before 1934: "Longshoremen were hired on the docks, and the Embarcadero [the street running along the water's edge] was known as the 'slave mart.' Men hung around the docks all day, often in the rain, and then received two or three hours' work in the late afternoon—if they received anything." Historian David Selvin concluded that "Irregular job distribution—feast and famine, side by side—was inherent in longshore employment." Hence, although the hourly wage was decent for a manual laborer, getting sufficient and consistent hours often proved frustrating.[31]

Labor surpluses traditionally defined the industry, which drove down wages, made organizing harder, and opened hiring to tremendous abuses. The work involved impressive skills—most notably, fitting cargo of endlessly varied shapes and sizes into holds of different sizes and to do so in a way that the ship remained balanced—along with the fact that, at its essence, the task demanded a strong back. Fortunately for employers, large-scale European immigration and the migration of rural Americans to US cities guaranteed huge labor surpluses in industrial cities even before the Great Depression sent unemployment to unprecedented levels. In the words of Frank P. Foisie, head of labor relations for Seattle shippers, in 1934 "the waterfront is 'the scapegoat of competitive industry'—the dumping ground of human surplusage from all other industries and the last refuge of the down-and-outer." In South Africa, the Native Lands Act of 1913 pushed millions of rural blacks (almost 80 percent of the total population) into about 10 percent of the nation's land, among the least arable at that, ensuring massive overpopulation and suffering in "native reserves" such as Zululand and Pondoland. Thus, South African blacks might have flooded cities without strict state controls designed to prevent such an occurrence to both ensure cheap labor for white farmers and maintain cities as white preserves. During World War II, however, South Africa "needed" many more blacks for urban industrial work to support the British war effort. Not coincidentally, a worsening of conditions and tightening of regulations also pushed rural blacks into the urban wage economy. These policies guaranteed that vast numbers of impoverished blacks needed to migrate to cities for work—when allowed by the state's pass laws, which strictly managed the movement of blacks into urban areas. The state, thus, worked closely with urban employers to ensure sufficiently large, constant flows of cheap black male migrant labor. When apartheid arose in the late 1940s and 1950s, the state more fully codified and tightened the existing racist restrictions. In both ports, hence, employers greatly benefited from labor surpluses.[32]

Combined with the vagaries of the boom-bust cycle of market economies, hiring bosses picked friends, men who had something in common with the boss (race, ethnicity, birthplace, etc.), or those willing to kick back some money, that is, pay a bribe. In San Francisco before 1934, hundreds to thousands of men appeared at the "shape-up" along the Embarcadero, the waterfront's main thoroughfare, near the Ferry Building. Each morning between 7 and 8 a.m., after walking bosses received their assignments, they hired gang bosses, who then picked their gangs. Those not hired might try "prospecting," going from pier to pier to replace anyone hurt on the job or otherwise not available. Some steady gangs had a regular meeting spot to wait for their gang boss. The majority not in a steady gang might wait around to see whether a place might open up in a steady gang. This process was as hated by longshoremen as it was loved by the bosses. Though perhaps an exaggeration, especially if he was in a steady gang, one San Francisco longshoreman testified about the shape-up: "We have been hired off the streets like a bunch of sheep, standing there from 6 o'clock in the morning, in all kinds of weather; at the moment of 8 o'clock, we were herded along the street by the police to allow the commuters to go across the street from the Ferry Building, more or less like a slave market in some of the Old World countries of Europe."[33]

Durban dockworkers also worked casually and received housing in large company- and city-owned hostels near various wharves, mostly at the Point, despite being casual laborers. As in San Francisco and every other port in the "casual" era, individual workers decided whether to seek work for a particular shift; of course, if one did not work, one did not get paid. In Durban and across Natal, casual laborers were called *togt* laborers, a system that emerged in the mid-nineteenth century to meet the needs of white employers and colonial authorities. British colonials created conditions and laws that forced (some) Africans to migrate to cities for work as cheap laborers in white-owned industries and homes. Zulu workers, however, continued to assert independence, as recounted in a "Brief History of the Durban Municipal Department of Bantu Administration" in 1974: "The Natal Government's Secretary for Native Affairs (Theophilus Shepstone) issued a memorandum on 'The Evils arising out of the practice now becoming so general among the Native labourers in the towns of Pietermaritzburg and Durban of refusing employment except as jobbers.'" Hence, this "Brief History" described how, to exert further control, Shepstone created a system for "registering of kafirs," a pejorative and racist term for Africans.

As for the term *togt*, following Keletso Atkins, Ralph Callebert aptly wrote, "The name *togt* is Dutch for journey or trip and points at the link between the rural and the urban." Atkins suggested *togt* was something of a compromise, in that colonial powers proved unable to exert total control over the native peoples, and Africans frequently resisted the imposition of wage labor. Accordingly, *togt* laborers could refuse work anytime they wished—that is, they had some independence in remaining casual. In Durban, the demand for *togt* labor was greatest on the wharves and ships; the city was already the nation's leader for exports and a major one for imports. Though *togt* labor was somewhat unique, as in other ports around the globe, job prospects depended on the number of ships in the harbor as well as the competition for work. In the hostels, black men called *indunas*, an isiZulu word meaning headman or foreman, ran the compounds (on behalf of white-owned shippers), and other *indunas* acted as hiring bosses; as in San Francisco and elsewhere, *indunas* had their favorites and, despite also being Zulu, often were despised and mistrusted by workers. Generally, dockworkers worked for and were housed by one stevedoring company but could seek work with others.[34]

To sum up, the lives of dockworkers seemed "poor, nasty, brutish, and short," following philosopher Thomas Hobbes's famous dictum. Employers exploited huge labor surpluses to keep wages low and unions weak (or nonexistent). Once hired, the work proved quite difficult, often dangerous, and accompanied by poor treatment; as one Durban dockworker complained, "The bosses treat us like oranges. They suck out the juice of our labour, then they throw us away." Yet, for many, such work remained their best option. Hobbes's quote describing the lives of humans did not fit dockworkers in at least one crucial way, for he described most people's lives as miserable for being "solitary" but nothing could be further from the truth for dockworkers.[35]

Indeed, dockworkers mostly labored in gangs of ten or even twenty and often hauled cargo in pairs, both of which contributed to a collective identity. Literally for thousands of years, workers loaded and unloaded cargo in gangs. Often, multiple gangs were deployed to a single ship, with one gang per hatch, so that there might be 150 men working at one time. Much, perhaps most, work was done in pairs. Sidney Roger, who worked for and belonged to the ILWU, explained, "no longshoreman works alone." In San Francisco, many longshoremen had regular partners, and they worked together exclusively, sometimes for years; it was not uncommon to refuse a job if one's partner was not dispatched. One retired longshoreman, John Fern, even wrote a poem when his partner died or "crossed the bar." Further, dangerous workplaces, like waterfronts, often inculcate in workers a sense of each other as family. These traits proved important in the rise of unions and prompted members, once in unions, to act with impressive solidarity. Be it

Genoa, Mombasa, or elsewhere, dockworkers often have organized, formally or informally, to improve wages, safety, and other work conditions. Essentially, the gang nature of dock work encouraged a collective identity and deep bonds.[36]

Not only did they frequently see each other as family, dockworkers were unusually cosmopolitan, knowing much more about the world than many in other occupations. The nature of marine transport—moving goods, people, and information—explains why dockworkers (and sailors) are so worldly, often more so than people with (far) greater wealth or more formal education. The 1958–59 journal of San Francisco's Eric Hoffer, nicknamed the "longshoreman philosopher" for writing ten books and countless articles, offers a window into this world. Hoffer worked ships arriving from Germany, Chile, Japan, Norway, Holland, and elsewhere; met sailors from Sweden and the Philippines; unloaded coffee from Colombia, hides from New Zealand, and copra (coconut meat) from the South Pacific. Many longshore workers had access to information and people who traveled the world and, thus, interpreted their lives, work, and worldview through a global lens. Often, they become internationalist in their thoughts and, occasionally, actions. Moreover, certain political ideologies are overtly international in their imagination and intention; many dockworkers in the Bay Area and Durban embraced leftist or Pan-African ideologies, or both. Leftist ideologies did not inspire all activism; during the Cold War, New York longshoremen protested ships from the Soviet Union. Of course, not all dockworkers were political or internationalist, though their propensity to think in such ways is remarkable.[37]

Since the 1960s, containerization transformed marine transport and its workforce. Seeking larger profits and facilitated by governmental allies, shipping corporations introduced a new technological process that loaded and unloaded cargo in standardized metal boxes using ever larger cranes onto ever larger ships. Economist Marc Levinson brilliantly summarized the profound impacts in *The Box*: "The container made shipping cheap, and by doing so changed the shape of the world economy." He described the new, more seamless system for shipping freight worldwide:

> A 25-ton container of coffeemakers can leave a factory in Malaysia, be loaded aboard a ship, and cover the 9,000 miles to Los Angeles in 16 days. A day later, the container is on a unit train to Chicago, where it is transferred immediately to a truck headed for Cincinnati. The 11,000-mile trip from the factory gate to the Ohio warehouse can take as little as 22 days, a rate of 500 miles per day, at a cost lower than that of a single first-class air ticket. More than likely, no one has touched the contents or even opened the container, along the way.

As a result, "In the decade after the container first came into international use, in 1966, the volume of international trade in manufactured goods grew more than twice as fast as the volume of global manufacturing production, and two and a half times as fast as global economic output." Dockworkers, as a result, found themselves in the "eye of the storm" of modern globalization, moving ever more containers with ever fewer fellow workers. Not coincidentally, containers caused a massive decline in dockworkers and weakened their unions across the planet, although those who survived, in many nations, now earn higher wages. Moreover, because of their vital role in global trade, organized dockworkers still command significant power.[38]

A few comments on the terminology demand attention. In the late nineteenth century in San Francisco and across the United States, the terms *stevedore* and *longshoreman* were interchangeable, though, over time, the former became anachronistic despite its use in the commercially and critically acclaimed television show *The Wire* for the International Brotherhood of Stevedores, a fictionalized version of the International Longshoreman's Association. By the early twentieth century, *stevedore* often referred to employers who hired dockworkers on behalf of shipping agents and companies. The US term generally has been *longshoreman*, but in recent years the gender-neutral longshore worker sometimes is employed, and the ILWU made its name gender-neutral in 1997 with a resolution—approved unanimously—at its biennial convention. As for Durban, historian Ralph Callebert wrote, "there were two types of dock workers in Durban. Stevedores worked in the holds of the ships, stacking or unloading cargo. Shore workers handled the cargo on the wharf. The term 'dock worker' can refer either to both groups of workers or specifically to the latter group. In Durban, [some] shore workers were referred to as railway workers as well, as they were employed by the South African Railways and Harbours. Shore work generally required less skill, was less dangerous, and earned lower wages." Traditionally, dockworkers in Durban and across South Africa were men, but the union currently representing dockworkers in every port, the South African Transport and Allied Workers Union (SATAWU), also chose a gender-neutral name and seeks to recruit more women into both its ranks and its leadership. In this book, the term *stevedore* never will be used to refer to dockworkers, because the meaning varied in time and place. Rather, the term *dockworker* generally will be used. In the United States, however, *longshoreman* and *longshore worker* are the most common ones and so also will be used in that context. In South Africa (as in Britain and some other places), people regularly use the term *docker* and so I will do so in sections on South Africa.[39]

For many centuries, dockworkers in Durban, the Bay Area, and globally were almost entirely male and that disproportionality typified other sorts of maritime work, including seafaring and shipbuilding. As in many other occupations and cultures, men identified dock work as "manly" *because* it was physically hard, quite dangerous, and exclusively male. Though writing about the ports of Los Angeles–Long Beach, sociologist Jake Alimahomed-Wilson's words apply: "the industry, waterfront, and union local were thus shaped and influenced exclusively *by* and *for* men. The male-dominated longshore industry, along with the union local, was thereby defined within this exclusionary masculinist context." William W. Pilcher, an anthropologist and former longshoreman, examined dockworker manliness, including how the all-male Portland waterfront workforce made fun of each other's masculinity or lack thereof. Pilcher suggested that this manner of talking with co-workers proved central to the creation of a tightly knit occupational community and to building trust among partners, who literally put their lives into their fellow workers' hands. Pat Ayers examined Liverpool, whose dockworkers based their manly identities upon their physically difficult and dangerous labor; their drinking cultures, as in Pilcher's Portland, also factored into their masculine identities. Despite the gender-neutral names of the ILWU and SATAWU, few women have worked on the waterfront, though both unions now attempt to recruit some. In SATAWU, the national organizer for its maritime sector in 2009 was Veronica Mesatywa, though she came to unionism as a railway worker, and at least one Durban shop steward in the port was female. The ILWU, meanwhile, created a short video called "Women of the Waterfront" and undertook some effort to ensure equal treatment between the sexes in the union and on jobsites. Of course, the fact that the waterfront was entirely male did not mean that gender did not matter; in fact, quite the opposite, as Pilcher argued; historian Daniel Letwin elaborated that, at least in the US context, the *absence* of women made organizing across racial lines somewhat easier. Similarly, David Roediger noted the absence of racial diversity in a specific US locale did not, in any way, mean that race did not matter among an all-white group. So, too, the fact that dockworkers were exclusively men did matter in Durban and San Francisco. Though gender is not a central theme of this book, it periodically shall be examined.[40]

On the Durban Waterfront

That Durban dockers possess a long history of activism and self-organization is no secret. This section briefly describes their militancy from the late nineteenth century into the early post–World War II years, highlighting tactics used in organizing themselves while integrating them into the social history of Durban. As discussed earlier, the first employment of Zulu men as *togt* laborers occurred in the mid-1800s. Almost as soon as they started working on the waterfront, they began walking off it. The booklet *Sifuna Imali Yethu*, published in 1983 and based upon extensive interviews with Durban dockers, declared, "The first fight was over 100 years ago. In 1879 the workers at Durban docks went on strike. They demanded more money. Since then the fight hasn't stopped." In 1895, they struck again, demanding a raise; academic H. G. Ringrose wrote, "There is no evidence of the outcomes, beyond that the Agent in question ordered the Natives to report to his representative on the Docks, but the comment of the press is noteworthy: 'It is evident that the Natives are fully alive to the scarcity of labour and want to take advantage of it.'" Ringrose also documented a dock strike in 1903 in which workers challenged their bosses on workload. More than a thousand dockers struck in 1919 but failed to win a raise. Predictably, Durban's economic and political elites did not like docker activism. Robert Jameson, a Durban town councilor, complained to the South African Native Affairs Commission in 1905 that the *togt* worker "is left very much to his own devices . . . he is undisciplined, he is impatient of control, he is lazy . . . it would be in the interest of the native himself if he were located in the compound, where he would be *under proper discipline and control*." In Jameson's words can be read the fear that whites had of black worker agency and power. Indeed, the entirety of South African history, before 1994, can be read as the white minority using its capital and state power to exploit and dominate the black majority.[41]

Numerous factors explain the militancy of Durban's dockers. First and foremost, as discussed, the work inculcated a group identity with shared interests as opposed to individuals focused solely upon self-interest. Second, dockers, like other African workers, were paid extremely low wages and therefore lived in desperate poverty and, thus, always had material reasons to demand greater earnings. Third, dockers lived together, meaning they got to know each other even better and identify with each other that much more. Fourth, their shared interests, on the job and off, were buttressed by the reality that nearly all of them were of the same ethnic group, the Zulus, and thus spoke the same language, shared a culture, and generally understood each other; literally, they all came from rural KwaZulu (or Pondoland), with which they maintained family and other connections. Fifth, they were all men, meaning they shared a gender identity, which made it easier to organize than in a multisex workforce. Sixth, they suffered from shared racial oppression, blacks in a society dominated by whites. Finally, the very nature of African men migrating from their rural, agrarian lives to the industrial city of Durban meant they were bold. Scholar-activist Bernard Magubane explained how he viewed his father, who moved (with his family) to Durban in the late 1930s:

> Looking back at my father's decision to abscond with us from the farm, I think it was not only an act of courage, but also a "revolutionary" act on his part, although he would not have seen it in that light. White farmers in South Africa, especially during the Great Depression, had an insatiable appetite for cheap black labour and to lose even one family was a gross loss. My father had deprived the farmer not only of his labour power, but also of the labour of his children and nephews.

Hence, such people might have been predisposed toward action and protest.[42]

Durban dockers built upon this strong foundation through collective action on the job, exerting significant pressure despite rarely belonging to a union. Before

1959, dockers simply could refuse to make themselves available for work because, officially, they were casual; thus, they could—and sometimes did—organize together so that none reported for work. Being *togt*, their action was not, legally, a strike and hence they could not be fired by their bosses, arrested by the police, or deported back to their rural homelands. They also could engage in variations on this tactic, like not accepting overtime or Sunday work. Dockers repeatedly used an overtime ban, perhaps more effective than a strike, in that it was safer for the workers. Similarly, in his influential study of mid-twentieth century Mombasa, Frederick Cooper demonstrated how the casual employment provided dockers some independence and power.[43]

Second, dockers occasionally slowed the pace at which they worked, which provided many advantages. Because they were on the clock when they disrupted the loading or unloading of cargo, they simultaneously earned wages while hurting their employer's pocketbook. Protesting and earning money, generally, was far more attractive than striking with no strike fund or financial reserves. Of course, workers all over the world sometimes used work slowdowns to express discontent over wages, treatment, safety, and the like. When workers, unionized or not, engage in this tactic, it is called "working to rule" or "the conscious withdrawal of efficiency," that is, workers follow company rules (or union contract) to the letter and never take initiative—unlike normally, when workers often use their skills and knowledge to save time or effort in ways possibly unknown to managers. The effect, of course, is the same: lower productivity. In marine transport, where the credo is "the ship must sail on time," slowing down remains among the workers' best tactics.[44]

Finally, Durban's dockers sometimes engaged in a tactic called "robbing the hold," in which they pretend to finish loading cargo but did not do so. Tina Sideris, editor of a wonderful history of Durban dockers, quoted one: "'Robbing the hold happens deep down in the ship,' explains the stevedore. 'The hold is the place where the goods are stored. The workers take the goods on one side and pile them up to the roof. In this way they want to make it look as though the job is finished. Yet there is an empty space on the other side. Even the foreman can't see that the workers robbed the job. Because he sees the hold filled up.'" "Robbing the hold" and similar tactics confirm that, while dockers were strong like buffalo, they also possessed the intelligence of humans. Ralph Callebert contended that "pilferage," a related subject, "falls in a grey zone between theft, which is clearly illegal, and a perk," which is legal. Callebert thoughtfully analyzed this "livelihood strategy," which was quite common in the mid-twentieth century and engaged in "without shame." Dockers participated in actions for their financial benefit, predictably, but also joined with other blacks in actions primarily political.[45]

Perhaps the dockers' first overtly political action was their deep involvement in the well-known 1929 Durban "beer riots." Historian Bill Freund noted Durban was renowned "for its invention of the so-called 'Durban system' of municipal beer halls for Africans. Municipally controlled brewing of 'native' beer was set to be the source of welfare spending on African needs in the city such as it was." Maynard Swanson elaborated: Durban "was a pioneer in developing a self-financing system for segregation and controlling its African population." Thanks to the Native Beer Act of 1908, profits from municipally owned, male-only beer halls (along with "native eating halls") fully financed the city bureaucracy—including police—that oversaw blacks along with the municipally owned hostel that Durban dockers lived in, for example, the Bell Street *Togt* Barracks. The city literally profited from its sale of food and drink to Africans while disempowering them. It should come as no surprise that every hostel was within walking distance of a native beer hall like the Point Beer Hall, one of few recreational outlets dockers had when not working.

Durban dockers understood and resented this system's controlling effects. So, on weekends, they traveled to the city's outskirts to African-owned "shebeens," a South African adaptation of the Irish word *síbín* for an illicit bar, often in a private house and generally operated by a black woman. The shebeen system worked well, for African women traditionally brewed beer, *tshwala* in isiZulu. In cities, brewing and selling beer became an increasingly important source of income for African women. Bernard Magubane, later a prominent historian who grew up in Durban townships, recalled that his mother "who was a very enterprising woman, started to brew African beer to sell to migrant labourers who worked at the docks and in the Durban factories." Predictably, city elites hated that black dockers spent much of their free time and money in shebeens—outside white control and profit. To attack this "problem," in the 1920s government officials passed another law that granted itself a monopoly over beer brewing and sales. In response, African women, with support from dockers and other black men and with some leadership offered by the Industrial and Commercial Workers' Union of Africa (ICU), boycotted municipal beer halls. The 1983 oral history of Durban dockers described what followed: "In the 1920s the dockers refused to pay taxes. And they stopped buying beer from the municipality. This went on for many weeks. Until the police and army arrested hundreds of workers." In May 1929, the issue came to a head as ICU-led marchers protested on multiple Sundays. Then, in June, the growing conflict exploded into the Beer Hall Riot, in which six blacks and two whites were killed and more than a hundred injured when the police intervened. By all accounts, dockers were heavily involved, confirming their militancy and organizational ability. The state understood the political ramifications of blacks protesting state laws and institutions and, thus, acted accordingly. It did so again shortly thereafter.[46]

In 1930, Durban experienced another political clash—against racist-inspired taxes and passes—with major involvement by dockers, this one led by Johannes

Nkosi, Durban's first black working-class martyr. Born in rural KwaZulu in 1905, Nkosi was among the first black leaders in the Communist Party of South Africa (CPSA). He became involved in antipass law protests in 1919 and, in the 1920s, was an activist in both the CPSA and ICU, the first union to sign up a large number of Africans. Notably, the ICU emerged out of a strike of dockers in Cape Town after World War I before the union spread across southern Africa. The ICU—influenced by both the US-founded IWW and Marcus Garvey's US-based Universal Negro Improvement Association—had a significant presence in Durban and Natal along with some influence on the docks. Early in 1929, the CPSA sent Nkosi to Durban, who quickly became the most popular black leader, among dockers as among others. In 1929 and 1930, Nkosi frequently spoke at protests of the municipal monopoly on beer brewing and "called for a *South African native republic* and the burning of passbooks." Nkosi effectively promoted the party's nationwide effort to burn passbooks on December 16, 1930, a holiday at that time called the Day of the Covenant (or Dingaan's Day), which celebrated the Afrikaner *Voortrekkers'* defeat of a Zulu army in the 1838 Battle of Blood River. The passbook demonstration that the Durban CPSA organized was impressive but, causing no surprise, the Durban police responded with violence. Nkoski was stabbed and brutally beaten, dying a few days later, as did three other black protesters. This incident revealed, yet again, that the use of force was the government's last and best resort against black protest. In fact, Nkosi's killing and further police repression resulted in the disappearance of the CPSA from Durban in the 1930s. Through their active participation in both the 1929 beer hall riots and 1930 passbook protests, however, Durban dockers demonstrated they understood the system as the ultimate source of their oppression. The 1930s were quieter, though it did include a brief strike in solidarity with Ethiopians fighting Italian invaders.[47]

World War II sparked the largest and most sustained examples yet of docker power on behalf of their material and political interests. The British military desperately depended on the port of Durban to link Europe, Africa, and Asia, as Jon Hyslop wrote: "With the Mediterranean near impassable for the Allies because of air and submarine attacks, the route around the Cape became crucial to supplying the Commonwealth forces in Egypt and in India and the Far East." Peter Johnston noted that twenty thousand vessels docked at and six million service men and women traveled through Durban. To handle this surging traffic, about four thousand *togt* workers were employed by four major stevedoring companies and the government's own South African Railways and Harbours Administration, along with thousands in related work such as the railroads. Despite the traffic, dockers generally worked three or four days a week because employers preferred a permanent surplus to weaken workers' power; another method for employers to maintain power was recruitment from the "Native reserves," a clear signal should dockers prove too demanding. Nevertheless, their actions during the war years led Hemson to conclude that "In a broader context they had taken up issues of wider economic and political struggle."[48]

Despite employers' best efforts, war-induced labor shortages and soaring inflation, in Durban as elsewhere, triggered a series of waterfront strikes led by Zulu Phungula, the first docker to take a bold leadership role and, accordingly, singled out for persecution. In 1939, a thousand *togt* workers elected Phungula as their leader. Like other dockers, he was a migrant, hailing from the iXcopo district in rural Natal. As Hemson noted, Phungula was a working-class leader quite different from "the urbanized intelligentsia who led the African trade unions during the war years." He also differed from the urban elites who led the African National Congress (ANC) and could be considered an "organic intellectual," as Frederick Cooper used the term. In 1941, multiple short strikes erupted, with Phungula loudly demanding a doubling of the basic wage. Hemson attributed this strike wave to "increased organization, rising prices, and expanded production." The largest strike occurred in August, first at the large Bell Street *Togt* Barracks and then spreading to other hostels and shutting down the port. This crisis—for South African goods supported the British who, at that time, were the only ones left fighting Germany—resulted in the state intervening and the dockers "agreeing" to return to work without a raise.[49]

Negotiations heated up again in 1942, the employers' willingness to talk a clear indication they feared another strike. Dockers demanded a major raise with Phungula forcefully declaring this at a meeting at the native commissioner's office:

> We have been taught by the Europeans what to eat and we like to eat the same things as the European, for instance eggs and tea in the mornings, we would like to fly in aeroplanes and drive round in motor cars. The shops are full of clothes and motor cars, but we cannot buy these things because we have no money. . . . We do not want 8s a day, we want 25s a day (the wage of white clerks employed by the stevedoring companies). Even if we get 8s a day we will not be satisfied. If we had not agreed with our masters for 8s we would not have asked for that today . . . the government only gives us an empty dish to lick.

Phungula's passion and logic proved insufficient to carry the day, no agreement was reached and another strike erupted, which he referred to as a "strike called *inyathi*," a strike of the buffalo. Under the wartime emergency, the government pressed employers to negotiate with a committee of eleven dockers, including Phungula. Meanwhile, an organizer from the Cape Town Stevedoring and Dock Workers Union (CTSDWU) arrived and tried to establish a Durban branch, with Phungula as the leader, though this initiative failed. The government again resorted to force and arrests of Phungula and others. In a shocking move, when released by the police on condition that he cajole the dockers back to work, Phungula encouraged his fellow workers to remain on strike: "Look, we now dig gold for them, diamonds for them, and all they do is sit on the chairs which can even reach heaven. What makes them not to give us enough money to feed our children?" Finally, the state deployed stronger measures: massive fines, imprisonment, and Phungula's banishment from Durban for five years—someone other than he would have to lead what he called the SS *Inyathi* or steamship *Buffalo*. "Ivan Walker, the Controller of Industrial Manpower," Callebert noted, "declared stevedoring a Controlled Industry after the first war-time strike, as it was crucial to the war effort," and near the end of the year, Pretoria issued War Measure 145 of 1942, outlawing all strikes by Africans. Though this strike failed and future ones had been criminalized, *togt* workers still possessed some power, because they were not under contract with any specific employer. Thus, they could coordinate their actions and not report for duty. In response to Phungula's banishing, they learned a powerful lesson, one described later by Archie Sibeko, Cape Town docker and future global anti-apartheid and labor activist: "As a result trade union organisation was forced underground." Although these wartime actions suggest a workforce seeking to improve their material conditions and expand their power, not all their actions were positive.[50]

In 1949, many dockers joined in the historic Cato Manor riots that pitted working-class Africans and Indians against each other, resulting in about 140 people killed and thousands wounded—roughly equally from both groups—and fifty thousand Indians left homeless. Cato Manor, about five kilometers west of the city center, had been a predominantly Indian area. As ever-more Africans, mostly Zulus, moved from the countryside to the city during and after World War II, however, the housing situation worsened considerably. Peter Johnston wrote that Cato Manor's population increased more than 500 percent during the war. As a result, tens of thousands of Africans lived in "shacks," poorly built homes constructed from found objects, across the city, thousands of whom settled in Cato Manor's eMkhumbane area. Some Africans who lived in shacks on Indian-owned lands in Cato Manor were dock and railway workers who took buses down to the harbor, one of whom was the father of Curnick Ndlovu, a docker who became an important labor and political leader in Durban in the 1950s and an underground military leader in the 1960s. Describing the area as freer because it was beyond the city limits, Iain Edwards quoted docker Brutus Mthethwe: "it was the African city, uMkhumbane. It was not Thekwini [Durban], it was ours. That was what Cato Manor was for." In this setting, thousands of Africans and Indians lived in close proximity and somewhat reasonable harmony.[51]

African-Indian relations in Durban also exhibited tremendous tensions, however. Of course, the dominant white population primarily benefited from keeping Africans and Indians as cheap, exploited labor as well as at odds with each other.

These conflicts were particularly common and dangerous in Durban, possessing, by far, the largest Indian population in the nation. There, Africans and Indians frequently eyed each other suspiciously, especially as competitors for jobs but also in housing and trading. Africans were quite resentful that Indians had more political rights and, accordingly, more economic and social opportunities.[52]

African and Indian working-class leaders were mindful of these problems and understood that the possibility of cross-racial alliances did exist, especially on the job. Occasionally in the 1930s and 1940s, African and Indian workers in Durban struck together, for example, in 1937 at Falkirk Iron and Steel, where four hundred Africans and Indians downed tools after sixteen union members were retrenched. Notably, the CPSA long had become multiracial with numerous prominent Indian radicals in Durban. Iain Edwards suggested that African workers were radicalized by Indians, who possessed a much longer history of trade unionism and more rights (than blacks) under the Industrial Conciliation Act. Further, the leaders of the ANC and Natal Indian Congress (NIC) also embraced "nonracialism" in 1947 (though both the ANC and NIC, at the time, remained all-black and all-Indian, respectively), signing a formal alliance nicknamed the "Doctors' Pact," as the signatories were medical doctors. During the war, Indian and African workers engaged in many strikes, some being multiracial or "nonracial." Yet sometimes Africans were used to break Indian or Indian-African strikes. Historian Goolam Vahed explained, "the identity of non-racialism did not permeate to the masses. In their daily lives, Indians and Africans were not only socially apart but competed for very limited resources as Durban's population more than doubled between 1936 and 1951."[53]

In 1949, tensions boiled over in reaction to overcrowding and inflation (particularly of rent, but also of other goods, generally purchased by Africans in Indian-owned shops), along with the heightened racialization of South African society precipitated by the Nationalist Party. Curnick Ndlovu noted that blacks in eMkhumbane suffered from massive overcrowding, abject poverty, unemployment (albeit they fared better than in rural areas), and repeated police raids in which a great many blacks were arrested and deported from the city for pass violations. So, when an Indian shopkeeper, downtown, beat a young African in a petty dispute, other Africans immediately responded by looting Indian shops and attacking Indian people. This spark set off three days of massive rioting, citywide, in which Africans angrily turned on slightly better-off Indians. As Curnick Ndlovu, who lived with his parents in "eMkhumbane, the worst place ever," recalled in 2001, "They [Africans] burnt property belonging to the municipality, buses, and some of the [Indian] shops in the vicinity [Grey Street, downtown]. It spread all over like fire."[54]

Dockers, including those who lived in barracks at the Point, played a conspicuous role in the rioting. A report by the South African Institute of Race Relations noted that "The rioters were drawn from those who lived in single Native quarters (barracks) or in the shacks of Cato Manor." Citing testimony from the official investigation of the riots, Hemson wrote, "the worst attackers of Indian property in Cato Manor came from the Point barracks in the dock area through the central area of the town into Booth Road and then on into Cato Manor itself." He suggested that the failure of nonracial strikes in the 1940s resulted in "African workers [who] turned toward more nationalistic forms of action. Instead of class action the African workers turned against Indian people; both petty bourgeois shopkeepers and landowners, and Indian workers." In the aftermath, even those Indians who had sought to forge African-Indian unity turned away from such efforts. In his excellent dissertation on Durban's Indian community, Vahed quoted a working-class Indian born and raised in Cato Manor who belonged to the NIC and identified his politics as "left": "The 1949 riots made us having nothing to do with the African. That suffering we underwent, the misery which has been caused at the hands of the Africans made us more anti-Africa. Our feelings became more bitter. That is why you find the Cato Manor Indian is anti-black. We hate Africans to be quite honest with you and you can't blame us." In this moment, Durban dockers also chose their racial identity over class.[55]

The Cato Manor riots were a defining moment in the history of Durban, especially traumatizing for the city's Indian population. The riots also greatly harmed relations among Durban's multiracial working class, with severe implications for the future ability of Africans and Indians to form alliances, political or otherwise. Vahed highlighted the fact that, for Indians, "the riot resulted in an important and definite change with Africans," and Keith Breckenridge perceptively commented that Indians found themselves "caught between the racist white elite and the rapidly increasing African urban population." Perhaps ironically, the riots confirmed to Nationalist Party leaders, winners of the 1948 elections, the "wisdom" of apartheid, as Freund wrote: "The 1949 race riots were taken as a token of the need to separate the races in the interests of the harmonious development of the city." The following year, the national government passed the Group Areas Act to do just that, though, as geographer Brij Maharaj documented, the municipal government repeatedly and forcefully acted on its own to eliminate multiracial areas and construct a segregated city, before and after apartheid's emergence.[56]

The Cato Manor riots also serve as the logical endpoint for this section. Durban dockers had displayed a long history of militancy and activism, for their own benefit and as part of larger political struggles. From 1950 until 1994, the history of Durban docker activism was part of the larger struggle against apartheid. That is, every strike or other organizational effort of waterfront workers inevitably became caught up in—or consciously belonged to—the freedom struggle.

On the San Francisco Waterfront

Before 1934, waterfront employers had enjoyed near-total power in San Francisco and across the Pacific Coast. That year's "Big Strike" rocked the West Coast, however, and from the workers' stunning victory ultimately came a new union that drastically improved the lives of dockworkers. The strike originated among San Francisco longshoremen, some in a newly emboldened Local 38–79 of the International Longshoremen's Association (ILA), before spreading to other maritime workers, especially sailors, and crippling the entire region's economy. After weeks of brutal repression, on July 5 the San Francisco police killed two men— one a striking longshoreman, the other a union cook who supported the strike; a total of six workers were killed, coastwide, during the strike. Now called "Bloody Thursday," the ILWU still annually conducts memorial events and it remains a legal—paid—holiday for its members, written into its longshore master contract at least since 1990. The killings ignited the historic four-day San Francisco General Strike involving more than 125,000 workers. Sixty years later, Sam Kagel, a strike supporter, recalled, "I can still see it and feel it. It was an exhilarating moment at the beginning. I looked up Market Street and there was nothing moving. It was like in the movies, where something happens and all of a sudden the film shows blank." All told, the Big Strike lasted nearly twelve weeks, ending only after federal government intervention. Federal arbitration took several more months, with the workers ultimately winning many of their demands. A few years later, in 1937, most Pacific Coast ports, led by the San Franciscans, split from the East Coast–dominated and more conservative ILA to form the ILWU. The ILWU quickly affiliated with the left-leaning Congress of Industrial Organizations (CIO), itself born out of a break with the more moderate American Federation of Labor (AFL); in both the ILA-ILWU and larger AFL-CIO divisions, similar arguments existed over organizing tactics and ideologies.[57]

San Francisco and all West Coast longshoremen won unprecedented gains, most importantly a hiring hall, ostensibly jointly managed but largely controlled by the union. In wresting control of the hiring process, the union ended the hated shape-up, a tremendous victory. Instead, each year the rank-and-file in each local elected dispatchers, who assigned work to union members in good standing when they presented themselves at their hiring hall, several times a day, on a "low man out" basis. Other gains included recognition of the union (in 1934, the ILA and, from 1937 onward, the ILWU) as the workers' bargaining agent; a six-hour day and thirty-hour week; major raises in the hourly wage and time and a half for overtime (since shifts, ultimately, remained eight hours, that meant all workers were paid overtime for the final quarter of each shift); a coastwide contract with the same wages, hours, and general conditions in all ports; and preference of employment for union members and rotating job assignments through hiring halls operated by each local. To apply historian Joshua Freeman's quote about the impressive New York City public sector union contracts of a later generation, "In the dry details of contract language, a revolution took place."[58]

A sacred principle upon which the union's hiring hall operated involved equalization of work, meaning the union member with the fewest number of hours worked (in that quarter) was dispatched first. This "low man out" system was—and remains—quite radical and gives a clear sense of how the ILWU implemented, in a practical way, its ideological commitment to equality. In the words of later Local 10 leader and historian Herb Mills, "The hiring hall was indeed 'the union.' It was *the* institution whereby the reality of community could be fashioned and maintained by men who had agreed to structure and divide their work on a fair and equal basis and who, through great strife and conflict, had won the right to do so." With these ideals, it should come as little surprise that numerous ILWU members belonged to or were influenced by various socialist traditions, particularly those of the Communist Party of the United States (CPUSA) and the anarcho-syndicalist Industrial Workers of the World (IWW or Wobblies). Despite massive governmental and employer repression of the IWW during and after World War I, Wobbly ideas circulated aboard ships and on waterfronts along the West Coast at least into the mid-twentieth century. IWW influence is most evident in the motto the ILWU adopted, verbatim, from the Wobblies: "an injury to one is an injury to all." This motto adorns a gigantic banner in Local 10's hall to this very day. Notably, this example of working-class praxis also adorns the masthead of the union that Durban dockworkers belong to, SATAWU, as well as the largest labor federation in South Africa, the Congress of South African Trade Unions (COSATU). As for the CPUSA, many in the ILWU belonged to it or were "fellow travelers," Harry Bridges being the most important.[59]

Another major development that emerged, between 1934 and around 1940, involved the creation of an arbitration system as rare as it was interesting. In the wake of the Big Strike, newly empowered longshoremen engaged in countless "quickie strikes" over workplace disputes, another major strike during 1936–37 (at the end of the first two-year contract), and further quickie strikes afterward. Workers sought greater control over gang size, maximum weight per sling-load, and the like, which led some employers to blacklist gangs and threaten to set up their own hiring hall. As early as 1935, to put limits on such job actions, Bridges and ILA Local 38–79 took the lead within the Maritime Federation of the Pacific, another product of the Big Strike that united longshoremen, sailors, and other maritime workers. Bridges was troubled by job actions of members of the allied Sailors Union of the Pacific, who designated various loads as "hot cargo" as part of their own efforts to expand their power; once designated as such, longshoremen (and all other workers) were supposed to refused to handle "hot cargo" as a matter of solidarity. That is, Bridges's union had no control over which cargo the Sailors Union of the Pacific might label as "hot," yet were expected to respect (not work) said cargo, thereby causing shipping firms more headaches. To hold onto their gains from 1934, particularly the hiring hall, the ILA—and, then, ILWU—agreed to a new arbitration system that ruled on the legitimacy of such work stoppages. Prior to World War II, after a series of rulings, both sides came to accept some basic work rules; these exist alongside the union's coastwide contract and sometimes were called "hip pocket" rules. Crucially, employers accepted the right of longshoremen to stop work for "health and safety" reasons and the union accepted the right of employers to an efficient loading and unloading process. At first, the US secretary of labor appointed arbitrators but, after a long strike in 1948, a revamped system created port arbitrators, regional arbitrators (for southern California, northern California, Oregon, and Washington), and a coastwide one (with final authority). This system exists, albeit in a somewhat different form, to this very day.[60]

Out of the Big Strike, Harry Bridges, the ILWU's outsized leader, stormed onto the scene. Bridges's storied and controversial life remains deeply intertwined with the ILWU even though he retired in 1977 and "crossed the bar," that is, passed away, in 1990. Still known simply as "Harry" by ILWU members, Bridges was born in Australia in 1901. Possessing the wanderlust of many a youngster, he started working ships as a teenager and traveled throughout the South Pacific. His experiences, predictably, shaped his politics: "the more I saw the more I knew that there was something wrong with the system." In 1920, Bridges arrived aboard a cargo ship in the greatest US Pacific Coast port. What he found on the San Francisco waterfront, though, was a broken shell of what had been: The San Francisco Riggers and Stevedores' union had struck in 1919 but had been crushed, replaced by a company or "fink" organization nicknamed the Blue Book union for the color of its dues book (the Riggers and Stevedores' cards were red). At that time, Bridges did not plan to remain in the United States. The following year, 1921, Bridges ended up "on the beach," that is, living ashore instead of working aboard a ship, in New Orleans and joined the IWW, still the most radical union. His uncle's and fellow seamen's politics already had primed him and the Wobblies further shaped his views on unions and socialism. The next year, he started working along the shore in San Francisco, a typical trajectory for a sailor looking for his "snug harbor" as a longshoreman. Bridges worked there for the rest of the decade and into the 1930s. Cherny quoted Bridges about that era: "'All we were doing,' he later recalled, 'was struggling to make it.'"[61]

During the Big Strike, Bridges emerged as a nationally known working-class radical. Bridges belonged to a group of leftist rank-and-filers, many of whom belonged to the CPUSA. During the strike, they successfully resisted pressure from the

ILA's top leadership, in New York City, to accept the employers' offer and end the strike. His organizational abilities quickly earned him great respect and a large following. After the victory, Bridges parlayed this influence into becoming the leader of those in San Francisco—and along the entire West Coast—rebelling against the far more conservative, less democratic, corrupt ILA. First, Bridges was elected president of the San Francisco local, then of the ILA's Pacific Coast District, and, after secession, ILWU international president. Despite maritime labor historian Frank Broeze's generalization that union leaders act more conservatively than rank-and-filers, Bridges helped pull the ILWU leftward. He is frequently described as "the most radical labor leader ever to assume major proportions in this country," a label he likely deserved into the 1950s. Often accused of being a communist, Bridges denied the charge until his death, all the while saying that his views and those of the CPUSA were 95 percent alike. The federal government spent literally twenty years trying to deport him as a communist—no unionist suffered such intense scrutiny for so long—but the rank-and-file gave him unwavering loyalty, including the conservative members, whose numbers were not insignificant. Some scholars, notably Michael Johns, argued that, Bridges's assertions notwithstanding, he belonged to the CPUSA; but Cherny and another important historian of the ILWU, Harvey Schwartz, remain unconvinced.[62]

As international president, Bridges led the ongoing expansion of the union's numbers and strength, built upon the solidarity and pride of the "'34 men," veterans of the Big Strike who became legends inside the union. Although the ILWU remains dominated by the Longshore Division, its name acknowledges the Warehouse Division, too. Amid the labor and political militancy of the mid-1930s, and with new federal protections for workers, longshoremen lined up others in what now is called the logistics or supply chain. First organizing warehouse workers near the docks, the union proceeded to "march inland," hundreds and even thousands of miles from any waterfront. These efforts jibed with the CIO practice of organizing industrially, not by craft, in this case the transportation industry. The ILWU won recognition for new locals that translated into significant material gains and power for both longshore and warehouse workers with the longshoremen's successes earning them the nickname "lords of the docks." Reg Theriault, in Local 10 for thirty years, boasted that "To other workers in the western United States longshoremen on the West Coast had, since the knock-down-drag-out strikes of the mid-1930s, achieved a mythical, almost heroic status, much of it deserved. They had very good wages and just about the best working conditions one could find in any industry. And they did not take crap off of anyone, starting with the stevedore companies and shipping interests that employed them."

ILWU members appreciated that their power was built upon a strong ideological foundation and demanded constant vigilance; they also remained committed to using direct action at the point of production, a syndicalist approach that flowed from the Wobblies. That is, to enforce and strengthen the contract, West Coast longshoremen engaged in myriad, quick, and localized strikes that resulted in the creation of informal or "hip-pocket" rules, for instance, to reduce the maximum weight allowed for any sling-load of cargo.[63]

In addition, shortly after the Big Strike, left-wing whites in the rank-and-file and leadership actively promoted racial equality and built an interracial union, with what became Local 10 particularly committed to this cause. During the union's founding strike, Bridges and others sought to overcome a troubled history of race relations on the waterfront. In the previous generation, a "lily-white" union denied admission to blacks who, thus, felt little compunction about acting as strikebreakers. Bridges, though, reached out to forge alliances with the Bay Area's black community. Pragmatically, the striking longshoremen wanted to prevent African Americans from crossing picket lines again. In addition, Bridges and many other whites in the fledgling union were ideologically committed—as socialists of various persuasions—to organize workers irrespective of race. This groundwork laid, as work swelled during World War II, several thousand African Americans found jobs on the San Francisco waterfront and entered the union. After the war, leftist whites in Local 10 continued pushing for racial inclusion despite declining work. Cleophas Williams, the first black president of any ILWU local, recalled that not only was it racially inclusive and integrated, "Local 10 was the most democratic organization I've ever belonged to." Although not everyone in the ILWU proved equally committed to racial inclusion, as Isaac "Ike" Morrow, an African American longshoreman in Tacoma, once declared, "Sure, there are racists on the waterfront, but the union is not racist."[64]

Conclusions

This chapter contends that both Durban and San Francisco were important ports, regionally, nationally, and globally. These ports facilitated the emergence of other large industries that helped both cities grow and prosper. This chapter also suggests that these port cities (and others in South Africa, the United States, and worldwide) share much even though every place is unique. Of course, the myriad similarities between Durban and San Francisco dockworkers should be apparent.

Simply put, the men who worked along the waterfront in both Durban and San Francisco developed strong bonds with each other. First and foremost, the collective nature of dock work created a common culture and, accordingly, a common identity. Lifting and loading heavy items required working together. Working in tandem and gangs, dockworkers labored toward a common goal (finishing the job), again and again. They also experienced oppressive hiring conditions, labored "causally," felt threatened by perpetual labor surpluses, shared all sorts of dangers, and believed themselves drastically underpaid. Another way to consider these workers is that shared suffering solidified their identity—in the hiring process, on the job, and after work. As a result of shared identities and troubles, both sets of dockworkers started organizing themselves and, despite repeated pushback from employers, never stopped acting collectively, most visibly through repeated strikes and union building. Further, their work experiences shared enough to make comparisons viable.

No doubt, profound differences between these two sets of dockworkers also existed. For one, Durban dockworkers were all black and mostly Zulu while San Francisco longshoremen—before 1934—were almost all white and of many different ethnicities. Second, white Americans were entitled to a set of political rights that ensured them a set of protections and freedoms that, when the New Deal drastically expanded citizenship to include labor rights, saw San Francisco longshoremen quickly seize the moment. African Americans suffered from profound discrimination albeit less so outside the South. By contrast, Durban's all-black dockworkers systematically were denied legal protections created by and for the sole benefit of white South Africans. Among the many inequalities that Durban's dockworkers suffered was the denial of labor rights such as striking or unionizing.

Housing also revealed dramatic differences. Most obviously, Durban dockworkers were compelled to live in seaside hostels whereas San Francisco longshoremen found their own accommodations and commuted to the waterfront. Hostels inculcated an even closer identity in Durban dockworkers, a shared experience that included moments of pleasure, no doubt, but especially shared hardships. In the United States, some textile workers, loggers, and miners lived in company housing, but never dockworkers. Instead, many white longshoremen in San Francisco lived within walking distance of their work, but most African Americans could not; rather, they suffered from pervasive residential segregation. Generally, blacks in the Bay Area lived in racial ghettoes (on both sides of the bay) with more living in Oakland than San Francisco even though most of the work was on the San Francisco side, translating into longer and costlier commutes for blacks.

A related difference involves the migration patterns of these workers. Durban dockworkers, according to law, "belonged" in a native "homeland" such as Kwa-Zulu, even though many worked in the city for years. David Hemson argued that, accordingly, they were among the first fully urbanized Africans, self-consciously so, and invoked some choice quotes from Zulu Phungula as evidence. Quite recently, however, Ralph Callebert profoundly challenged this aspect of Hemson's much earlier scholarship. Citing a series of more than fifty interviews with Durban dockworkers who started working no later than the 1950s, Callebert documented how nearly all of them maintained firm ties to their rural homes and, almost to a man, retired to their original rural homes. Of course, the apartheid state actively worked to keep blacks in rural areas by making it nearly impossible for them to establish permanent urban residence. By contrast, African Americans in Oakland and San Francisco became fully urban despite being mostly rural Southerners by birth and ancestry. African Americans, whether they moved as individuals or in families, never imagined returning to their southern homes because of the horrors of Jim Crow. Once they moved to the Bay Area (and cities across the North, Midwest, and West), African Americans had no intention of moving back to their birthplaces. Thus, the desire of African Americans to remain in the Bay Area, outside the rural South, diverged from that of Zulus to return to their rural KwaZulu homes after retiring.[65]

Yet despite these differences, what also seems clear is that both sets of dockworkers were well organized on the job and willing to frequently agitate for changes in their workplaces. What the Canadian anti-apartheid activists Ken Luckhardt and Brenda Wall wrote about the long history of resistance by Durban dockworkers equally applies to San Francisco: "the history of their involvement in both industrial actions and political protests over the years, has revealed that these workers, despite the disabilities forced upon them, do possess an advanced proletarian consciousness, perhaps even fostered by the system of controlled barracks and compounds." It is to these matters that now we turn.[66]

2

FIGHTING RACIAL OPPRESSION
IN THE 1940S AND 1950S

A victory for the dock workers is a victory for the
entire working class of South Africa.
—Congress of Democrats, in David Hemson, "Dock Workers"

When I first came on the waterfront, many black workers
felt that Local 10 was a utopia.
—Cleophas Williams, in Schwartz, *Solidarity Stories*

World War II and its aftermath helped launch social movements in South Africa, the United States, and worldwide—particularly for independence in much
of the southern hemisphere—that grew in the 1950s and exploded in the 1960s
as a New Left emerged. In both Durban and the San Francisco Bay Area, increasingly bold movements reshaped each city and nation as black freedom struggles
dominated the discourse in both societies. In South Africa, apartheid proved so
all-encompassing that every social movement, including labor, intersected with
race matters. In the postwar United States, civil rights became the leading social
movement—though unionism, undeniably, had been largest and most significant before World War II. This chapter examines how dockworkers in both places
played central roles in struggles for racial equality, often called social movement
unionism in South Africa and civil-rights unionism in the United States. In the
words of South African journalist Azad Essa, social movement unionism "defined
the union movement at the height of the liberation struggle. It was a time when
workplace bread-and-butter issues were not separated from the socio-political
inequities and challenges that existed outside the workplace." This chapter uses
the term "social movement unionism" before dockworkers unionized, for they

demonstrated extensive, informal organization and even coordinated with the South African Congress of Trade Unions (SACTU) that embodied the concept in the 1950s. In short, Durban dockworkers played an important role in the fight against apartheid. Similarly, Bay Area longshoremen committed themselves to what historian US historian Robert Korstad called "civil rights unionism," meaning a union that simultaneously fought for civil and labor rights in a bid for social justice. Starting in the 1930s and continuing through the 1950s, the leftist ILWU and increasingly large black membership in Local 10 became a battering ram fighting racist hiring practices and unequal treatment of African American workers across the city and region.[1]

In their influential work, *The Many-Headed Hydra*, Peter Linebaugh and Marcus Rediker brilliantly documented a multiethnic, multiracial working class overcoming national and racial prejudices, particularly in harbors and aboard ships, as capitalism—in no small part thanks to shipping—started dominating the global economy. Linebaugh and Rediker's study of the Atlantic world ended with the nineteenth century, but marine transport workers continued their struggles in the twentieth century and beyond the Atlantic. This chapter positions Durban and San Francisco dockworkers in this larger history, especially as part of black freedom struggles for, as Alice Mah recently wrote, "Port cities are particularly interesting political sites of struggle, with strong traditions of working-class solidarity and grassroots social movements."[2]

Curiously, although historians of Durban and South Africa generally appreciate the importance—even centrality—of organized (dock)workers in the fight against apartheid, historians of the Bay Area and the United States less frequently "connect the dots" between labor unions and civil rights. Indeed, one of this book's historiographical interventions is that the central role played by South African workers generally and Durban dockworkers particularly in the struggle offers a corrective to the US historiography in that workers and unions rarely appear in accounts of postwar social movements. But the ILWU, especially in San Francisco, committed itself from its inception to black equality. Hence, what the history of Durban dockworkers offers Americanists is that worker movements, including ILWU Local 10, cannot be ignored. Similarly, although scholars of both nations acknowledge the importance of these metro areas, when histories move from local to national, somehow dockworkers—their strikes, unions, and impacts—disappear. The valuable contributions to equal-rights movements by Durban and San Francisco dockworkers have been excluded from national histories. This book challenges traditional interpretations by positioning dockworker activism in these major ports as central to the history of each nation.[3]

Before going down into a metaphorical ship's hold to examine this cargo, however, recall that racial capitalism ruled in both nations. Racism proved so pervasive that not only did employers and the state work to maintain white supremacy, unions and working-class whites in both countries also generally embraced white supremacy. Nearly all unions in South Africa were white-only, though some colored and Indian workers unionized, as black workers legally were denied the right to unionize and strike. Similarly, before the 1930s, most US unions excluded blacks from their ranks or segregated them. It is not surprising that many African Americans, most famously Booker T. Washington, distrusted unions and had little compunction about strikebreaking. Considering race's centrality in South Africa, the overwhelmingly black working class and exclusively white economic and political elite all saw labor and race as inextricably linked. Hence, on "African struggles in Durban," Paul Maylam argued, "It would be a mistake, however, to draw too sharp a distinction between worker action and popular [political] protest." Though fewer whites in the United States made this connection, historians widely agree that racial divisions acted as the primary fault line in US society, including its workplaces. Leaders and many rank-and-filers in the ILWU, particularly its largest branch, Local 10, also saw economic and racial struggles as linked. As Bay Area longshoremen fought long and hard against white supremacy in their own ranks and society at large, black members became deeply loyal and the union much stronger. In both societies, attacking white supremacy demanded a powerful working class.[4]

It also must be understood that, despite many commonalities between Durban and San Francisco dockworkers, crucial differences existed, for instance, that South Africa still could be considered a colonial society until 1994. When South Africa gained independence from the United Kingdom in 1910, 85 percent of its people, that is, the non-Europeans, were not citizens until multiracial democracy arose in 1994. Before then, the white minority dominated the state and economy, arguably still a white settler colony. As Jack and Ray Simons wrote in their classic, *Class and Colour in South Africa*, "White South Africans do behave as though they were imperial masters of a distant colony." Thus, the anti-apartheid movement should be considered part of the independence wave that swept across Africa after World War II. In many of these African freedom struggles, workers—dockworkers in particular—played vital roles. For instance, in Guinea-Bissau, Basil Davidson wrote, "on 3 August 1959, Bissau dock workers at Pidgiguiti began a strike for higher wages. They were shot back to work by the police with the loss of some fifty lives. The whole situation suddenly sharpened." One month later, the revolutionary leader and Pan-Africanist Amilcar Cabral returned to Bissau (after having organized in Angola, where he helped found the Popular Movement for the Liberation of Angola), met with others in the African Independence Party of Guinea and the Cape Verde Islands, and "declared for a struggle against the Portuguese 'by all possible means including war.'" The Pidgiguiti dockworker strike, in retrospect, proved instrumental in convincing Cabral and others to embrace armed struggle. Similarly, labor activism of dockworkers in Mombasa in the 1950s cannot be divorced from the larger anticolonial struggle in Kenya, as Fred Cooper forcefully argued in his groundbreaking book. The situation in South Africa moved far less quickly, but the key point is that labor struggles—particularly of dockworkers—often precipitated and contributed to struggles for black freedom. So, too, in Durban, where this chapter now moves, documenting and analyzing a decade of militancy on the part of dockworkers and their role in the nascent anti-apartheid struggle. After that section will be one examining how San Francisco longshoremen integrated their union, Local 10, helped bust open a fellow local reluctant to do so, and fought to expand job opportunities for African Americans throughout the Bay Area.[5]

Fighting Apartheid on the Durban Waterfront

Docker actions sought to improve the lives of a vital part of Durban's black working class and contributed to the struggle against apartheid—social movement unionism without a formal union. Their actions are especially notable, for they occurred despite drastic efforts by employers and the state to contain them. Indeed, dockers struck five times in eleven years, in 1949, 1954, 1956, 1958, and 1959. They did so with Zulu Phungula as their leader and after his banishment. They struck for wage hikes but also to improve hiring conditions and perhaps decasualize the waterfront—to end the *togt* system. Simply put, no other group of black workers in Durban did what the dockers did; nationwide, perhaps only gold miners around Johannesburg proved as militant. Each time the dockers rose, repression quickly followed with firings, police arrests and beatings, and threats of deportation. Attacks against Durban's dockers, particularly in 1958–59, also foreshadowed broader repression against the anti-apartheid movement in the early 1960s, resulting in a largely quiescent black population later in the decade.

The emergence of apartheid merged with surging anticommunism, early in the global Cold War, to further limit the options of black activists and white allies, especially communists, fighting for equality. The great comparative historian George Fredrickson wrote, "Although they never achieved the mass support that the Garvey movement or the ICU had attracted during the '20s, Communists did manage to play a significant role in the struggle against white racism." Scholar-activist Bernard Magubane, whose father worked on the Durban docks, recalled that "My father and his friends responded warmly to the fighting stand taken by communists on behalf of African rights. They referred to the members of the Communist Party as *Amabomvu*—the 'Red Ones.'" The CPSA and communists across Africa, as well as in the Soviet Union, provided major support for independence movements throughout the developing world, including South Africa. Almost immediately upon assuming power, though, the Nationalist Party undertook a massive campaign against the CPSA, hand-in-glove with the first wave of apartheid legislation. As historian Nicholas Grant recently wrote, "the National Party regularly framed the containment of black protest in South African in the language of anticommunism." Most drastically, the Suppression of Communism Act of 1950 banned the CPSA and defined communism in the broadest of possible terms; literally, a communist was anyone who advocated "any political, industrial, social or economic change within the Union [of South Africa] by the promotion of disturbances or disorder." Just prior to this law's passage, the CPSA dissolved itself but, in 1953, returned as the South African Communist Party and operated underground until it was unbanned in 1990.[6]

Durban dockers agitated against white minority rule for decades but became increasingly involved as apartheid's grip expanded in the 1950s. Billy Nair, a legendary Durban communist and labor and anti-apartheid activist, summarized the dockers' vital role:

> This has a history because in the thirties and forties the workers themselves organised secretly. This is largely because one of their leaders exposed himself by actually becoming a spokesman, a famous Zulu Pungula [*sic*]. When it was found that he was the ringleader in organising the workers he was actually deported, never to come back to Durban again.
>
> The workers learnt a bitter lesson from this and decided to organise secretly so their leaders were never exposed again. But annually, especially during the peak period, when the ships used to dock in the Durban harbour by the hundreds, the workers used to strike at the right moment, in order to push their demands. The workers were met with hostility on the part of the authorities. Police, sometimes the army, were called and even the security [force] of the Stevedoring Company was also let loose, to bash their heads and pressure them to get back to work and so on. Force was one of the themes that ran through the reaction to workers' struggles for improvements.

Beyond the obvious point—the dockers' major role—Nair's quote highlights the historian's challenge in unearthing subaltern history.[7]

In 1949 and throughout the 1950s, dockers proved among the first and most prominent Africans in Durban to challenge apartheid. The regime's labor and urban policies served twin purposes: maintain surpluses of black labor in rural areas (for white farmers) and limit blacks in the cities (to shield white workers while preserving cities as white spaces). Scholar-activists Simons and Simons provided further context: "The perpetual rotation of Africans under intensive police surveillance has had a crippling effect on African labour and political organization. The fear of being 'endorsed out' of towns has been a major deterrent to mass action against apartheid. Labour migration accordingly delays the process of consolidating Africans into a class-conscious proletariat." Although African residents of cities had much to consider before protesting, dockers acted boldly and repeatedly on the job—where they had power—understanding themselves as political actors. Tina Sideris, who interviewed some in the early 1980s, reiterated: "The dockworkers faced some very big problems. One of the biggest problems was the police. During every struggle the government sent the police to break strikes. Sometimes they even sent the army to force workers to go back to work." Whites also understood that black working-class power had the potential to upend apartheid. B. J. Schoeman, a prominent National Party politician who served as minister of labour in the House of Assembly, said as much as early as 1953: "It is obvious that the stronger the Native trade union movement becomes, the more dangerous it would be to the Europeans in South Africa. . . . We would probably be committing race suicide if we give them that incentive."[8]

In 1949, after the horrible Cato Manor riots, Durban was predictably tense. Nevertheless, Zulu Phungula, newly returned after his five-year banishment, is-sued "A notice to all workers in the Province of Natal" urging them not report to work on May 1 unless they received 1.5£ per day. Eight hundred dockers responded by striking the day after May Day and black workers in related industries also struck. These actions occurred despite Phungula's arrest. Rowley Israel Arenstein, a well-known communist Jewish lawyer in Durban, served as his defense attorney; Phungula stood little chance. Once again, Phungula was banished to Ixopo, this time for ten years and, as far as is known, he never returned. The city government also reduced the number of "surplus" Africans by more strictly limiting the entry of Africans into Durban, which hurt employers of *togt* labor. The national govern-ment also aided the employers, when it introduced labor bureaus in rural areas and agreed that *togt* employers need not register their workers daily.[9]

The banishment of Phungula, no doubt, gave the dockers serious pause and resulted in an ingenious new tactic that tens of thousands of black workers in Durban copied in 1973. As Sideris wrote, on the basis of interviews conducted in the early 1980s, "The dockworkers learnt one big lesson from their fight in the 1940's. They saw what the government did to their leaders. So they had to find a way to protect their leaders. In the 1950's they made a plan." That plan turned out to be as simple as it proved effective, "When we are talking to our employers the government interferes. The man we want to speak for us has been taken away. We are still looking for him. [Henceforth] We won't have spokesmen." Dockers first refused to select leaders during their 1952 strike. The Native Affairs Com-missioner in Durban, R. Watling, reported on this strategy to his superior: "I re-quested the gathering to elect two or three spokesmen to appear and put their case to the Council at the meeting to be held on Monday next. This was rejected on the ground that a spokesman would be victimised and deported from Durban." As an

Fig. 1. Durban dockworkers, ca. 1950. Photograph by David Goldblatt. University of Witwatersrand Historical Papers, Johannesburg. Image used with permission of Goldblatt.

alternative, Watling arranged a gathering at which employers and government officials addressed a group of "some 400 to 500 Natives . . . [who] were most orderly and well behaved." Hemson later discussed this tactic: "These organizational forms were able to survive longer among these workers than among those with more formal methods of organization." They continued using this strategy and, in 1973, the workers at Coronation Brick—widely credited for launching the Durban Strikes—adopted an identical approach.[10]

In 1954, nearly three thousand waterfront workers—mostly *togt* but also some members of the South African Railway and Harbour Workers Union (SARHWU)—struck, marking the largest industrial action of 1950s Durban to that date. Their primary demand was a raise, of nearly 50 percent, though they also asked to be represented by their banished leader, Zulu Phungula. It is interesting to note that the government blamed the African National Congress (ANC), a South African police official claiming, "there is little doubt that this organisation had much to do with bringing about the stoppage of work"; though no extant evidence for ANC involvement exists, it would add further heft to this chapter's thesis if the ANC had coordinated with the dockers. Under the newly passed Native Labour (Settlement of Dispute) Act, African workers could not legally strike, and so the dockers were threatened with firings; the *togt* workers, as casuals, *legally* were not striking, however, and so they were within their rights in refusing to return to work. Employers and the Central Native Labour Board (CNLB) then threatened to evict the workers from their hostels, asserting that *togt* workers were required to be on call for work as a condition of housing. After facing down both barrels of this employer-state shotgun, the dockers returned to work, but not before the CNLB "granted" a raise of nearly 20 percent—a major gain and evidence that employers understood that their workers possessed some power. Yet, in a final show of employer strength, nearly one hundred strikers were fined one day's wages for their actions. Further proof of this strike's national import came from the Transvaal Council of Non-European Trade Unions and Congress of Democrats, the latter of which declared "A victory for the dock workers is a victory for the entire working class of South Africa."[11]

Two years later, in 1956, several groups of dockers struck or threatened to do so—to gain a raise, have a hostel *induna* fired, and eliminate the *togt* system—suggesting a heightened sense of militancy in an era of surging anti-apartheid activism nationwide. One action resulted in a raise, without a strike, confirming docker power though CNLB Chair S. D. Mentz asserted, seemingly without irony, "the reason [for the raise] was that they [dockers] had been obedient." Mentz also revealed his paternalism: "if they continued to do so [stay within the law] he would remain their father." Another strike, which failed, sought to pressure one stevedoring company to fire an *induna* who changed the rules that previously allowed residents to host visitors, such as wives. Some dockers also proposed to work on monthly contracts with a steady income, in other words, decasualize the waterfront, with mixed results. Later that year, some struck after a few employers hired a small group of workers on a permanent basis—albeit at reduced wages—apparently trading security for money. Employers acted cleverly, playing workers off each other in hiring some permanently while leaving others casual and cutting wages for the new permanents. Such tactics paralleled the pre-1934 San Francisco waterfront. There, hiring bosses chose some longshoremen for "star gangs" that received the most regular employment; in exchange, bosses expected these gangs to bolster productivity and "encourage" other workers to do the same. Harry Bridges belonged to a star gang in the 1920s, and so he knew how nefarious they were in dividing workers. In Durban, dockers also understood the issue for the newly permanent workers and struck to protest the cuts with many *togt* workers striking in sympathy. This contentious matter continued to animate labor relations for the remainder of the decade.[12]

Local and national government officials, along with waterfront employers, understandably were desperate to end these blatant and repeated examples of black (docker) power. Hemson wrote, "In November 1957, the Minister of Native Affairs, Dr. H. F. Verwoerd announced his intention to remove most of the stevedoring compounds in the Point Dock area, and allow only 2,000 African stevedores in the area." Verwoerd's plan, not surprising from the person widely considered to be the father of apartheid, called for relocating them to the new black township of Kwa-Mashu, created to further segregate Durban's population. Apart from the workers' opposition, though, employers expressed major concern that their workers would not report for overtime, nighttime, and weekend shifts if they had to travel twenty kilometers between the Point and this far northern township. The *Natal Mercury*, always in line with local business interests, led its "news" story with the following: "It would be impossible to work the stevedoring industry in Durban with anything like the present efficiency if Native labour was moved out to Kwa Mashu, Mr. R. C. Lloyd, a representative of stevedore employers, told the Wage Board in Durban yesterday." The Stevedores' Association, which housed more than a thousand dockers, formally protested against the government proposal and countered that the resulting decline in efficiency would result in ships skipping Durban for Lourenço Marques. In a perhaps surprising statement, CNLB chairman Mentz concurred: "it would be a gross mistake to upset the balance of work at the port because of an ideological view." In this instance, economics trumped ideology and dockers continued to be housed at the Point.[13]

While government officials and employers debated housing policy, dockers heeded the call of SACTU, a core member of the anti-apartheid Congress Alliance, in a three-day "Stay-at-Home" in April 1958. SACTU organized black workers into unions even though, legally, they had almost no workplace rights. Muriel Horrell noted that "the S.A. Railways and Harbours Administration and many private employers, are openly hostile [to SACTU]. . . . The Wage Board does not allow African unions, including the Sactu ones, to appear at its meetings to give evidence." SACTU devoted much of its energy to the political struggle for racial equality, collaborating with the ANC in organizing worker stay-aways (recall that African workers legally could not strike). Employers, government officials (local and national), and police all attempted to dissuade Durban dockers from joining the stay-away, as did the paramount chief of the Zulus, the latter on the front page of the *Mercury*. Nevertheless, 75 percent of dockers left their hostels and demanded a massive raise, to £1 per day, the SACTU version of a living wage campaign. Magubane put a human face on these actions: "The introduction of the stay-at-home as a political tactic tested the will of my father and other poorly paid workers. They risked losing a day or two's wages, if not their jobs. The police acted viciously against those they found 'loitering' in the streets."

When SACTU called off the stay-away, because of low participation nationwide, dockers continued with an "overtime ban" and refusal to work Sunday shifts for several weeks. A few short strikes also erupted. These actions caused massive delays at the port, idling dozens of ships. The *Mercury* asserted, "It is understood that this decision [overtime ban] was not directly connected with the 'stay away from work' campaign" though the timing and identical wage demand suggest otherwise. Finally, in late May, employers and dockers reached a settlement that raised wages to 14s. per day—meaning *togt* workers drove their wages up nearly 65 percent in the 1950s. Overall, the national stay-away was not that successful, though the Durban dockers, again, had displayed their militancy even though few belonged to SACTU.[14]

Durban dockers, in fact, provided significant support to SACTU, a major player in fighting apartheid during the 1950s. Robert Lambert, the historian who created the label "political unionism" and who is the expert on SACTU in Natal, wrote, "SACTU leadership consistently argued that the struggle against economic exploitation in the factory, and the related but wider political oppression, must be developed simultaneously." In the 1950s, SACTU became the leading voice of black workers, explicitly fighting apartheid, declaring the following at its first annual conference:

> Sactu is conscious of the fact that the organising of the mass of workers for higher wages, better conditions of life and labour is inextricably bound up with a determined struggle for political rights and liberation from all oppressive laws and practices. It follows that a mere struggle for the economic rights of all the workers without participation in the general struggle for political emancipation would condemn the Trade Union movement to uselessness and to a betrayal of the interests of the workers.

More prosaically, Chief Albert Luthuli, ANC president-general (and future Nobel Peace Prize winner), stated at another SACTU conference, "SACTU is the spear, ANC the shield." This phrase became quite popular in explaining their relationship, suggesting that SACTU did not take orders from the ANC. For example, in this era, the ANC remained black-only though philosophically committed to nonracialism; by contrast, Africans, coloreds, and Indians populated the ranks and leadership of SACTU. Regarding Durban's multiracial working class, Hemson noted, "new relationships between Indian and African political and industrial organizations were born in the aftermath of the riots of January 1949. In Durban the base was laid for the mass organization of industrial workers which developed in the 1950s with the growth of SACTU" and the period saw the development of the "Durban area as a leading centre of militant trade unionism, mass political action, and a high level of strike activity." Bill Freund, though, qualified this characterization in highlighting the fact that few Indians joined SACTU because of the lingering effects of the Cato Manor riots and earlier failed joint strikes of black and Indian workers. Historian Tom Lodge added, quoting the stalwart Durban communist Arenstein, "Indian workers were left in the cold" in the 1950s, despite their earlier activism in unions and CPSA, because the underground Communist Party deemphasized unions to the chagrin of Durbanites. Indian workers played little role on the Durban waterfront.[15]

Some dockers, though, were active in SACTU, most prominently Curnick Ndlovu, a key figure from the mid-1950s until his imprisonment in the mid-1960s. His father moved the family to Cato Manor after the war and found casual work on the railways at the Point. In 1953, Ndlovu found a job as a casual docker which he held for a decade. In 1955, he joined SARHWU, an African union dating back to the 1930s. Although SARHWU had limited influence among Durban dockers (that is, those who worked on the ships), about five hundred pier-side railway workers belonged. SARHWU helped found SACTU with its Cape Town branch most active. Ndlovu soon became involved in SACTU, ANC, and the Communist Party (then an underground organization). When the government declared a national state of emergency—right after the notorious 1960 Sharpeville Massacre, in which the police killed at least sixty-nine black anti-apartheid protesters—the Natal secretary general of SARHWU hastily left South Africa (as had ANC vice president Oliver Tambo), and so Ndlovu was elected to serve in that role, also becoming a member of the SACTU National Executive Committee. In these capacities, he organized workers in Durban and KwaMashu and was "instrumental in exposing agents sent by the government to disrupt anti-apartheid activities in the trade union movement." In the immediate aftermath of Sharpeville, however, organizing workers proved impossible. Nelson Sambureni discussed how the underground ANC and allies planned a three-day national stay-away in May 1961 to protest South Africa's declaration of a republic (despite the fact that the great majority of South Africans were not citizens nor ensured equal rights); however, in Durban, "the stay-away was a failure" and even the dockers reported for work, suggesting the new labor regime and retrenchments effectively quieted activism for the moment.[16]

Though the ANC was banned after Sharpeville, in 1961 Nelson Mandela and other ANC leaders created an armed underground wing, Umkhonto we Sizwe (Spear of the Nation or MK). Ndlovu became the leader of the Natal Regional Command of MK. Like Ndlovu, most MK leaders in Natal also were SACTU activists. In a 2001 interview, Ndlovu recounted that "We started forming operational units, arranging for their training technically on how to mix the ingredients for making pipe bombs, petrol bombs and all those things." The MK announced itself to the nation on December 16, 1961, when cadre members started blowing buildings up nationwide. Ndlovu gave these highlights: "the main targets were government properties and government installations. But there was a stern warning that there should be no loss of lives. In Durban we targeted the Department of Home Affairs," a symbol of apartheid. A government agent provocateur inside the MK Natal command, however, tried to convince Ndlovu to bomb commuter trains at

Georgedale and Hammersdale, but he refused: "Are you crazy? Do you know what is going to happen there? You will kill those train drivers and that is not our policy." Ndlovu emphasized that "We continued to mess up the rail lines, like the one on Old Berea Road, where there was no threat to human life." In April 1963, Ndlovu was banned just prior to a speech he was to give at the downtown Bantu Men's Social Centre; under the Suppression of Communism Act of 1950, African trade unions regularly were harassed, had their offices raided, had their records confiscated, and the like. Soon thereafter, Ndlovu was arrested and put on trial, where he defended the use of sabotage as the last resort after decades of using nonviolence to end white supremacy. Predictably, Ndlovu was found guilty of sabotage and sentenced to twenty-four years in prison, ultimately serving twenty on notorious Robben Island. Though he made no mention of it, a typical experience of arrest, interrogations, and imprisonment involved both brutality and torture. Ndlovu's story exemplifies how labor and political activism were part and parcel of the same struggle.[17]

Ndlovu's actions also reveal how at least some waterfront workers were committed to both racial equality and socialism. Billy Nair, Ndlovu's second in command in the Natal MK as well as a leader in the Natal Indian Congress and SACTU, spoke at the historic Congress of the People, where the Freedom Charter was released, in Kliptown (in the Johannesburg township of Soweto) in 1955:

> Now, comrades, the biggest difficulty we are facing in South Africa is that one of capitalism in all its oppressive measures versus the ordinary people—the ordinary workers in the country. We find in this country . . . the means of production, the factories, the lands, the industries, and everything possible is owned by a small group of people who are the capitalists in this country. They skin the people, as a matter of fact in exploitation. They oppress in order to keep them as slaves in the land of their birth.

Nair, Ndlovu, and others in and around the Congress Alliance envisioned socialism as the solution to racial capitalism. These leaders exemplified the interconnections of the anti-apartheid and labor movements and how the latter dominated both in Durban. Rob Lambert's important dissertation lends further heft to the contentions that Durban's working class stood at the forefront of the nation's labor movement and SACTU played a leading role in the era's struggle, including its armed underground, the MK. In this moment—as it would in the early 1970s—Durban dockers played a significant role in the national story, part of a major upsurge in activism in the late 1950s and 1960 that then was suppressed brutally.[18]

Back on the waterfront, in 1959, a strike broke out with ramifications for both the fight against apartheid and dock work in Durban, in that it evolved out of another national stay-away campaign waged by the ANC and SACTU. In February 1959, more than fifteen hundred dockers struck for another raise, complaining that their recent one was far less than what *indunas* received, though not everyone joined. Callebert cited one docker who chose not to protest because "you would be arrested if you are against the white people." Though the job action did not anoint formal leaders and dockers used nicknames to avoid identification, employers responded with mass firings and orders to leave the hostels. In response, the dockers called a meeting at what was called Bamboo Square, one of the oldest "informal settlements" in the Point near the hostels, where the chief native commissioner, A. L. Schaeffer, admonished those gathered because "It is illegal to go on strike." The strikers then suffered a baton charge by the police that broke up the meeting and left four workers bleeding on the ground. Police arrested scores who were soon found guilty of trespassing and sentenced to twenty-five days in prison or a fine of £5: because no docker possessed such a sum, they all served the time. Most of those who were fired were rehired later but under an entirely new system in which all workers were "permanently" employed by a single newly created firm and paid weekly rather than daily. To welcome this new public-private organization, named the Durban Stevedoring Labour Supply Company (DSLSC), many former *togt* workers struck yet again, for they believed the new system translated into a pay cut. Technically, the dockers refused overtime and, as Muriel Horrell reported, "Congestion in the harbour resulted. The employers did not undertake further negotiations, but dismissed the entire labour force, recruiting new workers from Zululand to take their places." Durban's stevedores and government decasualized the waterfront, fired the entire workforce, and recruited a new group of workers from rural KwaZulu.[19]

The dramatic events on the Durban waterfront created new problems for dockers and foreshadowed wider repression. David Hemson wrote, "the comparatively 'free' form of labour [*togt*] was transformed into contract labour under a strict labour regime," controlled by the newly created DSLSC. After hiring thousands of new and inexperienced workers, "the conditions were very poor . . . people got injured. They broke legs and arms," according to Mr. Khanye, one of those hired under the new regime. Tina Sideris connected the 1960s Durban docks to the broader struggle: "The bosses used the controls very well. For a while things were quiet at the docks. And things were quiet all over South Africa." Indeed, the nationwide protests of the late 1950s and 1960 resulted in the fiercest repression yet seen in South Africa, when every anti-apartheid organization was banned and most activists arrested, driven underground, exiled, imprisoned, or killed. The effects upon black workers during the "quiet decade" were stark: "In the 1960s there were very few strikes. When workers went on strike, the government acted strongly and quickly to keep workers weak and afraid. Very few workers were members of unions. They remembered how SACTU had organised, but they also remembered the government repression. Some workers were afraid to join unions. They had seen too many of their leaders banned, banished and put in jail. Some workers did not want to trust trade unions any more. They said that the leaders had fled and gone overseas." On the Durban waterfront and across the nation, the power of the apartheid state and employers—tightly aligned—proved momentarily triumphant.[20]

To conclude, this section argues that docker activism in 1949 and the 1950s played a central role in local and national efforts against apartheid. Durban dockers helped lead the charge, repeatedly striking to raise their wages but also for overtly political ends, spearheading SACTU stay-aways in Durban in 1958 and 1959. They understood their own power—crucial cogs of the marine transport industry—as evidenced in the tactics they used: refusing overtime, not reporting for work, and timing their stoppages during heavy ship traffic. After the banishment of Zulu Phungula, their radical leader, they developed new forms of organizing, informally and secretly, in ship's holds and their hostels. It should come as little surprise that Durban dockers played a major part of the struggle. Callebert, echoing Fred Cooper, linked docker resistance to liberation movements elsewhere: "Throughout colonial Africa transport workers have been particularly militant as well. . . . Port and railway workers occupied a strategic position in the infrastructure of empire, a fact of which they were acutely conscious, not least because they felt a strong presence of the colonial state in their workplace." It also is unsurprising that employers and the state deployed drastic measures to suppress dissent, bolster profits, and maintain apartheid. Notably, the targeting of dockers in 1959 foreshadowed repression against the wider movement in subsequent years. Consider one Native Affairs official who named the waterfront in 1961 as a "strategic centre for subversive elements." And just as they were among the first suppressed, dockers proved among the very first to return to the struggle. San Francisco longshoremen also fought racial capitalism in the mid-twentieth century, the subject to which we now turn.[21]

ILWU Local 10 Fighting White Supremacy

ILWU Local 10 committed itself to racial equality in its own ranks and fought for it in the Bay Area and nationwide, setting the bar for civil-rights unionism. Generally, coalitions of left-leaning or communist African Americans and European Americans drove the racially progressive policies of labor unions like the ILWU. Starting in 1934, during and after World War II, and through the 1960s, left radicals turned the San Francisco waterfront upside down—transforming a workforce from only 1 percent black to about 50 percent by the mid-1960s. The membership also started electing black leaders to local offices. A combination of factors, ideological and pragmatic, explains how Local 10 became one of the most integrated

unions—indeed, institutions—in the nation. But the ILWU's record on race relations revealed problems, too, the most troublesome being the international's
decades-long toleration of systematic racial discrimination in some longshore
locals, especially Los Angeles and Portland. Nevertheless, the ILWU, led by Local
10, proved staunch advocates of racial equality.

In the 1930s and 1940s, endemic racism existed in San Francisco and throughout the Bay Area both on the docks and in other workplaces. As discussed, before
World War II, few African Americans lived in San Francisco or Oakland. Yet, as
Bruce Nelson perceptively wrote, "Although blacks were—relatively speaking—absent, race was omnipresent. The region was, after all, settled by Anglo-Protestant
migrants who brought their whiteness with them and by European immigrants
who found the West a congenial environment in which to negotiate their citizenship in the White Republic." Only during World War II did many African Americans migrate to the Bay Area, and several thousand found jobs on the waterfront,
where race relations already had been tainted. In 1919, the white-only Riggers and
Stevedores' Union struck but, according to Robin Dearmon Jenkins (now Muham-
mad), "Jamaican strikebreakers brought in by Bay Area shipping companies and
guarded on ships just off port in San Francisco Bay weakened the strikers' resolve."
The replacements helped defeat the strike, but Jenkins contends these Jamaican
dockworkers later allied with black railroaders in the East Bay, hoping "to turn the
tide of white nativism and employment discrimination within the AFL," albeit to
no avail. Nelson summarized race relations in the Bay Area on the eve of the Big
Strike: "for the most part, wherever unions prevailed, black workers were excluded.
Indeed, in the early 1930s John Pittman, editor of the [black] *San Francisco Spokesman*, complained bitterly that 'for Aframerican workers in the Bay cities, union
labor has been and still is the chief obstacle to employment.'" In 1934, only a few
dozen African Americans worked on the San Francisco waterfront, having gotten
these jobs via strikebreaking fifteen years earlier, and all in "Jim Crow," that is, all-
black, gangs. In the Bay Area, few blacks belonged to unions with most of those
in the Brotherhood of Sleeping Car Porters, led by C. L. Dellums, Oakland's most
prominent black labor leader.[22]

It is perhaps surprising, then, that white longshoremen on strike reached out
to African Americans—in a time when white supremacy was the norm. First, left-
wing militants among the strikers lined up the existing black dockworkers. Henry
Schmidt, a long-time leader alongside Harry Bridges, recalled "efforts made" to
persuade them to join the strike and union. Bridges described this event this way: "I
went directly to them. I said: 'Our union means a new deal for Negroes. Stick with
us and we'll stand for your inclusion in industry'." Then Bridges, who emerged out
of the rank-and-file to lead the Big Strike, reached out to the broader black community and asked for their support. No doubt, it helped tremendously that Dellums,

the most important black civil-rights and labor leader around, implored African Americans not to take jobs as replacements; appreciating the potential for trouble, striking longshoremen even acted as his bodyguards. Forty years later, Dellums remembered: "I was interested in them having a real union again because all the workers needed a union. Of course I was interested in breaking up the segregation on the waterfront and breaking up the shape-up system and providing for Negroes to be allowed to work on there, because they were human beings and had a right to work—and should work without discrimination." Particularly in San Francisco, the ILWU made good on that promise.[23]

Shortly after the Big Strike, the San Francisco local instituted new rules that promoted racial integration. Before 1934, ethnicity and race often played a major role in hiring and on the job. It was common practice, in San Francisco and other ports, for employers to hire ethnically and racially homogeneous gangs that, once on the job, were pitted against other gangs of another composition. For employers, this practice increased productivity and reduced worker solidarity, thereby making strikes and unionism less likely. For workers, this system increased ethnic and racial tensions as well as accident rates. African Americans suffered greatly under this old system, either from exclusion or segregation. Shortly after the Big Strike, however, the San Francisco local prohibited gangs composed exclusively of ethnic or racial minorities, essentially mandating that African Americans be integrated into gangs. This initiative—and, more generally, the opening of the union to African Americans—met some resistance. Long-time Local 10 and ILWU leader Henry Schmidt recalled that "many, many of our [white] members were opposed to those [black] people coming in." Historian Bruce Nelson credited left-wing militants, including Bridges and Schmidt, for promoting integration, which remained in place; writing about the 1940s, labor economist Herbert Northrup wrote, "segregated gangs are not permitted, and the union's non-discrimination policy is strictly enforced." By contrast, the ILA in New York City and some of its other ports forced black members to shape up as "extras," rather than as part of gangs, and segregated them into all-black locals well into the postwar era. Meanwhile, in San Francisco, "a few white-black partnerships" started to dispatch regularly from the hall as early as the 1930s.[24]

What had been a small black membership in Local 10 soared during World War II. Unprecedented labor shortages sparked the second wave of the Great Migration of African Americans to cities outside the South, including the Bay Area. Historian Jim Gregory argued that "The Southern Diaspora transformed American racial hierarchies, as black migrants in the great cities of the North and West developed institutions and political practices that enabled the modern civil rights movement." The Bay Area, for instance, became the leading industrial and military center for the war effort in the Pacific theater, with perhaps two thousand African Americans joining Local 10 as "permit men," fully one-quarter of its war-inflated membership. These black men earned more than they previously could have imagined, hailing from economically (and politically) desperate portions of the rural South, especially Arkansas, Louisiana, Missouri, and Texas. Historical sociologist Howard Kimeldorf noted that some had previous experience as dockworkers, "One of the largest and most politically important groups to enter the union at this time was made up of black longshoremen from the Gulf. . . . By the middle of 1943 several hundred black dockworkers from Louisiana and southern Texas were at work on the waterfront."[25]

Though everyone's life is unique, the stories of two black migrants fairly represent thousands. Born in 1914 in Shreveport, William Chester grew up around Kansas City. His father's death, when Chester was just eleven, and the Great Depression ensured that he entered the workforce as a teen. He "chose" the US Army, as so many working-class blacks (and others) had before him and still do. In 1940, after unhappily serving in a segregated unit, Chester moved to San Francisco, where he worked on barges and then the docks, both organized by the ILWU. Similarly, Cleophas Williams came from rural Arkansas where he had suffered from the plague of Jim Crow. Despite a thirst for education, his family struggled and his father died prematurely as a result of the atrocious health care then available to southern blacks. Williams moved to Oakland in 1942, found work on the waterfront in early 1944, and joined Local 10. ILWU members later elected both Chester and Williams to local and international leadership positions. Blacks in other local industries, by contrast, experienced vastly different conditions.[26]

Tens of thousands of African Americans found jobs during the wartime boom in the Bay Area, particularly its massive shipbuilding industry, though they still suffered from racism. They earned much higher wages than ever before and no longer suffered under the horrors of Jim Crow, and so they embraced their new homes. Moreover, some industrial unions affiliated with the recently born CIO (which included the ILWU) actively organized African Americans. Most other unions, however, continued ignoring black workers or segregating them. In particular, AFL craft unions in shipbuilding came under criticism for pervasive racism; this industry was the most important one because it employed about two hundred thousand people in the Bay Area at its World War II peak. The primary shipbuilders' union was notorious for denying blacks access to many skilled jobs and for segregating them in lower-paying and less skilled categories. Civil-rights activist Cy Record offered a contemporary indictment of such racism in his feature on Willie Stokes, who worked in the East Bay's huge Kaiser shipyard. Stokes was forced into an auxiliary local of the AFL's local shipyard union: "He did not know much about unions, but he knew Jim-Crow, segregation, discrimination, and second-class citizenship when he saw it." Racism persisted despite vigorous efforts by local activists in the A. Philip Randolph–led March on Washington movement, the National Association for the Advancement of Colored People (NAACP), and national CIO. In the Bay Area and nationwide, many unions remained closed to blacks or treated them as second-class members. Bill Chester, for one, reiterated the well-known fact that the building trade unions, affiliated with the AFL, controlled entry into these lucrative fields and preserved them as white-only. Off the job, most African Americans were pushed, via a variety of legal and extralegal ways, into highly segregated, poorer neighborhoods on both sides of the San Francisco Bay. Local racial tensions remained common—further heightened after Japanese and Japanese Americans were forcibly removed to internment camps in the interior West.[27]

By contrast, the racial policies of the ILWU, especially Local 10, appear decades "ahead" of the times. The union committed itself from its founding to being inclusive to all ethnic and racial groups. Once in the union, workers of color were dispatched as all others, i.e. "low man out," essentially putting the Christian socialist notion of the "last shall be first" into practice. No doubt, the gap between theory and practice can be yawning, but African Americans found themselves treated quite well in Local 10, far better than any other white-majority union, business, church, or government institution. The first real test was World War II, when the African American membership skyrocketed to 25 percent of Local 10. The figure is astounding in a city where blacks had risen from less than 1 percent of the population to only 5 percent in the 1940s; even in Oakland during that decade, African Americans increased from about 3 percent to a little more than 12 percent. The union not only took in blacks but also defended them; for example, in 1943, one US Naval officer ordered a longshore gang to stop loading oranges because one worker was black; Jesse Merritt, the African American in question, reported the officer called him a "God-damned black nigger!" In response, Local 10 held an investigation at which Local 10 President Germain Bulcke found the naval officer "guilty of discrimination" and called for his court-martial. Beyond inclusion, Cleophas Williams later declared, "Local 10 was the most democratic organization I've ever belonged to." Elected leaders could serve only two consecutive years before, as Local 10 leader Bulcke noted, "The third year you go back to work on the docks." Williams found himself impressed with union meetings where blacks participated equally and, more generally, that leaders "believe in educating the rank-and-file." In the 1950s, blacks started getting elected to Local 10 offices such as dispatcher, business agent, and chief dispatcher. In 1967, Cleophas Williams was the first black elected local president, going so far as to declare, "This union was the greatest thing in my life, other than my family."[28]

The primary explanation for the ILWU's strong commitment to racial equality is the politics of the original leaders and rank-and-filers, many of whom believed in democracy and socialism. Perhaps most famous was Harry Bridges's declaration, "If things reached a point where only two men were left on the waterfront," if he had anything to say about it, "one would be a black man." Since San Francisco was his "home local" and the international based itself there (as the coast's busiest port), Bridges commanded outsized influence in Local 10. Though leadership matters greatly, many other leftists populated the union's ranks, particularly Local 10—well-known as a hotbed for communists, Trotskyists, socialists, and even a few Wobblies. In fact, when the local expanded during the war, "many of the earliest recruits were radicals of one type or another" who desired, as Kimeldorf documented, admission to the ILWU *because* of its left politics. For decades after the war, Local 10 and the ILWU remained magnets for leftists. Also notable was the ideological influence of the IWW, despite its miniscule membership by the 1930s. The IWW was the first union in the twentieth century United States to seriously combat white supremacy (in the 1920s, the CPUSA also embraced this ideal); the ILWU clearly modeled its commitment to racial equality after the IWW (and CPUSA), as already evidenced in adopting the Wobbly motto, Bridges's and others' previous membership in the IWW, and its democratic practices. The ILWU embraced (in modified fashion) the Wobbly practices of holding frequent local elections to prevent leaders from losing appreciation for what ordinary members experienced; thus, though it varied by local, elected leaders went "back to the bench" after serving a single one- or two-year term in office. Also, officials never were paid more than the highest-paid rank-and-filers; Bridges was perhaps the least-well-paid union president in the nation. The ILWU was not unique in the 1930s, for new CIO unions in auto, meatpacking, steel, and other industries also reached out to African Americans, Mexican Americans, women, and other historically oppressed groups. Just as in the ILWU, communist, Trotskyist, and other left activists (themselves of a variety of racial and ethnic backgrounds) generally led the push for full inclusion in other unions.[29]

Of course, pragmatism also helps explain why the ILWU opened itself up to blacks—what David Roediger referred to as "stomach equality." Like most organizations, unions are stronger with more members and, if some are excluded, those who are excluded can be used against them, most obviously as strikebreakers. Examples of pragmatic interracial or biracial unions include New Orleans dockworkers in the late nineteenth century and coal miners in Alabama and West Virginia who belonged to the United Mine Workers of America. Yet America's racist history is replete with examples conclusively demonstrating that practicality, by itself, did *not* usually convince white workers to stand with black ones. Hence, ideology mattered. In the case of racial equality on the San Francisco waterfront, historian Robert Self concluded the ILWU "forged an intense solidarity, and Harry Bridges and cosmopolitan radicals of both communist and syndicalist persuasion turned this solidarity into a force for racial equality."[30]

During the Cold War, an anticommunist crusade merged with white supremacy in the US government's massive effort to deport Harry Bridges, a naturalized
citizen. Many rank-and-file leftists were investigated or "screened" off jobs, particularly early in the Cold War, and Bridges started to experience governmental
harassment in the 1930s. For twenty years, the San Francisco Police Department,
the US Immigration and Naturalization Service, the US Department of Labor, the
US Department of Justice, US Congress, and various federal courts investigated,
prosecuted, and sought to deport or imprison him—alternately for being a member of the CPUSA or lying about it. Many supporters suspected the government
of doing the employers' dirty work, as Woody Guthrie wrote in his "The Ballad of
Harry Bridges," later modified by Pete Seeger and the Almanac Singers:

> Harry's organized thousands more and made them union men.
> "We must try to bribe him," the shipping bosses said.
> And if he won't accept a bribe, we'll say that he's a red!"
>
> The bosses brought a trial to deport him over the sea,
> But the judge said, "He's an honest man, I got to set him free."
> Then they brought another trial to frame him if they can,
> But right by Harry Bridges stands every working man!

Bridges refused to be cowed and continued criticizing the US government during
the Cold War. Most dramatically, after condemning President Truman's decision to
commit US armed forces to the Korean Conflict, federal authorities threw Bridges
into prison for three weeks. Huge majorities of ILWU members—including those
who disagreed with his politics—saw the government investigation as a witch hunt
and Bridges as a martyr. Bridges suffered through five lengthy trials in twenty years
and was found innocent in all of them. He commented, ironically, "I don't deny
that I've had due process. I've had all the due process I want." US Supreme Court
Justice Frank Murphy agreed in 1945: "Seldom if ever in the history of this nation
has there been such a concentrated and relentless crusade to deport an individual
because he dared to exercise that freedom which belongs to him as a human being
and is guaranteed him by the Constitution." Among other factors explaining this
persecution, one ILWU pamphlet pointedly asked in 1955, "Is it because the ILWU
banned racial discrimination and segregation twenty years before the United States
Supreme Court found the courage to do so?" What is interesting in the Bridges-
ILWU example is that it provides something of an exception to the argument pow-
erfully made by Alex Lichtenstein, namely that interracial unionism failed to take
hold in most of the US labor movement because of a series of interrelated factors,
including the postwar anti–Communist Party purge inside the CIO; the passage of
the fiercely antiunion Taft-Hartley Act of 1947 and the anticommunist Smith Act of

1950, as well as the more general co-optation and repression of unions and radicals in the domestic war against communism called McCarthyism or the second Red Scare. Despite the numerous factors that undergirded the failure of the US labor movement to embrace racial equality, the ILWU remained committed to this goal.[31]

Despite the postwar surging anticommunism in the United States, blacks in and around the ILWU attributed the union's racially inclusive policies to its left politics. Bill Chester, for instance, commented in 1969 that "a group of well-meaning 'progressive' whites" supported the struggle for racial equality. After two decades of McCarthyism and his own more mainstream liberal views, it is not surprising that Chester used the term *progressive* rather than communist or socialist. Cleophas Williams, a leader in Local 10 for forty years, spoke more forthrightly: "Those [whites] who were more active in expressing concern [for African Americans], I later found out, were considered to be left-wingers. They were the ones who would come over and speak to you and ask you about your housing and your transportation." Remarking on Bridges's claim that, if there were only two longshoremen left, he would prefer one to be black, Williams found it "very shocking to me because there was no political gain for him by making this statement," because whites made up the vast majority of longshoremen in a city and nation where racism reigned supreme. Williams, who told Kimeldorf that many blacks in the union felt similarly, continued: "I had read and been exposed to some of the left-wing forces, but I had never heard anyone [white] put his neck out on the chopping block by making a public statement of this kind." Similarly, in 1949, Cy Record noted in the *Crisis*, the NAACP monthly, "Whatever one may think of the left-wing tendencies of the Bridges-controlled International Longshoremen and Warehousemen Workers union, the fact remains that through it Negroes have obtained a fair break in job opportunities and union participation." The NAACP already had moved rightward amid the Cold War–induced Red Scare, going so far as to expel, essentially, the legendary cofounder and long-time editor of *Crisis*, W. E. B. DuBois. Of course, black membership and equal treatment in Local 10 did not happen solely because of white solidarity but also because African Americans advocated for themselves and achieved a critical mass that neither the local nor the international leadership could ignore.[32]

African Americans proved among the most ardent defenders of Harry Bridges and other ILWU members accused of being communists. The federal government investigated Bridges for twenty years, and the presence and visibility of African Americans in the groups created to defend Bridges is striking. Cleophas Williams's viewpoint typified that of other African Americans in the union: "They were after Bridges," who needed to be defended because "he was our leader." This stance was seconded by Bill Chester, who chaired the committee defending Bridges and other prosecuted ILWU leaders. Numerous other blacks in Local 10, including Albert

James, Claude Sanders, and John E. "Johnny" Walker, actively involved themselves in the Bridges Defense Committee; James chaired the Committee against Water-front Screening in the early 1950s.[33]

Yet the union's overall practices on race relations failed to live up to its lofty ideals, especially in the ports of Los Angeles and Portland, where pervasive racism existed. The most thorough and damning indictment appeared in Bruce Nelson's powerful *Divided We Stand: American Workers and the Struggle for Black Equality*. Nelson spent much of one chapter examining Los Angeles Local 13 that, after World War II, purged hundreds of African Americans who joined during the wartime boom. Nelson convincingly argued that, despite claims the local reduced its ranks in a race-neutral manner, what happened was anything but. In fact, European Ameri-can, Mexican American, and Mexican members went out of their way to ensure that few blacks remained in Local 13. Although this local's white majority saw its actions as protecting jobs for sons and neighbors, blacks and most outsiders interpret(ed) it as designed to eradicate blacks. In the case of the significant Mexi-can membership, following Neil Foley, Nelson suggested they made a "Faustian pact with whiteness." Even worse, Portland's Local 8 remained lily-white into the 1960s, widely known for doing so, despite rhetorical pressure from Bridges and the international. The decentralized and democratic nature of the ILWU, accord-ing to Nelson, limited the power of Bridges and the international to impose racial equality from above, and so prejudice flourished in locals where white members were racist or treated the union as a job trust for sons, nephews, and neighbors. The ILWU, of course, hardly was alone; inside the AFL and CIO, even in its most progressive unions, institutionalized structures limited black opportunities. In the ILA, African Americans suffered pervasive racism before, during, and after World War II, most notably in the nation's largest port and ILA's headquarters, New York City. In recent decades, ILWU Locals 8 and 13 have become more inclusive though, still today, Local 10 remains the most diverse longshore branch, particularly as regards African Americans.[34]

Blacks (and whites) up and down the coast, of course, knew about racism inside the ILWU. Bill Chester, the most prominent African American in Local 10 and the ILWU, politely lamented in 1969 that "On the other hand, policies of discrimination existed in the ILWU on the West Coast, although the union's International consti-tution forbade it. The Portland longshore local excluded Negroes for a number of years." Before Bridges appointed Chester to direct the northern California region of the union, he and other African Americans, including Albert James and Johnny Walker, fought racism in Local 10. Chester remarked, "To bring about equality and truly eliminate discrimination, a group of us San Francisco Area blacks formed ourselves into what nowadays you'd call a Black Caucus. But in those days, in the 1940s, we just called it getting the boys together to talk over a problem." Chester and Williams and other blacks learned from more experienced ones like James and Walker, who, as Kimeldorf wrote, "had belonged to dissident locals of the ILA, particularly around the ports of New Orleans and Houston, which had long histories of opposing the Jim Crow and collaborationist policies of international union leaders." That is, black dockworkers from Gulf Coast ports, especially New Orleans, had decades-long experiences with unions and the battle for racial equality, which they brought with them to the Bay Area. The historical memory of overt racism earlier in ILWU history still exists among black and white members, including numerous ones who spoke at a 2013 memorial gathering for Local 10's Leo Robinson, a leading anti-apartheid and civil-rights activist. Racial tensions inside Local 10 also threatened to worsen after World War II, when work precipitously declined. How the local responded reveals volumes about race relations inside the union.[35]

The notion of a zero sum game often has heightened racial divisions in the United States, and not only in its working class. Centuries of racism have conditioned many white workers to see blacks as competition and, accordingly, sided with white workers over black ones, especially during times of job scarcity. After World War II in ports up and down the West Coast, this matter threatened to rip the union apart. Of course, the matter hardly was unique to the docks; NAACP activist Cy Record described the postwar reality for black shipyard workers: "They were in industries born of war and doomed to collapse with its end." Bruce Nelson documented how, after the war, Local 13 systematically and drastically reduced its black membership. Even when work later picked up, Local 13 ignored blacks with more seniority to give union cards to whites with less. In 1949, Local 10 confronted this same issue and how it responded offers further evidence of its firm commitment to racial equality.[36]

The postwar decline in shipping combined with a bruising, hundred-day coastwide strike in 1948 to force the question of reducing Local 10's ranks, which—everyone understood—would disproportionately hurt African Americans. Although San Francisco retained its place as the coast's leading port, the amount of shipping—and work—had declined dramatically. Clark Kerr and Lloyd Fisher outlined the problem in 1949: "With union control over the hiring hall and a system of work equalization through rotary dispatch, the available work opportunities are divided evenly among the registered longshoremen. When aggregate employment declines seriously, all longshoremen are underemployed." Addressing the issue in the *Local 10 Longshore Bulletin*, Bridges proclaimed, "many men on the front" asked him to "remedy the situation, as they could no longer make a living." Seniority seemed the answer to many, in other words, deregister the least experienced members, a policy, Bridges asserted, "no fair-minded, honest union member can oppose." Kimeldorf, who interviewed Local 10 veterans of the 1940s, framed it differently—namely that older, more conservative, white members pushed for reductions, precisely as in

Local 13, from which hundreds of African Americans were expunged. Led by James Kearney, white conservatives in Local 10, who always made up a significant minority, belonged to a "Blue Slate." In contrast to the "Reds," that is, communists (and other leftists), the Blue Slate pushed for sharp reductions based upon seniority and Bridges, apparently, agreed. When black workers expressed concerns, Kimeldorf cited Blue Slate supporters who responded, "We can work together, we can eat together, but we can't starve together." Nelson juxtaposed Bridges's commitment to racial equality as clashing with, and taking a back seat to, another sacred principle of his and many other unionists, seniority.[37]

Instead, white leftists in Local 10 united with blacks to reject Bridges's proposal and, in the words of one later activist, "extend their community." This matter was so important that Local 10 rented the San Francisco (now Bill Graham) Civic Auditorium, because it did not (yet) have a hall that could accommodate its entire membership. Five thousand attended this meeting to debate several proposals, including one presented by Henry Schmidt, Local 10 president and a widely respected leftist. Schmidt "proposed cutting equally from 'the top, middle, and bottom' of the seniority ladder," in other words, reducing some of the older folks who, truthfully, might not be as physically strong as younger members. The other point of contention was the voting method. Williams recalled that votes generally were conducted by secret ballot, which was how conservatives like Kearney wanted it; Bridges, however, successfully pushed to have proposals decided by standing vote, so that everyone would see who voted which way. That day, after hours of heated discussion, both proposals were defeated overwhelmingly, and no one lost his union card.[38]

Though subject to interpretation, the most convincing and reasonable reading is that the members of Local 10, black and white, chose to stick together rather than eliminate some of their own. Curiously, Nelson only briefly acknowledged this historic outcome, perhaps because it places the ILWU in a vastly different—and more positive light—than his also-important example from Local 13; Nelson framed Local 10's vote as proof that Bridges could not dictatorially impose his will on a local. Nelson is correct, but more important is that white leftists, of whom there were many, acted as "race traitors" and confirmed their civil-rights-union bona fides by voting to support their fellow black unionists. Herb Mills, an important Local 10 leader and intellectual, later interpreted these events in this way: "For the members of Local 10 their vote on his [Bridges's] motion was a truly historic and profoundly important expression of their sense of community." Simply put, most (white) members of Local 10 now considered the black members part of the union, Mills's "community." Having earned their place by working the job and supporting the union (including during strikes in 1946 and 1948), black members had earned their place and could not be tossed aside when the economy worsened. Bridges, in 1955, described the meeting in a way similar to Mills and framed himself as the "heavy":

> They figured I had just completely sold them out and I was lucky to get out of that meeting alive. I was all on my own. I didn't get one single supporter in the meeting. When I marched in with the idea of laying off a thousand men. I am just telling you not one single person voted for me. They still preferred to go on and work 26, 28 hours a week. We had just been through a strike. This was the spring of 1949, and they said, "This is fine thing, for you to come around after all of us have stuck together and fought together, and propose now a thousand of us to be thrown away." And to make it worse, the bulk of the thousand were Negro men and they had no chance of getting any other kind of work at that time. Things were very slack.

Bridges having zero support is unlikely in light of the fact that he wrote, prior to the meeting, about being asked by Local 10 members, the Blue Slate, to resolve the matter. But what Bridges's recounting also indicates is that he viewed the members of Local 10—as Mills did—as united. To put a fine point on it, Local 10, with its large white majority, voted to retain a significant black minority even though doing so, at least in the short run, reduced the earnings of the more senior, mostly white members. This event does not just prove that Bridges had limited authority. Rather, it proves Local 10 committed itself to the principles of racial equality. Ironically, it was Korea, a war Bridges condemned—for which he took enormous criticism— that resulted in a surge of work that ended the "need" to cut the union's ranks.[39]

Not only did Local 10 integrate itself and increase the number of African Americans in its own ranks, starting in the late 1930s Local 10 members organized workers in the newly created Warehouse Division, in the Bay Area and as part of the "march inland." In both San Francisco and Oakland, warehouses lined streets near the Bay and their workers easily could have found their way to the docks and been hired by employers to destroy the nascent longshore union. Efforts by San Francisco longshoremen to organize warehousemen can, in part, be seen as defensive, yet these workers also toiled under onerous and dangerous conditions for low pay and so had good reason to unionize. They toiled in grain and flourmills, canneries, food-processing plants, cold storage and grocery warehouses. As Lou Goldblatt recalled, "some of the older waterfront houses floated on pilings—and probably were still floating on the sweat of the old-time waterfront warehousemen." Before the ILWU, few blacks worked in warehousing, though, in the words of historical sociologist Chris Rhomberg, many were "immigrant and second-generation ethnic workers." As in longshoring, and as a result of the racial politics of the ILWU, a growing number of warehousemen were African American, much more so once the war began. Bay Area warehouse workers formed ILWU Local 6 and, under the leadership of Goldblatt, the march inland spread into the food-processing and canning centers throughout the Bay Area, then into California's heavily agricultural Central Valley, to the Great Plains, and even parts of the South. ILWU leaders, thus, created an industrial union in transportation, as Harvey Schwartz wrote: "The logic of this national organizing campaign followed naturally from the logic of the Bay Area march inland. It had been necessary to organize inland warehousemen in San Francisco to protect the city's waterfront warehousemen; similarly, it was seen as important to organize warehousemen in other states to protect the Bay region's warehousemen." While marching inland, the Warehouse Division found black and Latino workers. For instance, during the 1950s, the international dispatched Chester to organize African American and Mexican American cotton-compress workers in California's Central Valley and help with contract negotiations. During and after World War II, Local 6 became a Bay Area force for racial equality and other social-justice movements. In 1947, for example, Robert Self noted that "Paul Heide of ILWU, Local 6, delivered a stinging indictment of police brutality against African Americans before the Oakland City Council." Not only did the Bay Area longshoremen recruit black workers into the ILWU, they also agitated on their behalf in other industries.[40]

As World War II wound down, the ILWU successfully pressured the San Francisco Municipal Railway System (MUNI) to hire its first black driver, Audley Cole, and literally rode the rails to defend him from racist vigilantes. Historians Robin D. G. Kelley and Danielle McGuire both have discussed how mid-twentieth century streetcars were racial (and gender) battlegrounds in the US South. San Francisco proved little different. Two years before Cole drove a car, members of the Amalgamated Association of Street, Electric Railway, and Motor Coach Employees of America—at the time lily-white—attacked several of their colleagues for agitating on behalf of hiring black drivers. Then, in 1944, on the very first shift he drove, hostile whites dragged Cole off his streetcar and whipped him! After that incident, Bill Chester recalled, "guys in our union—there were always four or five of us— would ride the streetcar whenever he was driving. We rode in shifts. . . . He didn't have any more trouble." Kelley, in an important 1993 essay, argued such streetcar battles "form an important yet neglected part of African-American political history," particularly of its urban working class. Local 10 activists' defense of a black streetcar driver is another example. By 1970, Chester reported African Americans made up more than half of all MUNI drivers.[41]

The ILWU also pushed local maritime employers to hire more African Americans and pushed other unions to open their membership. In the World War II era, historian Daniel Crowe reiterated, "Rather than being champions of the rights of all workers, unions in the San Francisco Bay Area were largely enclaves of white working-class power," as across the country. Chester, the leading civil-rights activist in the ILWU during the 1950s and 1960s, agreed: "San Francisco happens to be one of the most unionized towns in this United States. But my experience has been that the American labor movement, with the exception of some unions [like the ILWU], the American labor movement is very discriminatory." Chester and others singled out the San Francisco–based Marine Firemen, Oilers, Watertenders, and Wipers Association and Sailors' Union of the Pacific for excluding blacks, but both opened their ranks to African Americans after ILWU advocacy. Even some of the Bay Area's most notoriously racist unions, such as the plumbers and electricians, began to hire at least a few African Americans. Similarly, the ILWU pushed for the hiring of black workers in various businesses (e.g., "Negro sales girls" at Sears, Roebuck department stores) and local governments. Chester described how "The union did business with Kaiser Hospital, so we met with Edgar Kaiser and said, 'We want some black interns and black physicians on the staff.' Everywhere we could, we made the union's weight felt." Moreover, Local 10 extended its own efforts to Latinos and Asian Americans when expanding its ranks, such as in 1969: "In selecting the 600 we gave representation to the black community, to the brown community, to the yellow community, and the white community where that's located in the poverty areas." In short, the ILWU Local 10 strove to live up to its antiracist ideology within its own ranks but also promoted this vision in the wider Bay Area labor movement and pushed employers on behalf of black advancement and equality at work.[42]

Closer to home, in the early 1960s, San Francisco longshoremen (and the ILWU international) pushed hard on the Bay Area's clerks, Local 34, to open its ranks to African Americans. In the words of a long-time Local 34 member and self-trained historian, Don Watson, "The clerk was to tell the longshoremen where to put the cargo," quite challenging as "keeping the count of all the goods [was a] very complicated process," especially before computers. Clerking generally required more formal education, particularly in mathematics, than longshoring. Numerous clerks usually worked a single ship and, in 1960, Local 34 had about one thousand members. Local 34's racial demographics, however, were almost lily-white. Although several thousand African Americans belonged to Local 10 by the early 1960s, Local 34 had but two black members and one, supposedly, "passed" for white. The ongoing resistance of Local 34 to African American membership troubled many blacks and whites in Local 10, as well as at the international. Watson, a left-wing white activist who had left the Communist Party and whose father served as founding editor of the union's *Dispatcher*, recalled, "there was a lot of complaints that the ship clerks were discriminatory." Bridges worked with allies in Local 34, what Watson called "a lunch group that was a caucus," along with Jimmy Herman, a white clerk and long-time left-wing unionist who became local president in 1961, to "encourage" change in Local 34. Considered a brilliant organizer, his *San Francisco Chronicle* obituary, much later, noted that Herman "had the oratorical gallop of a preacher and a fierce, lifelong commitment to workers' rights." In early 1963, a huge special meeting occurred whose purpose, Watson remembered, "was to pass a motion saying that we were opposed to discrimination according to race, creed or color. He [Herman] carried the vote. We had some people bitterly complaining about it, but it was basically carried. It was after that that a fair percentage of black clerks came in." With this endorsement, Bridges tapped Chester to recruit scores of young black men, via his extensive networks including local black churches. One recruit was Alex Bagwell, who arrived with his parents from rural Texas at the end of World War II. Though his family started in West Oakland, they soon moved to San Francisco's Fillmore neighborhood, the city's first black ghetto. After graduating from high school in the 1950s, Bagwell enrolled at San Francisco State College but then joined the US Army. Bagwell, however, left the military after suffering under a racist superior officer. He was playing organ at a Methodist church in the Fillmore when Bagwell's pastor connected him to Chester. Bagwell recalled, "They had pressure on Local 34 to put black clerks in." Many "old school" clerks (Bagwell's term), did not want blacks so made it very hard on Bagwell and other newcomers. Nevertheless, by the mid-1960s, Local 34 had enrolled many African Americans, with Herman doing an excellent job—according to Bagwell—at easing racial tensions until older white members became more used to this "new normal." How and why Local 34 became integrated deserves further examination.[43]

Simply put, the left politics of many black and white members of Local 10, along with pressure from the antiracist Bridges, caused Local 34 to open its ranks. Bagwell, in the first wave of blacks entering Local 34, already was politicized—after experiencing intense racism in the army—and quite educated. His thoughtful, multicausal interpretation of Local 34's integration merits consideration: (1) Jimmy Herman's leftwing leadership, (2) pressure from the (leftwing) international, (3) pressure from the militant, more racially progressive, and increasingly black membership of Local 10, and (4) growing pressure from the larger civil-rights movement. Bagwell attributed most of the credit to black activists in Local 10, like Albert James and Johnny Walker, for "putting pressure on Local 34" because longshoremen intimately worked with clerks daily. The second key factor, to Bagwell (and Watson), was Herman's politics—and that of other whites influenced by both the IWW and CP, including Bridges. Though Herman, originally from New Jersey, was new to the ILWU, he was no youngster, having been in the radical Marine, Cooks and Stewards before the ILWU. In the mid-twentieth century, the Marine, Cooks and Stewards, along with the ILWU, stood at the forefront of white-majority organizations on race matters, primarily because of the left radicalism of many leaders and rank-and-filers. In Bagwell's opinion, Herman was "absolutely antiracist" and had good friends among African Americans in Local 10, including Al Thibedeaux, another leftist who "had sailed with Jimmy" before both ended up "on the beach," that is, the waterfront. Herman also had mighty assistance from Bridges and Chester at the San Francisco–based international headquarters. One final point worth mentioning is that African Americans in Local 10 also helped themselves by pushing Local 34 to open its ranks, because many older longshoremen (black and white, then and now) aspired to become a clerk, which paid better and was less physically demanding. Around 1990, in fact, the rules were changed so that the only pathway into an ILWU clerks local was via a longshore local.[44]

Similarly, when Local 10 expanded its ranks in the late 1950s and 1960s (a result of an aging membership and increasing work), the union made a conscious effort to include people of color, especially from poor neighborhoods. In 1959, for the first time since World War II, and four times more in the 1960s, Local 10 added members. When Local 10 announced its plan, literally thousands applied; for instance, in 1963, ninety-seven hundred applied for four hundred slots and in 1967 twenty-one thousand applied for seven hundred openings! Though it need not have done so, the union actively recruited African Americans from the poorest and most racially segregated parts of the Bay Area. Technically, when the union took in new members, the process was jointly administered by employers and, according to Chester, the union's racially inclusive policies created more sympathetic employers: "The committee on the union's side has had progressive-minded, thinking whites. The strangest thing is that we've educated the employers, too. When we get ready to register men now, the employers will say, 'Bill, did you make sure you got some black people from [Bayview–]Hunter's Point in San Francisco? Did you take care of the black people from West Oakland?'" West Oakland was the poorest and blackest area of that city; African American activist Paul Cobb, the son of an ILWU member, referred to West Oakland as an "urban plantation" while Bayview–Hunter's Point, quite possibly, had become the most ghettoized part of San Francisco and experienced a race rebellion in 1966. As already detailed, Local 10 went from having fewer than a hundred blacks in 1940 to having a black majority by 1970. Further, Local 10's rank-and-file started electing African Americans to leadership positions in the late 1930s (decades before they were the majority). In the 1960s, the African American Joe Mosely became chief dispatcher, arguably the most powerful elected local position in that it dictates who works where and how much.[45]

Summing up ILWU Local 10's race politics, Chester—one of the most important players in the local and the international—contended they were "a group of workers who didn't just look at their own selfish points of view as far as what they had economically. We were willing to participate and spread the experience that we had learned in the trade union movement." The ILWU story stood in marked contrast with most unions on both sides of the San Francisco Bay and nationally. Daniel Crowe, a historian of civil rights in San Francisco, wrote, "Workers and activists who dared speak out against the white unions or tried to integrate their ranks faced violent reprisals and scathing verbal attacks." Robert Self, author of one of the finest books on race relations in postwar Oakland, criticized "[t]he duplicity of Oakland's labor movement" that, even into the 1970s, "continued to undermine civil rights efforts." The ILWU and particularly Local 10 stood in stark contrast by actively seeking to integrate its own ranks without any outside black or government pressure.[46]

Conclusions

The movement against apartheid in South Africa and for civil rights in the United States each received mighty assistance from dockworkers in San Francisco and Durban, respectively. That explains why the Congress of Democrats, which helped organize the legendary Congress of the People that created the Freedom Charter, proclaimed, "A victory for the dock workers [in Durban] is a victory for the entire working class of South Africa." As they repeatedly struck from 1949 to 1959, despite massive repression from employers and the state, dockworkers contributed mightily to the struggle. In response to their power, employers and the government completely overhauled labor relations and decasualized the waterfront. Essentially, black dockworker militancy threatened both the profits of shipping companies and maintenance of apartheid, a history that remains "under the radar." These events in Durban in the 1940s and 1950s echoed those happening in Mombasa, the most important port in British-controlled Kenya, where capital and the colonial state sought to weaken dockworkers (via economic, legislative, and police actions); Cooper noted that elites "found that the new world which emerged was no more theirs to forge than the one before." In both African port cities, dockworkers resisted the authority and power of political and economic elites and disrupted racial capitalism via collective action, particularly strikes. Cooper's subsequent book more broadly argued for the importance of labor activism in anticolonial struggles across Africa. The Durban story fits in neatly.[47]

Similarly, San Francisco longshoremen attacked white supremacy, inside their union and the wider metropolitan area. In the 1930s, with only a few black members, the ILWU committed itself to racial equality. Subsequently, war-induced labor shortages drew more than one hundred thousand southern-born African Americans to the Bay Area and a few thousand onto the waterfront, where they found a union willing to accept them as members and treat them as equals—unlike most unions, particularly the AFL shipbuilders. After the war and despite a reduction in work, Local 10 resisted the "logic" of zero-sum racial capitalism (in which if black workers benefited, white workers suffered) and recommitted itself to equality. By the late 1960s, most Bay Area longshoremen were African American.

Local 10 proceeded to push its fellow workers in ILWU Local 34 to open their ranks to African Americans, a significant achievement, and helped organize black and white warehouse workers in Local 6. They also promoted the hiring and equal treatment of blacks in other workplaces, including local governments, throughout the Bay Area. By contrast, the larger union did not always promote black equality, most egregiously in "looking the other way" at the overt racism of Portland Local 8 and Los Angeles Local 13. Yet the ILWU leadership generally was antiracist and put that ideal into practice, the best example being the many thousands of long-shoremen and farmworkers, mostly Asians or of Asian descent, who joined the ILWU in Hawaii after World War II. Within the ILWU, Local 10 clearly led the way; further evidence being the election of Cleophas Williams as local president in 1967. Local 10 had achieved what one *New Yorker* writer described in 1967 as "a regular league of nations on the waterfront." The achievements of ILWU Local 10 mark it as a leader among civil-rights unions, and its story deserves far more recognition than it has thus far received.[48]

The next chapter continues to (re)center dockworker power, positioning their activism into larger stories of race-based social movements that transformed each city and nation in the 1960s and 1970s. Chapter 3 expands on Local 10's civil-rights unionism by documenting and analyzing its support of other social movements in the "long 1960s." First, though, the chapter examines how Durban dockworkers helped reignite the fight against apartheid in the late 1960s and early 1970s, truly the signature cause of South Africa's troubled and dramatic history.

3

FIGHTING RACIAL OPPRESSION
IN THE 1960S AND 1970S

We found that, in a sense, the union is the community.
—Chester, interview by Martin

In 1969, O. P. F. Harwood, an economist at the (whites-only) University of Natal–Durban, boasted, "Labour at the Port of Durban is not a problem, as it is, for example, at the ports of the United Kingdom, where it is regarded as their most serious problem." Though he might be forgiven for so poorly predicting the future, Harwood continued, "In Durban harbour this problem hardly exists." Rather, that very year, Durban dockworkers struck—the first sign that the black working class in South Africa had reawakened. They threatened to do so in 1971 and again in late 1972. It seems reasonable to suggest that they, in fact, reignited a moribund labor movement, though few today know of their key role. Instead, every student of South African history "knows" that, in January 1973, workers at Coronation Brick struck and "officially" launched the Durban Strikes of January–March 1973, the largest strike wave of black workers since 1946. The legendary Durban Strikes involved upwards of one hundred thousand workers from more than 150 companies, shocked the nation, and restarted the national anti-apartheid movement that largely had been quiescent as a result of brutal repression a decade earlier. In the words of the editors of the quasi-official history of the struggle in South Africa, "The revival of the workers' movement in the factories, mines and stores was arguably the most important development of the 1970s." Left out of most histories, however, is that, under the surface just prior to the Durban Strikes, local dockworkers were rising. Although there is no doubt that the Durban Strikes shattered the deafening silence after the repression of early 1960s, dockworker activism preceded and helped inspire the Durban Strikes.[1]

Similarly, in the United States every student of history knows that a huge wave of social movements erupted in the 1960s and that the San Francisco Bay Area emerged as an epicenter, perhaps the center, of this radicalism. Historians know that "the sixties" did not emerge in a vacuum and, in fact, during the previous decade the southern-based civil-rights movement started thawing the consensus of the early Cold War. Subsequently, a series of important—in some cases quite radical—social movements emerged, many lasting well into the 1970s with San Francisco and the entire Bay Area a magnet of such activism. The laundry list of US social movements surging in the sixties included fights for equality for African Americans, women, Chicanos, American Indians, homosexuals, and others. The antiwar, student, environmental, counterculture, and other movements also found great support in the Bay Area. Yet organized labor often is left out of histories of 1960s US social movements, and the working-class background of countless movement participants is regularly ignored in a society where class analysis remains rare. In the San Francisco Bay Area, though, black and white rank-and-filers in Local 10, in conjunction with Harry Bridges and other international leaders, proved central to the local struggle for racial equality and contributed to the nationwide push. When civil-rights icon Dr. Martin Luther King Jr. wanted to champion unionism as a crucial way to uplift (poor) African Americans, he visited ILWU Local 10. The longshoremen did not stop with racial equality, however. They provided mighty assistance to many other social movements then exploding across the Bay Area and nation. This chapter's first section examines the role Durban dockworkers played in the resurgent anti-apartheid movement. The second part explores some—but not all—of the movements that Bay Area longshoremen engaged in; simply put, Local 10 and the ILWU intersected with so many social movements that this chapter cannot do justice to all their contributions.

Dockworkers: The (Surprising) Missing Link in the Durban Strikes

White elites understood Durban dockworkers' potential power and, therefore, entirely reorganized the labor regime in 1959. As scholar-activist David Hemson wrote, "The Divisional Inspector of [Department of] Labour had predicted, in 1958, that decasualization would help employers in 'weeding out troublemakers' in order to achieve 'peace in the industry for the rest of your lives.'" Subsequently, the state squashed the entire anti-apartheid movement, which lasted roughly from 1964 to 1973, as Rob Lambert summarized: "Social movements were repressed and civil society disempowered during the 1960s and, as a consequence, movement capacity to impose change appeared fanciful." Recently, Julian Brown contended that state repression did not fully destroy opposition to apartheid, making a particularly strong case for pockets of university students. Nevertheless, it is undeniable that the mass-based labor and political protests of the 1950s quickly disappeared once a state of emergency was declared after the Sharpeville repression. Moreover, poverty wages and high inflation made mere survival a challenge, as blacks became truly desperate. Hence, when Durban waterfront workers struck in 1969, threatened to do so in 1971, and struck again in 1972, their actions were as impressive as they were rare. It is interesting to note that, just as repression against the dockworkers in the late 1950s foreshadowed the state's response to black activism in 1960, a decade later Durban dockers helped lead a resurgent black working class back to the metaphorical barricades. Although to many, at the time and subsequently, the mammoth Durban Strikes of 1973 appeared out of nowhere, this chapter contends that the dockworkers are the missing link and helped ignite the black militancy that marked the reemergence of a domestic struggle against apartheid in the 1970s. In retrospect, what employers and government officials bought with decasualization was one decade.[2]

With the long-standing militant tradition at the Point, it should come as no surprise that Durban dockworkers returned to the struggle in 1969, in advance of nearly all other black workers. That April, two thousand dockers struck for a raise, driven by their abject poverty combined with a recent slowdown in port traffic. As D. M. Ross-Watt, in his University of Natal honors thesis, wrote in 1970, "The work is hard and the wages are low. In common with most other non-white workers, there is virtually a 'legislated-inability' for the stevedores to secure a better wage." *Isisebenzi*, the publication of the Student Wages Commission (SWC), explained the strikers' demand in simple terms: "Since they were working 14 hours a day they had better earn R14 a week instead of R6.50." The bold and unexpected strike proved effective, shutting down work on thirty-five ships in the harbor. Employers and the government responded in typical fashion: a refusal to negotiate and mass retrenchments, accompanied by machine-gun-toting police who "escorted" fired workers to trains. The gigantic font and top-of-the-fold headline in the *Natal Mercury*, Durban's paper of record, screamed: HALF DURBAN DOCKWORKERS SET OFF HOME, EMPLOYERS SAY NO TO PAY DEMAND, and, more hopefully, HARBOUR "BACK TO NORMAL SOON." As soon as the strike began, P. J. Kemp, manager of the Durban Stevedoring Labour Supply Company (DSLSC), met with "officials from the Department of Labour and Bantu Affairs and senior police officers"; in other words, the city's economic and political elites quickly swung into action. Riot police armed with machine guns were deployed to the Point, but the strikers remained peaceful and undaunted. Two days into the strike, "When they were told to return to work by officials from the Department of Labour they jeered at the officials and repeated their demands for more money."[3]

Evidence of the strike's sophisticated organization quickly became evident. First, they launched the strike on Good Friday, the Friday before Easter, which "could hardly have come at a more embarrassing time for the authorities," the *Mercury* reported. The paper described a "lightning stoppage by African stevedores which brought work to a standstill at the weekend." It might seem obvious that pulling off a strike involving thousands of workers must have been coordinated, which explained why "Mr. A. H. Pettit, Secretary of the DSLSC, 'was convinced the strike had been caused by agitators,'" with the *Mercury* asserting most workers were "blown along in the wind . . . frightened of intimidation." The newspaper also claimed, "Africans feared intimidation in their kraals," a commonly used Afrikaner word for a livestock enclosure—but a curious and seemingly pejorative reference to the workers' hostels. Hemson offered a different interpretation: "The concentration of workers in increasingly centralized and controlled barracks . . . facilitates greater communication among workers." *Isisebenzi* later reported that strike leaders "spread word" of the issues and demands by writing "on the walls" of hostels in addition to, no doubt, planning on the job.[4]

The strike confirms the dockworkers' continual militancy despite decasualization, repression, and the inevitable labor turnover for a decade. As for the response, that also suggests little had changed; once again, the police threatened and beat strikers and the DSLSC fired fifteen hundred. Those retrenched were "given" four hours to leave the city, because black people without jobs were not legally allowed in the city. Presumably, the retrenched returned to their homes in KwaZulu that, along with other Bantustans, were desperately poor, overcrowded "dumping grounds for 'discarded people.'" As in prior clashes, employers hired fresh recruits, first from nearby townships and then rural KwaZulu. Scholar Bernard Dubbeld pointed out that "By the 1960s, and especially with the 1964 Bantu Labour Act, workers in urban areas had to be recruited through networks of homeland authority." Urban employers believed rural Africans to be more "traditional" in their outlook, loyal to both Zulu royalty and the apartheid state, and without class consciousness. Mass firings of dockworkers followed by a new batch of rural Zulu recruits proved only a temporary palliative, though. Dubbeld also documented a significant drop in worker productivity after the strike, as well as a concomitant rise in workers' injuries, reconfirming that work aboard ships involved many skills despite assertions otherwise. The new recruits, presumably, were happy to learn that, shortly after the strike, the DSLSC raised both standard and overtime rates by 20 percent.[5]

The 1969 strike was of tremendous significance, for it marked the first hints of a resurgent anti-apartheid movement inside the country that, in the early 1960s, largely had been squashed. The South African Congress of Trade Unions, part of the anti-apartheid Congress movement, never was banned officially but had been destroyed inside South Africa, as reported in the South African Institute of Race Relations' (SAIRR) 1968 *Survey*: "Sactu now exists in name only: all its leading members (mainly non-whites) have been banned or have left the country, and a large proportion of the unions that at one time were affiliates have gone out of existence." Subsequently, almost no nationwide strikes occurred from the early 1960s into the early 1970s. Steven Friedman noted that "For more than a decade, African workers had been seen but rarely heard. . . . [S]trikes were so rare that each was a major event. Employers were free to run their factories as they chose and to pay Africans what they pleased." All that said, this action was neither widely heralded nor bemoaned at the time.[6]

In the 1960s, the South African economy boomed, at least partially a result of the defanging of black workers. Afrikaner nationalists—united with capitalists—committed an immense state bureaucracy to enforcing apartheid and maintaining their cheap labor system, resulting in immense profits largely on the backs of black workers. Western corporations, however, did not seem concerned, as N. Mandred Shaffer, a Northwestern University geographer, wrote in 1965: "Although the apartheid policies of the South African Government are in disfavor throughout most of the world, there has been no indication that it has adversely affected the total foreign trade of the country." In fact, although the state had squashed the anti-apartheid movement, Shaffer reported, "Exports from South Africa, via the ports, have increased at a faster rate within the past five years than during the previous five-year period." South Africa's gross national product during the 1960s grew at an impressive annual rate of 6 percent—among the highest rates in the world. Historian Bill Freund thoughtfully juxtaposed apartheid and prosperity in the 1960s: South Africa "looked especially menacing and potentially triumphant when it coincided with the unprecedented boom in world trade during the decade of the 1960s," which also implicitly highlighted Durban's centrality, being the nation's largest port.[7]

Thus, when several thousand black dockworkers struck in 1969, not only did Durban shipping agents express concern, so did other economic elites during "the golden age of apartheid for those class forces that benefitted from this system." In retrospect, the strike suggested the reawakening of the black working class after its brutal suppression at the decade's start. Tina Sideris, editor of a collection of interviews with Durban dockworkers, offered a similar analysis: "They broke the silence of the sixties. And they showed that workers must take up the struggle for their rights again." David Hemson also pointed to the strike's ironic timing, which occurred at "precisely the same time as the ANC and SACP [South African Communist Party] had concluded at the Morogoro [Tanzania] Conference that mass action among the working class had been exhausted as a means of resistance to apartheid." At that conference, however, long-time union and communist organizer Ray Alexander sent a letter on how to revive the labor movement: "We must organise under any name—the Mutual Benefit Societies, Co-ops. We may even have to consider utilising the 'Works Committee.' It was the Works Committee at

Durban Docks that led the dockworkers' strike this month." Subsequent (dock) worker actions must be seen in this context—the first drops of rain before the deluge that followed. Indeed, Hemson suggested as much on the fortieth anniversary of the Durban Strikes of 1973, "the sign was there that there was life and resistance among the workers which would eventually crack the granite and break down the system of apartheid."[8]

The dockers resumed their struggle, still without formal organization, in 1971. That September, two thousand threatened to strike unless they received a raise to R14 per week, still well below the Poverty Datum Line of R18, the amount considered enough for subsistence. The dockworkers' latest effort surfaced, as in 1969, when pamphlets appeared on notice boards around the Point with the wage demands. Recall that no such action should have been possible, for the authorities had retrenched more than a thousand dockworkers in 1969 and changed recruitment patterns. After the 1969 strike, the DSLSC established stricter controls for labor recruiting, doing so in areas with close ties to the Department of Native Affairs and where traditional Zulu values supposedly reigned supreme; KwaZulu areas like Nongoma and Mahlabatini were attractive because supposedly men from there were "traditional," "conservative," and loyal to Zulu royalty—unlike Pondo areas like Mount Ayliff, where some radicals had come from, and so no longer a site for recruitment. Clearly, those policy changes had failed in several ways, first in a decline of productivity. The *Mercury* reported, in January 1970, of "diminishing productivity have been causing concern to the Durban Chamber of Commerce for a long time." Second, the supposedly more loyal workforce threatened to strike just two years after mass retrenchments. With their current difficulties, waterfront employers had little choice and agreed to a 30 percent wage hike, though the DSLSC "manager maintained that the increase had been under consideration since May and did not result from the threatened strike." The 1971 action further suggests that the dockworkers maintained their organizational structure and militancy while developing new strategies, for instance, placing anonymous notices in public places rather than demands presented by "leaders." Also widely noted at the time, a major strike of thousands of miners in Ovamboland, in South African–controlled Southwest Africa (now Namibia), inspired many black South Africans. The early 1970s seemed to promise a renewed push for black freedom across southern Africa.[9]

Indeed, when Durban dockworkers struck again, in October 1972, they offered a vitally important contribution to the larger struggle against racial capitalism and paved the way for the far better known Durban Strikes of January–March 1973. Their strike demonstrated a memory of and respect for their own history, seeking to avenge their fired comrades in 1969, itself echoing demands of the 1950s for the return of their deported leader, Zulu Phungula. Despite assertions otherwise, the

1972 strike was not spontaneous but, rather, the culmination of months of growing agitation to increase wage rates, and it demonstrated remarkable organization
even without a formal union, unlike the larger strike wave that was unplanned. As
in 1969, this dock strike was illegal because Africans did not possess the right to
strike or unionize.[10]

In July 1972, three months before their strike, dockworkers took an unprecedented step and audaciously demanded a raise at a hearing of the Department of
Labour's Wage Board. The government Wage Board set rates for African workers
in specific industries yet, because it met once every four years, wages rarely kept
up with inflation. The Wage Board's existence, in fact, offered another example of
the apartheid state's heavy hand over the nation's so-called free-market economy.
Historian Robert Ross wrote, "There were few, if any, countries outside the Communist bloc in which the state had a greater direct involvement in the economy."
At the July 1972 Wage Board meeting on dock wages, student activist David Davis
recalled, "workers filled the room set aside for the hearing to overflowing" and
demanded a raise from R8.50 a week to R18, the poverty datum line, along with
higher rates for dangerous and holiday work and shorter shifts. Dockers claimed
they would reach out to their "homeland" governments if they did not receive sat-
isfaction. In the dockworkers' written testimony, submitted on their behalf by
sympathetic white student activists, "The money which we earn doesn't satisfy
us because it is very low and the work is very hard."[11]

When hundreds of dockworkers appeared at the hearing, they did so with the
active support of the newly formed SWC. David Hemson, who became the key
student organizer on the waterfront, declared that his initial inspiration came from
the 1969 dock strike: "a flash of lightning illuminating the path ahead. . . . [I]t
changed my political understanding and the direction of my studies and political
work." A handful of other radical white students at the University of Natal–Durban
(UND) found each other, equally inspired by the horrors of apartheid, the emergence of a global New Left in the 1960s, and influential professors. Radical white
UND students formed the SWC in 1971 and soon engaged in an array of activities
to support dockers and other black workers. Mindful that African unions remained
illegal and following the advice of Harriett Bolton, a veteran white labor organizer,
they did not initially seek to unionize black workers. Instead, they formed the SWC,
officially sanctioned by the UND Student Representative Council, and researched
African wages and conditions to gather evidence on the need for raises. They also
established the General Factory Workers Benefit Fund that attracted hundreds,
subsequently thousands, of workers (including some dockworkers), paying
monthly dues that they could access in the event of sickness, death, or firing. The
benefit fund was a proto-union and brilliant organizing tool in an environment in
which unionism was not yet possible. Students also visited workers in their

Fig. 2. Dockworkers demanding a raise from the Wage Board, 1972. The (Durban) Student Wages Commission published *Isisebenzi* (*Worker* in isiZulu), with stories in English and isiZulu, periodically in the early 1970s. Image used with permission from the University of Cape Town.

hostels, wrote pamphlets for and distributed them to workers, and presented their research findings at Wage Board hearings. They also created a newspaper for black workers, *Isisebenzi*, meaning *The Worker* in isiZulu, with most stories written in Zulu. After the Durban Strikes resulted in an explosion of African worker activism, these white radicals, including Hemson and Rob Lambert, helped create black trade unions despite their not being legal yet. Lambert singled out "Hemson [who] was also engaged in exceptional work on the Durban docks dissolving racial, cultural and language barriers through his knowledge of unionism and scope for organis- ing despite the narrow limits of racial industrial law." Though Grace Davie, author of a wonderful article on the Durban SWC, pushed her argument too far—in insist- ing that white university students' research on the poverty datum line played a crucial role in the dock strike and, by extension, the Durban Strikes—she convinc- ingly proved they cannot be discounted.[12]

The stirrings of black workers, a global New Left, and Dr. Rick Turner—a legendary white professor who arrived at UND in 1970—all influenced these students. Billy Keniston, Turner's most recent biographer, summarized the philosophy professor's view on overthrowing apartheid: "Turner was convinced that the economy was the only sphere in which the power of Africans was growing, a power that could potentially be made greater through trade unions and other forms of organized working-class action." UND students including Hemson, Lambert, and Halton Cheadle came to share Turner's Marxist analysis, which he first developed in his Sorbonne dissertation on Jean-Paul Sartre. For instance, Cheadle echoed Turner, "Workers are absolutely critical for the national democratic revolution." Inspired by Turner and a few other leftist professors, they formed the SWC, which undertook research on wages and conditions in Durban's industrial workplaces and reached out to black workers. Eddie Webster, a sociologist and labor activist who arrived in Durban shortly thereafter, recalled "heady days when university-based intellectuals distributed pamphlets at factory gates at 6.00 a.m. in the morning, strategized with activists during the day and discussed Hegel's relationship to Marx late into the night." SWC members leafleted the Point, organized meetings with dockers to formulate demands for the Wage Board hearings, and engaged in countless other tasks.[13]

A high point came in July 1972 when the Wage Board met and hundreds of dockworkers boldly attended to push for wage increases. Although their 1969 strike had resulted in mass firings, four testified at the hearing. They also challenged the authority of Zulu foremen (*indunas*), widely detested for collaboration with management and corruption, though they particularly hated the senior *induna*, J. B. Buthelezi. Harriett Bolton, an influential local labor activist, recollected that "for years, the board's hearing had been attended by an 'induna' or African foreman who employers had appointed to represent workers—his chief role was to thank the employers for their efforts on workers' behalf. To the consternation of the board, the stevedores angrily challenged his right to speak for them—and his claim to be a dock worker." She continued: "The board's faces were a picture. . . . I don't think they'd ever heard a real worker speak at a hearing before." Cheadle, an SWC activist, also recalled that meeting as being remarkable, especially Buthelezi's testimony. "When he got up to speak for the workers, they all shouted him down. It was absolute chaos. After that the government changed the law so that the chairman of the Wage Board could decide whether he would allow people to come to the meeting." Cheadle added for an American interviewer much later that "it was all organized in typical colonial style. What they did was to reproduce the tribal structures as part of the authoritarian structure inside the factory. So, the supervisor was your *induna*. It was disgusting." This hearing proved to be of great importance for the dockworkers, as Morris Ndlovu later observed: "It was at that meeting where we realised our power because we were talking for ourselves at that sitting." Ndlovu credited the "Wage Com" radicals for his participation: "It is because I was actually encouraged by the advice I received from the students about organisation, that without uniting and speaking with one voice we were not going to win. I actually wanted to hear on my own and to speak out about higher wage."[14]

Quite possibly, an underground group existed among dockworkers and readied them to act, but little solid evidence exists. This line of thinking also was applied to the subsequent worker uprising, as the authors of the first and only book on the subject, *The Durban Strikes, 1973,* have noted: "The beginnings of the strikes are shrouded in mystery." Johann Maree, in his critical review of this book, argued the workers *must* have had some organization and leadership; while no evidence exists for 1973, some does for the dockworkers' strike just prior. David Hemson, uniquely qualified by his role as a central activist, which he followed up with a lengthy, never-published dissertation, credited a secret organization of dockers that partook in the Wage Board hearings. Hemson recounted "an extraordinary [anonymous] letter from 'The Stevedoring Workers' to the Wage Board in 1972 who demanded the return of 'those who stood for us in 1969.'" Hemson also pointed to petitions, pamphlets, and the like that were posted to notice boards to the attention of workers and employers that never were attributed to any person or group. Such details, he argued, "provided concrete evidence of an underground network which did not declare itself even when open trade-unionism started among dock-workers at about that time" (actually, a few years later). Underground cells consisting of members of SACTU, Umkhonto weSizwe in isiXhosa (translated into English as "Spear of the Nation," simplified as MK), ANC, or SACP all seem possible. In the 1950s and 1960s, many SACTU activists worked with the underground Communist Party and MK, and so it seems conceivable that such was the case in the early 1970s too. These underground efforts offer hints about how action on the scale of the Durban Strikes "happen," that is, not entirely spontaneous but, rather, with prior organizing, as Maree noted. Of course, conversations and communications constantly occurred among fellow workers on the job, in the street, at the beer and eating halls, at the bus stop, and in their hostels. For instance, D. M. Ross-Watt, in his 1970 UND honors thesis, highlighted the beer hall's importance: "Apart from sleeping, spare time is spent largely in the [hostel's] beer garden. This appears to be the focal point of all activities outside of work." He continued, "the men are able to select their workmates and friends, the bonds being of considerable importance to the individuals." Clearly, they had plenty of chances and places to organize themselves.[15]

The experience of Harold Bhekisisa "Bheki" Nxasana offers an illuminating example of links between SACTU, underground elements, and dockworkers. Nxasana, along with the Robben Island veteran and long-time union leader Stephen

Dlamini and a few other SACTU veterans, wanted to revive SACTU in the early 1970s, first issuing a pamphlet encouraging black workers to unionize. In 1972, according to Hemson et al.: "Nxasana was employed by the Benefit Fund as an organiser, speaker, and translator. Interviewed in 1981, he recalled that after they had re-established SACTU: 'The Special Branch arrived and took me to their offices and told me we couldn't do this and must disband. So we contacted the Wages Commission and they took over our members and established a Benefit Fund. This was the start of the unions.'" After the Durban Strikes, Nxasana—coincidentally born in Ixopo, where Zulu Phungula was from—worked as a labor organizer and translator (from English into isiZulu) for texts written by the SWC and Institute for Industrial Education, another of Turner's creations and a vital site for promoting black unions.[16]

Further evidence of dockworker organizing comes from Omar Badsha, a Durban native, artist, ANC underground member, and labor activist. Badsha recalled that, in October 1972, about a dozen dockworkers—including militants from the Wage Board hearing—participated in a retreat at a Catholic mission outside Durban, near Pietermaritzburg. That weekend, Turner, Hemson, and a few others held workshops with the dockworkers. Badsha remembered Turner leading a discussion on Karl Marx's labor theory of value in which he broke down the theory in brilliant fashion late on Saturday night. On Sunday evening, as Badsha as drove the dockworkers back to the city, one told him that they intended to strike the next morning! Though they had spent the entire weekend with allies, the workers had maintained strict discipline in not revealing their plans. Only a few hours before the strike had the plan emerged from the shadows.[17]

Because the Wage Board had not yet issued its ruling, the dockworkers decided they would not wait any longer and struck. First, dockers struck at Maydon Wharf, an important part of the port distinct from the Point, followed by a strike at the Point. All harbor traffic shut down. One dockworker identified only as Mr. Zulu recounted in 1983 the strike's beginnings:

> There was a pamphlet in Buthelezi's office (a "welfare officer," perhaps an *induna*) [actually the head *induna*], and other pamphlets on the walls. The pamphlets said there was going to be a strike. When the date of the strike came we heard a voice and a whistle. Somebody was shouting and whistling in the compound [workers lived in nearby hostels]. Somebody was shouting "Nobody is going to work." And somebody answered on the other side.
>
> All the compounds were shouting like that. They were saying: "Asiyi emsebenzini, sifuna imali yethu" [roughly: "We do not go to work, we want our money"]. Those who tried to go to work were met with bottles which were thrown at them, and they ran back. Everybody moved out of the compounds.

When this happened Buthelezi disappeared. The workers shouted for him. They said: "He is always standing like a god at the gates, but look today. He will if only we find him in the streets."

In addition to providing further evidence of the pamphlets and secret networks that Hemson, Badsha, and others mentioned, Mr. Zulu also revealed how the workers communicated and organized, seamlessly, between the job and hostels. Also noteworthy is the fact that at least some strikers previously were strikebreakers hired after the 1969 strike when the entire workforce was retrenched. Or, as Hemson wrote in 1990, "The bosses' strategy had backfired!"[18]

No doubt, poverty was the most pressing concern for Durban dockworkers, but, truly, the same could be said for most black South Africans in 1972. The South African Institute of Race Relations estimated, in 1971, that 60–75 percent of urban African households earned income under the poverty datum line. Moreover, workers already suffering from low wages were whipsawed by soaring inflation in the early 1970s, causing one worker to lament, "It even costs more to sleep!" For dockworkers specifically, Bernard Dubbeld noted a slowing South African economy, in the late 1960s and early 1970s, meant declining exports and, thus, fewer ships and hours for dockworkers. As for the dockers themselves, Morris Ndlovu, who started on the Durban waterfront around 1963, claimed the strikes in 1972–73 were caused by "poverty, hard work, poor treatment." Another dockworker, S. K. Ngubese, echoed Ndlovu, "the salaries were very low, in fact, far below the bread line, and these people realised that they were merely working, going up and down, paying busfares, they were not even able to pay school fees for their children, food for the families and all that. That was the major cause of the strikes." No one disputed black people's material suffering. Even the Durban Chamber of Commerce, in a confidential memo to members in February 1973, suggested 11.4 percent inflation in 1972 combined with "low wages which workers have been receiving—in many cases without review or appreciable revision for a number of years" as the principal causes of "Bantu labour stoppages." The historiographical question that frequently has arisen, though, is why *Durban's* black workers rose up when African poverty existed nationwide. The answer very possibly lies with the dockworkers' strikes in October and December 1972.[19]

Crucially for the subsequent Durban Strikes of January–March 1973, the dockworkers refused to elect a delegation—a tactic they pioneered in the 1950s—instead shouting their demands, as a group, to management. The SAIRR reported that "When an executive of the Labour Supply Company addressed the angry workers and asked to be allowed to negotiate with a few spokesmen, there were shouts from the crowd of 'We will be fired.'" Morris Ndlovu concurred, recalling how all the strikers went to management to demand a raise to R18 per week, the poverty datum line. Ndlovu made no mention that he was aware that this tactic—of not electing leaders to negotiate—predated 1972. As discussed previously, however, they had used it as early as 1954 after the banishing of their leader, Zulu Phungula. That this tactic remained in use for decades also is fascinating because employers had fired many thousands of dockworkers over that time in addition to typical turnover; in other words, the collective memory remained, perhaps whispered among the buffalo in their hostels?[20]

Though the strikers returned to work after a few days to avoid firings, they soon won a significant raise. Responding to the strike, the Wage Board sped up its investigation and in November raised wages to R14.50, a raise of nearly 50 percent; as the SAIRR soon noted, however, when adjusted for inflation, the raise was about 23 percent. Some employers supposedly paid slightly more, though the dockworkers still earned much less than their demanded R18. Tensions remained high, fifteen more dockworkers were retrenched, and, two thousand dockers struck again briefly in December for R18. When police intervened, dockworkers attacked several policemen and threw empty bottles at a police vehicle, which was followed by arrests and twenty more firings. Wage Commission members, meanwhile, started distributing a new pamphlet encouraging the dockworkers to unionize.[21]

Even more significant, the dockworkers influenced the far better known Coronation Brick workers, who universally receive credit for "officially" launching the Durban Strikes of 1973, a turning point in the struggle against apartheid. Undeniably, black workers throughout the country suffered from grinding poverty and frustration, so why did black workers first arise *in Durban*? One year later, the editors of *The Durban Strikes, 1973*, did not answer that question, though they did claim, "What is clear is that there was no organised body such as a trade union which called for a strike to occur at a particular time over particular demands." They are correct. But the growing activism of the dockworkers, which culminated in two strikes late in 1972, is the logical—if almost never credited—missing link. That is, the dockworkers' militancy made Durban unique. Moreover, Robinduth Toli, in his fascinating if almost unknown 1991 master's thesis, convincingly argued that "the strike at Coronation was made possible when African workers, having been emboldened by the 1972 dock workers strike and having become acutely conscious of their problems were encouraged to take militant action." That is, the Coronation strike proved central to the Durban Strikes that reenergized the national struggle, and because the dockers inspired the Coronation Brick workers to act, then the dockworkers also were integral.[22]

The dockworkers' militancy and actions influenced Coronation Brick workers, and by extension the Durban Strikes, in many ways. First, Coronation workers clearly paid close attention to the dockers' strike. Durban's *Daily News* quoted one Coronation striker: "We know what happened to the stevedores," for their action was the biggest news story in the city when it occurred and, unquestionably, the largest strike of black workers in Durban since the dockworkers' 1969 strike, the biggest one of that year too. Second, dockworkers possessed contacts among and knew African migrants who worked in Durban's many factories, including Coronation. Consider that most African workers in Durban were Zulu, hailed from KwaZulu, lived in similar hostels (though dockers lived in separate ones), drank at the same African beer halls, and moved about the city and away from the city on the same buses and trains. Third, Coronation strikers modeled their strike slogan and tactics on those of the dockworkers. Toli wrote, "As the dock workers had done, brickworkers downed tools, assembled on company premises, shouted their demands to management and refused to elect a strike leadership or a delega-tion of worker representatives to management for fear of victimization." One of the most famous moments of the Durban Strikes occurred when several thousand Coronation workers met on their company's football field on their first day out and refused to elect a delegation to negotiate with management—precisely like the dockworkers. Morris Ndlovu, who participated in the 1972 dock strike, recalled in 1979 how he and others joined in the negotiations: "everybody went. We just standing there because there was no any worker committee, no nothing, just all the workers just standing. I went to see the management." Even labor historian Steven Friedman noted the parallel yet neglected to suggest that the dockwork-ers' strike—which preceded Coronation Brick—influenced the latter: "Like the 1973 strikers, the stevedores refused to elect spokesmen—when they were asked to do so by a company executive, the crowd shouted back: 'We will be fired.'" As discussed, this tactic had been used on the waterfront for decades. Fourth, the Zulu Royal House mediated both strikes; without getting sidetracked, at that time the KwaZulu government served as an important interlocutor between the over-whelmingly Zulu workforce in Durban and apartheid government, though later in the 1970s and 1980s the Zulu government, by way of Inkatha, often criticized black strikes and unions. Fifth, the dockworkers actively spread the subsequent Durban Strikes when they broke out; Hemson recalled that "Dockworkers then were transported around in open trucks rather than buses. This became a factor against the bosses because from the back of the trucks they would see workers on strike and greet them. As they were driven further, they would shout the news of the strike to other workers across the street and so on. Eventually workers were coming out everywhere." Sixth, Coronation strikers knew the possibility of repres-sion, as did one Coronation worker, who feared "the men would be victimized," as the dockworkers had been. Essentially, the dockworkers showed Coronation and other black workers in Durban that collective resistance was (again) possible as evidenced in how closely the Coronation strike resembled the earlier dock strike. Coronation workers did not, however, strike immediately after the dockworkers' second strike, in December, because of the annual Christmas break, when many companies closed and migrant workers visited family in "homelands." Instead, the Coronation strike began in early January.[23]

Because of the nature of apartheid, almost any strike of African workers had political dimensions, but the mammoth Durban Strikes quickly forced changes to national labor law. In particular, the dockworkers' and other strikers' demand for wage hikes directly assaulted the cheap labor system that formed a key pillar of apartheid. To keep black workers weak, the Native Labour (Settlement of Disputes) Act of 1953 had declared African strikes illegal, but, shortly after the Durban Strikes, the government made a major concession and issued a new law, the Native Labour Relations Regulations Act of 1973. This new law, in some circumstances, allowed African workers to strike—a small but not insignificant gain. The law also created several types of committees (works and liaison) to represent African workers in negotiating with employers, though Africans nicknamed them "tea and toilet committees" because of the trivial topics open to negotiation; Mike Morris, a dock labor organizer in the 1980s, described works committees as follows: "Half the workers' representatives were appointed by management" and the other half were "elected" among those hand-picked by the employer-dependent *induna*. The government also responded with repression in 1973 by banning numerous activists, including Rick Turner and David Hemson, as well as Black Consciousness founder Steve Biko, although he had no direct involvement in the strikes.[24]

The rampant racism of white unionists also merits observation. Shortly after the Durban Strikes, James Zurichm, president of the Artisan Staff Association, which represented some white workers in South Africa's transportation industry, spoke at his union's annual conference. Zurichm denied that black workers wished to unionize, "As we know them, I doubt whether the Bantu is interested in forming trade unions. If he is interested in forming his own union I doubt whether he has progressed far enough to be able to be able to fully appreciate the workings of the Industrial Conciliation Act." His condescension toward black people continued: "The Bantu is emerging from his primitive state and it is no easy for him to understand the white man's ways. They are a people who are strange to our concept of disciplined work, hours of duty, etc., and they are also a superstitious people." Racism among white unionists remained the norm, confirming the impossibility of a multiracial labor movement involving most white South African workers at that time. Such racist views also confirm the radicalism of those (few) whites in the SWC who fought for black workers.[25]

Despite Zurichm's assertions, dockworkers continued organizing, as did a growing number of black workers, creating the first cracks in the apartheid wall. Shortly after the Durban Strikes, dockers joined black railway workers in a march downtown, demanding that SACTU be made legal again (technically, SACTU never was banned, despite suffering tremendous repression). The dockworkers' activity continued unabated, still pushing for wage hikes and an actual union. In fact, in the aftermath of the 1972 dock strikes and 1973 Durban Strikes, stevedore firms increased wages annually the rest of the decade so that they had more than doubled by 1980. Organizer Morris suggests the impressive increases were attributable to how low wages had been along with dockworker power. As for unionism, although the matter is complex, two unions soon emerged in Durban and other ports, the Transport and General Workers Union (TGWU) and the General Workers Union (GWU), both of which gained members in various ports, though by the early 1980s most in Durban belonged to the GWU. Off the waterfront, worker activism exploded nationwide in the wake of the Durban Strikes, though "Unions grew quickest in Natal." It seems fair to conclude that Durban's dockworkers were a forerunner of unleashing working class resistance in 1970s South Africa and played a central role in it.[26]

The significance of the 1972 dock strikes, then, was far greater than its wage increase. Arguably, the strike helped launch the legendary Durban Strikes that erupted just weeks later, although the historiography still understates the dockworkers' import. That the Durban Strikes unleashed a domino effect of anti-apartheid protests, however, is widely accepted. The classics by Steven Friedman and Jeremy Baskin—as well as Jabulani Sithole and Sifiso Ndlovu's recent chapter in the monumental survey of the anti-apartheid movement, *The Road to Democracy in South Africa*—acknowledge the role of Durban dockworkers, even if they downplay the size of their contribution. Worse, general histories omit the dockworkers' 1972 strike entirely, instead crediting the Coronation workers for launching the Durban Strikes. For instance, Mahmood Mamdani, in his influential chapter on migrant workers in South Africa, says, "Durban 1973 and Soweto 1976 were the two events that symbolized, dramatized, and concretized this shift in the perspective of resistance." More accurate is the argument first presented by Hemson, "On October 23, 1972 1,000 stevedores went on strike and signalled the beginnings of mass opposition to apartheid."[27]

That the dockers struck prior to Coronation should be instrumental to an understanding of how and why they and other blacks in Durban struck soon thereafter. One should think of the late 1972 dock strikes as tremors preceding the larger earthquake of early 1973. One interesting observation was that of long-time noted journalist Allister Sparks, who saw "Forces under the Surface" between the two 1972 dock strikes: "If you look carefully you will notice beneath the static surface of our formal political scene, there is some movement . . . These are the inexorable forces of socio-economic change working away all the time beneath the surface . . . the growing movement towards Black trade unionism is becoming significant: here are Black people beginning to sense their new power." Sparks accurately predicted the eruption of black workers shortly thereafter. Yet Sparks and even the latest scholarly contributions continue to ignore the dockworkers' role. In his generally wonderful 2015 article on black worker activism after the Durban Strikes, Alex Lichtenstein makes no mention of the dockworkers or their 1972 strikes, despite lamenting that none of the recent scholarship "casts much light on the reasons for the outbreak of the strikes themselves." Indeed, he includes a laundry list of possible factors that did not include the dockworkers' strikes but did name the white activists who supported them.[28]

Also demanding mention, in the same era and same city in which black dockworkers reignited the black working class, the legendary Stephen Biko helped create the Black Consciousness Movement. Academic and activist Tony Morphet labeled the convergence of many people and events in the early to mid-1970s who became influential in the struggle against apartheid the "Durban Moment." Biko, however, had little to no direct contact with or influence over dockworkers—or other black workers in Durban. Biko, himself a medical student, offered a brilliant and radical critique of both apartheid and the anti-apartheid movement. At least initially, however, those who embraced black consciousness were primarily educated middle-class blacks who did not seek to organize the overwhelming black majority in Durban, that is, the workers. In fact, no evidence exists that the Black Consciousness Movement influenced, in any manner or degree, the Durban Strikes. And when black consciousness student activists attempted to organize black workers, they had little success. The Black Workers Project was established, as well as an independent trade union, the Black Allied Workers Union, but neither gained traction, though some black community programs strove to reduce the intense suffering of the rural poor. As the white student activist and, later, scholar Dan O'Meara noted, "Biko's group could have done this, but they didn't have a class analysis, and Black Consciousness was focused more on community projects, not in factories." Moreover, whereas black consciousness adherents rejected the assistance of white radicals (though Biko and Rick Turner were on good terms), black workers did not. For instance, hundreds and then thousands of dockworkers and other black workers gladly joined the benefit fund and unions that white activists helped create. Nevertheless, the government presumed that Biko and the Black Consciousness Movement were involved in the Durban Strikes, and so many black consciousness activists, including Biko, were arrested, banned, or both immediately after the strike wave. Similarly, in March 1973 Turner was banned and Cheadle, Hemson, and others in the SWC were banned in 1974. Worse, Nxasana was arrested under the Terrorism Act in 1975 for five hundred days and, all too typically, brutally tortured while imprisoned. Finally, Turner was murdered while still under a banning order, with the case never resolved, though nearly all believe the government ordered his killing.[29]

To conclude, it seems safe to say that the dockworkers played a key role in the subsequent Durban Strikes. David Hemson, writing about the 1969 and 1972 strikes, made a different yet complementary point: The resurgent labor and anti-apartheid movements after 1973 "demonstrated effectively the capacity of the dockworkers to reorganise after defeat, indicated the tendency for the dock-work-ers to act in advance of the workers of Durban and, indeed, of the entire coun-try." Subsequently, the struggle against apartheid gained new life after a so-called quiet decade. Moreover, as Sithole and Ndlovu wrote, "The Natal strikes created an enabling environment for the revival of the political unionism that was first established by SACTU in the 1950s." Black working-class activism directly and indirectly challenged the apartheid state, as Rick Turner and Fozia Fisher, his wife, wrote in 1978: "It is worth stressing that in South Africa, managerial prerogative over African workers has traditionally been virtually absolute. Under these circum-stances, all issues are issues of control, whether they concern the right of workers to negotiate for higher wages, or to have recognized trade unions, or to take away the managerial right to hire and fire at will. Because they are perceived by manage-ment as issues of control, they may at least come to be perceived in the same way by workers." Dockworkers in Durban helped usher the South African working class into a new era. Bill Freund, the great scholar of African political economy, wrote of dockworkers generally as "pioneers of unionisation and the spread of socialist ideas in Africa."[30]

By contrast, San Francisco Bay Area dockworkers seemed to swim against the prevailing current of union movements in the Bay Area and the United States. In the 1960s and 1970s, ILWU Local 10 stood front and center among many social movements, most particularly the black freedom struggle. Most US labor unions at the time, however, moved slowly to embrace racial equality. Whereas Local 10 epitomized social-movement unionism, in the 1960s the mainstream AFL-CIO—"Big Labor"—seemed completely opposed to accepting—let alone supporting—the changes demanded by African Americans and their white allies. In a famous incident, George Meany, AFL-CIO president for much of the Cold War period, castigated A. Philip Randolph, perhaps the most important African American unionist in US history, for pushing unions to open their ranks to black workers. "Meany angrily dismissed his concerns: 'Who the hell appointed you as the guard-ian of all the Negroes in America?'" Bay Area longshore workers challenged the racism of white America, within the labor movement in particular.[31]

Local 10 and the Black Freedom Struggle in the 1960s

The ILWU leadership and many rank-and-file members in Local 10 advocated racial equality in many of the intersectional social movements during the 1960s and 1970s. The previous chapter examined Local 10's dramatic increase in African American membership and then how black and white longshoremen agitated on behalf of hiring blacks in other Bay Area workplaces. This section examines other aspects of Local 10's civil-rights unionism, along with its efforts on behalf of and commitment to other social movements. Rather than deeply exploring a single topic, this section traces how the ILWU, Local 10, and rank-and-file members (not just following but leaders in their own rights) participated in many social movements in the heady sixties, thereby demonstrating the breadth of their activism. The longshoremen, their local, and the international became deeply involved in struggles too numerous to cover, and so this section examines a representative sample: fighting against discrimination and for equal rights for Japanese Americans and African Americans; helping create the first major protest against the Red Scare; organizing a massive civil-rights march in solidarity with "the movement" in Birmingham; supporting the Sheraton Palace sit-ins, the largest civil-rights protests outside the South up to that time; creating the St. Francis Housing Cooperative, the first privately financed, racially integrated, and affordable housing development in San Francisco; welcoming Dr. Martin Luther King Jr. to Local 10's hall; contributing to the Pan-Indian occupation of Alcatraz, and supporting California farmworkers, who were heavily Latino and Filipino, to build the United Farm Workers (UFW). In short, San Francisco longshore workers and their union greatly affected Bay Area social movements during a pivotal time in US history. Their efforts also had larger influence, for what happened in the Bay Area shaped struggles nationwide.

The tremendous historical significance of Bay Area longshore workers and Local 10 largely has been ignored by historians. Although scholars of labor—particularly Bruce Nelson and Howard Kimeldorf—wrote quite insightful books about the early ILWU, precious little about the union's postwar history and its connections to social movements exists. Similarly, histories of postwar US social movements generally ignore the labor movement, including its intersection with civil rights. For instance, Paul T. Miller's book on civil rights in postwar San Francisco includes a few brief mentions of the ILWU, an organization with thousands of African Americans who were fully integrated—and had black leaders—and promoted racial equality beyond their union. The same goes for Daniel Crowe's and Albert S. Broussard's books on civil rights in the Bay Area. Perhaps because the ILWU was exceptional, it receives a quick nod and then promptly is ignored. This omission is further revealed via comparative histories; that is, histories of postwar Durban and South Africa devote far more attention to the labor movement (albeit not Durban dockworkers) in the anti-apartheid struggle. Instead, when US unions are mentioned, they are scoffed at—first criticized, sometimes justly so, for being "part of the problem" as "Big Labor" by New Left adherents. Second, less justifiably, most scholars follow this interpretation as laid out by Maurice Isserman and Michael Kazin: "Institutional stability brought many benefits to the unions and their members, but these came at the cost of a sense of social mission. Every year at annual conventions, delegates adopted resolutions pledging support for a wide range of ambitious social reforms, but few people in or out of the labor movement took them very seriously. Unions existed primarily to service the needs and represent the interests of their own members, not to wage crusades on the behalf of non-dues payers, however just their cause or dire their plight."[32]

The tremendous economic benefits that unions won for their millions of members, namely uplifting them into the blue-collar middle class, should not be discarded. And, sadly, when Nixon ended conscription, many in the US middle class stopped protesting the war in Vietnam. Unlike most unions and other organizations, though, the ILWU has, for decades, dedicated itself to a social mission, provided mighty support for equal rights, and influenced the Bay Area and beyond. The ILWU may (sometimes) receive a brief nod for being different, but its history generally is ignored and this book seeks to correct such glaring omissions.

An early, poignant example of the union's commitment to ethnic and racial equality came in its principled if controversial opposition to the persecution of Japanese Americans during World War II. In 1942, the ILWU condemned the internment of 125,000 Japanese and Japanese Americans, ordered by President Franklin D. Roosevelt shortly after the surprise Japanese attack on the US naval base at Pearl Harbor, Hawai'i. Hostility toward Japanese immigrants (by law, never allowed to become US citizens) and Japanese Americans quickly reached fever pitch, and very few came to their defense, although more recently most Americans acknowledge the trampling of their constitutional rights. In sworn testimony before Congress in February 1942, only three months after Pearl Harbor, ILWU leader Lou Goldblatt sagely predicted, "this entire episode of hysteria and mob chant against the native-born Japanese will form a dark page of American history. It may well appear as one of the victories won by the Axis powers." Similarly, in May 1945, the month Germany surrendered and three months before Japan did, Bridges pushed to have a few Japanese Americans, interned for most of the war, admitted to the Stockton division of Local 6 (Bay Area warehouse) in conjunction with the government's War Relocation Authority. When the white majority division refused to allow them into the union, Bridges and Goldblatt pulled the charter until the seven hundred members accepted them into the local. The union's commitment to equality for Japanese Americans was rare, to say the least, and remains largely unknown.[33]

African Americans, though, made up the largest minority population in the United States, and their fight against discrimination provides the main evidence of how the ILWU helped lead the fight in the Bay Area to end segregation and other legal forms of racism. The union's commitment, rooted in its founding ideals of solidarity and equality ("an injury to one is an injury to all"), played out in a great many ways. In addition to the workplace matters discussed in an earlier section of this chapter, ILWU members publicly condemned racism in their local communities. For instance, in 1947 Paul Heide, a white activist in Local 6, testified in front of the Oakland City Council to attack racist police brutality. The ILWU engaged in city and state politics, collaborating with civil-rights organizations and other unions to get bellwether fair housing and fair employment laws passed (both outlawing racial discrimination) in the 1950s and 1960s. In 1951, Local 10 activist and later ILWU international officer Bill Chester testified before the San Francisco Board of Supervisors in favor of a strong fair employment practices ordinance. When employers took credit for blacks working on the waterfront, Chester offered a corrective: "It was the ILWU and its leaders that fought to see to it that men and women were hired without discrimination." By contrast, he declared, "there is not a single Negro woman hired by the employers to work in their offices, and there is not one Negro hired as a walking boss, who work directly under the employers' supervision. The employers should be ashamed of themselves." Historian Robert Self—generally highly critical of the region's racist white people and institutions— wrote that the ILWU "stood at the center of the Bay Area's African American trade union culture and remained an influential force in all of the region's midcentury black community." Indeed, "the importance of the Bay Area locals of the ILWU and MCSU [Marine Cooks and Stewards, a racially integrated, left-wing union that merged with the ILWU in the 1950s] to shopfloor racial equality and civil rights is definitive." Although primarily focused on (black) workers' economic conditions, the ILWU also committed itself to African Americans' legal and political equality. As labor historian William Jones convincingly argues about the 1963 March on Washington for Jobs and Freedom, unions including the ILWU were "insisting that social democracy and civil rights were not only compatible but mutually reinforcing."[34]

Examples of how the ILWU worked in solidarity with the largely southern-based black freedom struggle are too numerous to recount, but the union's commitment was real and long-standing. Bridges regularly wrote in support of racial equality in his column "On the Beam" that appeared in the union's newspaper, *Dispatcher*. For instance, in 1954, after the US Supreme Court issued its historic ruling against Jim Crow segregation in *Brown v. Board of Education*, Bridges lauded it as "a victory for all decent and progressive Americans—whether Negro, white or any other color" because the Jim Crow "system has been a cancer on America." Whereas President Dwight D. Eisenhower did not even make a public comment upon the ruling and privately expressed doubts, Bridges condemned racial segregation that humiliated and degraded "many of our Negro brothers" in the ILWU who hailed from the South. Wisely if unfortunately, he pointed out that, in and of itself, *Brown* would not end racism; rather, people still must fight to make integration a reality and suggested that the Supreme Court ruled as it had only because it was forced to so, that is, because of the power of the civil-rights movement. A few years later, in 1960, after the Sharpeville Massacre, when South African police killed at least sixty-nine peaceful anti-apartheid protesters, a *Dispatcher* editorial drew an apt parallel between opponents of racial equality in the USA and its opponents in South Africa: "South African segregation practices carry to an extreme the segregation practices of our own South. . . . There is a brutality inherent in the conduct of Southern police against Negro students which is akin to the conduct of the South African police. There is, moreover, a terrible kinship between South Africa's racism and the kind which is still depriving Southern Negroes of equality in education or anything else." Following up, the ILWU Dock Caucus voted in 1960 to boycott South African cargo though little came of that pronouncement save one single action by Local 10 in 1962.[35]

Many black longshoremen, led by Chester, collaborated with the San Francisco chapter of the National Association for the Advancement of Colored People (NAACP), the nation's most prominent civil-rights organization. Chester, in a 1969 interview, discussed ILWU support: "We found that many members of our union, practically all of the blacks, were members of the NAACP, many of them contributed to the Urban League [another mainstream civil-rights organization]." Blacks in Local 10 supported the NAACP even though, earlier in the Cold War, the local chapter actively distanced itself from the ILWU, as historian Daniel Crowe wrote: "In 1954, the moderate civil rights organization proclaimed that the International Longshoremen's and Warehousemen's Union (ILWU) 'does not have their support, and furthermore authorizes no one from the ILWU to use their organization as a front for the Communist Party.'" The NAACP took this stance irrespective of Local 10's voluntary integration decades before nearly every other union or institution. As the longshoremen fought for civil rights so, too, did they fight for civil liberties.[36]

ILWU Local 10 found itself at the forefront of the first mass protest, anywhere across the nation, against domestic anticommunism, helping launch the 1960s as the most important decade for social protest in postwar America. In 1960, the ILWU remained square in the sights of the US House Un-American Committee (HUAC), as evidenced by HUAC Chair Francis E. Walter calling Bridges a "Communist agent" in hearings on *Communist Activities among Seamen and on Waterfront Facilities*. That year, HUAC held hearings in San Francisco and subpoenaed Local 10 member Archie Brown, an open Communist Party member. Much of the national media, and a hysterical government propaganda film *Operation Abolition* created about the events, highlighted that a large number of students from the University of California–Berkeley (and San Francisco State College) protested the hearings. Lost in this coverage, though, was that Brown—a long-time Local 10 activist and well-known communist—was the primary subject of this HUAC investigation, and attacking him also was a clear attack on the ILWU, the most powerful left-wing union in both the Bay Area and the nation. Brown understood the stakes and castigated the congressional representatives for their Red Scare tactics. Brown refused to be intimidated by the committee's questions and, when HUAC members sought to close the hearings to the public, Brown shouted, "What are you hiding? Let the people in, let them hear!" After his testimony became more heated, the police literally dragged Brown out the door as he yelled, "Here comes the goon squad! This is Americanism. Watch this Americanism in action!" Although it is undeniably important that many students protested the hearing's first day, Brown's arrest resulted in hundreds of longshoremen appearing on the second day. Few in Local 10 belonged to the Communist Party, but the overwhelming majority defended their right to do so. The Bay Area's social movement culture, with the ILWU at the forefront, helped thaw the domestic Cold War that had forced Americans into fifteen years of conformity. Local 10 should be centered in the history of these protests, alongside students, who—together—made the Bay Area, in the early 1960s, an epicenter of the New Left, an important national and global phenomenon.[37]

Another fascinating link between the anti-HUAC protests, UC–Berkeley, and the ILWU was Herb Mills, a Berkeley political science PhD student, leader of the anti-HUAC protests, and (future) leader in Local 10. Mills, a white man from Detroit, had dropped out of high school to work at Ford's River Rouge factory, where communists in his United Auto Workers (UAW) local appreciated his intellectual gifts and so encouraged him to return to school. Upon graduation from the University of Michigan in the mid-1950s, he joined the army on the assumption—like many young working-class men—that he would be drafted anyway, and so better to volunteer while the nation was not in a shooting war. After an honorable discharge in California, he decided to stay and, like many a veteran, used the GI Bill to enroll at Berkeley. Soon he helped create and become a leader of SLATE (not an acronym), a graduate student organization, and its anti-HUAC protests; SLATE is far more famous for helping organize the Free Speech Movement in 1964, but by then Mills had dropped out after being accepted into Local 10. It is interesting to note that, while still at Berkeley, Mills had written an essay on the student movement's "use of direct action" as "a very conscious and radical comment on present political institutions," a tactic pioneered by sailors and dockworkers centuries earlier and still deployed to this day. Mills continued participating in and, sometimes leading, such actions for the next thirty years in Local 10. He also became a leading critic of the ILWU's response to containerization and helped lead Local 10's successful boycott of ships loading US military equipment for fascist Chile.[38]

In 1963, the same year Mills joined Local 10, the ILWU began selling units in the housing cooperative that its leaders conceived and financed in response to urban redevelopment and a lack of affordable housing. Though not the first in the nation (several clothing worker unions constructed thousands of such units in New York City), the St. Francis Square Housing Cooperative was the Bay Area's first. Beginning in 1960, the ILWU invested some of its pension funds in property that was part of a forty-five-block area cleared, notoriously, by city and federal housing agencies in a move criticized by the legendary African American writer and activist James Baldwin as "urban renewal which means moving Negroes out; it means Negro removal." The redevelopment of the Fillmore (or Western Addition), the city's largest black neighborhood, began in the 1950s and continued into the early 1970s, razing about twenty-five hundred Victorian structures and displacing more than ten thousand people—overwhelmingly African Americans—including hundreds of Local 6 and 10 members. ILWU secretary-treasurer Lou Goldblatt later explained why he developed this project: "what they were not doing was replacing the slums with anything that any of the people who had lived there could have any chance under the sun of coming back to." St. Francis's three hundred units were open to every ethnicity and race, the first integrated housing development in San Francisco. Its first manager was Revels Cayton, a black left-wing activist and ILWU member. ILWU members who lived in the Fillmore continued to resist further clearings, albeit with limited success. Ultimately, the character of the Fillmore changed forever, with far fewer blacks. The co-op, though, recently celebrated its fiftieth anniversary, commemorated by a small exhibit at the San Francisco Public Library's main branch, and remains home to some ILWU pensioners, including Leroy King, an African American leader in Local 6, and until recently a former ILWU librarian and historian, the late Carol Cuénod.[39]

Also in 1963, the ILWU and Local 10 helped organize a huge civil-rights demonstration in San Francisco and supported another, the legendary March on Washington for Jobs and Freedom. Early that year, the nation's eyes focused upon Birmingham, Alabama, nicknamed "America's Johannesburg" for being the most segregated big city in the South. The Southern Christian Leadership Conference, headed by Dr. Martin Luther King Jr., collaborated with local activists for several months of nonviolent civil disobedience to highlight the persistence of racial segregation, nearly ten years after *Brown v. Board*. Chester, utilizing his many contacts, helped create the Church-Labor Conference that, on May 26, 1963, brought together twenty thousand people to march with a giant banner reading "We March in Unity for Freedom in Birmingham and Equality in San Francisco" An additional ten thousand joined at the march's end to rally—the largest civil-rights demonstration in the region's history. Three months later, the ILWU donated money and sent a delegation to the nation's capital (as did some other unions, most notably the UAW) for what became the largest political gathering in US history up to that time. One quarter of a million Americans, mostly black but with many whites, participated in the March on Washington to pressure the Congress and the president to pass a comprehensive civil-rights bill outlawing racial discrimination once and for all. Tragically, the response of some unreconstructed segregationists was the blowing up of a black church in Birmingham closely associated with the movement that killed four black girls. When word reached San Francisco, Local 10 members quickly shut down the port for a "stop work meeting" in front of the US Federal Building to protest this terrorist attack.[40]

The rhetoric notwithstanding, equal rights proved elusive, and so the movement continued and the ILWU became involved in the largest civil-rights event in San Francisco, the 1964 effort to pressure hotels to hire more African Americans and employ them in more skilled jobs. Upwards of fifteen hundred black and white demonstrators, especially students from Berkeley and San Francisco City College, joined the Sheraton-Palace Hotel protests, with perhaps five hundred engaging in civil disobedience (sit-ins), resulting in the arrest of more than one hundred fifty. Far less known is that the ILWU played multiple roles in this struggle. Starting in the 1960s, the ILWU cultivated deep connections with the city's political establishment, becoming quite liberal by US standards. Jo Freeman, an important Berkeley leader in these demonstrations and the Free Speech Movement, later wrote, "While we were still in jail, leaders in the ILWU had phoned Mayor [John F.] Shelley, who had enjoyed major union support for his recent election [the first Democrat elected mayor since 1908], and urged him to resolve the conflict. Several children of the ILWU leadership were in the Sheraton demonstrations, and many Negroes were among its members." ILWU Northern California Regional Director Bill Chester helped bring together representatives from businesses and the government with civil-rights advocates. Citing Mike Myerson, another important activist, Freeman credited the ILWU with "creating a network of familiarity among the mayor, the unions, and the protestors." Local 10's lawyer Norman Leonard later defended some of the sit-in protesters arrested for trespassing. Ultimately, an unprecedented agreement occurred in which thirty-three hotels committed to making 15 to 20 percent of its workforce "minorities." In the Bay Area history of the 1960s, the Sheraton-Palace victory is legendary and another example of how the ILWU worked to diversify the workforces of local businesses.[41]

Because of the union's many efforts to fight racism, in 1967 Dr. King visited Local 10 and became an honorary member, like Paul Robeson before him. King, best known for his "I Have a Dream" speech, long had been interested in and supportive of unions and proved increasingly so in his final years. He repeatedly encouraged black workers to join and form unions, calling them "the first anti-poverty program." King regularly supported and spoke to racially inclusive unions, and so it was not surprising that he visited Local 10's hiring hall. Addressing a large gathering of dockworkers, King declared, "I don't feel like a stranger here in the midst of the

Fig. 3. Dr. Martin Luther King Jr. speaking at Local 10's hall in 1967, when he was made an honorary member of the union, like Paul Robeson before him. Image used with permission from ILWU Library.

ILWU. We have been strengthened and energized by the support you have given to our struggles. . . . We've learned from labor the meaning of power." More than forty years later, Cleophas Williams remembered the speech: "He talked about the economics of discrimination," insightfully pointing out that "What he said, is what Bridges had been saying all along" about all workers benefiting by attacking racism and forming interracial unions. King's vigorous support for unions resulted in losing some support among middle-class white Americans or, as Williams said, "He wasn't very popular when he was talking about pork chops." Both King and the ILWU considered the civil-rights and labor movements "twins"—Williams's term. The following year, King spent a lot of time in Memphis to support striking sanitation workers (mostly black men), where he was murdered by a racist white man. The day after his stunning death, April 9, 1968, the Bay Area was quiet when more than one hundred fifty cities and towns erupted into flames. Longshoremen shut down the ports of San Francisco and Oakland for their newest (honorary) member, as they still do when one of their own dies on the job. Nine ILWU members attended King's funeral, in Atlanta, including Bridges, Chester, and Williams, the last-named elected the local's first black president the previous year.[42]

Similarly, it is neither incidental nor coincidental that ILWU members in the Bay Area gave major support to Californians seeking to form the United Farm Workers (UFW). It is widely known that migratory farmworkers were heavily nonwhite (particularly Mexican and Filipino Americans) and immigrant (Mexican but also smatterings of other nationalities, including Arabs). When Filipino American farmworkers struck large table and wine grape growers in and around Delano, California, in 1965, they quickly joined forces with Chavez's fledgling union, mostly Mexican Americans. Thus began a five-year saga that—like the predominantly African American sanitation workers in the Memphis "I Am a Man" campaign—combined elements of labor and civil-rights activism. On November 17, 1965, a few strikers stood at the foot of San Francisco Pier 50, hoping to convince longshoremen not to load Delano grapes aboard the *President Wilson*, headed for Asia. One key activist, Gilbert Padilla, described what happened next:

> We went there as the grapes were being loaded onto ships to Japan . . . and I'm standing out there with a little cardboard, with a picket [sign], "Don't eat grapes." Then some of the longshoremen asked, "Is this a labor dispute?" And I said, "No, no, no labor dispute." So they would walk in. Jimmy Herman came over and asked me, "What the hell you doing?" And I told him we were striking. He knew about the strike but wanted to know "what are you asking for?" And I was telling him, and then he says, "Come with me." He took me to his office; he was president of the clerks (a longshoremen's union local). He took me to his office and he got on his hands and knees, Jimmy Herman, and he made picket signs. And he told me, "You go back there and don't tell nobody about who gave you this. But you just stand there. [You] don't [have to] say a goddamned thing." The sign said, "Farm Workers on Strike." And everybody walked out of that fucking place, man! That's the first time I felt like I was 10 feet tall, man! Everybody walked out. So then they asked what's happening and we were telling them, and Jesus Christ, man, I never seen anything like it. There were trucks all the way up to the bridge, man!

Herman, of course, was the Local 34 president who also proved instrumental in integrating Bay Area clerks. Two weeks later, a similar action happened in Oakland, when longshoremen refused to load twenty-five hundred cases of DiGorgio grapes. Social movement scholar Marshall Ganz suggested the longshoremen's respect for the farmworkers "was a powerful tonic to the strikers," coming at crucial point in the strike, right at the end of the harvest, after which there would be far less work. In short, organizers believed "interference with shipping could exert economic pressure on growers and thus sustain the strike" and, hence, ILWU members proved vital in strengthening the strike at a key moment. Subsequently, Bay Area ILWU locals collected clothing, food, and money for the strikers and their families. Local 34's Don Watson, the leading ILWU Bay Area activist on farmworker solidarity, as well as a historian of this chapter in his union's history, recalled that "There were a couple of Local 10 people that ran a five dollar a month club in support of the farm workers," to which he also belonged. That Bay Area longshoremen and clerks actively supported this movement comes as little surprise, especially as the ILWU organized farmworkers, overwhelmingly Asian Americans, in Hawai'i in the 1950s.[43]

Local 10 also played an integral, if hidden, role in the historic Pan-Indian oc-cupation of Alcatraz, an especially incredible chapter in Bay Area social move-ment history. Beginning in 1969, American Indians, some of whom studied at San Francisco State, planned and carried out the occupation of the legendary Alcatraz Island, a former federal penitentiary. They did so to raise awareness of the desper-ate plight of American Indians and promote cultural and political changes among both Indians and the nation at large. Long forgotten or never known is that Local 10 longshoreman "Indian Joe" Morris, born and raised on the Blackfoot reserva-tion in Montana, helped make the eighteen-month occupation possible. Alcatraz's twelve-acre "Rock" was lifeless, and so literally everything needed to sustain life, including water, had to come from the mainland (a main reason the federal gov-ernment stopped using it as a prison). Morris secured the unused San Francisco Pier 40 for the transfer of all people and supplies between the island and city. In his unpublished memoir, he wrote, "When the Indians occupied Alcatraz Island I was the Alcatraz troubleshooter and mainland coordinator." Morris also raised thousands of dollars from the ILWU and other unions and solicited donations at the Ferry Building (its plaza along the Embarcadero now named after Harry Bridges). Without Morris's unsung action, the occupation—simply put—could not have continued very long. Morris might have been the only American Indian in Local 10, but there was tremendous sympathy among other members; the ILWU execu-tive board praised the Indians occupying Alcatraz "as a haven and a symbol of the genocide they have suffered." Morris helped arrange for a delegation of Local 10 and other ILWU members to visit Alcatraz, where Lou Goldblatt proclaimed, "You folks are just like a labor union on strike. You have to last one day longer than the other guy." Winding down in 1971, the *Dispatcher* featured a photograph of Morris holding a painting—his first ever—commemorating the occupation, though few know this intersectional history.[44]

By contrast, among the best-known organizations that emerged in the 1960s out of the Bay Area was the Black Panther Party, the quintessential Black Power organization, which shared much in common ideologically with the ILWU. First and foremost, the leaders in both groups and many ordinary members saw the world in materialist terms and held explicitly anticapitalist views. Though the ILWU and Black Panthers originated out of different communities and generations, both saw the poverty and disempowerment of working people, including African Americans, as caused by an economic system neither just nor fair. Accordingly, both advocated, albeit vaguely, socialism to serve "the people" rather than economic and political elites, be it "the boss" or "The Man." Although the Black Panthers, obviously, fo-cused on empowering black people, its underlying materialist critique cannot be ignored—nor was it at the time. In 1967, Harry Bridges, an Australian immigrant then in his midsixties, did not do so when he thoughtfully analyzed Black Power and highlighted the values it shared with the ILWU. Bridges opined that "integration," in and of itself, "does not serve any truly significant interest," for it did not "change the basic economic and political system that forces Negroes into ghettoes, or discriminates against them on jobs or in schools, that denies them legal rights, or robs them and cheats them and beats them." Bridges pointedly concluded, "The trade union movement has always understood that the only reasonable way to win gains is to bargain and fight from a position of strength—and that means power!" Similarly, historian Robert Self began his "Black Power" chapter in *American Babylon* by quoting Paul Cobb, a young black Oaklander: "The time has come for a declaration of independence for West Oakland. We live on an urban plantation. We have to plan our liberation." Cobb, an important if forgotten local leader, was the son of a West Oakland longshoreman who grew up listening to black dockworkers and Pullman porters where he, according to Self, learned of his hometown's "cosmopolitan laborite culture that blended politics, trade unionism, and human rights." In keeping with their left-wing beliefs, both groups believed in the necessity of interracial alliances: the ILWU by recruiting blacks into the union and, in Local 10 at least, integrated its ranks while the Panthers allied with the predominantly white New Left Peace and Freedom Party in Bay Area elections. Panther chief of staff David Hilliard later told author Ishmael Reed, "We always worked with the white left." Finally, people in both organizations advocated what Donna Murch labeled in the Panthers' context "radical black internationalism." Black and white leftists in Local 10 proved quite internationalist, including supporting liberation struggles in Africa as evidenced by the formation of the Southern Africa Liberation Support Committee. Bobby Seale, a cofounder of the Panthers, summarized these issues in *Seize the Time*: "We do not fight racism with racism. We fight racism with solidarity. We do not fight exploitative capitalism with black capitalism. We fight capitalism with basic socialism. And we do not fight imperialism with more imperialism. We fight imperialism with proletarian internationalism."[45]

In addition to shared political values, both maintained power bases in Oakland, home to many Panthers as well as many hundreds of black longshoremen. The Panthers were founded and headquartered in Oakland, home to the largest number of Bay Area blacks, "ghettoized" in the flatlands in the western and northern parts of the city. Robert Self documented how blacks had few alternatives to Oakland in the East Bay and, inside the city, they suffered from hypersegregation. As a result, many black longshoremen—despite earning good wages—resided on the same West Oakland streets as Huey Newton, Bobby Seale, and many Panthers. Another shared trait of most blacks in Local 10 and the Panthers was that they had arrived in the Bay Area during the second Great Migration. Hence, not only did longshoremen and Panthers live near each other, some black Oaklanders belonged to both organizations. Cleophas Williams, who ended up in West Oakland when he arrived in the 1940s and later moved to North Oakland, recalled, "We had some of the Panthers in our union." Among the thousands of African Americans who belonged to Local 10, it seems reasonable to conclude that many were sympathetic to the Black Panthers and their agenda; but there is no evidence that many Local 10 members were Panthers. Leo Robinson, for instance, was a black communist in Local 10 who later applied his Marxist Pan-African sensibilities to solidarity with freedom struggles in southern Africa—but he was not a Panther. Supposedly, David Hilliard, an Oakland resident and Panther leader, worked as a casual on the waterfront in the 1970s, but he never fully registered in Local 10.[46]

The most tantalizing link between Local 10 and the Panthers was "Sweet" Jimmie Ward, whose story offers hints at other interconnections that, no doubt, existed among black radicals in Oakland in the 1960s and 1970s. Like Leo Robinson and Huey Newton before him, Ward moved to California from Louisiana in the 1950s, hoping to join Local 10 and finally doing so in 1963. Building on waterfront connections, he opened the Lamp Post, a nightclub, in Oakland's Uptown in 1969. Ward's fellow black longshoremen proved to be among his most valued friends and customers, but so were Black Panthers. Ward reportedly was a cousin and friend of Panther cofounder Huey Newton, and Panther members staffed his club. The Lamp Post was a popular hangout for Newton and other Panthers and supposedly had a silent investor who belonged to the group. These links easily lead one to imagine the Lamp Post as a popular place for longshoremen *and* Panthers to socialize together. (During this era, someone knifed Ward in the chest, thereby earning him a new nickname when his doctor declared "Sweet Jesus" had saved Ward's life; he later named another club of his Sweet Jimmie's, which operated until 2006.) Ward also received praise for using his money and influence to support a host of black community and political organizations, from mainstream to radical. In her excellent social history of the Panthers in Oakland, though, Donna Murch never mentioned the ILWU nor the Bay Area's long history of left-wing labor activism, concluding that these aspects of the Panthers need more research. The preceding paragraphs provide glimpses at the connections between the Panthers and ILWU, yet despite shared members, geography, and politics, Local 10 and the Black Panthers never aligned.[47]

Other black dockworkers took the politics they learned on the job and applied them off the waterfront—to integrate golf courses, admittedly not a traditional black pastime, and provide solidarity with other social justice causes by way of black dance traditions. In the early 1950s, Cleophas Williams barely averted injury while playing softball and then decided to switch sports. He bought a set of clubs at a pawnshop and started playing at the nearby Alameda Golf Course that, as was typical for West Coast clubs, denied black people membership. In response, Williams and his black golfing buddies organized the Bay Area Golf Club, open to all, but basically a black organization. They played at various courses and pushed to integrate them and for clubs to do so. He later helped organize chapters for the Western States Golf Association, which now stretches from Phoenix to Seattle. In contrast to many social clubs of the time, Williams boasted, "we didn't discriminate." Coincidentally, he first heard about the landmark *Brown v. Board* decision while on his way to play golf in Monterey. He claimed that "the fight was the same, it was just over a different scene." Similarly, black longshoremen brought their culture into the union to promote equality, as when Josh Williams (no relation to Cleophas) founded the Local 10 Drill Team—almost certainly, the first union drill team ever. Like many longshoremen, Williams was a veteran of the US Army; like many blacks, he suffered from racism in the military. After seeing combat in Korea and receiving an honorable discharge, he returned to the Bay Area and joined Local 10 in 1959, the first time since World War II it had opened its ranks. Williams created the union's drill team in 1965, which combined military precision and esprit de corps with African American step-dancing traditions among black fraternities; in fact, he had belonged to one such fraternity at San Francisco City College but dropped out when accepted into the union. Williams wanted the team to be diverse, though for many years only blacks (mostly military veterans) joined. In their very first performance, they marched with a thousand farmworkers at a San Francisco rally to raise support for the United Farm Workers, apropos for Williams who, while a child, joined other family members in working harvests in California's Central Valley and along the coast. In the late 1960s, the drill team performed frequently at Vietnam War protests and elsewhere with the endorsement of the local, because Williams had family members and knew other "good people" killed in Vietnam. They also marched at cultural events, especially in the black community (e.g., at West Oakland's McClymonds High School) and San Francisco's legendary Chinese New Year parade. Though "Captain Josh" has passed away, the Local 10 Drill Team continues to perform, for example in 2011 in Madison, Wisconsin, to support the right of government workers to belong to unions. Examples such as these prove how black members of Local 10 promoted a progressive, racially inclusive agenda off the waterfront.[48]

Conclusion

In 1969, the legendary African American activist Bayard Rustin wrote, "the Negro can never be socially and politically free until he is economically secure." Rustin could have been describing the civil-rights unionism of ILWU Local 10—or Durban dockworkers who struck that same year. For in South Africa, apartheid was inextricably linked to the economy, thereby creating a particularly virulent form of racial capitalism. Although their most pressing concern was ameliorating their poverty, the dockworkers surely understood their strikes as political acts. After all, as Nelson Sambureni wrote, no other black workers were agitating at that

Fig. 4. The ILWU Local 10 Drill Team participated in many political and cultural events throughout the Bay Area. In 1972, they marched in solidarity with the United Farm Workers, who opposed a state proposition promoted by agribusiness, which was defeated. Image used with permission from ILWU Library.

moment—indeed, almost no overt resistance to apartheid then existed: "In the 1960s, at the height of the repressive period, while the country's economy boomed, the apartheid state took a firm grip on a vast range of fronts." The Durban dock-workers who struck or threatened to do so three times in four years, despite mass retrenchments and police violence, were among the very first blacks anywhere in South Africa to loosen apartheid's grasp. The vehemence with which employers and the state cracked down on the dockworkers indicates that they also understood the gravity of the issue. The dockworkers' actions, thus, helped shatter the silence of the "quiet decade." This chapter further contends that, in contrast to the current historiography, in its 1972 strike, the dockworkers paved the way for the Durban Strikes of 1973 and, thus, contributed mightily to the national liberation struggle. They did so by inspiring the Coronation Brick workers to walk in the dockworkers' footsteps. The Durban Strikes shattered the era of high apartheid and, henceforth, black workers play a central role in the later fall of apartheid. In light of the fact that the workforce turned over several times since 1959 and also after the 1969 re-trenchments, the dockworkers' actions further reconfirm the pivotal role of work culture in their militancy.[49]

Similarly, black and white longshoremen in the San Francisco Bay Area worked in solidarity with and for a vast array of social movements, applying the experiences gained in their powerful and integrated leftist union. Bill Chester, an ILWU vice president and Local 10 member, noted in 1969 that "We also went outside the labor movement to bring our union programs to the wider community." He continued, "We found that, in a sense, the union is the community." Rank-and-filer Josh Williams embodied this ideal (what Korstad named civil-rights unionism) when he founded the Local 10 Drill Team that stepped on behalf of Mexican American and Filipino American farmworkers in a Market Street parade. In describing similar efforts by St. Louis Teamsters to promote interracial unionism and community activism, labor historian Bob Bussel coined the term "total-person unionism." To Bussel, "the other sixteen hours" of workers' lives, that is, the time off the job, should be equally important to any social justice-oriented union. The praxis of Local 10 explains why Dr. Martin Luther King Jr. made a pilgrimage to the San Francisco longshore union's hall, where he celebrated its efforts on behalf of (black) working-class power and equal rights. This chapter inserts dockworkers and their union into the Bay Area's and the nation's wider social movement history because they have received shockingly little attention. Some, of course, appreciate this history, including African American author Ishmael Reed, who wrote *Blues City* as a paean to Oakland. In his book, simultaneously a year in the life of Oakland and an exploration of its history, Reed praised Local 10 and the ILWU as being both "left" and committed to racial equality, unlike "the Old Left of the 1930s" or "New Left in the 1960s." Specifically, Reed described the union's participation in a 2003 rally against the US war in Iraq: "Apparently, the ILWU had not failed their black members, because not only was the moderator of ceremonies, union member Clarence Thomas, a black man, but a number of the speakers were black men, rare for a Left demonstration, where usually the only black males on the podium are hip-hop acts and entertainers." Following the lead of South African scholarship, this chapter contends that historians of the United States must more centrally position the ILWU and Local 10 when studying the civil-rights and other social movements.[50]

Finally, this chapter illuminates how militant dockworkers proved integral to the interconnected class-based and race-based social movements in these port cities. Because of their propensity to strike and organize, Durban and Bay Area dockworkers occupied the center of black freedom struggles in both cities. Events in these places helped shape national struggles, meaning these dockworkers profoundly affected each nation's history at key times. Just as Peter Linebaugh and Marcus Rediker labeled dockworkers and sailors "the motley crew in the American Revolution," so, too, in Durban and the Bay Area, a multiracial cast of maritime workers engaged in the revolutionary act of fighting for racial equality. They brought their notions of equality and radicalism and their commitment to it—steeped in their workplace culture and organizations—to black freedom struggles and, in the process, helped transform their nations.[51]

4

DECASUALIZATION AND CONTAINERIZATION

Used to be we'd unload Spanish cinnamon, Egyptian cotton,
Costa Rican coffee, and Scotch from
Cavernous bellies of rusty ships.

Not now.

Whiz kids with T-square, slide rules, and
Whips whirl warehouse cargo box and ship
Into new flat square molds.
—Dave Ramet, "Vans, Rain, and Wind"

The containerization of general cargo represents the most
promising innovation in the worldwide shipping industry.
—Carrabino, *Engineering Analysis of Cargo Handling*

In 1958, a Matson ship sailed out of San Francisco harbor loaded with twenty containers on its deck. Two years later, Matson launched its first ship carrying only containers,[1] 436 of them. In 1970, Matson's *Hawaiian Progress* embarked, from the ever-busier Port of Oakland, on its maiden voyage. This ship, the world's largest at the time, carried a thousand containers—the first purposefully constructed to haul these metal boxes. (The largest ship currently carries more than twenty-one thousand.) Among its many impacts, containerization radically changed the work of dockworkers (and other transport workers) in the San Francisco Bay Area, Durban, and across the globe. For millennia, the loading and unloading of ships had been, for all intents and purposes, remarkably similar. Ancient images on a Pharaonic Egyptian vase and an imperial Roman relief depict gangs of workers carrying cargo aboard ships. From those times through the mid-twentieth century, this work remained largely dependent upon the backbreaking manual labor of gangs of men, though it also involved great skills to properly and safely load and balance a ship's cargo. That model forever changed when entrepreneurs and engineers in the United States developed an entirely new method of moving cargo, in which twenty- and forty-foot standardized metal boxes or containers, whose contents were generally not loaded at the port and not by dockworkers, were hoisted onto ships and off them with huge dockside cranes.[2]

Containerization's effects are immense and, arguably, still underappreciated as perhaps the main factor in the past few generations' explosion of world trade. When people consider globalization, the widely used term to describe our increasingly "small" world, many think of the wonders of the Internet, smart phones, and e-mail. As economist Marc Levinson and sociologist Alice Mah convincingly argued, however, the centrality of shipping to global capitalism remains underestimated, for ships still transport fully 90 percent of world trade. Integral to the modern movement of goods—by rail and truck as well as by ship—is the process of containerization. How containers have affected the people who work along the shore is the focus of this chapter and the next. Basically, as productivity soared along with shipping companies' profits, the number of dockworkers plummeted. Because the ILWU was powerful enough that employers negotiated the transition, the 1960 Mechanization and Modernization Agreement (M&M), Bay Area longshoremen experienced a far less painful and more lucrative shift. Subsequent to this world-historic contract, dockworkers across the planet, port by port, experienced the container revolution. In Durban, the relatively late introduction of containers devastated dockworkers who were not strong enough to influence the process, made all the harder in that they still suffered under apartheid.[3]

The first major change in twentieth-century waterfront labor, though, was the ending of casual labor, and so this chapter starts with that topic. As discussed, in Durban, San Francisco, and most ports, the hiring of workers was done on a casual basis, meaning temporary and with no guarantee of any further work beyond that specific job. Also called contingent labor, employers hired dockworkers for a single shift or as long as it took to load or unload a particular ship. In many ports, dockworkers despised the hiring process, and the "shape-up" and longed for more job security, and so pushed to end casual labor. In the aftermath of the 1934 Big Strike, the nascent ILA (soon to be the ILWU) successfully achieved decasualization and, even better, a union-controlled hiring process. Although they received no guarantee of a minimum number of hours, with the union in control of the hiring hall and the dispatching of workers, longshoremen gained greater security. Simultaneously, they maintained a level of freedom quite rare, especially among manual laborers, for they chose which days or nights to seek work. By contrast, in 1959, Durban employers scrapped the casual (*togt*) system in favor of decasualization but controlled the entire process. Durban dockworkers wanted more work and security (and higher wages), but they appreciated that their casual status provided them with some measure of power, for they, essentially, could strike without punishment—and repeatedly had. As discussed, dockworkers and other Africans did not have the legal right to strike, but when *togt* laborers did not report for duty, they did not break any law or any condition of employment. To reduce such power, Durban shippers and government officials overhauled the hiring system, especially in response to a series of dockworker "strikes" coordinated with ANC-SACTU stay-aways in the late 1950s. Thus, San Francisco dockworkers pushed "from below" for decasualization, whereas in Durban employers instituted it "from above." Inherently, then, decasualization was neither proworker nor antiworker. By contrast and of utmost import, employers always drove containerization (as they did other forms of technological change), and so the issue became whether workers had the power to shape *how* the new regime proceeded.

Naturally, in both the hiring process and the use of technology, each side sought to expand their power vis-à-vis the other. To quote the preamble to the IWW Constitution, "Workers and employers share nothing in common." Some might take exception to this statement, but it accurately described labor relations in Durban, San Francisco, and other ports. Once one understands the veracity of that statement for dockworkers, another Wobbly mantra—more famous and perhaps more fundamental—can be understood: "an injury to one is an injury to all." Though coined by the Wobblies, it remains the official motto of the ILWU and flies high above Local 10 members at their hiring hall. Similarly, the signature image of several black workers turning a wheel of COSATU, the South African labor federation to which Durban dockworkers now belong, incorporates this slogan encircling the workers.

This chapter and the next one are more complex than the previous two, for these two analyze important shifts in labor relations that happened across several generations in San Francisco and Durban. Many labor regimens will be discussed, starting with casual labor, the typical regimen on global waterfronts for centuries. Curiously, dock labor historian Klaus Weinhauer noted that, though many study the late nineteenth and early twentieth centuries, "The highly interesting phase beginning with the introduction of relatively well-working decasualization schemes after World War II [in the global north and Australia] up until the beginning of containerisation of the mid-1960s is still waiting for similar attention." Precious little has changed since 2000 and, moreover, shockingly little has been written about the era after 1970. This chapter begins to correct these deficiencies, first focusing on decasualization in San Francisco and Durban, followed by an examination of containerization's rise in 1960s San Francisco. After millennia of relatively stability, this revolutionary new technology—in the historical equivalent of the blink of an eye—forever changed the working of cargo. The ILWU was the first union in the world to negotiate this transformation and San Francisco dockworkers, essentially, were the first to experience containerization and the myriad changes it wrought.[4]

Decasualization from Below in San Francisco

Before 1934, longshoremen had no control over whether they worked, when they worked, or for how long they worked—further worsened by the shape-up. Shaping up and irregular work were norms in every US port in the early twentieth century, as for most dockworkers elsewhere. Longshoremen particularly hated the shape-up for its arbitrariness, in which hiring bosses regularly played favorites (based upon race, ethnicity, religion, etc.) and sometimes solicited bribes. Naturally, workers wanted control over hiring—often called decasualization—though they also wished to retain some aspects of casual work. In the 1934 strike, the ILA Pacific Coast District successfully pushed for the creation of hiring halls in every port it represented. Under that system, workers still received no guarantee of minimum hours, but the new process ensured that hiring happened without discrimination. Further, and atypical of most decasualization schemes, the ILWU equalized work opportunities (not earnings) with its "low man out" rule. The union did not mandate that workers had to report for duty, say, five days a week. Instead, they retained that part of the earlier casual regime in which individuals decided when to report for work.[5]

In their first contract after the Big Strike, San Francisco and other West Coast longshoremen won many of their demands—in no small measure because of a sympathetic government. President Franklin Roosevelt and the US Congress, both more proworker than any before them (and since), helped make such gains happen, though increasingly militant workers also pushed them to act. In 1933, Section 7(a) of the National Industrial Relations Act meant that the federal government endorsed collective bargaining for the first time; in response, worker activism surged nationwide, pressing employers to recognize unions and bargain with them. In the case of the West Coast longshoremen, after almost three months on strike, employers and workers agreed to accept the rulings of the newly created National Longshoremen's Board (NLB), which Roosevelt created specifically to arbitrate the Big Strike. In late 1934, this board ruled in favor of the ILA's demands, especially for recognition of the union, reduction in hours, and major wage hikes. What was most significant was that the NLB ruling also created a hiring hall jointly maintained by the union and employers, though, crucially, the union selected job dispatchers. Gang bosses (also called walking bosses) also were included in the union, which meant that they no longer performed the managerial functions of foremen, particularly hiring and firing. These events also demonstrate the importance of the state to US labor relations, as in South Africa.[6]

The union replaced the hated shape-up with union-run hiring halls, promoted equal treatment among union members, and—most radically—implemented a socialistic "low man out" rotational hiring system. Hiring halls operated democratically and union members voted for dispatchers in annual elections held by each local. The ability to select their dispatchers, also fellow unionists, revolutionized the hiring process, for no longer did longshoremen have to bribe hiring bosses or appeal to their prejudices. Sam Kagel, the senior arbitrator between the ILWU employers for decades, described the root of the union's strength this way: "The Longshoremen were extremely strong because they had a real central point around which to gather." The union's success at achieving power even was acknowledged by Thomas "T. G." Plant, leader of the Waterfront Employers Association, who said at his organization's annual meeting in 1940, "joint control of the hiring hall and hiring policies has been converted into 100 percent union control. The union likewise controls work distribution." Plant was referring to the socialistic hiring system that Lou Goldblatt, long-time ILWU leader and one of its many leftists, more fully explained: "The whole principle of equalization of work opportunities is what it amounts to. We don't have equalization of earnings under the contract; we have equalization of work opportunity, the basic idea being that under the system of rotary dispatch a man took his job as his turn came along." Widely called "low man out," under this system the member with the fewest hours worked in that quarter of the year gained the first chance at a job when reporting for dispatch at the union hall. This system ensured equal treatment and, the union hoped, inculcated egalitarian ideals among members, as Bridges described in 1949: "Our union, which had its origin in the establishment of the Pacific Coast longshore locals and the 1934 strike, originally adopted, struck for, and has many times stood solidly on the principles that the longshore work of the port must be distributed through the machinery of the hiring hall as equitably as possible. No local has authority or autonomy to violate this principle." As discussed earlier, race no longer influenced the selection process, of particular importance to African Americans, who had suffered greatly from previous racist practices. Thus, from its inception, the union instilled practices that ensured fairness and equality, codified in 1953 as its Ten Guiding Principles.[7]

The hiring hall also provided a place for members to meet, see friends, catch up on the news of the day, and learn from one another—all the more so as they lived in one of the world's great port cities. Cleophas Williams, a long-time Local 10 member, described the hiring hall as the union's nerve center, for "that's where you told your stories." Like other maritime workers, who for centuries placed a premium on socialization, Williams fondly recalled that "there's always this interaction of stories" at the hall. A black man reflecting in his late eighties on arriving on the waterfront in the early 1940s, Williams claimed he did not understand, at first, the nature of the occupation he stumbled into: "I learned early that I was cut off from this kind of interaction, living in [rural, Jim Crow] Arkansas. I didn't live in a port city." Like maritime scholars, Williams highlighted the cosmopolitan nature of port cities and marine transport workers, "the real nature of interacting with sailors and people who were, had been to different parts of the world." Williams and countless others found "this interaction" both educational and empowering. Later, in 1994, Leo Robinson, a black activist in Local 10 and primary leader of the union's anti-apartheid efforts, helped get Local 10's hall named after Bill Chester, the first African American elected to the international ILWU leadership. Like Williams, Robinson believed in the power of the hiring hall, worker education, and symbols.[8]

Perhaps no one has thought longer or more deeply about the hiring hall than Local 10 leader and trained social scientist Herb Mills, who believed the union's egalitarian principles and policies emerged out of the nature of traditional (precontainerized) longshore work. Mills joined Local 10 in 1963 and, a few years later, received permission for a hiatus from the docks to complete his dissertation at the University of California–Irvine, graduating in 1967. Fully registered in Local 10 in 1968, he worked another twenty-five years, served in multiple elected positions in Local 10, and has not stopped writing, thinking, and talking about longshore work and his union. Mills contended that "The community which had been fashioned by and amongst the San Francisco longshoremen by the late 1930s was uniquely democratic and diverse, unified and stable, militant, impetuous, and audacious, progressive, and embattled because of an unusual unity that had come to exist between the daily occupational experience of its members and their organizational and political experience." In short, the work itself determined the politics of the longshoremen and the union they built. Mills continued: "the history of this community from the late 1930s forward simply cannot be understood except in the light of the concrete occupational experience of its members." Mills talked about praxis, how the nature of the work shaped the ideology of the ILWU with the hiring hall and "low man out" system serving as concrete representations of the union's ideals. In a 2011 interview, Mills concluded by saying, "The hiring hall is the cornerstone of fraternity and unity because it shares the work," while the dispatch system enshrined "equalizing opportunity to work and, therefore, some say equalizing income but also equalizing opportunity." To Mills, the introduction of containers irreparably changed the work, weakened longshore culture, and, thus, irreparably harmed the ILWU.[9]

Before containerization but also, to some extent, after it was introduced, the ILWU preserved attractive aspects of casual work—the most important being that members need not report on any particular day. Eric Hoffer, the famous longshoreman philosopher who wrote several books and countless syndicated newspaper columns while working on the San Francisco waterfront, repeatedly commented that he chose to work a few days and then took some days off to write; sometimes, when focused on a particular idea or on deadline, he did not report for a week or more. For those longshoremen not best-selling authors, Goldblatt added the following:

Conditions included working when you pleased. If you wanted a day off, you took a day off. If you didn't feel like working that morning, so you didn't turn to. The next day you'd plug in; the low man out system, you'd take your turn if you worked. We had guys who for years never worked the week when the horses were running; they'd work Friday night, Saturday and Sunday—figured they made themselves a paycheck with three days at overtime. Come Monday, they were down at the racetrack. Their way of living, that's all, and the waterfront meant that to them; other guys would work all the time.

Numerous longshoremen interviewed for this book described taking trips to California's Sierra Nevada or Alaska to camp and fish, often with children. ILWU members hardly were the only ones who valued such freedom. Historian Andrew Parnaby wrote of Vancouver dockworkers who also preferred to retain "the ability to choose when and where to work." No doubt, flexible scheduling is attractive to many workers, including those with families, but few workers—particularly manual laborers paid hourly wages—have the power to compel employers to operate such a system. The ILWU, however, proved strong enough to retain this aspect of casual work, though employers resented it and, in the mid-1960s, imposed a "steadier" system.[10]

Although the ILA Pacific Coast District eradicated the shape-up from its ports in 1934, Atlantic and Gulf Coast ports of the ILA did not do so until the 1960s. Thus, years after World War II, ILA longshoremen loudly complained about the shape-up and the most famous Hollywood film about longshoremen, Elia Kazan's *On the Waterfront*, depicted the abuses of the shape-up in one of its most classic scenes. Historian Colin Davis proved that "The murderous image of the mobster and union officials was based on a violent reality" and, as a result, "longshoremen both obtained employment and worked in an atmosphere of fear and intimidation." Because most ordinary longshoreman hated to shape up, another explanation for why a strong union, the ILA, did not replace this hiring process is needed. It is reasonable to conclude, from the well-documented corruption of its leaders and lack of democracy, that the leadership benefited from the shape-up: controlling a potentially rebellious rank-and-file while enriching themselves by inflating the rolls of dues-paying members because workforces with open hiring systems are several times larger than those with more controlled access. When it came to hiring, then, a stark contrast between the two longshore unions existed. Bridges described his view on these differences during a 1955 congressional hearing: "We readily admit that so long as the industry is decasualized the peaks and valleys of demand for longshoremen will present problems, but we are not prepared to return to the jungle of the New York waterfront and the west coast of pre-1934 in order to have a permanent surplus of men available at each dock gate. That way is the way of sharing starvation and with it comes the kickback, the payoff, the corruption and the racketeering. We will never return to this." From its inception, the ILA Pacific Coast District (and then ILWU, from 1937) sought to eliminate aspects of longshoring that workers detested (the shape-up) and retain those they liked (choosing when to report). Moreover, as discussed, the union's replacing of the shape-up with a dispatch system eliminated both favoritism and racism. Over time, as more blacks joined Local 10, their votes in the election of dispatchers provided a further check.[11]

By the mid-1950s, as a result of rank-and-file power and leadership savvy, San Francisco longshoremen became lords of the docks and their union became strong, and the Pacific Maritime Association (PMA) under the relatively liberal leadership of J. Paul St. Sure seemed to have reached an understanding with the ILWU. ILWU members, including those in Local 10, had created a hiring hall to eliminate discrimination and promote the equalization of work. Further, they were proud of their craft, as Mills described them: "the work which was performed by the San Francisco longshoremen in the 'good old days' [before containers] required initiative, ingenuity, a willingness to cooperatively innovate, and a wide range of skills and experience." However, a new technology to move cargo, containers, soon emerged. Could the ILWU continue to negotiate from a position of strength when facing the massive resources of shipping corporations, along with postwar redbaiting? Bridges had survived repeated efforts to deport him but, as late as 1960, the House Un-American Activities Committee released a report titled *Communist Activities among Seamen and on Waterfront Facilities*. Hence, as the Cold War continued in the late 1950s, Bridges undertook negotiations with St. Sure about the introduction of containers. The future seemed uncertain then, and, in retrospect, containerization proved a game-changer for dockworkers, unionism, the (marine) transport industry, and the entire global economy. Meanwhile, in late 1950s Durban, decasualization played out quite differently.

Apartheid Arrives on the Durban Waterfront, or Decasualization from Above

When South Africa was still a British colony, Durban employers developed casual or *togt* labor. This system developed not as a result of imperialism; instead, it was the cheapest and most efficient labor regime in an era when most Zulus had no desire to work for the British and maintained sufficient independence to avoid doing so. The British also used *togt*, under a different name, in Mombasa, its premier East African port, as historian Fred Cooper recounted. In Durban (and Mombasa), dockworkers organized themselves and repeatedly struck many times over many years despite mass firings, arrests, violence, and racist laws. Durban dockworkers exploited the casual labor regime for their own material benefit but also to protest apartheid. Durban employers and the state feared dockworker power and so, in 1959, decasualized the waterfront and instituted a new regime under the Durban Stevedoring Labour Supply Company (DSLSC). Hence, whereas waterfront workers in San Francisco pushed for decasualization, Durban dockworkers wished to retain *togt*. But Durban employers, in alliance with the state, eliminated casual dock labor.

In the mid-nineteenth century, Theophilus Shepstone had helped create the *togt* system, in which Zulus were brought from their homes in rural KwaZulu to serve as dockworkers, and shipping has remained the city's primary industry ever since. South Africa achieved formal independence in 1910, but the *togt* system changed little until 1959. Before decasualization, *togt* workers' numbers fluctuated. As in many industries, employers preferred the system that ensured labor surpluses, which kept wages low and workers weak. Moreover, casual workforces were "flexible," that is, they could be adjusted to accommodate the amount of traffic in the harbor. Dockworkers generally lived in company- or city-owned hostels around the Point and reported for work at different docks, operated by multiple stevedoring firms, across many miles of waterfront. The *togt* system allowed a dockworker to decide when and whether to work, on any particular day or night. Legally, if a dockworker did not report for work, individual employers could do nothing. The only method to punish a *togt* worker was deportation, as most Africans were migrant workers with legal permission to reside in the city only while holding a job. But permanent replacement was burdensome and complicated for employers, especially when no dockworker worked for a single employer. Ultimately, then, who controlled the dockworkers remained uncertain, which meant, as historian Ralph Callebert highlighted, they "were also a major concern of the authorities."[12]

For decades, Durban dockworkers demonstrated an impressive ability to utilize their casual status in this strategic industry to their advantage. Being casual was a major source of strength, for they could choose not to report and—legally—not be accused of striking. The dockworkers understood their ability to stop or slow down the flow of goods as a major source of their power, and Durban was the nation's busiest port. Economist Trevor Jones, for one, noted that in 1955 Durban shipped fully half the nation's cargo. Thus, dockworkers exploited a loophole in the labor laws designed to keep black workers weak and instead, periodically, stopped work. Generally, they did so for economic reasons, for wage hikes. Though dockworkers occasionally struck in the early twentieth century, they repeatedly did so during World War II. The war caused inflation to spike, which squeezed workers' pocketbooks. They also appreciated that the wartime labor shortage afforded them another opportunity. They knew that their actions affected South Africa's economy as well as the entire British Empire during a time of great crisis. Unlike San Francisco's patriotic longshoremen, who worked doubly hard and conducted no strikes during the war, few Africans in Durban had reason to pledge allegiance to the Allies. Employers responded, typically, with threats, replacements, and deportations.[13]

At least five times between 1949 and 1959, Durban dockworkers exploited their casual status by "striking" for economic and, increasingly, political objectives. In the mid- and late 1950s, Durban dockworkers coordinated with SACTU, ANC, and others in the Congress Alliance in efforts to overturn apartheid. Dockworkers joined in ANC-SACTU stay-away campaigns although, as casuals, technically they did not strike. For instance, for one week in April 1958 several thousand dockworkers refused to report for overtime in conjunction with a large, national stay-away. The *Natal Mercury* regretted that the overtime ban "may cause serious delay to shipping in the harbour" and reported that employers agreed to a wage increase under this "emergency" and after encouragement from the Natal Division of Labour. The *Mercury* claimed that "It is understood that this decision [dockworkers' overtime ban] was not directly connected with the 'stay away from work' campaign" but the timing, obviously, was not coincidental.[14]

As the anti-apartheid movement gained strength in the late 1950s, dockworkers stopped work twice in 1959, culminating in the end of *togt*. In February fifteen hundred dockworkers abruptly "downed tools," their largest strike in years, for a raise. On the second day, after refusing to disperse or return to work, police charged the dockworkers and wounded many. Employers then fired every single dockworker in the port, thereby ending the strike. To move some of the delayed cargo, replacements arrived from East London, who worked alongside "European stevedore officials" and ships' crews who "volunteered." Crucially, "employers decided to abolish the system of daily-paid labour, and took on all these men on a weekly basis." Employers essentially conceded that their workers were too powerful, abolished *togt*, and replaced it with the DSLSC to establish a permanent labor supply. Just one month into this new regime, though, dockworkers implemented another overtime ban over insufficient compensation for injuries caused during overtime. Very possibly, injuries had spiked after implementing the new system from the attempt to clear the backlog of cargo (from the strike) with new, inexperienced dockworkers. This action also confirmed that, despite employers' initial plan to hire an entirely new workforce, some—perhaps many—veterans had been rehired, as Muriel Horrell of the South African Institute on Race Relations reported. No doubt, the experienced dockworkers provided some of the leadership in the second labor action, timed just prior to Easter. With the holiday weekend fast approaching, ships crowded the harbor, necessitating more overtime to clear them, for the expeditious loading and unloading of ships depended on overtime. The overtime ban, which continued the following week, wreaked havoc, as the *Mercury* reported: "ships are packed stern-to-stern along the wharf, and trucks are crowded at the Point's marshalling yards." In the aftermath, the DSLSC fired every dockworker yet again, which also suggests that employers believed dockworkers possessed no special skills and so were easily replaceable.[15]

Of course, Durban's shipping firms and government created the DSLSC, which decasualized work, to reassert their authority over these surprisingly powerful black workers, finally ushering apartheid onto the waterfront. For a century, casual dockworkers had proved, as Callebert chronicled, "very prone to striking. They could not easily be disciplined, as the 'sanction of the sack' had little effect on them." Henceforth, the DSLSC, a company owned and operated by the local government, coordinated all dock labor. According to Mike Morris, who later organized dockworkers, "The DSLSC existed solely for the purpose of recruiting, employing, housing and controlling labour which it then subcontracted out on a daily basis to the various stevedoring companies." Thus, no longer could workers play different employers off each other because all worked for a single firm (with the exception of Maydon Wharf). No longer, furthermore, could they coordinate a "strike" by simultaneously not reporting for work or refusing overtime. Technically hired on a ten-month contract, dockworkers were supposed to be paid a guaranteed sum each week—along with additional wages for overtime and special cargo (e.g., hides). Yet, despite the wage policies allegedly established under the new regime, in actuality nothing changed, and dockworkers still were paid at a daily rate. The DSLSC remained in place for two decades before collapsing with the rise of containers.[16]

The decasualization of the waterfront marked a major turning point in the entire history of Durban, bringing the docks in line with apartheid labor policy. Employers and the government previously had discussed ending casual labor. Moreover, some white liberals appreciated that "the most brutal feature" of the *togt* system was that the burden of the shipping industry's inherent volatility fell largely on workers, whose earnings rose and fell with port traffic. But the larger concerns of employers and the state involved efficiency and power. Callebert wrote, "As early as 1937, the Mayor of Durban acknowledged that the instability of labour, the constant changing of jobs, was very inefficient. He pleaded for Labour Bureaux which could make sure that Africans were re-employed in jobs in which they had already acquired some skills." In addition, as already discussed, *togt* workers proved willing and able to disrupt the city's greatest industry, which affected every other one. Finally, the *togt* system allowed Africans to live as well as loiter near the city center, an affront to the National Party's vision for the apartheid city. Under the DSLSC, by contrast, dockworkers were much more fully controlled: recruited directly from rural KwaZulu, obligated to sign ten-month contracts, and, if one did not report for work, a worker could be liable for breach of contract and deported. As Morris later wrote, "The use of migrant labour from deep in the tribal heartland and the control mechanisms attached to that were developed to a fine art in Durban" by the DSLSC. Predictably, dockworkers hated the new system. David Hemson cited one who complained, not unlike Bay Area longshoremen: "In the past we used to take off a day or two whenever we felt tired, but now that we are employed [meaning paid] on a weekly basis we could not do this." Speaking in a newspaper sympathetic to SACTU, this docker believed, "that more workers should be employed by the stevedoring companies and at the same time we should be paid a decent wage for the hard work we do." The DSLSC, with its monopoly over hiring and tighter control of workers, was designed to eliminate dockworker power. The DSCLC should be described, following sociologist Karl von Holdt's term, as an "apartheid workplace regime." Employers effectively had seized the initiative, with key assistance from the state, and reestablished control—if, in retrospect, only for a decade.[17]

Though employed by a new entity, dockworkers still lived in hostels at the Point and, like most other Africans, remained legal migrants to the city with ongoing cultural ties to rural homelands. As nearly all dockworkers moved to the city from impoverished rural homelands, they "chose" to live in the hostels, rent-free, as opposed to paying for shoddy housing in the townships; ditto for the food, free if

Fig. 5. Unloading cargo, Durban Harbor, ca. 1960s. Transnet Heritage Library Photographic Collection.

insufficient and often disgusting. In their hostels, the Zulu foremen, *induna*, supervised, as they did on work gangs, which was intended to give dockworkers a (false) sense of the maintenance of traditional Zulu authority. To enshrine apartheid, literally "apartness" or "the state of being apart" in Afrikaans, the central government had sought to eliminate "black spots" from cities that, legally, were all white. Thus, in the late 1950s, the central government had proposed forcing Durban's Point-dwelling dockworkers out to the new black township of KwaMashu, nine miles from the Point. Unlike many large employers, however, that could (re-)locate their facilities to be near the townships, shippers very much wanted to keep compounds at the Point to address the twenty-four-hour-a-day, seven-day-a-week cycle in an industry in which "the ship must sail on time." An article in Durban's leading paper, the *Natal Mercury*, faithfully supported this view: "It would be impossible to work the stevedoring industry in Durban with anything like the present efficiency if Native labour was moved out to KwaMashu, Mr. R. C. Lloyd, a representative of stevedore employers, told the Wage Board in Durban yesterday." Such views carried great weight because shipping remained central to Durban's entire economy and was quite profitable; for instance, the South African Railways and Harbours Annual Report for 1956–57 reported Durban brought in £1,128,000 of profit on earnings of earnings of £3,262,000. No less a figure than S. D. Mentz, chairman of the Central Native Labour Board (which oversaw black labor policy at the national level), concurred: "it would be a gross mistake to upset the balance of work at the port because of an ideological view." With its clout, the shipping industry successfully dissuaded the government from relocating dockworkers to KwaMashu, unlike other Africans forcefully relocated there.[18]

Despite the presence of blacks in the heart of the white city, the DSLSC fit neatly into the "influx control" model established prior to the apartheid era and greatly tightened during it. The DSLSC coordinated with governmental labor bureaus in "homelands" (also called Bantustans) like KwaZulu, established in the 1950s by the apartheid state. The 1964 Bantu Labour Act reconfirmed that Africans who wished to work in cities first must register with traditional authorities in designated tribal areas. For example, Zulu men wanting to work in the Port of Durban needed an endorsement from Zulu authorities in KwaZulu—reinforcing the power of traditional, typically conservative, rural leaders. In the words of social anthropologist Bernard Dubbeld, "Close links were cemented between the particular homeland authorities in Zululand and senior officials in the labour supply company." In seeking to draw dockworkers from ever-more rural and remote portions of KwaZulu, the DSLSC followed what Deborah Posel described for urban employers, generally, who preferred Africans recently arrived from rural areas who were assumed to be "more obedient, harder working, and more easy to satisfy and control." Further, employers believed that rural Africans were less likely to support unionism or communism, had no experience with collective action, and were ignorant of what limited rights they possessed as workers. Even though the apartheid government tightened influx control to cities, including pass laws, the DSLSC received special exemptions to recruit more workers from reserves. Callebert concluded, "The DSLSC was a model apartheid institution that changed the labour regime from one with limited control over the labourers to one where the company controlled the workers' daily life in the compound, on the ship, and through increased rural recruitment even at home." The new regime concentrated employer control over recruitment, reaffirmed state and tribal authority, and more tightly regulated work. As a result, as activist-scholar David Hemson later recalled, "In the 1960s there was a desolate silence in resistance and the absence of political organisation." Dockworker militancy, indeed, was squashed in 1959, just prior to the repression of the larger anti-apartheid movement, though dockworkers resumed their militant actions in advance of others.[19]

In the 1960s, with the DSLSC engineering a stable and pliable workforce along with the larger crackdown on the black freedom struggle, the city's and nation's economy grew tremendously. Historian Nelson Tuzivaripi Sambureni contended that the creation of the DSLSC was foundational to the city's growth: "Two important employers, namely the Durban Stevedoring Labour Supply Company and especially the Frame Group of Companies, the key to the 1960s boom, were chief players who depended and survived largely on mobile labour." He pointed to massive corporate profits in South Africa "made possible by paying poverty wages to workers drawn from distant reserves who settled for anything, even wages below the going rate of pay. This labouring class was exploited on the basis that it was coming from remote reserves where homestead production had declined considerably and any form of wage employment was acceptable." Hemson added that the state granted immunity to the DSLSC to ignore labor bureau laws and regulations because it supplied labor to South Africa's leading port. Subsequently, Durban became so busy that the South African Railways and Harbours Administration, owner and operator of the nation's ports, undertook a major expansion in the mid-1960s, contributing to the doubling of cargo tonnage from 1965 to 1970. To accommodate this growth, and a decade before launching its container operations, the Railways and Harbours Administration built Pier 1—a complex of piers, actually—to handle increasing traffic and promote the South African economy, for, as Trevor Jones rightfully argued, "the ports have always been administered as national assets." Profitability and white supremacy went fist-in-glove in the Port of Durban and apartheid South Africa.[20]

Durban dockworkers, then, proved willing and able to demonstrate their power and discontent, repeatedly striking in the 1940s and 1950s by cleverly using their casual status. They did so to improve their own wages and conditions as well as in the struggle against apartheid. Although few, formally, belonged to SACTU, the dockworkers clearly supported the agenda of the SACTU-affiliated union federation, as evidenced by their joining the 1958 stay-away campaign. By 1959, after further large and well-coordinated work stoppages, waterfront employers and the state tired of this long-militant group and figured out a way to defang the dockworkers: decasualization. Henceforth, a city-owned company, the DSLSC, supplied the labor needs for the port's private shipping firms, once again demonstrating how closely the apartheid state worked with capital to ensure a cheap and pliable supply of black labor, the epitome of racial capitalism.

The strategy of decasualization to weaken dockworkers was hardly unique to Durban. Historian Fred Cooper documented similar efforts in Mombasa, the leading port in Kenya and crown jewel of British East Africa. Cooper described how dockworkers in Mombasa used their casual status to effectively resist colonial and employer oppression. Their strikes and, more generally, their ability to use their casual status "rekindled the state's concern with the need to maintain some authority over all dimensions of workers' lives." There, too, colonial authorities believed they could stabilize the workforce via descasualization, hoping to create workers with "better" values and habits—in other words, workers who were less truculent. Colonial officials in Kenya worked closely with private shipping companies to break the power of casual dockers and institute a new system to formally register workers. Just to the south of Kenya, in the British colony of Tanganyika, dockworkers in Tanga also experienced decasualization from above, with one worker calling the process an "exercise in total control." Similarly, Colin Davis chronicled how, in the British metropole, London dockworkers preferred their casual status and, despite the government's National Dock Labour Scheme imposed after World War II, resisted for many years. Klaus Weinhauer, who conducted the widest survey on the subject, suggested that, though every port is unique, decasualization followed a similar pattern generally, especially after World War II: "Many governmental reformers and port employers came to realize, that solving the complex problems of casual labour required more than just to restructuring some organisational features of dock work. Rather, the casuals' way of life had to be altered fundamentally. Disciplinary powers of the employers, the unions, and state had to be expanded deeper into the everyday routine of hiring, working and living." Weinhauer contended that whoever held the power to initiate decasualization controlled the future shape of dock labor. Hence, in Durban, where dockers never controlled the hiring process (despite the ability to manipulate it), the DSLSC ended casual labor and, simultaneously, disempowered dockworkers. In San Francisco, by contrast, the union successfully pushed for a hiring hall controlled by union job dispatchers elected by their fellow workers; thus, Local 10 essentially came to run the San Francisco waterfront.[21]

That dockworkers in San Francisco and Durban experienced casual labor differently is unsurprising. In San Francisco, decasualization occurred in the aftermath of a favorable federal ruling after the Big Strike, while in Durban it was imposed by employers after a failed strike. Moreover, in San Francisco, unionization emerged in tandem with decasualization, as in some other ports, but not Durban. Divergent experiences in different ports hardly are limited to North-South comparisons. Colin Davis, in his excellent comparative history of dockworkers in postwar London and New York City, concluded that "Paradoxically, what some New York dockworkers yearned for—stable, institutionalized union-employer relations—was resented by their London counterparts." The implementation of DSLSC echoed what Eddie Webster and Judson Kuzwayo described about a later phase of activism in which each "thrust" of African worker militancy "was followed by repressive legislation." Whereas in the United States, Franklin Roosevelt's New Deal included major gains for workers, including the rights to organize unions and to go on strike, government repression of African workers remained a "cardinal element of apartheid labour policy both ideologically and in practice." Because decasualization had not resulted in the weakening of San Francisco dockworkers—the opposite, in fact, occurred—employers deployed another time-tested tactic, introducing a new technology.[22]

Opening Pandora's Box: Local 10 and Containerization in San Francisco

San Francisco and other West Coast longshoremen, who soon founded the ILWU, followed up their "Big Strike" with many other work stoppages, thereby winning impressive financial and workplace gains and becoming "lords of the docks." The quiescence of unions in the twenty-first century might make it hard to imagine that "Between 1934 and 1948, Pacific Coast shipping suffered five protracted coastwide strikes, seventy-eight port-wide strikes, and 1,255 local stoppages. The five coastwide strikes alone [particularly 1934, 1936, and 1948] closed down the industry for 349 calendar days during these fifteen years." This era of combative labor relations peaked in the 1948 strike, the largest since 1934. That year, the Waterfront Employers Association (WEA), with some members still angry over the Big Strike, vigorously redbaited Harry Bridges and the entire ILWU, hoping to exploit the postwar rightward, McCarthyite turn in the United States. As J. Paul St. Sure, president of the Pacific Maritime Association (PMA) that formed after the 1948 strike, recounted, "Of course, the '48 strike was based upon the public position taken by the maritime industry that it would no longer, or could no longer, do business with Communists, with Mr. Bridges." Longshoremen, however, remained steadfastly loyal to Bridges, and the union emerged victorious. Employers tacitly surrendered, symbolized by the "new look" of the PMA that, as run by St. Sure, accepted Bridges and negotiated with the ILWU. Labor relations experts Clark Kerr, a future president of the University of

California, and Lloyd Fisher went so far as to refer to this turn of events as "the most extraordinary transformation in American labor history."

A decade later, though, massive technological changes provided the PMA with an opportunity to reverse everything the '34 union members had built. In 1960, the ILWU and PMA signed the world-historic Mechanization and Modernization Agreement (M&M). This contract resulted in the automation of longshoring, meaning that the loading and unloading of cargo piece by piece was replaced by cranes moving metal containers packed, or stuffed, far from the waterfront. This seemingly simple shift, in fact, was revolutionary and is now widely recognized as such, as the US Maritime Administration reported in 1985: "Overall, the single most important aspect of the container revolution has been the changing of the maritime industry from a labor-intensive to a capital-intensive one." The centrality of the United States (to the postwar world economy), the importance of San Francisco (West Coast's premier port), and the strength of the ILWU (widely seen as the nation's strongest, leftwing union) gave M&M international ramifications. For the first time—literally, worldwide—a dock union and shipping companies negotiated the transition to containers. Perhaps no one could have predicted just how integral containers would become to globalization, but, by helping increase global trade by several orders of magnitude, containerization remade the world economy.[23]

In agreeing to M&M, Harry Bridges played a singular role, hoping to control—or at least influence—the introduction, method, and pace of containerization. One clear priority was protecting the current generation of ILWU members from devastation, for many feared mass layoffs, lower wages for those not fired, and the death knell for their beloved union. Such fears were legitimate, and workers knew full well that technologies can, and have, killed jobs and entire occupations. The Local 10 *Bulletin* cautioned members in 1960, "Keep in mind that mechanization in a few years is going to result in a huge reduction of the present work force." Similarly, Eric Hoffer—author of the best-selling *True Believer*, "longshoreman philosopher," and Local 10 member—described in the *New York Times Magazine* how "one of the foremost manufacturers of automation equipment" testified at a 1963 congressional hearing that "automation was eliminating 40,000 jobs a week"! When real concerns like these threaten, perhaps only someone with Bridges's credentials as a left militant and his cachet among members of the union he helped found and lead (admiration for him bordered on hero worship) could have convinced a highly skeptical membership to go along with such enormous changes without striking in 1960 or 1966, when the second M&M was ratified. By persuading his members to accommodate rather than resist—voting for containerization—Bridges has been castigated by some in and around the ILWU for betrayal. Others in the union and beyond, perhaps most surprisingly in elite business circles, praised Bridges for his farsighted "vision" in adapting to "the inevitable." Undeniably, M&M caused huge changes. The remaining portion of this chapter examines how the first M&M reestablished employer control and sent productivity rates soaring while, over time, the numbers of workers plummeted and those remaining became better compensated. Containerization also resulted in the demise of the Port of San Francisco, then the West Coast's largest, and the concomitant rise of the (East Bay) Port of Oakland; later, the combined Port of Los Angeles and Long Beach became the dominant one on the West Coast. Before the decade ended, the seemingly simple metal box had become a case study in "the process of creative destruction," a term coined by noted economist Joseph Schumpeter.[24]

Considering these at least somewhat predictable changes, one might ask why Bridges decided to negotiate rather than fight, but, alas, he neither wrote a memoir nor sat for an interview on this topic. Or, as Harvard economist E. R. Livernash asked in 1971, "Just why this historically radical union leadership chose to go down this removal of restrictions and buy-out route cannot be clearly established." Bridges and the union faced a stark choice in the late 1950s, either try to slow down the transition via guerrilla resistance and hope for the best (essentially the ILA strategy) or negotiate with the PMA while the ILWU still possessed real power. Lincoln Fairley, an ILWU insider and important chronicler of this story, contended that Bridges believed technological changes no longer could be resisted and so sought to protect current union members in exchange for conceding to employers the prerogative of introducing new technology and, also important, ending old work rules. Shortly after retiring in 1978, Bridges offered a brief comment suggesting such an interpretation: "if we don't do something to meet this threat we'd put up a good fight to try to hold what we had won over the years and lose." Ben Seligman, an economist generally sympathetic to workers and quite knowledgeable about M&M, drew a more cynical conclusion: "By 1960, the P. M. A. was ready to buy out the union—it was as simple as that. The employers agreed to pay $5 million a year for five and a half years into a trust fund, the benefits of which were exclusively reserved to the A men. This sum was nothing more than a $29 million bribe to eliminate working conditions that had been in effect on the docks for years."

Bridges's sole biographer, Charles P. Larrowe, enumerated additional factors: the union was small, possessed few allies, and—most notably—still suffered redbaiting from the PMA, the government, its rival ILA, and even the Congress of Industrial Organizations (CIO), which ejected the ILWU in 1950. The union and its leadership very much believed redbaiting to be a subterfuge for attacks on the ILWU—witness the title of one publication defending its leaders, "The Real Target: Hiring Halls, Wage Increases, No Speedup, No Discrimination, Job Conditions." Larrowe concluded in 1972 that "With the union isolated from the official labor movement, its enemies waiting to pounce on it if its vulnerability were exposed, with the Administration in Washington hostile to him [Bridges] and to the union ('We don't even answer their letters,' a high government official said in 1957), a showdown with the employers [over automation] would be disastrous." The union said as much in its sixteen-page comment distributed immediately after signing M&M: "In our current negotiations, the union recognized a new factor. No matter which presidential candidate was elected, the climate for labor would worsen." Just as in the 1930s when the nation moved leftward and unions found organizing much easier, the Cold War made it harder on left, or even liberal, unions to survive, let alone thrive. Bridges and others in the ILWU leadership, therefore, chose to negotiate instead of "holding the line and 'hanging tough' on past practices and methods, of resisting the machine by guerilla warfare."[25]

The motivations of shipping company executives and the PMA appear clearer: Having failed to defeat the ILWU, a new technology seemed the best option for disempowering the union *and* reducing costs. Shippers had fought the ILWU for decades, using various tactics. After World War II, employers exploited rising anticommunism, as Wytze Gorter and George H. Hildebrand, business and economic researchers at UCLA and hardly ILWU sympathizers, wrote in 1954: "On the eve of the [1948] strike, the *Pacific Shipper* outlined editorially what in fact became the employers' strategy, by suggesting that in a major strike 'the industry can break the back of Communist domination of a minority of the maritime unions . . . notwithstanding previous defeats.'"

But the ILWU won that strike. Nor could employers use African Americans or immigrants to "divide and conquer" the ILWU, as so many other US employers did, for the union willingly integrated itself, thereby engendering tremendous solidarity among its ranks. Technology, thus, seemed the best, perhaps last, option. Although engineers might consider efficiency as value-neutral, in the words of the photographer and filmmaker Allan Sekula, "management experts in the shipping industry were beginning to dream of a fluid world of wealth without workers. In a period of declining profitability, postwar strikes, and increased labor costs, the petroleum tankship stood as the model for smooth automated operations for the entire shipping industry." In the 1950s, shipping firms collaborated with university engineers and business professors—underwritten by the US Navy's Office of Naval Research—to develop new cargo-handling methods on the model of the oil tanker: "They carry a very limited range of uniform types of cargo, which can be handled at very low terminal costs. Handling costs are low because the cargoes can be transferred by mechanical methods requiring very little labor. If similar improvements, now available, could be introduced in the technology of dry cargo transfers, the prospects for these [shipping] lines could become brighter." Many scholars, notably economist Marc Levinson in his powerful account *The Box*, gave primary credit to trucker Malcolm McLean for developing containers for ships

—from THE DISPATCHER

Fig. 6. In the early 1960s, the union's magazine published many stories, commentaries, and cartoons on automation and the M&M agreements. This cartoon by Phil Drew appeared in the *Dispatcher* in 1961. Image used with permission from ILWU Library.

steaming between New York City and Gulf ports. Other experiments with containers simultaneously and independently were underway, most notably by Matson, one of the largest Pacific Coast shippers and the pioneer of the world's first purpose-built container ship for its Hawaii–San Francisco run. Indeed, at the annual convention of the Propeller Club, held in San Francisco in 1958, St. Sure discussed containerization, as did US Senator Warren G. Magnuson, chair of the Senate Interstate and Foreign Commerce Committee, who "foresaw the rapid appearance of mechanical, labor-saving devices in the longshore industry."[26]

Certainly M&M included major union concessions on technology and work rules that workers had fought for—via repeated strikes, job actions, arbitrations, and negotiations—but Bridges saw no alternative. Once he decided the ILWU must adapt, he took it upon himself to convince the radical, ornery rank-and-file. The ILWU had a robust and democratic tradition with a transparent internal election process along with a great deal of rank-and-file participation in policymaking. Bridges frequently showed up at Local 10 meetings and received questions from members, who even had the right to knock on Harry's door at the nearby international offices. In 1957, with their contract up for renewal and containers on the horizon, Bridges formally sought permission from the Longshore Caucus, to which every local on the West Coast elected representatives and which "is the highest governing body of the Coast Longshore Division," to negotiate with the PMA over mechanization. Supposedly, those attending were "startled" but instructed him to study the problem and report back at a special meeting late that year. Because of the issue's complexity and significance, it took until 1960 to iron out the first M&M agreement, which lasted an unprecedented five and one-half years. A large minority quite consistently and vociferously opposed M&M—including the drastic work-rule changes—but Bridges convinced roughly two-thirds to vote for both the first and second M&M contracts. In retrospect, M&M clearly marked the successful return of employers to power on the waterfront, after twenty-five years when longshoremen had ruled.[27]

In the first M&M, the ILWU primarily protected current members, especially the oldest ones, who had the greatest incentive to support the contract. First, under the agreement the PMA established a $29 million fund to compensate longshoremen displaced by the introduction of new machines or work methods. Second, the PMA promised no layoffs of current, fully registered workers ("A" men); in 1978 Bridges described it powerfully: "When a man or woman went to work for any of these companies, he or she owned that job for life. There was no way a worker could lose that job because of the development of mechanization or automation." Third, fearing a major diminishment of work, the new contract created a wage guarantee for longshoremen; though this component was not renewed in the second M&M, it was restored, briefly and after a fashion, after the bitter 1971–72 strike. Finally, the PMA guaranteed that all future work on the waterfront would be performed exclusively by ILWU members—though that guarantee proved an utter fiction, to members' consternation and great detriment. Most important, the M&M fund induced older members to retire, widely referred to inside the union as "shrinking from the top" or, as Cleophas Williams described it, "a going-away present." Perhaps surprising for an occupation demanding heavy manual labor, Local 10 and several other large locals had quite old memberships—a product of the union having delivered such good wages and conditions.

In Local 10, more than 85 percent supported the agreement, but some old-timers, veterans of the Big Strike, had preferred to resist or "continue the guerrilla opposition." Lou Goldblatt, however, Bridges's long-time second in command, defended why M&M's approach was progressive: "our idea was that the way the worker shares in the saving of the machine is to shrink the work force from the top; let them retire with a substantially higher pension, as well as a cash-out," equivalent to about sixteen months' wages. It demands mention that "shrinking from the top" was exactly the opposite of what employers typically did and union contracts generally specified, which was a "last hired, first fired" approach. By contrast, Goldblatt contended M&M rewarded those with seniority while helping younger members move up the ranks. Under the first M&M, during its five-plus year duration, twenty-five hundred ILWU longshoremen in California, Oregon, and Washington retired—out of a workforce of about fifteen thousand. Seligman called this huge wave of retirements, cynically, a "bribe to eliminate working conditions that had been in effect on the docks for years." A not-so-dissimilar suggestion had been made by the US Navy–funded engineer who collaborated with shipping firms to study containers in the 1950s: "It is the author's experience that one of the best known motivational mediums is money." Although subject to interpretation, the union's concessions could be seen, particularly from the current members' perspective, as a very good deal—and much better than in many other industries when new technologies slashed jobs and decimated unions without workers earning any benefits whatsoever from the productivity gains.[28]

Bridges also strongly believed—and he was not alone—that the introduction of containers saved future workers from backbreaking, dangerous manual labor. Having toiled for more than a decade before helping form the union, Bridges appreciated the hard and risky nature of dock work, in which someone could die on the job for any number of reasons, on any day and at any time. And so, if containers could eliminate or, more likely, reduce health and safety risks, then he saw that as a real victory for workers. This case was made in *Men and Machines*, a coffee-table book jointly published by the ILWU and PMA, replete with dozens of full-page images and minimal text that sought to legitimize M&M by reminding longshoremen of their dangerous (yet impressive) labor. In the book's introduction, cosigned by Bridges and St. Sure, M&M is referred to as "a pioneering agreement—the first of its kind in American industry." The book put containers (somewhat disingenuously) into the context of a long march of technological progress to reduce the physical burdens on longshoremen, to wit, "Then came the rope sling, the oldest piece of hoisting equipment. It took some of the burden of packing cargo off the longshoremen's back." In *Men and Machines*, the ILWU and PMA leaders attempted to convince their target audience, union rank-and-filers, of containers' benefits.[29]

Many rank-and-filers, however, had serious concerns with M&M. First, members felt "uncertainty and suspicion," as long-time journalist and ILWU insider Sid Roger described, for they feared "the employer was going to do us in and that Bridges wasn't thinking about the old guys and the old rules." Such concerns had merit. Though Bridges negotiated the M&M in the belief that the union could not fight progress, only in 1967 did large numbers of containers start appearing in West Coast ports; curiously, the word *container* did not receive a single mention in the first agreement, though the first M in M&M stood for *mechanization*. Instead— which was shocking to many workers—employers moved quickly on the second M, *modernization* of work rules, some codified in the coastwide master longshore contract but others instituted informally port by port, nicknamed "hip pocket rules." Seemingly overnight, employers drastically increased the weight of cargo loads, sarcastically referred to as "Bridges loads."

For both practical and symbolic reasons, this issue mattered greatly. In the 1930s, the union had fought for, and won, a maximum weight of twenty-one hundred pounds per sling as a central health and safety protection for workers in their notoriously dangerous industry. Suddenly, this limit was eliminated, as ILWU leader Goldblatt explained: "I recall, for example, Bjorne Halling storming up to the office [in 1961]; he was just fit to be tied. Bjorne was a very good longshore-man. . . . And there was fire shooting out of his eyes, screaming at Harry, 'Three thousand—no, 30 sacks [each weighing 100 pounds]—on a goddam sling load"! Shipping executives had fiercely resented the rule that Halling considered gospel; in fact, the previously cited US Navy–funded study took aim at the twenty-one-hundred-pound limit: "The stated rationale for weight and height limitations on pallet loads is that they are predicated on safety considerations. However, the au-thor is not convinced"—though that author had never handled a single such sling. The union had fought to establish such workplace protections through strikes and countless, long-forgotten actions on the job but—overnight—such protections dis-appeared, forcing longshoremen to handle much heavier loads. The first productiv-ity gain to employers, then, was *not* due to technology but, rather, longshoremen working harder. Another effect, also not surprising, was soaring accident rates. Stan Weir, who belonged to Local 10 in the early 1960s, complained, "In the first year of the contract, the accident rate in what has become the nation's most danger-ous industry went up 20%," a stunning figure. Facing a speed-up, longshoremen found themselves conflicted, for, traditionally, they possessed a strong work ethic encapsulated by the phrase "always meet the hook," meaning always be ready for the next sling. But because "the hook never stops" and their loads suddenly be-came much heavier, longshoremen like Halling were enraged. Even Eric Hoffer, no militant or radical, declared, "This generation has no right to give away, or sell for money, conditions that were handed on to us by a previous generation." Anger on the waterfront triggered a series of wildcat strikes until industry arbitrators affirmed the new contract superseded older work rules.[30]

First, new work rules and, later, containerization resulted in an exponential rise in productivity and, over time, a tremendous decrease in longshoremen. From 1960 to 1965, economist Paul T. Hartman documented a 40 percent increase in productivity at West Coast ports, nearly all attributable to changing work rules. In fact, the Maritime Cargo Transportation Conference, a part of the National Academy of Sciences Division of Engineering and Industrial Research, issued a report in the early 1960s with eleven specific recommendations that, if firms implemented them, would result in "substantial improvement in cargo handling [that] was possible within the break-bulk system." Subsequent containerization in the late 1960s and 1970s resulted in additional, exponentially higher productivity gains. According to Lincoln Fairley, ILWU director of research, by the late 1970s the "estimated handling rate in terms of tons per hour" was about twenty times as great as in the precontainer era. It is not surprising, thus, that shipping firms shifted rapidly to containers. Fairley reported that West Coast container tonnage exploded from 494,000 tons in 1960 to 8,743,415 tons in 1970 and noncontainerized cargo plummeted to less than 15 percent of total cargo. Containerized tonnage increased at a similarly incredible pace in the 1970s and beyond.[31]

Predictably, technology-driven layoffs provoked the greatest fear and rage among workers. Squarely addressing this issue, *Men and Machines* declared, "all of the old fears [of the machine] return to the average worker when the machine threatens his job, his security, and his paycheck. If he is likely to be hurt he sees no difference between the machine and guillotine." Sure enough, the number of workers along West Coast waterfronts plummeted. The first wave came via early retirements, as prescribed by M&M, so few if any "lost" their jobs. But, in the long run, far fewer longshore workers existed, meaning that, as Fairley explained, "To the longshoremen, the rapid rise in productivity was a disaster." The combination of early retirements and greater productivity resulted in a drop in the number of fully registered "A" longshoremen of one-third to one-half from 1960 to 1971; this reality was masked, however, by a temporary boom in shipping caused by the escalation of the US war in Vietnam. The downward trend, in total hours worked, continued into the 1970s as tonnage handled in the Bay Area increased by more than 60 percent but the number of hours worked declined by more than 50 percent. Simply put, far fewer jobs existed starting in the 1970s, becoming a source of great frustration, as many rightly feared their sons and grandsons never would work on the waterfront. When Germain Bulcke, a legendary figure in the union and a long-time comrade of Bridges, was asked whether he thought ILWU members were better off because of M&M, he responded, "Well, yes, as far as it goes for those actually working, but as we know, there are millions of unemployed." Bulcke continued, "The waterfront employers have not added men for quite a number of years, and what's happening is that our membership is going down. For example, in my last term as president of Local 10 [late 1940s], we had 5800 members. At the present time [1983] we are down to 1800" or fewer. What nobody predicted, though, was that the drastic drop in the workforce did not happen immediately.[32]

A boom in cargo traffic in the 1960s, especially in the soon-ascendant Port of Oakland, resulted in a temporary demand for more longshore workers. First, in the early 1960s, the workforce dropped significantly from retirements, as designed by the first M&M. Second, the US war in Vietnam drastically escalated, causing Bay Area shipping to surge because it served as the primary West Coast location for the US Army and Navy. Oakland and neighboring Alameda saw major increases in traffic. Third, this rise in traffic was particularly of containerized cargo; both the US military and Japanese steamship lines heartily embraced containers. Though containerization likely would have surged eventually, Mark Rosenstein, in his thesis on the rise of the Port of Oakland, highlighted that McLean's SeaLand Corporation, which became the nation's largest container outfit, successfully lobbied the army to adopt containers, shipped from SeaLand's Oakland hub, to supply Vietnam. Shipping firms' profits demand(ed) that containers be filled in both directions, not just one way, and so the concomitant rise in US imports from Asia generally and Japan especially merged neatly with the widespread adoption of containers by Japanese firms. Rosenstein concluded, "By 1970, this new technology was well ensconced, entering an economies-of-scale phase that continues to the present." Unfortunately for Local 10 members, war-related work declined at the precise moment that containers rose, and therefore, as Fairley noted, "By 1968 the effect on work opportunity had become devastating." With job prospects and hours worsening, in the late 1960s and early 1970s the more youthful rank-and-file grew increasingly frustrated and struck as soon as the second M&M expired in 1971.[33]

The 1960s surge in Bay Area port traffic was ironic in that the ILWU, early on, condemned the war in Vietnam. As in Korea, the ILWU took a stand against Vietnam at its convention in 1965—when very few Americans opposed US involvement. Larrowe wrote that Bridges himself was hesitant, but convention delegates overwhelmingly voted to do so, "thereby confounding economic determinists who preach that a union will support a war because it provides jobs." The ILWU declared sympathy with North Vietnam, opposed US escalation, and asserted, "This terrifying concept ['negotiation through escalation'] is but one step removed from escalation to a world holocaust"! The ILWU position stood in marked contrast with President George Meany of the AFL-CIO, who loudly backed the US war effort. In addition, many members personally protested, and some—secretly and at great risk—took illegal actions while loading cargo. Longshoreman Gene Vrana summarized the options for Local 10 members, many of whom opposed the war: "Many guys simply chose to not accept jobs at those locations [where military cargo got loaded]." Others accepted such assignments because "a job was a job," and some longshoremen accepted those jobs "and did what they could on the job to make sure that the work did not proceed in a timely fashion. That's about all I will say about that." If the union had refused, categorically, to work ships at military facilities (e.g., Oakland Army Base or Alameda Naval Supply Depot), the government surely would have canceled its contracts and the ILWU would have lost those piers forever. Publicly, the Local 10 Drill Team marched at antiwar rallies even though many ILWU members were military veterans, including the team's founder, Josh Williams. The irony that many Local 10 members who opposed Vietnam saw their paychecks rise in the early and mid-1960s as a result of military escalation was not lost on them.[34]

Conclusions: Decasualization and Containerization

With containerization in San Francisco and decasualization in Durban, employers reasserted themselves over workforces that had repeatedly demonstrated great power. Employers in both ports believed—or perhaps hoped—that they no longer would have to deal with dockworkers who utilized their collective will for their own material gain as well as on behalf of racial equality. Indeed, after the implementation of the DSLSC, government officials boasted of how they had created a "model apartheid institution" that should be used as a prototype for other ports and workplaces. And, since Durban handled most of the nation's cargo, what happened in its port had national significance. In 1963, for instance, the general manager of the South African Railways and Harbours declared, "the expansion of the Republic's commercial and industrial activities has posed special problems in the field of port operations and management. Adequate port facilities are essential to ensure the free flow of import and export traffic and the ports must therefore be maintained and developed to keep abreast of the increasing demands." As previously demonstrated, however, the combined forces of shippers and the state only temporarily quieted Durban dockworkers, who struck in 1969 and remained among the nation's most militant African workers into the mid-1970s. Also, as argued, the implementation of the DSLSC in 1959 preceded the state's subsequent repression, in the early 1960s, of the larger anti-apartheid movement. Similarly, in San Francisco, although containerization clearly weakened the union and reduced its membership, it did not result in a quiescent workforce, as evidenced by a huge strike that erupted in 1971–72. Nevertheless, the ILWU undeniably was weakened by M&M, just as Durban dockworkers were when containers arrived in 1977. Thus, the effects of decasualization were contingent upon which party had the power to institute change. In Durban, the creation of the DSLSC resulted in nearly a decade of quiet on the waterfront. Similarly, the introduction of containers in San Francisco contributed to a strike-free 1960s. This matter's import and complexity, however, requires a much more extended discussion of containerization.[35]

M&M surprised many, especially in light of the well-known leftist politics of the ILWU and its leader, Harry Bridges. As a commentator summarized, "one of the most radical unions in America decided to abandon some of its hard-won work rules in order to maximize present earnings." Ironically, after decades of castigation as a supposed communist, Bridges received lots of praise from the mainstream. For instance, President Dwight D. Eisenhower's secretary of labor, James Mitchell, commented in *Time* in 1963, "Next only to John L. Lewis, Bridges has done the best job in American labor of coming to grips with the problems of automation." Even Stanley Powell, president of Matson, a powerful member of the PMA, opined, "I admire his ability to keep his word and get his union to back him up." The *Time* article, subtitled "The Man Who Made the Most of Automation," continued, "Such tributes stem from the fact that Bridges, far more than most labor leaders, has faced the challenge of automation." The article concluded that he negotiated the M&M "not precisely in any spirit of generosity" but, rather, for money. So much for communism, the article concluded: "'Harry will make a big speech at the table about [communist] Cuba,' says Matson Vice President Wayne Horvitz. 'We let him talk, and then we get back to business.'" ILWU membership became so attractive that twenty-five thousand people applied for twenty-six hundred openings in longshore locals in the 1960s. But another way to imagine that huge applicant pool was that America offered an insufficient number of good jobs and that automation threatened to take away more of them, as Dr. Martin Luther King Jr. asked in 1965: "Where are the unemployed automation has created?"[36]

Much like King's query echoing the Luddites, many San Francisco longshoremen deeply opposed the first M&M. Reg Theriault, a long-time Local 10 member who worked before and after containers emerged, explained why in his book, *The Unmaking of the American Working Class:* "'They're trying to buy our jobs, and our jobs aren't for sale,' was the longshore cry. They meant the next generation's jobs, of course, those of their sons, and later, daughters." Even Eric Hoffer, the darling of mainstream media in the Cold War 1950s and 1960s, initially feared M&M. Writing in the *New York Times Magazine*, he proclaimed, "After a lifetime of hardly ever sticking my nose outside the San Francisco waterfront, I found myself running around shooting my mouth off, telling people of an impending crisis, a turning point as fateful as any since the origin of society, and warning them that woe betides a society that reaches such a turning point and does not turn." Hoffer substantiated his fear with statistics, "Already in 1963 automation was eliminating between 2 and 2.5 million jobs a year." By 1965, however, Hoffer's view flipped 180 degrees, as evidenced by his essay's title, "Automation Is Here to Liberate Us." A caption in the article, underneath a large computer apparatus, read as follows: "Taking issue with the pessimists, a workingman argues automation really means the triumphant completion of a second, man-made Creation that began with the machine age: 'It can show us the way back to Eden, doing for man what no revolution, no doctrine, no prayer could do, but we are too afraid to realize that we have arrived.'" Hoffer's epiphany bordered on religious ecstasy, but economist Levinson concluded in 2006 that "As wage earners, on the other hand, workers have every reason to be ambivalent" about containerization. Theriault also pointed to the number of Local 10 members, which sank from five thousand when he started to fewer than fifteen hundred, many of whom periodically collected unemployment because of insufficient work during the 1980s.[37]

Because of the stakes, the ILWU leadership was mindful of the union's survival. One ILWU assistant very close to Bridges wrote, "unharnessed technological change possesses a vast potential for social catastrophe." As mentioned, Bridges never reflected, publicly, on containers, but Sid Roger, a long-time insider and confidante, made some telling points in the late 1980s, "Containerization was foreseen but not that it would come so fast and be so effective. We [the union] had some ideas that containerization would not be able to handle a great many types of cargos, which it finally managed to handle very well indeed. . . . As I saw it at close range, Bridges was almost among the last to recognize the enormity of the changes taking place." For instance, in the late 1950s while Bridges negotiated the first M&M, Roger claimed, "Harry really didn't seem to believe containerization was going to be that important," recalling an anecdote in which Bridges foretold how "port side loading," a long-forgotten alternative, "is the future, not containerization." Bridges did not offer his thoughts on containers, but Lou Goldblatt, his long-time second-in-command, did so in a series of interviews whose transcript runs more than one thousand pages. Goldblatt believed the first M&M "achieved certain positive results" and "was an attempt to meet the issue of mechanization without fighting a completely defensive fight until it destroyed you, as happened to many other unions, like the Railroad Firemen," who saw their jobs eventually disappear with the introduction of diesel-fueled engines. No doubt, new technologies have eliminated jobs many times, celebrated by economist Joseph Schumpeter as "creative destruction" that, in his view, remained "the essential fact about capitalism." Many workers and unionists decried this "fact," which Schumpeter also referred to as "the perennial gale," aptly a nautical term. Goldblatt reflected that "There was an attempt at least to grapple with the issue and use union power to get a piece of the machine. I think those aspects of it were good, but the degree of change which we allowed was excessive; we did not get all the things we thought we were entitled to under the agreement."[38]

Just how large a share of the machine would have been fair has been debated for a long time, but most analysts agree with Goldblatt that the PMA "won." In an interview decades later, Wayne Horvitz, a vice president of Matson, admitted that "I wouldn't disagree with people who've said—as I think Linc Fairley has said—that they [the longshoremen] settled cheap. I think they did settle cheap but I don't think the employers snookered them. *We didn't know how much that thing was worth.* We didn't know how much those work rules were worth. Nobody had ever measured this." Horvitz suggests that he, and other shippers, were surprised at the profits that containers generated, but it seems highly unlikely that Matson—the first Pacific shipping company to containerize—had not closely studied its potential. In fact, at least some shipping firms had conducted engineering studies in the 1950s. For instance, UCLA researchers collaborated with the San Francisco–based American President Lines and the US Navy and concluded as early as 1957, "The containerization of general cargo represents the most promising innovation in the worldwide shipping industry." So, what did PMA president and lead negotiator St. Sure, described by Goldblatt as wearing a "velvet glove on [a] steel hand" know? Goldblatt concluded later that "St. Sure knew perfectly well what he was doing." By contrast, in 1970, ILWU lawyer Norman Leonard reported asking Bill Ward, a coast committeeman (among the union's highest-ranking elected officials), about what the ILWU knew: "I said, 'Did you guys realize in 1960 when you went into M&M program, how it would work out.' Ward replied, '*We had no conception that it was going to develop this way*.' And I personally am sure that this is true." Far clearer were the surging profits of shippers, confirmed as soon as the first M&M ended, when Max D. Kossoris, director of the US Bureau of Labor Statistics Western Region, wrote, "A spokesman for the industry has estimated the gain to the industry thus far to be $120 million net," which Kossoris suggested was quite conservative. Bridges's biographer, in the early 1970s, suggested that "When the contract's five-and-a-half years were up, *they [PMA] had paid $29 million for M & M, and they had saved $200 million.*"[39]

Even Lincoln Fairley, who worked closely with Bridges in the ILWU and, later, wrote a book justifying the M&M, admitted they had not imagined the speed with which employers introduced "modernization" or the ferocity of the rank-and-file response. He wrote that "Particularly in view of the quite violent on-the-job reactions to the changes in work practices needed to give the employers additional flexibility of operation, it may properly be argued that in making very extensive changes in work practices in 1960 the parties were disregarding the pattern of the previous two decades. In retrospect, it appears that the 1960 changes on top of those in 1959 were too much for the Union membership to adjust to and too much for the operating employers to adjust to without going to excess." Fairley claimed even Bridges "admitted that the Employers are 'getting away with murder.' " Because the contract lasted for five and one-half years rather than the typical two or three, the workers who wanted to apply the brakes could not do so. It is perhaps surprising that the international leadership negotiated the second M&M for another five years and got that contract approved, albeit—again—with a significant, and increasing, minority voting against. As a result, the union leadership avoided a strike despite growing aggravation among the membership. Some criticized Bridges for not even threatening to strike in 1960 or 1966, thereby taking away their union's (any union's) strongest weapon during negotiations. In the first M&M, Henry Swados, a left critic, contended that Bridges "gave away" the tremendous gains the union previously had won without a fight, but Goldblatt disagreed: "the basic idea was of accommodating to change, but making the employer pay for it; of getting a good, substantial hunk of the machine. That, in my opinion, is a perfectly sound thing." Fairley probably offered the closest to an official justification in his 1977 book, *Facing Mechanization*:

> There followed, indeed, a relationship between the ILWU and the new PMA in the sharpest possible contrast to the 1930's. There was no coastal strike from 1948 to 1971, yet the Union made major gains in addition to steady wage increases, including unusually good welfare and pension plans, and, in 1960, the M & M Agreement. The employers had given up their long fight to eliminate or to hog-tie the union, while the union officers realized that the time had come to give up its program of harassment through work stoppages designed to win concessions.

Another ILWU insider, William Glazier, noted shortly after the first M&M went into effect that the West Coast longshoremen were lucky the PMA negotiated the introduction of technology, writing in the *Atlantic*: "A recent survey conducted among the presidents of selected nationwide firms revealed that 75 per cent feel that 'The company is entitled to all of the savings resulting from the introduction of labor-saving equipment'; and fewer than 10 per cent of them believe that the company is obligated to compensate workers displaced by mechanization." Glazier's defense of the PMA might seem surprising, for it did not read as if it came from a union considered, by friend and foe alike, as leftist. Swados was not alone in criticizing Bridges for becoming conservative, a charge he bristled at.[40]

Many people in the 1960s wondered about the costs of automation and who would pay them. Speaking before workers in Detroit, Dr. King declared, "Automation cannot be permitted to become a blind monster which grinds out more cars and simultaneously snuffs out the hopes and lives of the people by whom the industry was built. . . . When human values are subordinated to blind economic forces, human beings can become human scrap." King predicted the growing discontent among Local 10's rank-and-file—over containers as well as the "steady man" issue that arose in the second M&M—which resulted in a lengthy and bitter strike in 1971–72; rank-and-filers in Local 10 practically led this coastwide strike, essentially a rejection of both Bridges and M&M. Somewhat similarly, Durban dockworkers were whipsawed when containers arrived in 1977, albeit with immediate and huge retrenchments, for they were in no position to bargain over it. To these weighty matters we now turn.[41]

WORKING CONTAINERS OR GETTING WORKED BY THEM

My soul / has been sucked dry / and suffocated by / the shadow of a / forty-foot container, / Restored by outrage / at the mindless technology / unleashed by cash register computers So logical, / so methodical, / casting aside bent bodies / with poisoned lungs / to proceed with greed. / So technologically correct. / A heritage / caved in by the / ponderous pounding / of some psychopathic / robotonic / beast / clothed in the niceties of contractual compromise.

—Gene Dennis, "Footnotes to the Glory Years"

Perhaps the most important implication of containerisation to the container user is that he has become the stevedore.

—*Freighting/Containerising Weekly*, July 11, 1980

Revolution. This word, so overused, nevertheless accurately describes the effects of containerization, most obviously its signal contribution to the phenomenal explosion of global trade in the last half-century. The impacts on marine transport workers, by contrast, rarely receive attention, though longshoremen in the San Francisco Bay Area have had much to say about it. In 1971, after eleven years of accepting Harry Bridges's recommendations on containers, 96.4 percent of the rank-and-file, coastwide, voted to reject the third contract of the container era and unleashed the longest strike in US longshore history, spanning half a year in 1971–72. This strike reflected the anger that many dockworkers, especially younger ones, felt about containers and how employers had used them to regain power. Yet despite the impressive commitment of rank-and-filers, led by Local 10, the strike did not alter the terms of earlier M&M agreements. Instead, containerization continued, fewer dockworkers worked on the waterfront, more of them more beholden to employers, and—while well compensated—their union had been weakened, official statements to the contrary.[1]

Five years later, in 1977, containers officially arrived in Durban. Although the country's shipping industry and South African Railway and Harbour Administration (SARH) had been quite slow to embrace containerization, once begun, half of all Durban dockworkers lost their jobs in three years. They did not yet belong to a strong union—unions only recently had been legalized for blacks when the apartheid state "conceded" this right—and so employers had not negotiated the transition, and had not imagined doing so. When containers arrived, as the Luddites feared in nineteenth-century England, dockworkers lost their jobs. Hence, though the late 1970s saw a resurgence of black worker militancy, Durban dockworkers no longer marched in the vanguard. They did quickly join unions, which could only ameliorate problems, not solve them. Dockworkers struggled to survive the storm unleashed by a seemingly simple metal box. Ultimately, in 1994, multiracial democracy arrived, arguably the greatest social movement victory of the postwar world. Yet (dock)workers had been contained, as it were, for no second phase of the revolution happened, and dockworkers, like other (black) workers, found themselves dominated by global economic forces beyond their control. In Durban, an increasing number of containers worked by a decreasing number of dockworkers mirrored the reality of a growing number of workers around the globe.

Containers upended workers in both ports, as in every other, but Bay Area dockworkers proved far more capable of responding and shaping the process and its effects. The power the ILWU previously had accrued, engineered by a left-wing leadership and militant rank-and-file, meant that employers had no choice but to negotiate and give workers a "share of the machine." By contrast, Durban dockworkers simultaneously fought both employers and the apartheid state with insufficient power to resist either. By the 1980s, containerization was firmly entrenched. Call it automation, containerization, mechanization, or something else, this technology drastically reduced dockworker numbers and increased productivity, resulting in higher profits and far lower labor costs. This chapter will end in the 1980s as subsequent changes in shipping, undeniably important, followed the trajectory already charted. Employers had found a way to limit dockworker power by changing the very nature of the work. The late 1960s and 1970s proved pivotal, marking the end of one phase of global capitalism and the start of another. The stagnation of worker wages, ever-increasing precariousness of workers wearing both blue and white collars, and the steady decline of unions—all topics much discussed in the 2010s—began then. Containers had remade one of the world's greatest industries, shipping.

Containers and Their Discontents: Second M&M and Clause 9.43

Although the first M&M was historic, containerization did not take off in the early 1960s. Instead, employers instituted major changes to work rules, labeled "modernization," resulting in decreasing numbers of workers in gangs, heavier loads, and dramatic increases in productivity. The ILWU and PMA then negotiated the second M&M, another five-year contract that commenced in 1966. The second M&M echoed the first in that PMA members—benefiting from massive profits from modernization—again traded more money (in wages and benefits) in exchange for more control and work-rule changes. It cannot be discounted that longshore workers earned higher wages than other manual laborers; almost certainly, money explains why the majority voted for the contract. But, as the usage of containers ramped up dramatically in the late 1960s and the Vietnam War–induced shipping boom slowed, the number of work hours declined sharply coastwide. Perhaps members of Local 10 suffered more than other West Coast longshoremen because the PMA moved fastest with containerization in the Bay Area. Moreover, a provision new to the second M&M provoked an increasing volume of criticism, particularly in the Bay Area, where the PMA pushed hardest to hire "steady men." The second M&M also saw the abandonment of a guaranteed wage, supposedly because there would be no decline in the work (though, in fact, soon there was). These issues caused concern, then outrage, among many ILWU members, ultimately resulting in more than 96 percent of them voting to strike in 1971 for the first time since 1948.[2]

In the second M&M, Clause 9.43, the "steady man" clause, allowed employers to circumvent hiring workers from the union hall. In the new contract, Section 9 (on promotions), Clause 43, read as follows: "In addition to other steady employees provided for elsewhere in this Agreement, the Employers shall be entitled to employ steady, skilled mechanical or powered equipment operators without limit as to number or length of time in steady employment." Further, "The employer shall be entitled to assign and shift such steady men to all equipment for which, in the opinion of the employer, they are qualified." Recall that, from its founding in 1934, the union essentially controlled job dispatch and instituted a "low man out" system that placed a premium on the equitable sharing of work though seniority and skill qualifications also factored into dispatching. The second M&M, however, superseded the old system and allowed employers to select specific workers and employ them for as long as employers saw fit, instead of workers dispatched anew each shift from the hall. Employers loudly asserted that their investment in expensive new machinery (containerization being quite capital-intensive) demanded that only highly skilled workers—hand-picked by employers—be allowed to operate them. In ILWU Research Director Lincoln Fairley's words, as he later wrote, the

PMA "argued that on the new expensive and sophisticated equipment they needed steady men, trained to operate it." The employers' assertion may seem reasonable, but others argued that conventional, or precontainer, longshore work involved far more skill than driving a crane, no one more convincingly than Herb Mills, one of Local 10's strike leaders in 1971, who possessed a PhD in labor sociology to boot. Mills and others contended that, traditionally, since every ship and commodity was unique, loading and unloading cargo effectively and safely involved tremendous skills, especially the proper loading of a ship to ensure proper balance for a sea voyage. Granted, not every longshoreman needed such skills, but anyone working in the field for a sufficient time developed them along with pride in that know-how. Such knowledge and skills meant that longshoring *was* a craft despite being labeled unskilled and involving brute manual labor. Further, to a great many longshoremen, 9.43 threatened the hiring hall, perhaps the single most important factor in ensuring the strength and egalitarian nature of the ILWU. Mills passionately described it thus: "the social roots and bonds of the [longshore] community . . . were destined to be rent asunder, however, once the individual employer secured the contractual right to remove men from the functioning of the hiring hall by offering steady machine operator work (and a monthly pay guarantee) to those of his own choosing." Opponents of 9.43 asked how the union could equalize work opportunities when some worked steady and others were dispatched from the hall? Indeed, shortly after the second M&M went into effect, Sam Kagel, the coastwide arbitrator between the ILWU and PMA, heard a case about 9.43. James Kearney, Local 10 president at the time and considered a conservative, gave this testimony at the hearing:

> We went on record, we approved of the machine, of modernizing the hiring hall. But we had a different understanding. That if the hiring hall would be modernized that we could still use the low-man-out system. I was one of those delegates, I voted for it. I went back to my Union [Local 10] and I sold it to my Union with that belief. And all the other delegates that were there with me, they had that belief. And the Union believed it when we told them that. And we still want the low-man-out system.

Even though, in this case, on a minor aspect of the contract, Kagel ruled in favor of Local 10, it also revealed the larger ways that 9.43 soon bedeviled dockworkers and their union.[3]

Containerization also resulted in the Port of Oakland supplanting San Francisco as the dominant port in the Bay Area, which demands mention even though not this chapter's focus. As has been said many times, geography is destiny, and so with containers. Few have heard of Felixstowe, but it became England's largest container operation, supplanting London, for centuries one of the world's greatest ports. Similarly, New York City lost its entire cargo industry to neighboring ports in New Jersey. So, too, in San Francisco—the US West Coast's greatest port for more than a century. Physically, San Francisco is quite small, just forty-nine square miles and at the tip of a long, narrow peninsula, making it an unattractive place for a modern container port that demands huge acreage near the docks. As Herb Mills explained in the *San Francisco Examiner* in 1979, "a full and efficient utilization of modern longshore technology requires up to 20 times the acreage afforded by the finger piers of the old Embarcadero. Thus, for example, when SeaLand opened its Oakland operation in 1962, it did so on 13.5 acres. Within a decade, that was expanded to its present 60 acres." The San Francisco Port Authority boldly predicted, in 1966, that it would retain the port. The city simply did not have the space for a modern container port, however. By contrast, Oakland did and also benefited from the massive amount of dirt from the construction of the Bay Area Rapid Transit tunnel that connects San Francisco and Oakland, which was used to expand its port into the Bay. Oakland also provided easier access to railroad lines and highways when moving containers from ships to rails or trucks and vice versa, unlike San Francisco, sited at the northern corner of a peninsula. Though the San Francisco Port Authority failed to see containers as the future, San Francisco's demise as a great port largely can be ascribed to geography. Notably, Local 10 represented all dockworkers in the Bay Area ports, and so this geographic shift did not alter union representation. Ironically, because modern shipping requires so little labor, the tourist industry along the old waterfront, most famously "Fishermen's Wharf" and Pier 39, might create more, albeit more poorly paid, jobs than containers do for dockworkers. Another impact was that working-class neighborhoods tied to the shipping industry, as in New York, Baltimore, and elsewhere have been gentrified with devastating consequences for workers and residents in San Francisco. In contrast, while containerization forced a geographic shift in the Port of Durban—away from the Point, the busiest area traditionally—to the southern harbor, that location also lies within the city limits. In 1970, though, few considered the extensive impacts of containerization on cities, for dockworkers and employers were fixated on who controlled this technology.[4]

San Francisco Bay Area Longshore Workers Strike

The 1971–72 strike, lasting a mammoth 134 days, revealed the impacts of and conflicts over containers, both between the ILWU and PMA and between the rank-and-file and union leadership. Despite major concessions in the two M&M contracts, many had hailed President Harry Bridges for foresight and leadership in gaining a "share of the machine" for workers, no mean feat when employers rarely consult(ed) with—let alone pay workers for—introducing new technologies. Yet, throughout the 1960s, tremendous controversy boiled inside the union, especially Local 10, still its largest longshore branch. Because the PMA moved fastest to containerize in the Bay Area, Local 10's frustration is not surprising. ILWU members demonstrated their profound hatred of M&M when nearly every single longshoreman and clerk—not just in the Bay Area—voted to strike, with fully 9,317 in favor and just 343 opposed. This vote also was understood as a stunning rebuke to Bridges, who counseled against striking. During the strike, many longshoremen felt that Bridges and the international disappeared despite the near-unanimous strike vote; Bridges literally refused to meet with PMA representatives for a few months during the strike. With the international silent, Local 10 sought to fill the vacuum, and the words of its first pamphlet crystallized why longshoremen struck: "What would you do if . . . your jobs were being taken over by the 'progress' of new 'labor saving' devices and modes of operation (machines and containers)?" Other Local 10 strike documents, often reprinted by other locals in the absence of international press releases, bemoaned that their material benefits had not kept up with those of other industries and they "faced injury or death every working day because [their] industry's accident rate is second only to underground mining."[5]

In the Bay Area, as all along the West Coast, rank-and-filers believed they deserved a much larger "share of the machine." To them, the issue seemed abundantly clear and quite reasonable: In 1960 and 1966, at the urging of Bridges, they had not struck, in other words, *not* waged war against containers or other "modernization" methods—despite their considerable power and sacrifices. Thus, they had "earned" a significant chunk of the profits derived from productivity gains, particularly because these changes resulted, ultimately, in far fewer workers. One Local 10 strike pamphlet declared, "if this 'progress' is left unchecked, it will simply mean that our employer will line up at the bank with ever bigger profits while we line up at the unemployment and welfare office." An added wrinkle was that, in the late 1960s, another wave of retirements of workers occurred among those who mostly had started during World War II. The question in 1971 became, then, how would longshoremen who still had many years, even decades, of work ahead of them respond to an industry being remade before their eyes? Labor economist Max Kossoris focused upon this group: "Will the younger men still be satisfied with a long deferred retirement benefit," which had been so attractive to older members, who presumably voted overwhelmingly for the contracts in 1960 and 1966? The answer—a resounding no—came in the 1971 strike vote. Bridges, generally a brilliant tactician, clearly erred when asking the membership in 1971 to support the contract, as Kossoris predicted: "Even though aware of the discontent of the younger men, the union made no move in this direction, except to obtain an immediate sizable wage increase." In short, many younger members thought Bridges sold them—and their union—out.[6] Moreover, some believed that the union's longtime rival, the ILA, had won a better deal via a combination of wildcat strikes and

Fig. 7. Since the ILWU international provided almost no assistance, Local 10 member Jake Arnautoff, whose father was the prominent muralist and painter Victor Arnautoff, created this poster for the 1971–72 strike.

its leadership dragging out an agreement on containers for most of the 1960s. East Coast work gangs remained significantly larger into the early 1970s, in other words, with more workers, and the ILA negotiated a "container royalty fund" in the late 1960s (like the M&M Fund).[7]

The second fundamental issue was with the union's desire to eliminate "steady men," who threatened to undermine worker solidarity, the hiring hall, and maybe the union itself. When the ILWU agreed to 9.43, a fundamental shift occurred that permanently altered power dynamics on the waterfront by threatening to undermine workers' commitment to each other. Indeed, as soon as the second M&M went into effect in 1966, Matson hired forty steady lift operators in San Francisco. Local 10 quickly voted that 9.43 violated its rules and pressured this first crop to quit; instead, all workers must be dispatched from the hall, though some initially resisted. The PMA claimed these actions violated the contract and the ILWU international agreed. Matson subsequently convinced a few dozen to go steady while resistance and resentment percolated beneath the surface. Bridges defended 9.43 at the 1967 Longshore Caucus, but critics claimed steady men became divorced from their fellow workers and more loyal to employers. Leo Robinson, an African American firebrand who joined Local 10, argued, "containerization shot that [solidarity] all to hell" because a steady man "becomes company oriented," which "broke down the commonality" among workers. Robinson added that, previously, machinery on the docks simply had starter buttons, but steady men did not want other workers—dispatched from the hall—to use "their" machines, and so employers installed keys assigned to specific steady men. Lou Goldblatt, the union's second-highest-ranking leader, later raised another critique, "the dilution of work opportunity for the other men in the hall." This issue came to a head in the Bay Area in 1970, when the amount of work plunged as containerization rapidly expanded. Locals tried to equalize work opportunities for those still dispatched out of the hall, but steady men worked more hours and, thus, earned more money. Goldblatt continued, "With the advent of steady men, the concept of equalization begins to go out the window. The split is most dangerous because the men are pitted against each other, with some of the guys attached to the union and some of the guys attached to the employer." San Francisco longshoreman Bill Bailey, an older leftist who fought in the Abraham Lincoln Battalion during the Spanish Civil War, hated the steady men concept because it threatened "the hiring hall[, which] is the whole essence of the union, that was what the rank and file was afraid of, lose the hiring hall and the union means nothing." Did employers understand this issue and, for that reason, push for 9.43? Notably, an immense study of cargo loading undertaken in San Francisco during the late 1950s and early 1960s by the Maritime Cargo Transportation Conference, a part of the National Academy of Sciences Division of Engineering and Industrial Research, suggested yes: "Management spokesmen claimed that these [traditional ILWU] hiring practices precluded establishment of company loyalty in the work force."[8]

Local 10 members, especially younger ones, complained about 9.43 most forcefully because Oakland experienced containerization more quickly than other West Coast ports. As discussed, San Francisco was rapidly losing cargo traffic to Oakland, which emerged as the nation's second-largest container port by 1970 (behind New York–New Jersey) and remained so through most of the decade. Matson and SeaLand, the largest East Coast container firm, invested heavily into making Oakland the West Coast's leading container port, at least for a time. The US war in Vietnam also contributed to Oakland's rise because the East Bay housed major US Army and US Navy facilities. As the war escalated, massive quantities of cargo (and troops) shipped out of Oakland and neighboring Alameda, increasingly in containers, once the army embraced the new technology; Local 10 members worked all military terminals. Because the PMA—like the ILWU, headquartered in San Francisco—quickly moved to containerize Oakland, Robinson correctly deduced that "we were the experiment." Some older workers, reportedly, found containers intimidating, but they continued to retire in greater and greater numbers. In contrast, younger workers held little trepidation; they believed the suggestion that only some possessed the skills to operate cranes, and so needed to go steady, was bogus. Mills contended that "the employers' rationale for Section 9.43 was also increasingly seen as nothing more than a rationale for injustice," to wit, the undermining of the hiring hall and union. "Young Turks" like Mills and Robinson hated 9.43, led the strike from below, and belonged to a generation of workers challenging (older) leaders in many unions. Much like the way historians Jefferson Cowie and Lane Windham have described for other workers in the early 1970s, younger dockworkers were more free thinking and independent—and *far* less likely than their predecessors to accept Bridges's word as gospel. As the epicenter of resistance to 9.43, Local 10 members followed in the footsteps of earlier ILWU generations as the most leftwing, but it also was the only black-majority local in the union. Revealing some internal tensions, some Bay Area activists believed that their views were disregarded in other locals considered more conservative and, possibly, racist. Since "divide and conquer" was a time-tested and effective tactic, employers might have been particularly clever to push steady men first in Oakland.[9]

Anger over steady men combined, in the late 1960s and early 1970s, with a decline in work due to the slow withdrawal of troops under President Nixon *and* the advent of large-scale containerization in Oakland. Longshoremen, especially in Local 10, watched as work diminished rapidly and, naturally, became increasingly concerned about their futures. The dire situation was complicated further when Local 10 took in another large group of new members, "B men," in 1969 that, in retrospect, confirms that the leadership did not understand containers' long-term consequences. Newer longshoremen, who entered the union in a series of four expansions from 1959 to 1969, found that they could not make ends meet solely by longshoring—tonnage shipped soared while, as a result of containerization, hours plummeted. Meanwhile, the PMA—knowing it had gained the upper hand—sought to extend its power or, as Josh Williams phrased it, "They just want to test the longshoremen once in a while. They always find a way to fuck around with the longshoremen. Fuck over, I should say."[10]

Tensions grew as Bridges, whom a growing number of longshoremen mistrusted, negotiated with the PMA in 1971. Many rank-and-filers feared Bridges had become too conservative and accommodating, which, according to Goldblatt, originated at least as far back as the second M&M negotiations: "At that phase of the game, Harry was pretty well going along with everything [PMA leader J. Paul] St. Sure wanted; at least it struck me that way." By 1970 even the mainstream, probusiness *San Francisco Chronicle* considered him neither militant nor radical:

> If Bridges is indeed immutable, his waterfront is not. Waterfront employers, once his mortal enemies, now regard his ILWU, which hasn't struck since 1948, as one of the more stabilizing elements of the Pacific maritime industry. It embraced rather than fought mechanization and acquired one of the coziest working agreements, including unprecedented bonuses and fringe benefits and pensions. It is possible to say that Port Authority appointment [in 1970] clinches and affirms Harry Bridges's romance with The Establishment, but it would not be prudent to do so in his presence.

That is, in 1970 Mayor Joseph Alioto appointed the once-renegade Bridges to the San Francisco Port Commission along with other ILWU leaders to various city commissions. To press both Bridges and the PMA in the last months before the contract expired, Local 10 activists conducted illegal work stoppages to protest 9.43 and the loading and unloading of containers (called "stuffing" and "unstuffing") by workers not in the ILWU. The Bay Area arbitrator ruled that Local 10 must not interfere with anyone working steady, but it seems clear that many were itching to strike regardless. Bridges's biographer, Charles Larrowe, wrote, "there was sentiment among the ranks that in the ten years of M & M, the union had been too cooperative with the employers, that it had done less than it could to protect them against loss of jobs due to the use of containers, and that it had allowed working conditions to deteriorate more than was necessary." When Bridges and the PMA presented a contract with wage hikes but nothing to redress complaints about containers or 9.43, 96 percent of longshoremen voted against it. Hence, on July 1, 1971, according to a PMA strike chronology, "For the first time in 23 years all 56 Pacific Coast ports are shut down." Longshoremen, angry and fearful, no longer trusted Bridges and so walked out, which created an untenable situation for the union in that the rank-and-file did not trust their president and he resented the membership for striking.[11]

Though the dockworkers felt compelled to strike, clear problems existed from the start. First, rather than taking his cue from the nearly unanimous strike vote, Bridges continued bickering with his own membership, lashing out at those who disagreed with him. Larrowe noted, "Bridges's reaction to these criticisms was to counterattack" denigrating his critics (who elected him) in his *Dispatcher* column as "super-militants" and "hot shot radicals . . . advocating impossible demands to provoke an unnecessary strike." Arguably, as a long-time advocate of union democracy, Bridges should have respected his members' decision to strike but, truly, he did not. Even Cleophas Williams, a former Local 10 president and staunch supporter of Bridges, sounded mildly critical of Bridges and others in the international leadership who backed away during the strike. Second, though the strike vote suggested unity, divisions among the ranks existed over containers and 9.43. Williams was hardly alone in believing that the union could not roll back 9.43 or any of the other changes wrought by the two M&M agreements. Alex Bagwell, a clerk in Local 34, also recalled that the steady men issue "split the union," with some concern that racial divisions might emerge because many Local 10 members who went steady were African American (though many others were not). Bagwell joined other strikers who worried that "you'd be out of a fucking job" from mechanization and that employers wanted to "get rid of the hall." Third, without leadership from the international, locals were forced to fend for themselves, sometimes at odds with each other. Don Watson, a veteran Local 34 activist, recounted that "When Local 10 in San Francisco put out a four-page newspaper giving their reasons for the strike, I would notice you'd get something else from Portland." They all understood, as Goldblatt explained, that "The West Coast longshoremen are engaged in a struggle which will determine the course of labor in dealing with the impact of mechanization and automation—it is part of the endless fight between human rights and property rights." Disunity remained a major problem throughout the strike.[12]

ILWU strikers faced challenges from their own international leaders, the PMA, and the federal government. Despite knowing of their members' desire to strike, the ILWU international did little to prepare and issued no statements about demands. After three weeks of silence from the international, the Local 10 Publicity Committee, chaired by Mills, started issuing pamphlets that other locals reprinted, including the first, "Why Strike?" Locals organized mass picketing at piers up and down the coast that waylaid hundreds of ships, but the international had promised not to strike military cargo (with the US still at war in Vietnam, doing so surely would have resulted in government repression) and, surprising to note, perishable cargo. Because many shipping firms made large profits from military contracts, they suffered little economic pressure to negotiate. Even worse for the strikers, the Canadian ILWU, representing dockworkers in British Columbia, had a separate contract and so could not strike. Though, initially, they voted to refuse handling "hot cargo," the Canadian government compelled them to work—after a British Columbia court ruled against the union—under threats of imprisonment and massive fines. Subsequently, the PMA diverted some cargo to Vancouver and, then, placed goods on trains and trucks to move south across the border. Similarly, the PMA diverted some ships to Ensenada, Mexico, though ILWU and Teamster allies effectively dissuaded many US truck drivers from working this hot cargo. Further, the ILWU had no strike fund and so strikers made do by dividing working on military cargo with finding other jobs during the strike. They also lived on savings, support from neighborhood merchants who issued strikers credit, and food stamps. These disadvantages notwithstanding, the strike might have lasted even longer had not President Nixon intervened forcefully. During the strike's sixth week, Nixon announced unprecedented nationwide freezes on wages and prices to combat inflation, which precluded the wage increases the strikers might win. Later, on October 6, the strike's hundredth day, Nixon declared an eighty-day cooling-off period, forcing the strikers back to work while the union and employers resumed negotiations. The Labor Management Relations Act of 1947 (nicknamed Taft-Hartley) gave presidents the power to halt strikes for eighty days, ostensibly to protect the nation's economy, as Nixon claimed in this case. In the words of the affidavit justifying Nixon's declaration, the strike "affected, and if permitted to continue or to be resumed, will continue to affect a substantial part of the maritime industry of the United States engaged in trade, commerce, transportation, transmission, and communication among the several States and with foreign nations, and engaged in the production of goods for commerce." Of course, that was the whole point of the strike. Predictably, the longshoremen fiercely resented Nixon's intrusion for denying them their best tactic.[13]

In a shocking move during the strike, Bridges suggested that the ILWU should merge with its counterpart, the ILA (which was about to strike when Nixon slapped it with another Taft-Hartley injunction) or International Brotherhood of Teamsters (IBT). To many observers and ILWU members, Bridges's initiatives seemed perverse, desperate, or both because the ILWU had been bitter rivals of both unions for decades; recall that a young Bridges led West Coast longshoremen out of the ILA to create the ILWU in 1937. After World War II, the ILWU frequently squared off in nasty jurisdictional disputes (with the Teamsters), over politics (both the ILA and IBT were conservative and supported the Cold War), and democracy (with the ILA and IBT accused, including by the government, of rampant corruption). Thus, many saw the ILWU and ILA as polar opposites. Still, Bridges claimed—not incorrectly—that the ILWU was isolated from most of the labor movement (expelled from the CIO in 1949, it had never joined the AFL-CIO) and small, and therefore in need of allies, with the most logical ones being other transport workers' unions. Some considered Bridges's suggestions more a bluff because of dichotomous ideologies and the nasty feuds the ILWU had with both unions. Nothing came of Bridges's musings, although, if the ILWU and ILA had coordinated, all the nation's ports could have been shut down for the first time ever, which undeniably would have had demonstrated dockworker power.[14]

Ongoing federal pressure and the cooling-off period notwithstanding, neither side budged. In December, the longshoremen voted on an offer they had rejected in October, again overwhelmingly rejecting it: 10,072 to 746. Bridges asked "what next?" in his late December *Dispatcher*: "Was it a strike vote? Will it soften up the employers enough to offer us a contract we can accept? Not in my opinion." Hardly an endorsement of his members' wishes. Instead, Bridges continued discussing an ILA merger because, he claimed, the ILWU could not "stand by ourselves." Considering Bridges's utter lack of support, the rank-and-file's commitment to stay out seems that much more impressive. Because no agreement had been reached, the strike resumed in January 1972, though, as Don Watson recalled, "the enthusiasm had worn off quite a bit." In February, after marathon negotiations involving third-party mediation, the members ratified a new contract with about one-third still voting against or, as one former San Francisco longshoreman put it, "only after the ranks were many times outmaneuvered and long without paychecks."[15]

Despite enormous effort by and solidarity among rank-and-file longshoremen to alter power relations, the mammoth strike was at best a draw and, at worst, a defeat despite improvements to pay scales and fringe benefits. Charles Larrowe strongly argued that the two-year contract was a victory, for the worker "would have job security for life, a good pension waiting for him at retirement, virtually complete prepaid medical and dental care for himself and his family. And with the new wage rate, if he worked fairly regularly, he would be making almost $12,000 a year. That's not bad, considering he had qualified for the job without even a high school diploma." Employers also agreed to pay a $1.00 per ton royalty on any container loaded or unloaded within a fifty-mile radius of a West Coast port with the money going into a fund from which employers paid a wage guarantee of $180 a week to A-men and $90 a week to B-men. Crucially, the wage guarantee was lost in a subsequent contract and a future court ruling outlawed efforts by both the ILWU and ILA to draw "rings" around ports, as it were, and collect royalties from containers stuffed and unstuffed inside them, that is, not right at the port. Larrowe's points notwithstanding, the workers' gains were but a fraction of the profits employers made from containerization as ILWU research director Fairley, who helped negotiate the original M&M, wrote in 1977: "Tonnage almost tripled between 1960 and 1977. . . . [T]he shippers appear to have benefited handsomely. In this regard the M. & M. Plan has been a great success." By all accounts, the 1972 contract was similar to proposals the membership twice voted down—raising the question of what the workers won, if anything, by striking. Pouring salt into their wounds, after the strike ended, Nixon's newly created Pay Board drastically lowered the agreed-upon wage increase. Bridges, hinting at his earlier fire, threatened to lead the ILWU out on strike again if the Pay Board reduced the agreement by even one cent, but he did not follow through. "'In the old days, Harry'd never have let 'em call his bluff like that,' one of his close associates said." Cleophas Williams, a Local 10 president in this era, reflected, "youngsters and some of the older guys thought they could resist changes. We took a beating in that strike," at least partially because Bridges and the international "backed away," though Williams was being generous. Some, including Local 10 activists like Herb Mills, believed Bridges intentionally subverted the strike to punish the members for striking against his wishes. This theory may seem far-fetched, but many in and around the union believe it to be true.[16]

Coast arbitrator Sam Kagel, a confidant of Bridges for fifty years and nicknamed the "king of arbitrators," also suggested that Bridges intentionally undermined the strike. Kagel's friendship with Bridges dated back to the Big Strike of 1934. Few people were as respected and important to longshore labor relations from the 1930s until 2002 as Kagel. Among other accomplishments, Kagel mediated the marathon negotiations that ended the 1971–72 strike. In the mid-1980s, historian

Robert Cherny interviewed Kagel for a book on Bridges. Kagel recalled that PMA president Ed Flynn, who had succeeded St. Sure, repeatedly asked Kagel to set up a meeting with Bridges, who refused—for several months—to do so; the PMA strike timeline, on its website, confirms that no negotiations occurred for two months in late 1971. Kagel further recalled that once, when he called Bridges, Kagel suggested that the employers already had suffered from the months-long shutdown. Bridges replied that his reticence to meet with the PMA was not about punishing the employers but, rather, his own members. Kagel concluded that Bridges seemed driven by his desire to punish the longshoremen for striking against his advice![17]

Despite the strikers' best efforts, then, the 9.43 clause remained and many longshore workers continued to fear that steady men would divide the union and increase employer power. Rank-and-file activists in Local 10 contended there was no reason that skilled workers, including crane operators, could not be dispatched through the hall instead of going steady, an argument designed to preserve its low-man-out system. Although the PMA pushed hard to get steady men in the Bay Area (and Los Angeles), it is interesting that not all ports instituted 9.43, and the ILWU did not push locals to accept steady men. Howard Keylor, a long-time Trotskyist militant in Local 10, reported that in a closed meeting of Local 8 members in Portland, threats were made that any member who took a steady-man job would be shot out of his crane. Whether Keylor exaggerated or not, Goldblatt noted, "Portland has container piers now [1979] and they do a lot of container work. They are all convinced that no man should work steady for an employer. So the crane drivers [who must go through training and pass a test] are all rotated through the hall." Nevertheless, Bridges's negotiating team did not push to remove steady men from the coast's two largest ports, and probably they did not try. As Stan Weir, a fierce critic of Bridges, wrote, "That the contract that was finally approved still contained 9.43 was a monument to the ability of bureaucracies to close ranks against the rank and file."[18]

The PMA continued its strategy, starting with the first M&M, to offer financial sweeteners in exchange for the prerogative to maintain control over the hiring and work processes. Although ILWU members were paid more, easily financed with growing profits in the container era, by the late 1970s Local 10 possessed far fewer members. Fairley suggested that productivity was at least twenty times as great by the late 1970s as in the precontainer era. Whereas in the mid-1960s Local 10 had more than four thousand members, by the end of the 1970s it had less than half as many. Hence, labor costs dropped considerably. Fairley later tried to put the best possible spin on the results: "They still enjoy what for them is the greatest benefit of longshore work, the right and the opportunity to work only when they please, and to go hunting or fishing if they want to. They have no fear of layoff and any slack in work is taken up by the wage guarantee adopted in 1972 after the 1971–1972 strike. With good wages and the prospect of an adequate pension, they are among the elite of the workers in their areas." Some of Fairley's conclusions are curious—asserting workers value the chance to go hunting at will over equality—but he is correct in asserting that dockworkers earned more money and better benefits than nearly all other blue-collar workers. Of course, activists in Local 10 had promoted a different vision, as in their first strike pamphlet:

> It is essential for labor to challenge the notion that the employer—in the name of "progress"—can simply go ahead and slash his workforce or close his factory or, as is being planned in our industry, close an entire port, and to do this without any regard for the people and community involved. We in Local 10 also have the particular responsibility of presenting such a challenge to our employer because the majority of us are from minority communities which have already been engulfed by "the progress" of massive unemployment.

The 1971–72 strike failed to achieve this more radical vision, as Mark Rosenstein thoughtfully concluded: "The M&M agreement provided the basis for all of the other activities of containerization. Without the consent of labor, a very different path to adopting containerization would have almost certainly taken place." The ILWU won significant economic benefits but ultimately could not prevent the steep decline in the number of workers and, thus, unionists and political influence, which continued through the 1970s.[19]

Containers Arrive on the Durban Waterfront

Durban's transition to containers proved far more chaotic and harmful for its dock-workers, especially in the short run, because they were unable to shape the process. Whereas the ILWU negotiated from a position of strength that protected the generation that experienced the shift, Durban's dockworkers had no such power and, accordingly, suffered more. In Durban, containerization also must be understood in the context of black challenges to employers and the state. In 1977, when containers finally arrived in Durban, dockworkers had yet to form a union despite their pivotal role in inspiring other black workers to strike and unionize. Though slow to containerize, when it happened, the timing was fortuitous for South Africa's employers and government in that this technology devastated dockworkers, who suffered massive retrenchments that also prevented them from participating in the nationwide resurgence of black workers. Even still, black workers had become such a force that the government's Wiehahn Commission had little choice in 1979 but to recommend major reforms that legalized black unions in the Labour Relations Act. Black unionism continued at a frenetic pace including, by the early 1980s, at the Point. When dockworkers finally unionized, immediately after the container-induced retrenchments, the nascent union struggled. It took the better part of two decades for a strong union to emerge. Durban dockworkers, at the forefront of black worker militancy since the 1930s, no longer played a leading role precisely when the struggle reached epic proportions in the mid-1980s.[20]

Durban in the 1970s remained vitally important to South Africa, the nation's umbilical cord to the global economy, with dockworkers loading and unloading most of the country's exports and imports. The harbor and its large, low-wage workforce resulted in the emergence of Durban as a thriving industrial center. Steven Friedman succinctly described this coastal city as "South Africa's major port, its third largest city and its second most important industrial area." Geographer Errol Haarhoff elaborated: "Durban harbour commands a hinterland which includes all Natal, the Transvaal (the Witwatersrand in particular), the North-East Orange Free State and East Griqualand. These areas are all determined by natural, economic and political factors." Durban contributed even more to the global economy, as Haarhoff continued, because of geopolitical factors in the late 1960s: "Since the closure of the Suez Canal in June 1967 the sea route around the Cape has been intensified and South African ports have benefited from the increased traffic of diverted shipping. Durban has become the main port of all diverted ships, but again this increase of traffic only goes to aggravate the already congested port. Congestion in the harbour is becoming more and more critical each year." South African Railways and Harbours (SARH) moved quite deliberately, which worsened the port's existing congestion, where waits of seventy-two hours for ship berths were common. The global shipping industry, thus, "needed" Durban to containerize, but forces at the local and national level also created incentives.[21]

Containers officially launched in Durban in 1977. As early as 1970, Durban business and political elites begged for "rapid mechanisation." One story in the *Natal Mercury* started "Durban harbour should be mechanised to beat the throttling skilled [white] labour shortage and steadily decreasing worker output." The same piece complained that "The port is not equipped to handle the present traffic." Years prior to arriving in Durban, though, containers were radically remaking shipping and South Africans understood it. One 1972 *Rand Daily Mail* article described how "new" older vessels were transferred to shipping runs to South Africa, displaced from European routes served by more modern ships. Another article noted "a demand from foreign charterers for container vessels" that would not appear for more than half a decade. The 1970 *Mercury* article rightly concluded that "Durban is in between two periods. The whole pattern is changing from physical handling to mechanical handling, and we have not yet reached the stage of fully containerised or palletised cargoes."[22]

SARH studied containerization, for Durban and other ports, albeit in typically authoritarian fashion, that is, in detail and secret. In 1965, the Division Planning and Productivity department issued its confidential "Report of Committee of Investigation into Congestion in Durban Harbour," conducted—also typically—in conjunction with the Durban Chamber of Commerce, Natal Chamber of Industries, and South African Conference Lines. Dockworkers were not the primary or even second-most-pressing issue, though "staff shortages," meaning of supervisors, crane operators, engine crews—all white, in accordance with apartheid labor policy—received significant attention. The report noted some employers still resented the DSLSC, six years after its creation, claiming that decasualization along with the "tendency amongst non-White labourers towards slackness" caused lower productivity, the latter a pervasive view among white South Africans. In 1968, SARH appointed W. F. J. Steenkamp, professor of economics at the University of South Africa and formerly in charge of the Wage Board, to head a commission to investigate containerization. The commission took several years, and made a fact-finding trip to Australia, before issuing a hundred-page report in 1970 that concluded, "there is no doubt that it is the transport system of the future." The Steenkamp Commission warned, "In postponing containerisation, a country may well jeopardise its position in overseas markets, thereby suffering greater long-run loss than the short-run loss it would have incurred by containerising sooner." Steenkamp came down firmly in favor of containerization as soon as possible, in no small part because of spectacular productivity gains. Acknowledging the huge capital investment, the report reminded its readers, "the foreign trade dependence of South Africa is one of the highest in the world." Thus, the nation could not afford to be complacent which explains its very first recommendation: "Containerisation should be introduced into the South African trade at the earliest possible date." Moving in its typically slow, bureaucratic manner, however, only in 1974 did the South African government and South African–European Conference (Europe being South Africa's largest trading partner) sign an agreement that set the target for the main sea routes with Europe to be 70 percent containerized by 1979. Officially, SARH simultaneously launched four container ports, including Durban, on July 1, 1977—seven years after the Steenkamp Commission tabled its report (meaning filed, in South Africa), and a decade after initial discussions.[23]

Some still failed to anticipate the significant role containers would play in South Africa. D. M. Ross-Watt, generally a thoughtful analyst, made the following suggestion in 1970: "Although there are definite advantages to containerisation, the most important being the incredibly short turn around time, it is generally only suitable to specific trading routes. This is chiefly an economic consideration. The container ship, the special ship berth facilities and the containers themselves are expensive to construct and maintain." Unspoken was that, in Durban, firms exploited thousands of incredibly low-paid black workers, as the Steenkamp Report noted, "for ours is a developing country with a dual economic structure

Fig. 8. The South African Railways and Harbours Administration worked closely with foreign shipping corporations to containerize South African ports. Transnet Heritage Library Photographic Collection.

and, basically, an easy supply of unskilled [cheap] labour." Despite the remaking of shipping by containers, Ross-Watt was not alone in failing to predict the future. Even Dr. J. J. Burger, president of the (South Africa) Motor Transport Owners' Association, wrote in 1971 that "The use of containers on flat bed road vehicles over long distance [trucking] will never become very popular." In Ross-Watt's defense, he did suggest that, "with the introduction of more sophisticated cargo handling methods it may be anticipated that eventually the work of the Bantu stevedore will become a skilled occupation and result in an upgrading of the situation of the stevedore in terms of his wages and welfare." Admittedly, that advance took another thirty years.[24]

In hindsight, it seems impossible that any country imagined it could resist this transformation, especially when, as in South Africa, global firms pushed the process. After the Steenkamp Report, the South Africa government signed a fifteen-year Ocean Freight Agreement with corporations belonging to the Europe/South and South-East Africa Conference that commenced in 1977. Whereas in the United States, corporations like SeaLand and Matson largely drove containerization (with assistance from the US Navy early in the process), in South Africa the state played a central role, for it owned the nation's ports, investing R1.3 billion in the mid-1970s. The other factor in South African containerization, of course, was the power of Durban dockworkers.[25]

Though containers already were being shipped across the seven seas, the strikes carried out by Durban dockworkers demand mention. Recall that South African elites hoped that decasualization, instituted in 1959, would silence dockworkers and, as late as 1969, University of Natal economist O. P. F. Horwood asserted, "Labour at the Port of Durban is not a problem." Similarly, colonial authorities in Mombasa had hoped decasualization would tame workers but, as Fred Cooper concluded, the colonial state "found that the new world which emerged was no more theirs to forge than the one before." As in Mombasa, decasualization in Durban "bought" a "quiet decade" but only one. As discussed, major actions erupted on the Durban waterfront from 1969 to 1973 that both predicted and shaped the mammoth Durban Strikes of 1973. After the latter wave subsided, Durban-based shipping firms and government officials constantly fretted about dockworkers, as revealed in countless meetings and reports throughout the 1970s. For instance, M. J. Swales, an official of the Port Natal Bantu Affairs Administration, complained in 1974 that "Some Stevedoring firms and cartage contractors are not taking proper steps in complying with the law when they manage this type of labour." To which R. F. Drew, a Labour Officer in the same bureaucracy, replied, "I believe that the only solution to this problem is control of casual labour," a most curious reference confirming that the DSLSC did not fully control waterfront labor. Surely, then, shippers and SARH understood that, among other major benefits, containerization could silence troublesome dockworkers. Labor was on employers' minds, including the mind of J. J. Burger, president of the country's organization of truckers, who wrote in 1971 that, in some countries, labor was "the main driving force behind the container revolution." Burger cited the United States and the United Kingdom, "where the cost of labour is high and port activities are completely disrupted every now and again by dock worker strikes." Burger did not mention the 1969 strike and can be forgiven for not predicting 1972. Clearly, employers understood full well that new technologies can weaken workers.[26]

With the Steenkamp Commission report "tabled"—that is, presented—and the Ocean Freight Agreement signed, SARH moved forward with building container infrastructure in South African ports including Durban, where Pier No. 2, really a complex of piers, provided much more space for large container ships and ever-more container storage. Much as in the San Francisco Bay Area, rather than renovate existing terminals, SARH built a new quay far from the port's traditional center; whereas the Point lies along the northern side of the harbor, Pier No. 2 lies in the southern portion. Shippers and the state considered containerization an unbridled success. In a retrospective commemorating the twenty-fifth anniversary of the launch, South Africa's logistics industry magazine boldly declared,

"C[ontainer] Day was a triumph of centralised planning that even a communist country would admire. Having started behind the rest of our trading partners, South Africa was in a position to learn from them and commit resources to a big bang conversion to containerisation on a scale that had never been seen before and would not be seen again." This telling statement, of course, seems unaware of the many similarities between the fascist apartheid regime in South Africa and a Soviet-style communist one. It also seems problematic, to say the least, to loudly praise apartheid planning in the postapartheid era.[27]

Curiously, during its planning for containers, SARH made no mention of growing domestic and global resistance to apartheid. The subject simply does not appear in any of the reports generated by SARH, suggesting, perhaps, that apartheid simply was taken for granted by white elites. Yet South Africa's shipping executives fully knew of apartheid's poor reputation around the globe as well as the growing boycott movement. For instance, in 1978 Richard Siedle, managing director of Zambezi Africa Line, admitted of being "mindful of ever-increasing pressure for boycotts of South Africa and her exports," and so recommended that "shipping lines involved (Zambezi Africa Line and Zambezi Maritime Line) as well as exporters maintain a low political profile." South Africa's shipping firms and SARH might have wished to ignore this matter but the global movement against apartheid drastically expanded in the 1980s, and anti-apartheid actions included the targeting of South African cargo. Of course, South Africa's shippers hardly were alone in wanting to counteract negative publicity. Journalist Ron Nixon documented how, in the 1970s, Eschel Rhoodie, "the Joseph Goebbels of the apartheid government," led the global propaganda war that spent hundreds of millions of dollars in "a worldwide media and lobbying operation run with military precision." Because of their exposure, no one understood better than shipping executives that transportation provided a direct, effective, and powerful method of applying economic pressure upon South Africa. G. F. Baker, a high-level official in the government's Bantu Administration, noted in 1974, "Durban, as a harbour, apparently caters for 52% of cargo movement in this country and therefore, this is a factor that must be protected in the national interest." Throughout SARH planning for containers, Durban's dominant status was presumed and, sure enough, it continued handling most of the nation's cargo. Thus, that dockworkers could interrupt the nation's premier transportation hub mattered greatly.[28]

Containerization went hand in hand with the collapse of the DSLSC and consolidation of companies managing dockworkers. The DSLSC failed to adapt to the revolutionary changes in global shipping. Mike Morris, a leading waterfront organizer, noted in 1986 that the "centralisation of capital in [South African] stevedoring" largely was driven by international factors. These forces overwhelmed the DSLSC, the local monopoly of dock labor, causing Captain Gordon Stockley, general manager of the South African Stevedoring Services Company (SASSCO), to complain to other shipping executives at a Durban Club gathering, "I refuse to travel at the speed of the slowest ship in the convoy." In 1979, the DSLSC shut down. Scholar Bernard Dubbeld attributed the collapse to a period of increasing competition among small stevedoring firms, dating back to the 1969 dock strike, along with growing pressure from international shipping lines to adapt to containers. By 1976, what had been twelve companies had dwindled to four and, by 1980, SASSCO (itself a product of mid-1970s mergers) controlled 60 percent of the Durban market. SASSCO, which also faced international pressure during an(other) era in which a surplus of ships cut into profits, pushed for further consolidation. Accordingly, in the early 1980s, SASSCO took over Rennies and Grindrod Cotts, which had merged to compete with SASSCO. By the mid-1980s, the newly renamed South African Stevedores (SAS) stood alone. This consolidation, ultimately with SAS as a monopsony, had huge ramifications for dockworkers. Most painfully, further retrenchments occurred, as Morris decried, "This process of monopolisation has also resulted in massive redundancy of the stevedoring workforce internationally," itself sparked by containerization.[29]

The advent of containers devastated Durban dockworkers. As in many ports worldwide, the arrival of containers resulted in massive layoffs. Pete Williams, managing director of the large Safcor Panalpina logistics firm, reflected in 2002 on the multitudinous impacts of containers in Durban, "suddenly the whole supply chain changed. The breakbulk system of bags, crates, boxes and bales which was highly labour intensive was suddenly largely redundant." Williams continued, "Gone was the need for multiple handling of the product, *traditional stevedoring was substantially reduced*, claims virtually disappeared and ship turnaround time reduced from days or weeks to hours." One need not have waited twenty-five years after introduction, of course, to understand this reality. Even before launching, SARH, dock employers, and shipping companies all knew containerization would drastically increase productivity and decrease the number of workers. One mid-1970s SARH report noted, "It is estimated that containerised cargo will be handled 7 to 8 times faster than break-bulk cargo." Or, as Durban dockworker Mr. Khanye declared in 1983, "Workers loose [sic] their jobs because of these containers." Dubbeld provided the numbers: "at the height of the DSLSC in 1965 stevedoring labour force peaked at 3500 workers, by 1978 this had shrunk to an average of 2500 workers employed, and by 1985 the labour force was some 1200 workers." Thus, fewer than seven years after containerization launched, the workforce plunged by more than half! (Retrenchments at least as severe also occurred in Cape Town, Port Elizabeth, and East London.) The technological changes lessened the physical brutality and danger but, as Dubbeld concluded, "work became increasingly casualized, marginalized, and ultimately redundant." As in the San Francisco Bay Area, containerization diminished the traditional skills of dockworkers and undermined their collective identity created by work gangs. Unlike results in the Bay Area, however, containerization forced some Durban dockworkers to become more "flexible," that is, casual, once again. Perhaps it is surprising that Captain Stockley, a South African shipping executive interviewed by Dubbeld in 2001, harshly criticized these changes, blaming the global industry: "What these guys in the shipping industry knew about was the effects of containerization . . . they knew what was going to happen to the labour and that we would have a massive problem, but they weren't too interested in helping or showing us the direction to go. They just ripped the guts out of it to get better profits." The industry's *Freight and Trading Weekly* issue, commemorating twenty years in South Africa, offered its assessment: "The only word that adequately describes the influence of containerisation on International shipping over the last 25 or so years is 'Revolution'. Its impact on the way shipping companies and ports operate is without precedent."[30]

Dockworkers also grasped the implications and, after organizing informally for decades, embraced formal unionism in the early 1980s. Like other black workers, dockworkers gained the right to unionize in 1980; arguably, their earlier militancy helped create the conditions that forced the state to expand black worker rights. In the 1970s, employers established "liaison committees" that, according to labor organizer Morris, employers and the DSLSC dominated; half the committee's members were selected by management, the other half cherry-picked by the head *induna*. Black workers, generally, saw liaison and work committees as cynical efforts by employers and the state to co-opt black worker insurgency and power. Several unions emerged around 1980 on the nation's waterfronts, including the General Workers Union (GWU), born on Cape Town's docks, and Transport and General Workers Union (TGWU or T&G). Ethnic differences impaired the GWU organizing drive, as Tina Sideris reported: "When the GWU came to Durban [in 1982] it did not have an easy job. Many of the workers were scared to join trade unions. And many workers did not trust the Xhosas from Cape Town." Sideris quoted one: "'The workers were suspicious,' says Mr. Khanye. 'They didn't know whether the Xhosas had come to rob them. Because there is a belief that Xhosas are very clever.'" Such ethnic suspicions cut both ways. David Lewis, GWU general secretary in the era, recalled, after one large meeting, that some Xhosa activists complained of Durban's Zulu dockworkers: "what do you expect from a bunch of boys?" Xhosa men practiced circumcision and considered it an essential rite of passage into manhood; in other words, because Zulu men were not circumcised, they still children. Despite this conflict, the GWU earned the dockworkers' loyalty, as Hemson recounted it:

> The early organisers of the GWU in Durban came with a sense of mission broad enough, but also a practice sufficiently narrowed and concentrated, to make a difference. An office was found adjoining the docks, "Rev" Marawu (an early organiser)

wore the overalls of SASSCO (the main employer, the South African Stevedoring Services Company), and slept in the offices. The workers found this union approachable and able to follow up their concrete concerns. They gave it a name *dekle* (literally "to sit flat on the floor") because the union did not have any chairs; the word also has an association with a sit-down strike.

The GWU also convinced some dockworkers who served on different companies' liaison committees to become union activists. By the mid-1980s, the GWU represented 90 percent of Durban dockworkers, as it already did in other ports. Morris, admittedly biased as its lead organizer, hailed these events: "Unifying them into a union with the internal organisational discipline that this entailed, and beginning the process of linking them up with the rest of the working class, was a watershed in the development and history of the stevedores." In 1986, after the creation of the Congress of South African Trade Unions, which advocated "one industry, one union," the GWU and TGWU merged. In 2000, TGWU joined with the South African Railways and Harbour Workers Union to form the South African Transport and Allied Workers Union (SATAWU), which currently represents Durban dockworkers.[31]

The GWU achieved some impressive gains for Durban (and other) dockworkers. First, the union negotiated raises from about R12 to R21 per day, truly massive gains in just three years. Such wage increases paralleled results in other ports in the container era, in which a much smaller workforce earning higher wages; because of enormous productivity gains, employers' labor costs still plunged. Second, because containerization drastically increased turnaround times, meaning fewer hours worked, the GWU negotiated wage guarantees in all four major ports for a minimum of four-and-a-half days regardless of the number of hours worked—like the ILWU's first M&M and 1972 contracts (though ILWU's benefit later was lost). The wage guarantee meant, according to Morris, "Conditions of service have altered so fundamentally that in no sense can these stevedores still be regarded as casuals." The union also won a pension for workers, a first, and advocated for the workers on gang sizes and health and safety issues. Because of the GWU, the same basic wage rates and conditions existed at all four main ports, an unprecedented situation in South Africa.[32]

Although the union delivered improvements in wages and conditions, the GWU could not prevent the devastation wrought by containers, and the union suffered accordingly. David Hemson, who earlier had organized on the Durban waterfront, argued in 1996 that "the agency of the working class is hemmed in by the material conditions of life which are increasingly articulated with the conditions of globalization." He referred to the irony that the GWU emerged precisely when massive, container-induced retrenchments began. The GWU defended those slated for firing and fought to get retrenched workers bigger buyouts based upon years of service on the waterfront. The union convinced employers to use the principle of "LIFO" or "last in, first out" to determine who would be retrenched; advocating for use of seniority in determining layoffs remains a typical union strategy, though the ILWU had taken the opposite approach in the first M&M. Watching most of their fellow workers fired as the industry underwent massive upheaval, those dockworkers remaining became confused, scared, divided, or depressed. Subsequent, bitter divisions arose while individuals did whatever they could to save their own jobs. Many lost faith in the union and dropped out of the GWU. Morris lamented, "The retrenchments killed us all the time, it was very hard to ever heal these divisions." Hence, the trajectory of Durban dockworkers in the 1980s ran counter to that of many other black workers, who increasingly embraced unionism and militancy in the 1980s. In the mid-1990s, Morris reflected that negotiating retrenchments proved "a disaster," which left workers stunned. "It would have been better if we had just refused point-blank and then fought against it, though I don't know how we would have dealt with it." Morris unwittingly endorsed the ILWU rank-and-file rebellion in their 1971–72 strike.[33]

Another disturbing trend emerged in the 1980s when the state started issuing stevedore licenses to new companies with no experience and that exclusively used casual workers. Some of their workers had no dock experience whatsoever, though others were retrenched veterans. As planned, no doubt, this increase in competition caused a depression of wages. Thus, although some black dockworkers started entering the ranks of skilled labor in the postapartheid era, many others remained casual laborers, with no job security whatsoever. Over time, a bifurcated labor market emerged with the most secure, best-paid dockworkers employed by the state's port authority, now called Transnet, while others became highly exploited, very low paid casuals; the latter did not operate cranes or other heavy machinery, rather performing other tasks, such as work on noncontainerized cargo. This transformation from secure to more casual employment diverged from the trajectory of many other ports, including in the San Francisco Bay Area, with its smaller, well-paid, skilled, and relatively secure workforce. It is important to note that the recasualization of some Durban dockworkers mirrors the experience of a growing number of blue- and white-collar workers in South Africa, the United States, and other societies where technological changes and massive deregulation overhauled earlier methods of work. And so, despite the emergence of multiracial democracy in 1994 and a brief boom in the South African economy in the late 1990s, the lifting of apartheid-era international sanctions made the lot of Durban dockworkers seem more precarious in 2016 than it had in decades. The recasualization and degradation of work on the Durban waterfront is but one of numerous ironies of recent South African history. Although apartheid-era controls on black labor and migration ended with the rise of political democracy, South Africa in the 2000s has experienced an extended period of economic stagnation and rising precariousness for tens of millions of mostly black South Africans. Accordingly, the deep economic and racial inequalities in South Africa—legacies of apartheid—persist. Yet all was not despair.[34]

In some ways, by 1990 Durban's dockworkers were worse off than in the era before containers—there definitely were far fewer of them. A subsequent series of twists and turns, beyond the scope of this book, has resulted in a relatively strong union to which they now belong. SATAWU helped stabilize the labor force and improved material conditions for its members. The dockworkers even went on strike in 2010, suggesting a not insignificant amount of strength and solidarity. SATAWU has flexed its political muscle on behalf of workers in neighboring Zimbabwe and Swaziland, and even in far-flung Palestine. Thus, with another twenty-five years of hindsight, one may conclude that containerization did not permanently undermine Durban dockworkers, despite the poignant title of Bernard Dubbeld's well-written 2003 article "Breaking the Buffalo." Similarly, the recasualization of some jobs on the waterfront also has not eliminated dockworker power. As with ILWU Local 10, a combination of factors helps explain dockworkers' ongoing strength and unionism. First, dockworkers inherited a long history of militancy and strength. Second, they fully appreciate the fundamental role they play in the economies of their city, nation, and world. Third, despite the precariousness of casual jobs in the harbor, many hundreds possess skills and experience that cannot be replaced by a person lining up for a job some random day: they are neither easily nor quickly replaceable. Equally undeniable are the enormous changes wrought by containers.[35]

Containerization: Is Resistance Futile?

No one can deny the import of containerization but, for dockworkers, that included some awful consequences. Though introduced in the previous decade, only in the 1970s did their full impact become apparent. Shipping firm executives, of course, understood sooner than nearly everyone else. As Allan Sekula reported in his photographic tour-de-force *Fish Story*, as early as 1970 the International Organization for Standardization had issued International Container Standards that exist to this very day. To Sekula and others, the transformations wrought were no cause for celebration—far from it—for containers remade the global economy in ways that mostly benefited corporations, not human beings. In *The Forgotten Space*, the powerful documentary film that Sekula created with Noël Burch, they declared, "The sea is forgotten until disaster strikes. But perhaps the biggest seagoing disaster is the global supply chain, which—maybe in a more fundamental way than financial speculation—leads the world economy to the abyss." Dockworkers the world over would agree, lamenting how this technology not only facilitated the loss of many millions of jobs and relocation of millions more, it also remade their own work and sent the majority to unemployment lines in the 1970s and 1980s. In the once-mighty Port of London, for instance, the number of dockworkers sank from twenty-three thousand to nine thousand between 1967 and 1977. This section offers conclusions on the specific effects of containerization in San Francisco and Durban with a focus on the former, as the experience there set the tone for the industry worldwide and opens fruitful discussion about "paths not taken" along with larger implications of technological effects on work and humanity.[36]

The ILWU was the first union in the world to negotiate the shift to containerization, which has had broader ramifications for how workers and unions respond to technological change. Harry Bridges, the long-time, legendary, once-radical leader, apparently could imagine no alternative and so, in the late 1950s, negotiated the first M&M and then strongly encouraged the union's rank-and-file to accept it and the second M&M. ILWU leadership claimed that members deserved a share of the machine for accepting this transformation but also acknowledged that they could not fight "progress." Bridges was not wrong—containers clearly were the future—but the proverbial devil, typically, lies in the details. Eric Hoffer, the "longshoreman philosopher," experienced this transition as he started on the San Francisco waterfront during World War II and remained there into the 1970s. Hoffer witnessed, thought deeply about, and wrote for two decades on containerization's impacts and implications. As containers started remaking his job, he fretted that "in America just now the masses are on their way out. With the coming of automation 90 percent of the common people will become unneeded and unwanted." Perhaps the central question is what, if anything, his union could have done differently—and, more generally, what will happen to humans in a neoliberal world in which technology eliminates ever-more workers. Even though M&M ensured that the old-timers got big payouts, younger workers received far less financial gain as their work radically changed (at least in some ways for the worse), and their numbers plunged. In San Francisco and ports encircling the globe, there are perhaps 20 percent of the number of workers there were half a century ago. Did alternatives exist? Two important ideas spring to mind. First, instead of mass layoffs, could the ILWU have convinced the PMA to reduce the hours of the basic workday to spread the work among more people? Second, could the ILWU have fought to ensure that all work, including operating cranes and other new machinery, be dispatched through the hiring hall?[37]

Reducing the standard number of hours labored has been a key goal of working people for at least 150 years. The fight for the eight-hour day dates to mid-nineteenth-century America, provoking one of the most powerful moments in all US history in the national strike for the eight-hour day on May 1, 1886, that resulted in the Haymarket Tragedy a few days later. The issue simmered for another fifty years until the Great Depression sparked renewed demands to limit hours and increase employment. Victory, for hourly workers, came with the 1938 Fair Labor Standards Act that established eight-hour days (and five-day weeks) as the norm and radical unionists and some liberal corporate leaders experimented with the six-hour day. In fact, one of the first demands of the Big Strike of 1934, out of which the ILWU emerged, was the six-hour day; the first contract the union signed with employers enshrined a six-hour day and five-day week, in other words, a thirty-hour workweek. Some corporations also experimented with the idea, most famously Kellogg, the cereal giant, which instituted a six-hour day in 1930. Whether driven by employers or workers, the idea was similar: when less work existed, it should be more widely and equitably shared. More people could work if standard shifts were set at a lower number of hours. The Kellogg experiment lasted until 1985, and the ILWU moved to longer shifts during World War II, essentially an eight-hour day with the final two hours of each shift paid at overtime rates. Since automation so drastically increased productivity, in addition to workers gaining a "share of the machine," might the union have fought to prevent drastic workforce cuts? Bridges could have advocated for spreading the remaining work around, returning to the real six-hour day that Bridges and the '34 men had enshrined. There is no evidence, however, that Bridges and ILWU leadership engaged in serious discussions on this matter, within the union or the PMA, in the late 1950s or 1960s. Fast forward to today, companies around the world continue shedding workers and countless millions (billions?) of people wonder what happens in a world without sufficient jobs. Reducing the workday seems like a logical option well worth considering. In fact, in 2017 at a conference discussing whether the ILWU should support a contract extension, some radicals in Local 10 proposed "to make automation benefit dockworkers by reducing the workweek to 30 hours while maintaining 40 hours pay."[38]

As for resisting the employers' push for steady men, critics—most notably Herb Mills—argued that 9.43 was both unnecessary and detrimental to the union. As discussed, no legitimate reason ever was provided by Bridges or the PMA for why people trained and qualified to work the cranes or other heavy, expensive machinery could not be dispatched from the hall rather than working steady. After all, Local 8 dispatched such workers out of its Portland hall in the same era that the PMA insisted that Local 10's San Francisco hall could not. Stan Weir, admittedly a fierce critic of Bridges, bemoaned the insertion of steady men into the second M&M: "In the advanced state of confusion, there was little debate over the contract's clause 9.43 that allowed the employers to return to the pre-1939 practice of hiring steady men. Union officials assured the workers that this practice would involve only a 'few handfuls' of men in each port. Actually, another sale was being made." With steady men, the ILWU lost control over daily hiring in the dispatch halls and equalization of work opportunities. When the rank-and-file overwhelmingly revolted—in rejecting the 1971 contract proposal—a primary reason was 9.43. That strike proved, however, that the union had been irreparably weakened, for despite strident efforts, especially in the Bay Area—the most heavily containerized West Coast port and where employers pushed hardest to sign up steady men—rank-and-filers could not get rid of 9.43. At this key moment, Bridges "doubled down" on containers, repeatedly insisting to "his" members that they could not "fight progress," though no one had suggested that. Rather, Local 10 wanted all work to go through the hiring hall.[39]

A central conclusion of this study is that the way containerization played out confirmed what previously was argued about decasualization. That is, whoever controlled the process benefited the most. Containers, like other technologies, are not inherently antiworker; rather, the question is, who reaps the benefits? One person who called himself an "S.F. Dock Striker" offered his analysis during the 1971–72 strike: "The heart of the problem, compounded by the political nature of the Bridges & Co. leadership, is that the tops approached mechanization as if it were progress as such and not basically contingent on who controlled it. It not only fragments us in the work, making it repetitive and boring, speeds us up, increases the accident rate, etc., but we also face a problem similar to the miners who were reduced from 600,000 to about 100,000." Durban waterfront organizer David Hemson understood the issue similarly: "In the advanced countries the concessions the workers had won in the struggle for decasualisation were to a large measure negated by the catastrophic loss in jobs in the 1970s and 1980s." Local 10 lost not only members but also control over hiring and sacrificed its commitment to equalization of work opportunities.[40]

Traditions of worker control and independence often have been threatened by the introduction of new modes of production. The great US labor historian David Montgomery—not unlike Herb Mills, an activist and machinist before earning his doctorate—eloquently wrote about such matters in *Workers' Control in America*, and Dana Frank recently noted in a thoughtful analysis of this classic, "Montgomery's great insight was that management, in crafting its assaults, was in fact acting on the defensive. 'Both workers' submerged resistance and their articulate programs have turned out to be causes, as much as effects, of the rapid evolution and diffusion of managerial practice,' he concluded." So, too, with the introduction of containers. A series of thoughtful San Francisco longshore intellectuals also wrote about the devastation of their work lives and culture that have resulted from containerization.[41]

Mills earned his doctorate in sociology from the University of California–Irvine, but for fifty years and counting, his primary passion—intellectual and otherwise—has been the waterfront. He wrote his dissertation while actually on leave from the docks and, upon graduation, returned to became a leader in Local 10. In a series of

essays written since the 1970s, starting with some of the strike pamphlets quoted
in this chapter, Mills lamented the destruction of traditional longshore work culture and fought for its preservation. Mills convincingly described the many and
varied skills that dockworkers possessed, which gave them both pride in their work
and power over it. Among other effects of their work culture was the creation of
a militant union out of which emerged, Mills argued, a community committed to
equality. After all, how many organizations of any sort (not just unions) seriously
work to ensure that those on the bottom—those who earn the least—have the first
chance at the next job? Sadly, to Mills, containerization devastated this work culture, the basis for their militant, democratic, rank-and-file-driven, and socialistic
union. Containers might have been inevitable but not *how* they were worked or
who benefited, mostly, from them. Mills particularly lambasted steady men: "The
employers fully breached the hiring hall in 1966 by securing the 9.43 job category
provision of the second M & M. By omitting such jointly stipulated seniority and
training and promotion requirements as had long been set out for dockers to work
in every other job category, they gained the right to steadily employ—*without limit as
to number or length of time—whoever they chose and also deemed as qualified to drive any or
all of their power equipment.*" Thus, to Mills, Bridges's greatest mistake was not with
the first but, rather, the second M&M, for containerization could have developed
quite differently.[42]

Two other working-class intellectuals of the San Francisco waterfront wrote
of their great respect for dockworkers' skills and (working-class) values that containerization undermined. Reg Theriault, active in Local 10 for thirty years, praised
longshoremen for knowing how to perform a hard job fast, masterfully, and safely.
Theriault regretted that containers made such skills obsolete but also that, as went
traditional work routines so, too, did older values. The loss of traditional working-
class skills and pride—he suggested—eroded humanity itself. Similarly, activist
and author Stan Weir, who worked in the San Francisco dock works in the early
1960s, lamented the "real sense of powerlessness in the face of this tremendous
change." Further, containerization, Weir argued, "makes for a lonely waterfront."
Where, previously, the conversations, jokes, and stories created deep and lasting
bonds among fellow workers, "in a containerized situation, you don't have any
audience. [Unlike] when I'm working break bulk cargo—manual ship-loading,"
wrote Weir, who later earned a PhD in sociology. In many jobs, he continued, what
workers enjoy the most is their fellow workers. Alas, "Those who are isolated and
can't socialize are usually the people with the biggest absentee problems and the
people who are least happy on the job." Of course, most members voted for both
the first and second M&M agreements; Local 10 leader Cleophas Williams, for one,
called Bridges "prophetic" for thoughtfully planning for the transition to machines.
Regardless of blame, as Theriault decried, "Ships and the way they were loaded,

waterfront practices that had existed almost unchanged for hundreds of years, disappeared completely in little over a decade. The waterfront would never be the same again."[43]

The glorification of the precontainer era by some Bay Area longshoremen has little parallel in Durban. Because of numerous economic and political factors—apartheid, most obviously, but also South Africa's version of racial capitalism—Durban dockworkers never experienced the loading and unloading of ships under a regime dominated by them. Although they possessed the power to disrupt work before and during the DSLSC era, dockworkers could not revel in their power the way Weir boasted about West Coast longshoremen: "During the following twenty-five years [from the Big Strike until the first M&M], these men would live the largest, longest, and most successful formal experiment in workers' control ever conducted in the United States." Durban dockworkers may have expressed pride in their collective strength and power, as embodied in the term *onyathi* (buffaloes), but they did not celebrate the "good old days" as Mills, Theriault, and Weir did. That said, dockworkers in Durban—as with gang laborers in other ports and industries—frequently shared great affection for each other, building intense friendships during years of shared hard, dangerous, collective labor. In Durban, dockworkers' attachments to each other were solidified by shared housing and suffering under apartheid's wrath. Without glorifying dangerous, backbreaking manual labor eliminated by new technologies, the social nature of dock labor undeniably enriched workers' lives.[44]

Employers introduced containers to speed up the turnaround time of ships but also to reset the power dynamic on the waterfront. Echoing the Wobbly "Big" Bill Haywood, Montgomery described how employers sought to remove "The manager's brain [from] under the workman's cap." Longshoremen had seized power in strikes starting in 1934 and expanded it via direct-action tactics and positive arbitration rulings until a successful 1948 strike convinced employers to more or less accept the union. As a result, the ILWU controlled the waterfront, to a shocking degree and to employers' chagrin. The ILWU relinquished much of its power, however, in the M&M agreements. Managers and employers, of course, have deployed what we may call deskillization via new technologies countless times to reduce worker numbers and union power. The original theoretician of scientific management, Frederick Winslow Taylor, strongly advocated this approach, believing employers should control the entire work process and workers should do as ordered, "I have you [workers] for your strength and mechanical ability, and we have other men [managers] paid for thinking." Even Lincoln Fairley, long-time head of ILWU research, concluded that M&M reduced the union's strength: "Not only did the gains to the Employers far outstrip the gains to the Union and its members, but it appeared that the Union was weakened while the Employers regained much of the ground they had lost in the thirties."[45]

This discussion about how members of ILWU Local 10 (and other ports) fared as a result of containerization continues. Unlike Cleophas Williams, Fairley occasionally questioned Bridges's (and his own) vision: "The failure to foresee and prepare for the rapid development of containerization proved to be a major error on the Union's part." Yet, although thousands of longshoremen voted against the first and second M&M agreements and then 96 percent voted to strike in 1971, Fairley still concluded that "The Union has probably survived the shock of this revolution in technology as well as any union faced with a similar problem." Fairley highlighted the material benefits: "more than five years after M. & M. ended [1971], though membership has declined, no one has been laid off, earnings have risen and with a wage guarantee and a good pension plan West Coast longshoremen continue to enjoy a unique degree of lifetime security." Undeniably, amid the whirlwind of containerization, longshore workers' average annual earnings rose dramatically, from $8,626 in 1970 to $16,410 in 1977 (Fairley's numbers); but solely adjusting for inflation, a worker earning that amount in 1970 would have earned $13,472 in 1977. Moreover, one must underline the huge number of jobs that disappeared—in the Bay Area alone, from about five thousand (before containers) to closer to 1,500. In 1976, Eric Hoffer, who retired during the second M&M, declared, "We are living in an epoch of great disillusionment. . . . For a moment it seemed to us that we had arrived, that we had solved all material problems and could sit back and enjoy an eternal Sabbath. But we are discovering that the more triumphant our technology, the less does society function automatically." In short, far fewer dockworkers but, in the Bay Area (and other US ports represented by the ILWU or ILA), paid more handsomely. From the perspective of 2018, with neoliberalism seemingly ascendant, Fairley's view seems reasonable, if cold comfort to the thousands who never worked on the waterfront.[46]

Despite clear similarities, containerization played out in vastly different ways in the San Francisco Bay Area than in Durban. The most obvious similarity is that the size of the workforce plummeted. Another is that the work in Durban and the work in the Bay Area became more alike as a result of this new technology, for capital imposes market "logic" on workers the world over. Containerization weakened dockworkers in both Durban and San Francisco Bay Area, but far more so in Durban, where they stopped being a force in the struggle against apartheid and remained disillusioned for several decades. Moreover, as Dubbeld thoughtfully argued, the term *globalization* can obscure as much as it might reveal about the experiences of dockworkers in different ports; hence, we must analyze the varied, local stories and not presume that "one size fits all" in containerization. This book always seeks to keep one eye on local histories and another on global trends in studying two important ports, one in the global North and the other in the South.[47]

Because the San Franciscans were among the very first dockworkers, worldwide, to experience containers, an ILWU leader deserves the final words. After retiring, Lou Goldblatt, the second-highest-ranking official during the M&M era, offered quite critical and somewhat nostalgic reflections:

> As to how you weigh these things; what it does to the whole historical background of the longshoreman, the tradition of the equalization of the work, the high degree of democracy, the willingness to walk off the job and exercise their economic power; as to how you measure these things over the long pull, I guess the best way to judge is to see how things change as the years go by.
>
> But it is a new era; longshoring is just not the same as it used to be. The container has made unbelievable changes. . . . The industry was bound to change; whether these changes would result in a kind of work force that was more highly subjected to discipline, more comparable to an ordinary factory job, would be an important determinant.
>
> How you measure that is hard to say. Some of the old timers just simply say, "Well, it's the end of an era—that's all."

Goldblatt's words also apply to Durban, for containerization marked a new era the world over. Harry Bridges, the man so hard to separate from the union he helped found and lead for more than forty years, also offered brief thoughts in a fascinating speech in Washington, DC, just after his retirement. In front of a crowd at the elite National Portrait Gallery, Bridges discussed M&M: "In classical Marxist terms, by the way, it could be called a sellout. There's no class struggle in it. I know that. It did lead to certain strains with the Communist Party. In typical ideological terms, of course, they're right. But the union is a bit more practical." The article covering his speech concluded with Bridges displaying some irony from a man known for his sense of humor: "'The contract,' he summed up with a mischievous grin that brought laughter from the audience, was a 'beautiful piece of class collaboration.'" Of course, after he admits as much, we should briefly return to Herb Mills, who channeled Marx in arguing that containerization "alienated" workers when jobs became deskilled and routinized with drastically less independent thought and initiative. Were he still alive, Bridges might remind us that dock work now is less physically demanding (if still dangerous—disturbingly so) and far more lucrative. Yet, as Marx, Bridges, and countless others understood, the work process is what generates working-class consciousness and solidarity. Assuming at least some truth to that idea, it seems impossible to contend that, overall, the ILWU—and other unions—benefited from containers. Paradoxically, what financially benefited individual members hurt the union and the larger cause.[48]

Fast forwarding to current times, it also cannot be denied that dockworkers remain among the most heavily unionized and militant workers in the world. The next chapter demonstrates that containers clearly did not eliminate dockworker power or cause them to forget their long histories of militancy and commitment to (black) labor internationalism. Far from it. Though weakened, dockworkers in both ports lost neither their will nor their ability to use their power on behalf of global solidarity struggles.

6

"STRIKING" FOR SOCIAL JUSTICE: BLACK AND LABOR INTERNATIONALISM ON THE WATERFRONTS

Interfere with the foreign policy of the country? Sure as hell! That's
our job, that's our privilege, that's our right, that's our duty.

—"Harry Bridges," *Bill Moyers' Journal*

There is a ghostly galleon / that plies the southern seas, / it carries
death for working folk, / cannons and RPGs
It tried to dock in Durban / To drop its deadly load / but the
Durban Dockers' Union / Upheld the workers' code

—John Eppel, "Ghostly Galleon"

On November 24, 1984, the Dutch cargo ship *Nedlloyd Kimberley* docked at San Francisco's Pier 80 loaded with goods from South Africa. Rather than do their job, the dockworkers—members of ILWU Local 10—refused to touch the South African auto parts, steel, and wine, though they unloaded the rest of the ship's cargo. For eleven days, as hundreds protested daily and the boycott made national news, the tainted goods remained in the hold. The workers timed their action quite well, just two weeks after the landslide reelection of President Ronald Reagan, widely seen as an opponent of US labor unions and ally of the apartheid regime. If Reagan intended to continue his assault on unions, the ILWU had given notice of its presence and power. Coincidentally, the boycott began just three days after several African American leaders were arrested for sitting in at the South African embassy in Washington, DC; their civil disobedience launched a year in which more than four thousand people were jailed as part of the burgeoning Free South

Africa Movement in the United States. Adding another chapter to its long history of fighting for social justice, the boycott reaffirmed Local 10's commitment to racial equality and freedom worldwide, though it proved among the few US unions willing to undertake such militant action on behalf of South Africa.[1]

On April 21, 2008, the Chinese ship *An Yue Jiang* docked in Durban, "Carrying three million rounds of ammunition for AK-47 assault rifles and small arms, 3,500 mortars and mortar tubes as well as 1,500 rocket propelled grenades." President Robert Mugabe of Zimbabwe, the authoritarian leader of South Africa's landlocked neighbor, had purchased this arsenal to retain power during that year's highly contested election, when Mugabe's military and police beat thousands and killed hundreds of Zimbabweans. A most shocking event occurred when Mugabe's forces brutally assaulted his political opponent, the recent winner of the election's first round and, not coincidentally, a trade union leader. Rather than unloading the military supplies, the Durban branch of SATAWU boycotted the ship in solidarity with the Zimbabwean workers then leading the opposition. Subsequently, dockworkers in several other southern African nations refused to work the ship, which returned to China with its cargo. This work stoppage was not the first or last time SATAWU used its power in solidarity with political causes in other lands and echoed Durban dockworkers' earlier activism in the struggle against apartheid.[2]

This chapter examines how and why dockworkers in both the San Francisco Bay Area and Durban engaged in repeated boycotts that demonstrated their robust working-class solidarity. For decades, perhaps even millennia, dockworkers have been international-minded, more inclined than most to see immediate, local struggles in larger contexts as a result of the global nature of shipping. Dockworkers in both ports combined their internationalist, antiauthoritarian ideals with power on the waterfront to advocate for black freedom abroad. "Labor internationalism," a concept defined by global labor history proponent Marcel van der Linden, refers to "*the collective actions of a group of workers in one country who set aside their short-term interests as a national group on behalf of a group of workers in another country, in order to promote their long-term interests as members of a transnational class.*" Such notions might seem outdated in the context of the global domination of neoliberalism in the twenty-first century, an era of hypercharged capitalism, and unionism's decline the world over in recent decades. These workers, however, grounded their ideals in the reality that they possessed vital skills and occupied a central position in the global economy. Together with their culture of militancy and long history of stopping trade, their actions challenge the notion that workers are powerless to shape their world.[3]

The main events in this chapter exemplified black internationalism, a global movement of politically conscious blacks, who believed they shared much with all people of African descent, which greatly expanded in the postwar era and continues today. The members of ILWU Local 10 who led their union's anti-apartheid efforts were leftist African Americans who fought for racial equality at home and liberation in African nations, which Russell Rickford called "Left Pan Africanism," an ideology that identified capitalism, imperialism, and racism as a triple-headed monster. Leftist whites, both old-style communists and New Leftists, also joined the fight against apartheid. In the Bay Area of the 1970s and 1980s, after much of the fervor of 1960s social movements dwindled, Local 10 continued inspiring others, especially in the anti-apartheid movement. So, too, Durban SATAWU members' refusal to unload weaponry in solidarity with the union-led Zimbabwean opposition seeking to defeat Mugabe, whose long reign had descended into authoritarianism. Their boycott was tinged with sadness from Mugabe's support for the anti-apartheid struggle as a leader of a "frontline" state. Though mindful that the Zimbabwean nation and people actively had opposed apartheid, Durban dockworkers condemned Mugabe for disregarding the will of Zimbabweans by brutally suppressing the peaceful democratic opposition. Dockworkers in both Durban and the San Francisco Bay Area held black internationalist beliefs and, enhanced by their central role at choke points of the global economy, sought to shape politics in lands outside their own.[4]

Dockworkers and Transnational Solidarity

As discussed, dockworkers are unusually cosmopolitan, for they know much more about the world, by virtue of their work, than many other humans. The nature of marine transport—moving goods, people, and information—explains why dockworkers (as well as sailors) are so worldly even if some lack access to much formal education. Of course, simply knowing people and becoming familiar with ideas from other lands hardly guarantees empathy or class unity and, as Philip Bonner, Jonathan Hyslop, and Lucien van der Walt have contended, might result in the opposite happening: "Cosmopolitan contexts can as easily accentuate differences as limit their significance." Although that possibility is undeniable, dockworkers led incredibly cosmopolitan lives. Indeed, they give the lie to the notion that only the middle or upper class can be cosmopolitan. Working-class activists might not fit Gramsci's notion of "organic intellectuals," but this chapter suggests they should be considered "blue-collar cosmopolitans," to use James Barrett's term. For instance, San Francisco longshoreman Eric Hoffer kept a journal in which he frequently jotted down where the ship he worked originated, its sort of cargo, and the nationalities of seamen he met, such as "December 31 [1958]: Six hours on the German ship *Ditmar Koel* at Pier 15–17. We discharged cars." He worked steel, copra, asbestos, automobiles, newsprint, frozen fish, rice, and other commodities from Chile, Germany, Holland, Japan, Norway, and elsewhere. He also read, constantly, about national and international events, as well as philosophy. He was hardly alone on the waterfront. Similarly, Durban dockworkers met sailors from other parts of Africa, Europe (especially Britain and Holland), and the Indian Ocean world, including Australia. Dockworkers, with their access to information and people who themselves traveled the seven seas, interpreted their lives, work, and world through a global lens.[5]

Occasionally, dockworkers become internationalist in both thought and deed, joining what Peter Linebaugh and Marcus Rediker called the "hydrarchy." In their classic work, *The Many-Headed Hydra*, they deployed this concept to describe "the self-organization" of maritime workers, who "had ways of their own—their own language, stories, and solidarity." Shipping was "both an engine of capitalism," they wrote, "*and* a setting of resistance" for the hydrarchy posed a serious challenge to capitalism. Some political ideologies might be more overtly international than others, but the socialism that emerged in the era of industrial capitalism clearly has international intentions. Many dockworkers, including those in Durban and San Francisco Bay Area, embraced the hydrarchy by way of communist, syndicalist (in unions including the IWW), and other socialist strands that demanded transnational thought and action. The IWW, for instance, understood capitalism as a global phenomenon and, thus, advocated a global movement of workers; witness their name: Industrial Workers of the World. Wobbly and other syndicalist-minded sailors traveled far and wide, from the 1900s through 1930s, spreading their internationalist ideas to South Africa and elsewhere, as Jonathan Hyslop explored. Following in Wobbly footsteps, if not always consciously, communist dockworkers and sailors continued some IWW traditions, especially in the Popular Front 1930s. Holger Weiss, for example, wrote extensively on the International of Seamen and Harbour Workers, part of the Communist International, which organized global protests against fascist Japan for invading China and, similarly, against fascist Italy after its invasion of Ethiopia. Independently, San Francisco longshoremen (with support from the Pacific Coast District) refused to load scrap iron for Japan in 1935 to protest the Manchurian invasion. Conservative ideologies also sometimes motivated dock activism; for instance, ILA locals in New York City occasionally boycotted Soviet cargo during the Cold War, most recently in 1980–81 after the Soviets invaded Afghanistan. Although many workers are not internationalist, the propensity of dockworkers to embrace such ideals is remarkable.[6]

In keeping with such ideals, dockworkers helped established a global transport workers' federation. Along with sailors, in 1896 dockworkers created an organization that, a few years later, expanded to include land-based transport and renamed itself the International Transport Workers' Federation (ITF), among the first multinational labor union federations in world history. It should come as little surprise after considering that goods move across municipal, regional, and national borders. Historian Johanna Wolf highlighted two other vital points in its creation.

First, "British workers wanted to limit the recruitment of cheap foreign labour and established this kind of cooperation to protect themselves against strike-breakers," though they also acted in solidarity with striking dockworkers in Rotterdam and Hamburg. Second, they organized the ITF prior to the establishment of national unions in marine transport, suggesting that the affinities of maritime workers from many countries trumped their national loyalties. Building on these links, van der Linden noted, "the International Transport Workers' Federation has frequently played a leading role in transnational collective action." Although apartheid might have been the primary target for decades, dock unions still undertake boycotts, strikes, and protests in transnational solidarity, notably in 1997 when dockworkers in many ports, including Oakland, refused to unload the *Neptune Jade*, which had been loaded by replacement workers during a nasty strike in Liverpool. Sociologist Katy Fox-Hodess recently investigated how Greek, Portuguese, and English affiliates of the International Dockworkers Council continue this tradition into the 2010s.[7]

Some dockworker (and sailor) unions belonged to other multinational labor organizations. In the 1920s and 1930s, communist dock and sailor unions affiliated with the Red International of Trade Unions (also known as Profintern), the trade union arm of the Comintern, when the Soviet Union sought to foster—and control—such networks. Weiss convincingly argued that the Profintern-affiliated International of Seamen and Harbor Workers "was intrinsically directed towards building international solidarity not only in words but in deeds by actively highlighting an anti-colonial, anti-imperial and anti-racial agenda." After World War II, organized dockworkers and sailors belonged to one of two rivals, the Soviet-led World Federation of Trade Unions or the International Confederation of Free Trade Unions, with members across the noncommunist world. Despite mutual hostility, unions in both the World Federation of Trade Unions and the International Confederation of Free Trade Unions provided financial, moral, and rhetorical assistance to the anti-apartheid struggle. For instance, historian Rebecca Gumbrell-McCormick claimed, "The victory of the South African people in their struggle for democracy, and of the South African workers in their fight for free trade unionism, was also one of the most important successes in the history of the ICFTU." However, Hakan Thorn countered that "the strong 'anti-communism' within ICFTU did not make ANC [African National Congress] popular, since its main union ally at this time was SACTU (South African Congress of Trade Unions), that was affiliated to the communist-dominated WFTU (World Federation of Trade Unions)."[8]

Cold War politics aside, dockworkers played a particularly important role in the global struggle against apartheid. Unions in many countries stood at the forefront of organizing yet have received short shrift in historical accounts of the global anti-apartheid movement. Thorn, in his comparative history of the struggles in Britain and Sweden, notes one potential obstacle: "support for isolation [via boycotts or divestment] might have been limited by the fact that it could be seen to contradict the 'self-interest' of the organizations, since it could have the consequence of creating unemployment." Perhaps that explained why dockworkers engaged in direct action. In addition to ILWU Local 10, dockworkers in Australia, Denmark, New Zealand, and elsewhere also refused to unload South African cargo. Australian dockworkers and sailors, as Peter Limb documented, stood at the forefront of anti-apartheid activism in their nation. I find it interesting to note that the ILA refused to work cargo from southern Africa a few times. On October 10, 1963, the year after Local 10 longshoremen refused to unload South African cargo (to be discussed shortly), nearly one hundred people protested a South African Marine Corporation ship in Brooklyn, and Local 1814 longshoremen—as planned—refused to cross this community picket line; this action consciously copied the earlier San Francisco one verbatim. A decade later, in 1974, ILA longshoremen in Mobile, Alabama, refused to unload South African coal. Although their primary motive was respecting a picket line of Alabama union miners (largely white and concerned about their own jobs), the mostly black longshoremen also sympathized with freedom movements in South Africa and Rhodesia, especially after hearing from the North American representative of the Zimbabwean African National Union. Also in the 1970s, radical black and white longshoremen in Baltimore and other ports occasionally protested Rhodesian chromium.[9]

Black dockworkers in Durban and the San Francisco Bay Area belonged to a centuries-long tradition of international-minded black mariners. Jeffery Bolster documented how well represented black men were at sea and Risa Faussette analyzed their "working-class radicalism" in port cities. Indeed, going back centuries, "The power of transatlantic Pan-Africanism," as Linebaugh and Rediker wrote, "frightened the slaveowning ruling class; in response, Charleston's rulers immediately passed the 1822 Negro Seamen Act, which permitted the sheriff to board any incoming vessel and to arrest any black sailor for the duration of the ship's stay." This fear was justified as black sailors boasted about the Haitian Revolution that, as Linebaugh and Rediker suggested, should be understood as "the first successful workers' revolt in modern history" and distributed abolitionist propaganda including David Walker's incendiary *Appeal*. In the twentieth century, Claude McKay, the Jamaican-born, Harlem-based leftist and author of *Banjo* (1929), which featured globetrotting radical black mariners, as did Senegalese filmmaker Ousmane Sembene in *Le Docker Noir* (1956), both set in Marseilles. McKay, for a while, was a sailor (so, too, the great African American poet Langston Hughes) and Sembene, a dockworker. The solidarity actions of black dockworkers in Durban and San Francisco, hence, must be placed in this long tradition of internationalism among black maritime workers, who also made the 1935 Italian invasion of Ethiopia a cause célèbre.[10]

The Praxis of Local 10: "Striking" Apartheid

Although South Africans led the struggle against apartheid, people around the globe contributed to perhaps the most impressive social movement in the postwar world. In the San Francisco Bay Area, a cadre of dockworkers helped lead the local fight. Despite anticommunist repression during the Cold War and the container revolution—either of which could have destroyed it—the ILWU, led by Local 10, condemned apartheid and periodically undertook direct actions in solidarity with South Africa's black majority. Most notably, in 1984, shortly after Ronald Reagan's reelection, members of the ILWU Bay Area branches, Locals 10 and 34, refused to handle South African cargo for eleven days. Arguably the defining event in the history of the Bay Area anti-apartheid movement, this action inspired growing numbers of people to join the cause. For many in Local 10's black majority, supporting the fight against apartheid can be explained by Komozi Woodward's notion of "fictive kinship" that existed between black peoples on the African continent and in the African diaspora. Believers in Pan-Africanism, Local 10's black anti-apartheid activists also took inspiration from the socialist ideal that all workers shared an identity and an agenda. Of course, their jobs made it easy for longshoremen—irrespective of their ethnicity, nationality, or race—to conceive of capitalism as a global system.[11]

Local 10's *Nedlloyd Kimberley* boycott belonged to their lengthy tradition of work stoppages for political ends. Since its inception, radicals in Local 10—sometimes with the support of elected leaders, local or international—boycotted ships in solidarity with workers suffering in other countries. Herb Mills, a Local 10 leader and historian, explained:

> The International Longshore and Warehouse Union (ILWU) has a long history of rank-and-file action in support of domestic and international issues of social justice. That history for its Local 10 of San Francisco dockworkers began in 1935—less than a year after the monumental 1934 west coast maritime strike—when it refused to load nickel, brass and zinc destined for the Italian Fascist war machine then ravaging Abyssinia [Ethiopia]. Shortly thereafter, the members of 10 also refused to load scrap iron destined for a Japan bent upon ruling the nations of Asia. Such actions were in part underwritten by the still very powerful spirit of the 1934 struggle.

Harry Bridges's quote introducing this chapter justified the ILWU refusal to load cargo intended for fascist Japan forty years earlier: Ordinary citizens and workers have the right and obligation, in a democracy, to engage in global politics, especially when elected leaders prioritize politics as well as trade over humans. Bridges' statement also should be understood in the context of the unpopular imperialist US war in Southeast Asia. Yet despite his bold claim, politically motivated work

stoppages by ILWU members ceased in the late 1930s until 1962, with the first boycott of South African cargo. A combination of factors explains this gap, including
the US involvement in World War II (in which Bridges and other communist and
communist-party-aligned unionists took a no-strike pledge), Cold War repression, and containerization, along with Bridges's shift toward moderation and accommodation.[12]

Rank-and-file activists—sometimes in opposition to elected leaders at the local or international level—resumed boycotting ships from authoritarian, fascist,
or racist nations. Local 10 rank-and-filers planned to boycott Chilean ships under
the regime of General Augusto Pinochet, although, as Lou Goldblatt commented,
"Some of the actions taken by the longshoremen, like the refusal to handle cargo
to Chile after the assassination of [Socialist] President [Salvador] Allende, were
a bit difficult to implement because of the penalty provisions involved." Nevertheless, in 1978, Local 10 activists, supported by a host of groups—including the
Bay Area Trade Union Committee for Chile—refused to load US-made military
supplies intended for Pinochet's military. In the 1980s, the ILWU also protested
military dictatorships in El Salvador, South Korea, and the Philippines. The stance
that Local 10 took against apartheid South Africa belongs to this tradition, eighty
years old so far.[13]

Notably, Bay Area dockworkers' actions totally contradicted those of the mainstream US labor movement, particularly the AFL-CIO's top leadership. The AFL-
CIO, which included nearly all labor unions in the United States, embraced a Cold
War, that is, more conservative form of internationalism—including in support of
the apartheid regime. Bill Minter, a leading US anti-apartheid activist and historian,
wrote, "The negative impact of the Cold War dominates this period. There is little
question that U.S.-Soviet rivalry fostered division among progressive groups and
reduced popular identification with anticolonialism and with Africa." Similarly,
Steve Striffler noted that, during the 1970s and 1980s, when Latin Americans sought
international allies to combat US-backed military regimes, the AFL-CIO proved
invisible or worse. Accordingly, almost no US-based labor solidarity occurred from
the 1950s into the 1990s. In short, Local 10's contributions to labor internationalism,
including the struggle against apartheid, are noteworthy for standing in opposition
to the mainstream US labor movement, particularly DC-based officials.[14]

South Africa's anti-apartheid community first developed the strategy to boycott South African products and businesses and, over time, sympathetic groups
and individuals around the world heeded their call. After the Sharpeville massacre in 1960, the American Committee on Africa (ACOA), the leading US organization involved in African liberation solidarity work, called upon consumers to
boycott South African goods and the government to enact sanctions. ACOA cited
ANC president Albert Luthuli, awarded the Nobel Prize that year, as justification:

"Economic boycott is one way in which the world at large can bring home to the South African authorities that they must either mend their ways or suffer for them." The ILWU Longshore Caucus endorsed such boycotts the same year. Luthuli also found an ally in Dr. Martin Luther King Jr., who coauthored a letter with Luthuli in 1962 that ruefully noted, "The apartheid republic is a reality today only because the peoples and governments of the world have been unwilling to place her in quarantine." Although the ILWU and Dr. King embraced boycotts, President John F. Kennedy opposed them so the US could maintain political and trade relations.[15]

Into this breach and in coordination with ACOA, Local 10 members stopped work to protest apartheid, the only exception to the cessation of direct action under Bridges. Mary Louise Hooper, a leading US anti-apartheid activist and friend of Luthuli's whom the South African government had expelled a few years prior, coordinated with the ILWU as part of a series of events commemorating Human Rights Day. On December 17, 1962, Hooper, the West Coast Representative of ACOA, led picketing of the Dutch ship *Raki*, which arrived at San Francisco Pier 19 loaded with asbestos, coffee, and hemp from South Africa. This action sought to raise awareness of the horrors of apartheid and encourage the United States

Fig. 9. This 1962 boycott of South African cargo probably was the first such action in the United States. Perhaps no US union proved more committed to the struggle against apartheid. Image used with permission from ILWU Library.

to join a global boycott of South African goods. Members of the National Association for the Advancement of Colored People, Northern California Committee for Africa, and the Congress of Racial Equality joined the ACOA in picketing the *Raki*, part of the long-standing tradition of African American support for African freedom struggles. More than one hundred Local 10 members refused to cross this community picket line, leaving the ship unloaded for several shifts. A South African newspaper, *Spark*, quoted one union official, quite possibly Bill Chester, who described this action thus: "We traditionally don't go through picket lines . . . We understand the situation in South Africa and we're certainly against what's going on down there." Chester, ILWU regional director for northern California and the international's highest-ranking African American, had worked closely with Hooper in planning the boycott. Chester had a long history of civil-rights activism in the Bay Area, having served on the ACOA's northern California board of directors, among other posts he held. A few months, later the *Dispatcher* published a thank-you from John Gaetsewe, the London-based acting secretary-general of SACTU, exiled after much bitter persecution. This letter partially illuminated the networks that existed among the ILWU, US anti-apartheid activists, and South African exiles in the United States, Great Britain, and across Africa. Almost certainly, Local 10's boycott was the first anti-apartheid action undertaken by a labor union in US history.[16]

Durban Dockers' Transnational Activism

For eighty years and counting, Durban dockers periodically have struck on behalf of equality and freedom for (black) workers in South Africa and beyond. They undertook these politically motivated stoppages despite racist oppression and threats to their livelihood from the emergence of containers. In South African historiography, the phrase "social-movement unionism" applies to unions that actively fought apartheid and, generally, engaged in actions in support of the larger community in the 1970s and '80s. In that era, vigorous debates existed among activists over whether unions should participate in the struggle; those labeled "workerist" generally wanted to keep union organizing separate and "populist" unions supported direct and coordinated involvement. Steven Friedman explained that "This debate had originally centred on the appropriate role for the union movement— 'workerists' wanted to shield the labour movement from the nationalism of the ANC and its United Democratic Front ally while 'populists' saw an alliance with the nationalist movement as essential to the defeat of apartheid." Friedman, though, falsely conflated a desire by unionists to act independently of the Congress Alliance with being apolitical; after all, nearly all black workers and their unions opposed apartheid, but some believed in using different means or wanted to keep political and economic activism distinct. Durban dockers, as discussed, frequently engaged in workplace actions that aided the struggle and in coordination with it before they belonged to a union. Much more recently, dockers in Durban's SATAWU branch (their union still belonging to COSATU) stopped work in solidarity with the labor-led opposition in both Zimbabwe and Swaziland.[17]

A political boycott in 1935 is the first documented case of Durban dockers' subaltern activism in solidarity with fellow Africans. That year, fascist Italy invaded Ethiopia, perhaps the last African nation free of imperialism's grip. Antifascists and leftists worldwide condemned the invasion and sought to support Ethiopia; naturally, many of the most vociferous and active supporters were black themselves. Indeed, black leftists in Africa, Europe, North America, and the West Indies—often in conjunction with communist unions and parties—took the lead. For instance, the International of Seamen and Harbour Workers and International Trade Union Committee of Negro Workers, both part of the Communist International, organized global protests against Italy as well as against fascist Japan for invading China. Durban dockers would have regularly talked with black sailors and others sympathetic to the Ethiopian cause; historian Gopalan Balachandran brilliantly documented the experiences of Indian sailors, some of whom possessed anti-imperialist and socialist views. They also could have read about the invasion and protests in the International of Seamen and Harbour Workers monthly; Peter Linebaugh wrote about its "revolutionary newspaper, *The Negro Worker*, on which George Padmore worked, was passed from hand-to-hand by black sailors in Hamburg, Marseilles, and African and North American ports."[18]

In response, Durban dockers refused to load frozen meat aboard the *Perla*, intended for Italian invaders in Ethiopia. When asked by a *Natal Mercury* reporter why they stopped work when the Italians would "civilize" the natives, one docker countered, "It would be civilisation for the financial gain of Italy at the expense of the Native." This worker continued: "you can be sure that the Native would get a very small look in anything which was being done for the apparent benefit of the country." Similarly, the Durban Committee of the South African Communist Party declared, "If we, workers of South Africa, allow this food to be sent to East Africa, we shall be helping Mussolini to conquer and enslave the people of Abyssinia." Though the possibility of being replaced amid a labor surplus did not intimidate the dockers, the police did. They loaded the *Perla* after police forcibly dispersed a picket line. Dockers in Cape Town also refused to load cargo for Italy's army. The *Negro Worker* reported that black dockers in Luderitz Bay, South-West Africa (now Namibia, but then controlled by the South African government under League of Nations mandate), refused to work an Italian vessel too. The dockers' actions reconfirm that they were well informed about international affairs *and* opposed European imperialism.[19]

That Durban dockers paid attention to world affairs and regularly spoke with other maritime workers is beyond question. Just as Eric Hoffer talked to foreign seamen on San Francisco piers and read the news voraciously, so did Durban dockers. Some of these Indian colonial sailors, whom Balachandran noted numbered in the tens of thousands, might have informed Durban dockers or, perhaps, African American sailors did. In the nineteenth century, Keletso Atkins discussed the many African American seafarers who worked US whaling ships and docked at Durban and other southern African ports. She wrote, "subversive information was conveyed [to South African dockers] we believe by 'sea kaffirs' from the African Diaspora." There is every reason to believe this practice continued into the early twentieth century, as proven by Robert Trent Vinson in his wonderful book, *The Americans Are Coming!* Vinson documented African American sailors who brought Marcus Garvey's ideas, including his cry of "Africa for the Africans" to South Africa. Further proof of Durban waterfront workers' interest in world affairs comes from Bernard Magubane, who became a leading historian and anti-apartheid activist in exile. In his memoir, Magubane recalled that his illiterate father, who worked as a Durban ship painter in the midtwentieth century, brought newspapers home to the family so that his son could read them aloud to keep up with current events.[20]

Not until the 1970s does evidence emerge of further transnational solidarity on the part of Durban dockers. In late 1971 and early 1972, as many as twenty thousand workers struck in Ovamboland in South-West Africa (now Namibia); they did so to protest apartheid conditions in workplaces, particularly the mines. To suppress these strikes that rocked the entire country, local police and South African military forces used brutal force that killed ten strikers and wounded numerous others. As historians Jabulani Sithole, Sifiso Ndlovu, and S. Mohlongo wrote, the Ovamboland strike inspired many South Africans, who viewed it as an assault on apartheid. Not coincidentally, less than one year later, Durban dockers struck, followed by nearly one hundred thousand additional black and Indian workers. All of South Africa shook and, as Robinduth Toli concluded, "the Durban dock worker strikes were a forerunner of the 1973 strikes and foreshadowed a reawakening of black worker struggles in the 1970s." The early 1970s, then, witnessed a renewed push for black freedom, led by workers, across southern Africa. Loet Douwes Dekker and others even more forcefully argue for the centrality of worker activism in that era: "in a political system as tightly controlled by a dominant minority as in South and South West Africa, one of the few points of leverage at the disposal of the dominated majority lies in the use of what here can be roughly termed as 'labour power.'"[21]

Also in the early 1970s, the armed struggle for independence in neighboring Mozambique and Angola, both Portuguese colonies, crescendoed as the apartheid regime feared the effects on blacks in South Africa and South-West Africa. Ships regularly stopped in both Durban and the Mozambican capital of Lourenço

Marques (now Maputo), and so it is unsurprising that authorities worried. In 1974, South African activists planned a series of rallies to celebrate the announcement of Mozambican independence. The South African Students' Organisation, cofounded by Black Consciousness leader Steven Biko, declared it, "a revelation that every bit of Africa shall yet be free." Yet before a South African Students' Organisation rally in support of Mozambican independence could occur in Durban, local and national authorities effectively undermined it. In 1975, the apartheid regime continued monitoring black South Africans who might celebrate formal Mozambican independence, which, everyone understood, also was a cry for freedom in South Africa. R. F. Drew, the acting manager of Bantu Affairs in Durban's Central District, sent a confidential memo to divisional heads about "Rumoured Strikes." The agency feared dockers and other black workers would strike "on or around 26th June 1975, to coincide with Mozambique independence day." The report warned activists also might use the celebration of freedom in Mozambique "for the distribution of subversive literature" and urged everyone to report any issues "immediately to the South African Police." Another special meeting of the city's Bantu Affairs' Sub-Committee on Labour and Transport, in 1975, reiterated that what transpired among Durban harbor workers "was of national importance in bringing in foreign capital." Their alarm was accentuated by the Pan-Africanist nature of the Mozambique Liberation Front (Frente de Libertação de Moçambique in Portuguese) and its leaders, Eduardo Mondlane and Samora Machel. Machel, the first president of the People's Republic of Mozambique, soon declared, "we will provide all necessary assistance to the ANC-led people's liberation struggle and the South African people's resistance to this inhumane form of racism known as apartheid, so that they can attain complete economic and social emancipation." Ultimately, Durban dockers did not strike, though the regime's ongoing fear continued even after containerization drastically reduced and weakened the workers.[22]

San Francisco Longshore Workers Boycott Apartheid, Again

The global struggle against apartheid also surged in the 1970s, as solidarity efforts expanded in the wake of protests inside South Africa. The 1973 Durban strikes, preceded and influenced by the 1972 dock strike, shook the nation out of a repression-induced "quiet decade." Then the 1976 uprising of black students in Soweto, despite ferocious repression, took the movement to the next level. Black freedom movements engulfed southern Africa, as Mozambique and Angola achieved freedom in 1975 and the armed struggle in southern Rhodesia heated up. Events across the subcontinent resulted in the dramatic expansion of global solidarity. In the San Francisco Bay Area, radical rank-and-filers in ILWU Local 10 created the Southern African Liberation Support Committee (SALSC) to support these struggles. Black and white longshoremen's efforts catapulted them to the front of the burgeoning global anti-apartheid movement. Far less well known than other US opponents of apartheid—and entirely ignored in the historiography—San Francisco Bay Area dockworkers proved deeply committed and, ultimately, contributed to the downfall of white minority rule in South Africa.

Black members of SALSC generally embraced Pan-Africanism or socialism if not both. Many of the black (and all the white) activists identified as socialists or radical unionists who saw South Africans as fellow members of the global working class exploited by white South Africans and multinationals solely interested in profits. At least some black dockworkers involved also expressed a shared identity, Komozi's "fictive kinship," for peoples in (southern) Africa who—in the 1970s— still suffered under colonialism's whip. Predictably, San Francisco Bay Area black longshoremen had much in common with other African American opponents of apartheid. Africana scholar Francis Njubi Nesbitt categorized blacks who joined the struggle as holding leftist, nationalist, or liberal beliefs—with the leftists and nationalists sharing anti-imperialist views and the nationalists divided into economic and cultural camps. Although not all black Local 10 members were socialists, SALSC leaders were, following Nesbitt's left side of the black nationalist spectrum. Rickford's recent exploration of black power schools in the late 1960s and 1970s refined Nesbitt—namely, in the 1970s black power adherents split into racial and left Pan-African groups with the latter describing those in the SALSC. Leo Robinson, for instance, was both an African American and a communist who regularly critiqued capitalism, imperialism, and racism and first became really interested in South Africa during the Soweto uprising in 1976. Shortly after, Local 10's membership voted in favor of Robinson's resolution and established a committee dedicated to helping free the peoples of southern Africa. Robinson, widely acknowledged as the ILWU leader of this cause, enjoyed pointing out that the rank-and-file created the SALSC, the first "anti-apartheid labor committee" (his term) in the US labor movement. The group's name highlights the fact that the fight against apartheid belonged to interlocking struggles across the subcontinent. Subsequently, this committee, consisting mostly of African Americans, engaged in numerous actions over fifteen years in solidarity with South Africa, Mozambique, Rhodesia, and beyond.[23]

Local 10 anti-apartheid activists held a variety of socialist ideologies, among them communist, syndicalist, and Trotskyist. In addition to Robinson, committed SALSC members included Dave Stewart, an African American active in the Coalition of Black Trade Unionists; Bill Proctor, a white leftist raised by a stepfather who was a well-known black communist in Local 10; Larry Wright, white, raised by communist parents, and deeply involved in New Left anti-imperialist politics, including the Liberation Support Movement; Howard Keylor, an older white leftist and former Communist Party member deeply committed to antiracist struggles; and Charlie Jones and Leron "Ned" Ingram, both African Americans and Coalition of Black Trade Unionist members. "Politically, our Committee is a diverse group," wrote core member Wright, "but we are all in support of peoples' struggles for self-determination and independence from imperialism." The SALSC and a separate, smaller Trotskyist group of Local 10 and Local 6 militants, with Keylor in a leading role, raised awareness about apartheid and colonialism while preparing dockworkers for direct action. The committee occasionally worked with the AFL-CIO via the Coalition of Black Trade Unionists, a caucus of militant African Americans that played a leading role in the US anti-apartheid movement in the 1970s and '80s. SALSC also worked with other unionists, students, and religious people in the Bay Area and all along the West Coast.[24]

All these longshoremen, those involved in the SALSC as well as the Trotskyists, saw black South Africans as workers oppressed by a racist, capitalist regime and believed direct action the best method to attack apartheid. Not opposed to consumer boycotts or government sanctions, radical unionists believed working-class power to be strongest on the job and so, accordingly, pushed to boycott South African cargo. Direct action tactics harkened back to the IWW, the most radical union in the early twentieth century; recall the ILWU motto and most basic principle was and remains "an injury to one is an injury to all," a slogan crafted by the Wobblies. The SALSC received rhetorical support for boycotts from the ILWU leadership, in July 1976, when the International Executive Board "instructed the titled officers to communicate with all locals regarding a boycott of all South African cargo, and to report back at the next meeting." SALSC laid further groundwork by getting Local 10 members to pass a resolution condemning "The white minority governments of South Africa and Rhodesia [that] have by so-called law denied to the black majority of people in both nations *basic human rights* that in effect makes the white minority state the master and the black majorities the slaves."[25]

Local 10 activists soon targeted South African cargo shipped by the Dutch company Nedlloyd. In late 1976 and early 1977, community activists coordinated with the Longshore-Warehouse Militant Caucus to protest the docking of the *Nedlloyd Kimberley*. Then, on Easter Sunday 1977, SALSC coordinated a two-day boycott of the *Kimberley*, part of a week of union actions worldwide against apartheid. A sympathetic Local 10 dispatcher selected workers committed to refusing to cross a community picket. Approximately five hundred people, many from churches, cheered the workers and hoisted banners declaring, "Apartheid is crucifixion." Though the protestors were friendly, the Local 10 workers invoked their contract's "health and safety" clause to justify not crossing the line, allowing them to pull off what outsiders might consider a strike without violating their contract with the PMA. It is interesting that the *Longshore-Warehouse Militant* floated the idea of a strike "to force recognition of black South African longshoremen's unions," though that demand went nowhere at the time.[26]

That same year SALSC collected tons of supplies on behalf of South Africans, Mozambicans, and Zimbabweans involved in liberation struggles. Robinson, Proctor, Stewart, Wright, and a few others worked with churches and community groups to collect clothing, food, medicine, and other essentials, using Local 10's hall in San Francisco as a central depot. They also convinced shipping companies to donate and transport two forty-foot containers free of charge to East Africa. A few dozen dockworkers loaded one of them with goods for ANC exiles in Tanzania, whose numbers soared after the South African government suppressed the Soweto uprising. (In 2006, Robinson met a South African, Steve Nakana, who lived in a Tanzanian camp and told him that SALSC members "had often slipped chewing gum, candy, or dollar bills into the pockets of clothes just before sealing them . . . Nakana, smiling broadly, stood up and said he was one of those who opened such packages. 'It felt like Christmas.'") The second container supplied Zimbabwean refugees in Mozambique during the long and bloody effort to overthrow the white minority government in Rhodesia. An ILWU committee also raised $50,000 for a maternity clinic in Mozambique, then emerging from centuries of brutal Portuguese colonial rule and on the cusp of two decades of war after South Africa sponsored antigovernment forces intended to destabilize a country where blacks had achieved freedom and that had pledged to help overthrow apartheid.[27]

Longshoremen also undertook numerous direct actions that left no paper trail. Sociologist David T. Wellman described Local 10 business agents who patrolled the waterfront, where they carried out what Wellman called "ambushes" to demonstrate union power, challenge employer control, and undermine apartheid. That is, some dockworkers proved particularly vigilant about even the most trifling contract violations on vessels carrying South African cargo in order to disrupt its flow. Richard Austin participated in several such actions in the early 1970s and recalled one: "The company wanted to know how it could get the ship worked. Here is what happened: Cargo from South Africa was discharged and cold-decked. Other non-S.A. cargo was off-loaded, then the S.A. cargo was put back onboard and sailed with the ship. It did not get discharged on the West Coast." San Francisco Bay Area dockworkers had used this below-the-radar method to protest the US war in Vietnam when huge quantities of war materials had shipped out of Oakland.[28]

ILWU activists also screened the documentary film *Last Grave at Dimbaza* to educate people about apartheid and motivate them to join the struggle against it. This powerful movie, secretly filmed in 1973 and smuggled out of South Africa, showed the horrible suffering of black people, who endured such high infant mortality rates that scores of extra graves routinely were dug in anticipation of future deaths. Wright and Robinson showed the film to dozens of audiences up and down the Pacific Coast in the 1970s and 1980s, laying the groundwork for future actions. They paired *Dimbaza* with the documentary *A Luta Continua*, by African American filmmaker Robert Van Lierop, to raise support for Mozambican independence and, more generally, expand support for liberation across southern Africa.[29]

Indeed, an October 1984 screening of *Last Grave at Dimbaza* before about four hundred Local 10 members, approximately half African American, sparked the longest and most important workplace boycott against apartheid in US history. When new business commenced, Keylor offered a motion to boycott the next Nedlloyd ship carrying South African cargo. Robinson seconded the motion with an amendment to boycott only the South African cargo, which passed resoundingly. The timing was apt because, that autumn, a group of black South African union miners had been arrested and faced long prison sentences. San Francisco Bay Area longshore workers had been educated about apartheid by SALSC and Longshore-Warehouse Militant Caucus for nearly a decade and so were primed to act, especially in solidarity with persecuted unionists, just as Local 10 protested authoritarianism in Chile, El Salvador, and elsewhere.[30]

On November 24, 1984, the *Nedlloyd Kimberley*, an older break-bulk (noncontainerized) ship, arrived at San Francisco's Pier 80 carrying South African cargo. Local 10 activists knew of its arrival thanks to Alex Bagwell, an African American in Local 34 (clerks) and Keylor's contacts in Los Angeles. A Local 10 dispatcher "in" on the plan assigned workers committed to the boycott while a sympathetic clerk (called the supercargo) in charge of unloading the entire ship identified the targeted goods. Bill Proctor, a principal activist, dramatically recounted this moment:

> As luck would have it, South African cargo was not the only cargo, so we worked some breakbulk cargo from Argentina as I recall, then after about two hours, from below deck I heard our Ship's Clerk yell up to me, "that's it Proctor, nothing left down here but Razor Wire (Cortina) and Auto Glass from South Africa." I then said, and I shall never forget it: "okay fellas, come on out of the hold, I ain't hoisting one ounce of cargo from South Africa" and the movement of cargo came to a halt, we then left the ship.

For the next ten days, a dispatcher assigned workers who supported the boycott.[31]

In solidarity, many Bay Area residents gathered daily at the pier's gate. Community activists, in fact, also had pushed the longshoremen to boycott. Proctor recalled a group of black women who taught in the San Francisco public schools (presumably unionists) who asked Robinson, "When are you Longshoremen going to do something, and not just take resolutions to your union's convention?" Every day during the boycott, these teachers joined hundreds of others to support the longshoremen, who—after all—were violating their contract. On December 2, for example, about seven hundred people, many from unions, religious groups, and civil-rights organizations, rallied. Much later, as part of the Local 10 education program required for all new members, Robinson described the scene, "You couldn't get from Army and 3rd Street to the gate of Pier 80 because it was jam packed with community organizations and people. A federal judge can't do anything about that." Some also joined the newly created Bay Area Free South Africa Movement. Among those who spoke that week were legendary activist and long-time Bay Area resident Angela Davis. Congressman Ron Dellums, who represented Oakland and Berkeley as perhaps the most radical House of Representatives member, also spoke, as did many others.[32]

As employers sought to end the standoff, and without overt support from international or Local 10 elected leaders, the dockworkers remained steadfast. When the PMA proposed that the ship unload elsewhere, ILWU locals in Stockton, Portland, and Seattle announced, in solidarity, their refusal to touch "hot cargo." The PMA then filed a federal injunction, labeling the work stoppage illegal. Workers forfeited their minimum guaranteed weekly pay, predictably, but—more important—the judge declared that Local 10 would be fined $200,000 per day for failure to comply with the injunction he granted. This injunction also singled out Robinson and Keylor for fines of thousands of dollars per day. By the end of the eleven-day standoff, Local 10 faced more than $2 million in fines. Fearing reprisals, in addition to potential prison time, Local 10 president Larry Wing and secretary-treasurer Tom Lupher asserted the stoppage was not union-sanctioned but, rather, undertaken by individual workers. The *Dispatcher* quoted Lupher, "the workers' boycott . . . was made on an 'individual basis,'" despite the membership clearly having voted to stop work. The international leadership also backed this disingenuous assertion. In addition, Local 10 leaders worked behind the scenes with the Coast Labor Relations Committee (part of the ILWU-PMA grievance machinery) to end the standoff by not contesting the employers' charge that the boycott violated the contract.[33]

Activists were chagrined by their elected leaders' statements, but the union risked enormous fines and, arguably, had few alternatives despite quite possibly (albeit privately) supporting the action. Wing and Lupher were leftists who sympathized with this cause, according to activists Robinson and Heyman, and provided some assistance behind the scenes. International president James R. "Jimmy" Herman, who remained conspicuously absent during the boycott (as did the elderly Bridges), had a long record of fighting for social justice. Bridges had assigned Herman, in the early 1960s, to integrate the nearly all-white Local 34. Along with many in the ILWU, Herman had actively supported the grape workers' strike. A few months after the *Nedlloyd Kimberley* action, as the anti-apartheid movement heated up nationwide in 1985, Herman even was arrested for civil disobedience.

Activists later recalled Herman beaming, in 1990, when Mandela thanked the ILWU for its support.[34]

Finally bowing on the eleventh day to the injunction, Local 10 members unloaded the South African cargo. Some, including Keylor, Heyman, and others in the Militant Longshore-Warehouse Caucus, argued the boycott should be expanded. Led by Robinson and SALSC, however, most ILWU members endorsed ending the action, believing they had greatly heightened awareness, in the Bay Area and nationwide, of what people could do to combat apartheid. Community activist David Bacon later reflected, "That was the real birth of the anti-apartheid movement in northern California," which became the Bay Area Free South Africa Movement.[35]

The ILWU also embraced divestment, which became increasingly popular in the 1980s. In 1978, the ILWU first discussed pulling investments in the ILWU-PMA Pension Fund from any company operating in South Africa. Similarly, energized residents in Berkeley, Oakland, and San Francisco successfully pushed their cities—the area's three largest—to adopt strong divestment policies (Berkeley's, well prior to the *Kimberley* boycott). In 1986, Oakland resident and SALSC leader Larry Wright addressed his city's council to follow Berkeley and divest. When Oakland later closed its accounts with Bank of America, which conducted business in South Africa, "it was the most dramatic application of the city's rigorous new South African divestment ordinance to date. Bank of America lost the city's $150 million investment portfolio and $120 million annual payroll."[36]

The dockworkers' boycott also helped inspire students at the University of California–Berkeley to expand their protests in 1985, the largest and most sustained bout of activism there since the Vietnam War era. Thousands rallied and hundreds erected a shantytown, meant to resemble a South African township, resulting in repeated clashes with police and a heightening of public awareness. Wright and Keylor spoke at rallies on the Berkeley campus with a huge ILWU banner bearing its slogan, "An injury to one is an injury to all," prominently displayed in front of legendary protest site Sproul Hall. Harry Bridges even showed up to support the Berkeley students, as did Herman. The Berkeley protests were among the most significant of any US university, ultimately forcing a very reluctant board of regents to divest relevant portions of its $3 billion endowment. Nobel Prize winner Desmond Tutu later commented, "There is no greater testament to the basic dignity of ordinary people everywhere than the divestment movement of the 1980s."[37]

Furthermore, Local 10 exerted influence on Congressman Ron Dellums, a leader in the effort to impose US sanctions on South Africa. Dellums's father belonged to Local 10, and his uncle Cottrell Laurence "C. L." Dellums probably was the most important black labor and civil-rights activist in California in the midtwentieth century. Elected to Congress in 1970 and ultimately serving thirteen terms, Congressman Dellums strongly supported civil rights, unionism, and African liberation.

Every session he served in Congress, Dellums introduced a sanctions bill and later joined the DC-based Free South Africa Movement, which, in 1984, launched daily sit-ins at the South African embassy just three days prior to the start of the *Kimberley* boycott. Dellums wrote about the latter event in his autobiography: "we were elated that people were acting on their own to seize the moment to express their outrage with U.S. foreign policy and the apartheid regime." Local 10's actions truly had national reach but perhaps never more so than when Congress, shepherded by Dellums, overrode President Reagan's controversial veto and passed sanctions.[38]

The ILWU—and the Bay Area—proved so important that Nelson Mandela visited Oakland during his first US tour in 1990, shortly after being released from twenty-seven years in prison. As Ben Magubane, who helped organize Mandela's visit, wrote, "Each city chosen had a particular significance for our struggle." After listening to freedom songs presented by local choir Vukani Mawethu, founded by an ANC exile and to which ILWU activist Alex Bagwell and his wife belonged, Mandela singled out the dockworkers before sixty thousand at the Oakland Coliseum: "We salute members of the International Longshore & Warehouse Union Local 10 who refused to unload a South African cargo ship in 1984. In response to this demonstration, other workers, church people, community activists, and educators gathered each day at the docks to express their solidarity with the dockworkers. They established themselves as the frontline of the anti-apartheid movement in the Bay area." Mandela later described how this action belonged to the larger fight: "We were part of a worldwide movement. . . . Just as we watched and learned from the continuing struggle within the United States, so too did activists there gain strength from our struggles." Though the role of unions in the movement has been underappreciated in the United States, that no less a figure as Mandela praised Local 10 speaks volumes.[39]

Durban Boycott in Support for Zimbabwean Democracy

Halfway across the world, Durban dockers repeatedly demonstrated a commitment to social-justice issues beyond their borders, particularly in support of working-class power. In the 1980s and after apartheid fell, they belonged to several unions such as the TGWU, a founding member of COSATU. The largest labor federation in South Africa since it was formed in 1985, COSATU played a central role in the defeat of apartheid and remains part of the ruling "tripartite alliance" with the ANC and the South African Communist Party, albeit as a very junior partner. Like ILWU, COSATU masthead broadcasts the Wobbly motto "An injury to one is an injury to all." Among COSATU unions, several in transportation merged to form the South African Transport and Allied Workers Union (SATAWU) in 2000, the dominant union for transportation workers—maritime, road, and rail. Though fewer in number as a result of containerization, dockers remain a powerful and militant component of SATAWU, with members in Durban, still the largest in the country and sub-Saharan Africa, and every other port. Most dramatically, in 2008, Durban dockers boycotted a ship on behalf of Zimbabwean workers and democracy. This action made tangible the ideal of working-class internationalism and what South African scholar-activists Patrick Bond and Ashwin Desai labeled "foreign policy, bottom-up."[40]

Like most workers in postapartheid South Africa, Durban dockers have experienced a chaotic few decades. At times, it seemed that their collective power had been broken only to rise again, ultimately in SATAWU. As discussed, the two most important factors weakening dockers were containerization and the partial return of casual labor. Millions of other South Africans experienced similar challenges, including new technologies, casualization, a growing informal economy, and a government still struggling to overcome the massive economic and racial inequalities inherited from apartheid. These issues weakened workers, COSATU, and unions generally. Durban dockers' 2008 action, then, demonstrated that they still possessed some power, as well as a commitment to African liberation. Although uncommon, this boycott demands investigation, especially considering growing precariousness, driven by neoliberal policies in South Africa and worldwide, experienced by countless workers.[41]

In 2008, the political crisis in neighboring Zimbabwe reached a boiling point, and many South Africans looked on with interest and sympathy. Elected after independence in 1980, Mugabe held power until 2017. In his final decade of power, he increasingly was condemned—outside Africa but also within—for being a brutal dictator who refused to relinquish power. The truth, of course, is more complicated, especially in the context of left internationalism and Pan-Africanism. First, the two nations share a border and countless cultural, demographic, economic, historical, and political ties. Second, President Mugabe, and the Zimbabwean people, provided much assistance to opponents of apartheid and to future South African president Thabo Mbeki, a long-time ANC leader in exile. Third, during his reign, Mugabe claimed he acted on behalf of the black masses using expressly Marxist rhetoric; for example, the major land redistribution program in which wealthy white farmers lost "their" land was praised by many black Zimbabweans and other Africans, though generally condemned in the West. Nevertheless, Zimbabwe's economic decline and lack of democracy had, over time, resulted in rising opposition to Mugabe in his country as well as South Africa. When Morgan Tsvangirai, the leader of the Movement for Democratic Change and a trade unionist, won a plurality in the 2008 presidential election, Mugabe's forces unleashed terror. A Human Rights Watch report documented that the "government was responsible, at the highest levels, for widespread and systematic abuses that led to the killing

Fig. 10. Dockworkers chose a different approach to promoting democracy in neighboring Zimbabwe than President Thabo Mbeki's "quiet diplomacy" initiative. This cartoon by David "Andy" Anderson appeared in the *Sunday Times* (Johannesburg), April 27, 2008. Image used with permission from David "Andy" Anderson, www.danderson illustration.com.

of up to 200 people, the beating and torture of 5,000 more, and the displacement of about 36,000 people." This ugly conflict regularly made the international news and particularly concerned South Africans and the several million Zimbabwean immigrants and refugees there. Across the world, people looked to Mbeki, a friend of Mugabe, to mediate, but Mbeki asserted that "no crisis" existed in Zimbabwe. Meanwhile, Mbeki's efforts at "quiet diplomacy" behind closed doors and without public criticism failed to resolve the crisis.[42]

Amid these events and less than three weeks after the election, Durban dockers sent shockwaves across southern Africa and made international news by refusing to unload a ship full of weapons intended for Mugabe's regime. Much like ILWU Local 10's actions, SATAWU members in the Planning Department of Transnet, the South African port authority, provided essential information, including which COSCO ship carried the cargo, when it arrived, and where it docked. SATAWU general secretary Randall Howard, also ITF president at the time, coordinated with Provincial Secretary Joseph V. "J. V." Dube, who jumped into action: "I called a meeting of the 20 shop stewards and they got word out to the workers" via text messaging. SATAWU quickly declared, "Our members employed at the Durban Container Terminal will not unload this cargo. Neither will any of our members in the truck driving sector move this cargo." Word quickly spread, and community activists, both Zimbabwean and South African, picketed in solidarity. The ship remained in harbor for several days with its decks still loaded with containers holding millions of rounds of AK-47 ammunition, thousands of mortars, and thousands of RPGs, as confirmed by ITF inspector Sprite Zungu. The South African government, meanwhile, attempted to wash its hands, the BBC quoting South African defence secretary January Masilela: "If the buyer is the Zimbabwean sovereign government and the seller is the Chinese sovereign government, South Africa has nothing to do with that." SATAWU's Howard countered, "The South African government cannot be seen as propping up a military regime." This standoff continued for several days until the *An Yue Jiang* raised anchor and left in search of another port to offload its cargo. A great many people in South Africa, across southern Africa, and worldwide considered this boycott a great victory for Zimbabwean democracy and proof of the potential of transnational solidarity—though Mugabe remained in power.[43]

The reasons for SATAWU's stand were myriad and paralleled the motives of Local 10 activists. In Dube's words, "Our members are very well informed. We opposed what was happening in Zimbabwe. Trade unions have no rights. There is no freedom. Union leaders are victimised, kidnapped, assaulted and arrested. We've been supporting the refugees coming into our country from Zimbabwe, fleeing the repression there." Breaking down Dube's comment, first, many South Africans knew of the crisis in Zimbabwe and sympathized with those challenging the authoritarian regime. They had appreciated Mugabe's and other Zimbabweans' support during the struggle and, thus, regretted the irony of a revolutionary ally acting in antidemocratic ways to maintain power. My interview with Dube and Bhekitemba Simon Gumede, a Transnet shop steward, reiterated their awareness that Zimbabwean unions actively supported the anti-apartheid struggle. Second, the SATAWU educational program for its members proved effective at motivating them to act in solidarity with other workers' struggles. The official slogan of SATAWU, once again, is the same Wobbly one that the ILWU and COSATU also adopted. This boycott, of course, belonged to a much longer and wider history, as Douwes Decker and other South African union activists earlier wrote: "From its earliest days, African trade unionism and worker action in South Africa acted as a vehicle for the articulation of both economic and political grievances."[44]

Another matter was that Durban dockers' commitment to working-class solidarity and peace took precedence over SATAWU's affiliation with COSATU and, thus, over the Tripartite Alliance in which the ANC supported Mugabe. The South African government, particularly the ANC, had been closely allied with Mugabe for decades. When Rhodesia's black majority overthrew its white minority in 1980, the labor movement had played an important role and Mugabe frequently claimed to rule on behalf of the masses. Later, however, when growing numbers of Zimbabweans demanded Mugabe's ouster, trade unionists led the opposition. Mugabe's earlier contributions to fighting apartheid (and other anticolonial struggles) made it painful for South Africans, particularly Mbeki, to criticize Mugabe. More and more, though, South Africans criticized Mbeki for doing nothing while Zimbabwe imploded, especially after Mugabe's Movement for Democratic Change won a plurality in the 2008 election. When asked for SATAWU's motive, Dube answered that they did so in solidarity with Zimbabwean workers and the belief that, if Mugabe acquired more weapons, they would be used to kill Zimbabwean unionists and other civilians. Sandile Gasa, a Durban shop steward, noted that his union acted in opposition to state violence: "As South Africans, by standing up and refusing to off-load these arms, we are proud that we have not contributed to increasing the violence in Zimbabwe." Another steward, Bushy Shandu, echoed Dube and Gasa: "Solidarity is important. . . . [W]e urge people of Africa and abroad to do the same in saving people's lives who are still oppressed by their countries."[45]

As with Local 10's boycotts, many individuals and organizations actively supported and subsequently praised SATAWU. With millions of South African and Zimbabwean members, the dockers received aid from the Anglican Church, particularly the Right Reverend Rubin Phillip, Anglican Bishop of Natal, who had grown up in the Indian township of Clairwood. He belonged to the Black Consciousness Movement led by Steve Biko and served as deputy president of the South African Students' Organisation. Phillip spearheaded legal action to prevent the movement of military supplies through South Africa, in the event dockers were forced to unload the vessel. Zimbabwean refugees and South African allies also demonstrated in solidarity with the dockers at Durban harbor and the Chinese embassy in Pretoria. During and after the boycott, many congratulatory e-mails and letters poured into SATAWU headquarters from Angola, Australia, Canada, China, Germany, Italy, Thailand, the United States, and especially Zimbabwe. One woman's e-mail subject header read "heartfelt thanks from Zimbawe [sic]," and her e-mail declared, "This is a small note with a BIG thank you—for helping stand with us on our road to peaceful change in Zimbabwe." Another woman e-mailed, "Thank you for your involvement in trying to stop arms from making their way to Zimbabwe. We appreciate it because their arrival here would only mean further loss of lives. God bless you." Complimentary e-mails arrived from beyond southern Africa, including one "long-dated friend of the Zimbabwean people in Germany, supporting actively and financially aids orphan organizations in that country"; this man favorably compared the dockers' action to Mbeki's: "since your president's quiet diplomacy has had no positive result in Zimbabwe where it seems 'that there is no crisis' [Mbeki's words]. Go on acting like this and the world will be better tomorrow." Reverend Phillip's petition to a Durban judge also proved a success and forbade the transportation of military supplies overland—though SATAWU also represented South African truck drivers who had promised to join the boycott. The legal situation in Durban proved quite different from that in the San Francisco Bay Area.[46]

Also unlike events in the United States, where Local 10's boycott was opposed or, at least, not celebrated by the ILWU or broader labor movement, COSATU fully embraced the Durban action. While events still unfolded, South Africa's dominant labor federation beamed: "The Congress of South African Trade Unions congratulates its affiliate, the SA Transport and Allied Workers Union, on its historic victory in the fight to prevent the Chinese vessel, *An Yue Jiang*, from unloading its deadly cargo of weapons and ammunition destined for the illegitimate government of Zimbabwe. We shall never know how many lives of Zimbabwean workers will have been saved thanks to SATAWU members' act of international solidarity." That COSATU—part of the ruling alliance—acted in opposition to the ruling ANC, which had secretly approved this military shipment, added another dimension to the political significance. (Indeed, some South Africans advocated that CO-SATU, the most organized branch of the working class, should act independently of or even break with the ANC.) The COSATU press release encouraged dockers in neighboring Mozambique and Angola to follow Durban's lead. COSATU used its connections with these labor federations that also refused to unload the military supplies, earning the praise of South African journalist-activist Azad Essa: "COSATU's resolve and desire to continue its internationalisation against oppressive forces around the world." Essa correctly pointed to the role of COSATU, but he should have focused more precisely upon SATAWU and its members, whose interest in political struggles around the world and willingness to engage in transnational activism initiated the entire boycott.[47]

SATAWU used its own networks, particularly the ITF, to expand the boycott across southern Africa. SATAWU quite actively participated in the ITF, to which the ILWU also belonged, and Durban had hosted its forty-first congress in 2006. Coincidentally, in 2008, SATAWU secretary-general Randall Howard served as ITF president and therefore had that much more sway among global transport workers. Labor unions in Mozambique and Angola belonged, too, and so Howard's advocacy to dockers in those ports fell on sympathetic ears. As noted, dock unions in the ports of Maputo and Luanda refused to work the *An Yue Jiang* that, ultimately, returned to China with its cargo still aboard. ITF unions throughout the world, including Australia, New Zealand, and the United States praised this outcome. In the words of ITF general secretary David Cockcroft, "For over two weeks, working men and women have kept these bullets and bombs out of the hands of Mugabe's killers."[48]

Their nations' legal structures proved another notable difference between the Durban and San Francisco Bay Area actions. The South African constitution legally protected the SATAWU action and a Durban judge ruled in favor of a potential road freight boycott, both in marked contrast to a federal judge in San Francisco, who slapped the ILWU and boycott leaders with injunctions. The constitution ratified in postapartheid South Africa guarantees the right to be in a union and strike (Section 23). By contrast, US worker rights are not enshrined in the US constitution, though one can read the right to collective action in the First Amendment's right to assemble; although most Americans still support unions, worker rights were (and remain) insecure, as witnessed by the PMA's successful legal action in 1984. Thus, SATAWU did not fear a government crackdown—despite blatantly challenging Mbeki and the ANC—but the ILWU did.[49]

Of course, neither SATAWU nor COSATU has the capacity to engineer regime change in Zimbabwe or any other foreign country, leading Geoffrey Wood, Pauline Dibben, and Gilton Klerck to explore the "limits of transnational solidarity." South African unionists, clearly, had only limited success in promoting democracy in Zimbabwe and neighboring Swaziland, the last absolute monarchy in Africa, and where unionists make up the most powerful opposition to its king. Wood et al. provide a vast number of reasons why COSATU's actions failed to create democracy in both Swaziland and Zimbabwe. Unfortunately, they completely ignore the Durban boycott, which offers one possible tactic that COSATU (and these academics) might consider further—direct action where workers do have power: on the job. Ultimately, as with the global movement to support South African liberation, apartheid ended only when a massive social movement, in country, made South Africa "ungovernable." So, too, in other countries. COSATU, alone, cannot democratize a foreign country, though that is quite a high standard to establish for judging transnational solidarity.[50]

Finally, what this incident suggests is that, despite the twin whipsaws of containerization and casualization, SATAWU remains a vital force on the Durban waterfront. Though some scholars, notably Bernard Dubbeld, thoughtfully and impressively chronicled containers' devastating impacts in Durban, his research stopped in the early 1990s, resulting in his conclusion that Durban dockers were permanently weakened. That conclusion proved incorrect. Similarly, though the profound impacts of casualization on South African workers are quite real, Durban dockers have managed to weather that storm, too. Quite recently, scholar Franco Barchiesi made a powerful case for the increasing precariousness of work (and life) in contemporary South Africa. No one who lives there or has visited can deny this troubling reality; his conclusions parallel what people around the world increasingly say about twenty-first-century work. Without contesting Barchiesi's overall thesis, this chapter argues that Durban dockers' actions in 2008—years after he conducted his interviews (none with dockers)—are quite impressive and demand consideration. Barchiesi convincingly wrote about the precariousness of workers and, thus, unions, but (marine) transport does not fit neatly into his model. Indeed, dockers in many ports still hold surprising power, and those in the San Francisco Bay Area and Durban have used theirs particularly well, suggesting the need to appreciate local context as well as the nature of (marine) transportation workers worldwide.[51]

Boycotts on Behalf of Palestinian Independence

Quite recently, the long trajectories of transnational activism by Durban and San Francisco Bay Area dockworkers converged on the cause of Palestinian statehood. From 2009 to 2014, SATAWU Durban and ILWU Local 10 boycotted and protested Israeli-owned ships to express discontent over Israeli military campaigns that mostly killed Palestinian civilians and pressurize Israel to recognize a Palestinian state. Their actions—and those of dockworkers elsewhere who protested Israeli ships—suggest that the labor internationalism of dockworkers remains quite real.[52]

In 2009, Israel bombarded the largely defenseless population of Gaza for three weeks, killing more than one thousand civilians and resulting in SATAWU's announcement that Durban members would not unload the *Johanna Russ*, an Antiguan-flagged ship sailing on behalf of the Israeli shipping company Zim. A COSATU press release criticized Israel's "flagrant breaches of international law, the bombing of densely populated neighbourhoods, the illegal deployment of chemical white phosphorous, and attacks on schools, ambulances, relief agencies, hospitals, universities and places of worship" and declared that "the momentum against apartheid Israel has become an irresistible force." The use of the term *apartheid* is noteworthy, if controversial. Many sympathetic to Israel point to numerous differences between the Palestinians' treatment by Israel and of blacks, coloreds, and Indians during apartheid. Nevertheless, many South Africans make this comparison and consciously use the term. For instance, Ahmed Kathrada, a legendary anti-apartheid activist who spent twenty-six years in prison and counted Mandela among his closest friends on Robben Island, wrote, "A South African who is not white does not need more than one day's stay in Palestine to be thrown back to pre-1994 and realize that apartheid is very much alive under Israel as a colonial power." Clearly, Palestinian independence has yet to arrive. The stance taken by COSATU, however, typifies its efforts at global solidarity as well as South Africans' sympathy for Palestinians.[53]

Similarly, in 2010 and 2014, major protests occurred at the Port of Oakland in advance of the arrival of Zim line ships as Local 10 members repeatedly refused to cross community picket lines. As early as its 1988 international convention, the

ILWU officially condemned Israeli treatment of Palestinians, proclaiming Israel guilty of "state-sponsored terrorism" and quoting Israeli journalist Amos Elon, who described Gaza as "the Soweto of the State of Israel." A 1991 resolution reaffirmed the union's support for Palestinian statehood; during discussion on this resolution, Brian McWilliams (a future president of the ILWU international) bemoaned "the oppression of workers in the occupied territories in the Gaza Strip and the violation of basic trade union rights and human rights all by the Israeli military occupation." So, when one thousand people converged on the port in 2010 to protest Israel's killing of ten civilians aboard the Gaza Freedom Flotilla, the ILWU already had taken a stand. Protesters marched to the terminal gates in advance of the arrival of the *Zim Shenzhen* and shouted, "An injury to one is an injury to all, bring down the apartheid wall." Local 10 members invoked their contract's "health and safety" provision and refused to cross the picket line. The ship departed without unloading its cargo—the first successful boycott of an Israeli ship in North American history. In 2014, fighting resumed between Israel and Gaza Palestinians, leaving more than twenty-one hundred dead, nearly all Palestinians and mostly civilians. In response, the Bay Area's Arab Resource and Organizing Center developed the "Block the Boat" campaign, which involved several thousand people in four days of actions at multiple piers, again preventing a Zim ship, *Piraeus*, from unloading. Local 10 members provided invaluable inside information about the port and the ship's arrival. Most Zim organizers and protesters were not dockworkers, but some belonged to Local 10 or other ILWU locals and many dockworkers sympathized with the Palestinians' plight.[54]

Very recently, then, and not coincidently, the ILWU and SATAWU engaged in solidarity actions on the same issue. Not only do both unions belong to the ITF, they pay attention to each other's actions, meet at ITF conferences, and issue press releases praising each other's stands. Another recent example occurred when dockworkers across the United States (particularly in Local 10) and Europe boycotted ships, threatened to boycott ships, and donated money in support of the unionized dockworkers of Charleston, South Carolina, then under assault by a company that (with government aid) sought to destroy their union. If the recent past is any indication, dockworker activism will continue.[55]

Conclusions: Working Class, Antiracist Internationalism

This chapter explored how—to this day—militant waterfront workers periodically wielded their power on behalf of social justice causes in other nations, a movement called transnational solidarity or labor internationalism. Their actions also possessed a race-driven flavor, part of a global struggle for black freedom, and working-class power. Dockworkers in both ports demonstrated an ability to combine local struggles with global ones, consistently rooting their actions in the context of (racial) equality, freedom, and power. Keylor, the Local 10 longshoreman who helped organize the 1984 action and marched in the 2014 one—at eighty-eight years of age—suggested that these efforts "sent reverberations around the world." Keylor's notion of working-class power and solidarity might seem outdated in the twenty-first century, but at a time when global capital seems ascendant and unions ever weaker, dockworkers remain quite aware of their central role to global trade and, thus, their potential power. San Francisco Bay Area and Durban dockworkers combined leftist and antiracist ideological beliefs with a pragmatic understanding of the importance of their work to the global economy to promote their political agendas.[56]

Durban dockworkers, now members of SATAWU and affiliated with COSATU, act in accordance with the principles of transnational solidarity. Their 2008 boycott confirmed their commitment to global activism and willingness to challenge the ANC. In the words of South African journalist Essa, "The actions of COSATU and its affiliate SATAWU suggest a dramatic shift back to the social movement unionism that defined the union movement at the height of the liberation struggle. It was a time when workplace bread-and-butter issues were not separated from the socio-political inequities and challenges that existed outside the workplace." Essa also quoted SATAWU general secretary Howard, who perhaps overstated his case: "I don't think COSATU has ever shifted away from the community issues. We always knew that our role was always going to be more than merely workplace based issues." Patrick Bond, a prominent activist-scholar, agreed: "COSATU's philosophy of internationalism is exceptional, far advanced amongst the world's working classes. We've seen great actions against oppression in Swaziland, Zimbabwe, Burma and now Palestine."[57]

This analysis of SATAWU echoed how many describe ILWU Local 10, such as the San Francisco Labor Council, which praised the dockworkers for being "the heart and soul of the San Francisco labor movement." Rank-and-file activists in Local 10, even more than their elected leaders (or other Bay Area unions), continue agitating on behalf of social justice causes they believe important, nationally and globally. For instance, in 2008, Local 10 activists convinced the Longshore Caucus, representing all ILWU locals on the West Coast, to stop work for an entire day to protest the US wars in Afghanistan and Iraq—the only US union to do so; that this action occurred on the international Labor Day, May 1, only heightened the drama. In 2011, rank-and-file activists in Local 10 refused to work, in solidarity with public-sector workers in Wisconsin then in danger of losing many of their legal rights from a newly elected governor; Local 10 proved the only union, nationwide, that struck (in violation of their contract) on April 4, not coincidentally the anniversary of the killing of Dr. Martin Luther King Jr. Finally, Local 10 still pays attention to events in South Africa; in 2012 and 2013, in the aftermath of the killing of thirty-four striking platinum miners in Marikana, South Africa, Local 10 hosted a speaker representing Marikana workers and wrote a letter to South African president Jacob Zuma condemning these police killings.[58]

The actions of dockworkers in the San Francisco Bay Area and Durban may not have resulted in the dismantling of apartheid or ending of Mugabe's reign, but workers in both ports demonstrated fierce commitment to black freedom struggles. Many dockworkers possessed black internationalist mindsets rooted in their cosmopolitan lives and work. They are the rightful heirs of Claude McKay's characters in *Banjo*, who hailed from Senegal, the West Indies, and the US South. McKay's black maritime workers came together "on the beach," that is, between jobs, in the Port of Marseilles in the 1920s, where they discussed Marcus Garvey's Back-to-Africa Movement and the mistreatment of blacks in Mississippi and French West Africa. Nowadays, San Francisco Bay Area and Durban dockworkers discuss the troubles of people of color in places such as Gaza, Oakland, South Africa (still), and Zimbabwe.[59]

Clearly, dockworkers have possessed enough power to act on behalf of workers in other nations. Rooted in their appreciation of their strategic niche in global trade, this power exists even though their industry continues to be transformed and traditional working-class port communities have disappeared. Combining leftist and antiracist ideologies, San Francisco Bay Area and Durban dockworkers translated their beliefs in the need for and possibilities of solidarity into tangible actions: boycotting ships to protest apartheid and other forms of authoritarianism. Such boycotts, arguably, are even more possible now as a result of the ever-greater links created by global trade, "just-in-time" production methods, corporate desires to maintain low inventories, and transnational labor organizations like the ITF. In the twenty-first century, employers, governments, and global capitalism present tremendous challenges to workers. Despite containerization, globalization, and other forces, dockworkers have held onto their unions better than many other blue-collar workers in both the United States and South Africa. Not to suggest that they represent the norm, but dockworkers' experiences are suggestive of what others can accomplish even as technology and powerful economic forces threaten to weaken and destroy the power of ordinary working people. In both the San Francisco Bay Area and Durban, dockworkers have demonstrated a robust sense of working-class internationalism.[60]

CONCLUSION

Racism will not be defeated nationally. It will be defeated globally or it will not be defeated.

—"Prof. Achille Mbembe on Racism in South Africa in 2016 is #ReportingRace"

When the masses become superfluous it means that humanity is superfluous, and that is something that staggers the mind.

—Hoffer, "Automation"

The future is unwritten.

—Joe Strummer

This book examines three themes that, hopefully, convey the long history of dockworker power in both Durban and the San Francisco Bay Area. First, these workers fought long and hard in their respective black freedom struggles, against apartheid in South Africa and for civil rights in the United States. Despite the significance of their actions, however, their contributions to these struggles remain severely underappreciated. Second, to increase worker productivity and regain their control, employers in the Bay Area and Durban—fully appreciating dockworker power—deployed containerization and new hiring practices. Workers responded as best they could and retained some power, but they could not unmake this technological revolution or its effects. Third, these dockworkers have engaged in transnational solidarity activism for eighty years and counting. In periodically refusing to move cargo being shipped to or from authoritarian regimes, dockworkers aided social movements overseas and demonstrated the possibilities when workers possess and use power at the point of production.

Dockworkers in San Francisco and Durban played leading roles in their nation's respective struggles for racial equality, starting in the 1930s and '40s. Such
efforts have been described alternately as social-movement unionism, civil-rights
unionism, or recently by sociologist Kim Scipes as "social justice unionism." Labor
activist and photojournalist David Bacon explained Local 10's social justice bona
fides: "One of the most important reasons why the Bay Area, and the cities of the
Pacific Coast, have a radical political tradition is because of the ILWU. But it's not
just the union as an institution. It's the fact that the union brought together and
educated a body of workers who then worked in political campaigns, civil rights
demonstrations, school and workplace integration, and a myriad of other social
struggles. And creating and maintaining that active membership was the job of
the leftwingers in the union." Chapter 2 demonstrates how and why Local 10 integrated its own ranks—more than a generation before the Civil Rights Act of 1964
compelled unions and other US institutions to do so—and chapter 3 shows how
Bay Area longshoremen expanded their fight for racial equality to their city and
nation by participating in the countless social movements flowering in the 1960s.
Although Bacon fully appreciated their importance, these workers' signal contributions remain largely unknown among the general public and undiscussed by
scholars. In particular, ILWU Local 10 still fails to receive nearly the attention it
deserves in a great diversity of historical subjects: the San Francisco Bay Area and
US urban history, social movements, African American history and civil rights,
maritime history, and, most broadly, the history of the postwar United States, during which time Local 10 might have been the most radical yet influential union,
bar none. Similarly, the major role Durban dockworkers played from the 1930s
through the 1970s, although it received serious attention from several scholars,
remains outside the general narrative of South African history and, specifically,
the history of the struggle against apartheid. Yet these black workers repeatedly
struck, particularly throughout the 1940s and 1950s, in the face of apartheid and
rising persecution. After a decade of silence and after top-down decasualization
and nationwide repression of anti-apartheid activists, dockworkers struck in 1969
and 1972 when literally almost no other black workers, in the city or nation, had
either the audacity or capacity. Their strikes in late 1972 paved the way for the
mammoth Durban Strikes that restarted the anti-apartheid movement. Simply
put, no other group of black workers in Durban did what dockworkers did and,
nationally, probably only the miners proved more influential. Considering the horrors of apartheid and labor turnover over time, dockworker militancy, for nearly
fifty years, is that much more impressive.[1]

The ongoing separation of the labor and civil-rights movements, in both the US
historiography and its mindset, is but one example of how South African scholarship offers much to American(ist)s. Despite a generation of excellent scholarship

on race and labor, there remains a divide between those who study civil rights and, more generally, African American history and those who study labor unions, work, and working-class people; no doubt, some historians of African America ably integrate class and work into their scholarship. But more general histories of postwar America, including the 1960s, make invisible the significant contributions that some unions like the ILWU made. By contrast, few historians of South Africa deny the import of unionism and worker power, particularly the Durban Strikes, in helping defeat apartheid. Fortunately, the trend toward intersectionality in studying social movements in the United States and elsewhere is promising and follows in the wake of scholarship on civil rights and social movement unionism, black feminism, and, much further back, W. E. B. Du Bois's magisterial *Black Reconstruction*. It also demands mention, as Bayard Rustin wrote in 1971 but which equally applies today, "Blacks *are* mostly a working people; they continue to need what labor needs, and they must fight side by side with unions to achieve these things." Durban and Bay Area dockworkers fought on economic and social (racial) fronts simultaneously and should be appreciated for doing so.[2]

This book also examines the effects of containerization and changes to hiring methods—both threats to dockworker power. Did Harry Bridges, the legendary "red" and firebrand, accommodate himself to the reality of capitalism by conceiving of, negotiating, and selling containers to his members? Perhaps he inserted the following into the ILWU comment about M&M, a pamphlet written for the membership: "the Union realizes that a complete and absolute solution to the problems resulting from machines displacing men can't be found under our present economic system." Perhaps he also wrote, "Let's never forget that what the worker fears is *the way the machine is used*, the manner in which his skills or job security is wiped away. He does not fear the machine as a producer of more goods, as a means of living a longer and happier life, as a provider of safe, cleaner and easier work. Workers who smashed machines in the past were not trying to 'hold up progress,' they were hitting back at a system which denied them any benefits from the new machines and from progress." While the author of these words remains shrouded, we do know, as Richard Boyden did in 1972, "Employers here [in the US] and overseas have always regarded dockworkers' unions among the most militant in the labor movement—as serious obstacles to their 'prerogatives' and profits. They have therefore sought to use containerization to debilitate these unions." This technological innovation accomplished that objective, at least partially, in both the San Francisco Bay Area and Durban.[3]

Despite its world-historical significance, though, precious little research has been conducted upon the workers most directly affected by containers, those who load them onto and unload them off ships. Reviewing Eddie Webster's classic analysis of metal workers of South Africa's East Rand, economic historian Bill Freund summarized the dangers, for workers, of technology: "New machinery reduces the numbers and skills of workers and re-asserts the control of the capitalists on the shop floor more effectively than any number of foremen." New technologies may sometimes create new skilled positions, such as heavy crane operator, but those introducing a new technology (and hiring system) control the process for their own benefit. Of course, new technologies continue shaping and reshaping South Africa, the United States, and the global economy, and thus hardly a day goes by without some businessperson, scholar, or thinker commenting upon the multitudinous ways technology remakes workplaces the world over. Eric Hoffer, for one, expressed concern over automation but later reversed course and contended, "automation is here to liberate us." Robert Carson, a member of Local 10 in the generation after Hoffer—the one that most experienced the shift to containers—thought quite differently, as evidenced by a short story he set in 1973 in which several sailors discuss the future of shipping. One character, a Catholic sailor from "Upper Ireland, the Occupied Part," lamented:

> "One day soon, I mean very soon, they'll throw a couple of lines around the Trans-America building, plug the ship into a computer and that's it for us."
> "There'll always be jobs," I said, half-heartedly.
> "No, laddie, no. This is the last gasp, you know. I can hear the death rattle, sounds like the electric whip of falls on cranes and people gettin' devoured by money and big homes."

Economist Ben Seligman preceded Carson in 1966: "If one thing is beyond dispute—despite the reluctance of economists to say it aloud—it is that technology is altering life to its existential roots before our very eyes." In recent years, we all can relate to Carson's fear because, for better or worse, we identify with it. Countless news stories discuss the imminence of "self-driving trucks" that will eliminate more than two million jobs in the United States alone as millions watch YouTube videos on robots replacing human workers, as in Amazon's ever-more dominant supply chain. Katja Grace, a researcher at Oxford's Future of Humanity Institute, predicts that 47 percent of all US jobs will disappear in the next twenty-five years as a result of automation.[4]

So, too, hiring systems that increasingly contribute to precariousness, a reality that many a dockworker could relate to, be it in Durban or Valparaiso, San Francisco or Singapore. In the United States, South Africa, and other industrialized societies during an era when neoliberalism increasingly dominates, corporations (often in alliance with governments) have weakened or destroyed unions that once challenged employer prerogatives and shaped public policies. A central feature much discussed in scholarly, policy, and popular circles is the explosion in casual and flexible—precarious—labor, at least partially heightened by technological changes in nearly every industry. Earlier than most, dockworkers were subjected to these changes. The shipping industry's promotion of containers in the 1960s and 1970s contributed to and, indeed, predicted the rise of neoliberalism, as Klaus Weinhauer thoughtfully wrote: "In the last decades of the twentieth century dock work mirrors prominently the far-reaching changes brought about by global deregulation of employment." Similarly, as a result of changing work conditions, smaller safety nets, and ongoing technological changes, hundreds of millions of blue- and white-collar workers today find themselves with lower wages, less security, and fewer if any benefits, as Local 10 activist Reg Theriault remarked: "I know of no blue-collar industry whose work forces have not been seriously depleted by new technology and automation." Similarly, white-collar workers already are finding their work lives affected by automation and precarity.[5]

Human relationships to machines have a long and storied history in scholarly circles, the popular press, and the science fiction genre. Human fears of the robot date to the early twentieth century, as historian Toby Higbie brilliantly showed in analyzing Czech writer Karel Čapek's 1920 play, *R.U.R. (Rossum's Universal Robots)*, about the replacement of humans in factories and armies by more powerful and efficient robots. After gaining consciousness, Čapek described how these robots rebelled and nearly wiped out humanity. Science-fiction stories following in the wake of R.U.R. are legion—*Terminator, Blade Runner, and Battlestar Galactica* spring to mind—and include a 1960 cartoon from the ILWU *Dispatcher* addressing dockworkers' fear of replacement by robots.[6]

Discussions about automation have heated up recently. In his 2015 essay "The Robots Are Coming," labor journalist David Moberg correctly noted that the fears of technology as job killers are real and date back to the English Luddites in the early nineteenth century; but "Robots can be good—and bad. They fuel both fantasies and fears." Not unlike (de)casualization, arguably technology is a neutral force indifferent to human needs or desires, thus its greatly varied effects depend on who controls it. Moberg rightly added public policy to the mix: "Much will depend on whether we humans leave robotization to the free market or whether we take deliberate steps to shape our future relationships with robots, work and each other." Perhaps he was too sanguine? Economist Jed Kolko cautioned in 2016 that "More and more work activities and even entire jobs are at risk of being automated by algorithms, computers and robots, raising concerns that more and more humans will be put out of work. The fear of automation is widespread—President Obama cited it as the No. 1 reason Americans feel anxious about the economy in his 2016 State of the Union address." Moberg, Kolko, and Obama failed to mention whether workers themselves will (and should) have any input into the process, but geographer David Harvey added class analysis to his contribution: "Capital unleashes the powers of 'creative destruction' upon the land. Some factions benefit from the creativity, while others suffer the brunt of the destruction. Invariably, this involves a class disparity." Because workers, generally, do not dictate technological innovation, the odds that they will be the primary victims of creative destruction remain high. Another crucial matter relates to the meaning of work, as Manuel Castells, a prominent sociologist of information and globalization, suggested: "The process of work is at the core of social structure." Both Hoffer and I share Castells's view and, hence, remain deeply concerned about automation-induced unemployment. Of late, interest in and calls for universal basic income schemes are growing. I, for one, see wisdom and viability in Finland's 2017 pilot program. But, since work matters greatly to many humans' sense of self-worth, its noneconomic aspects also must be considered by any society not driven solely by short-term profit. The ongoing role of technological changes to the global economy offers another reason that the history of containerization remains relevant.[7]

Similarly, precariousness plays out both on the job and in society at large. The gigantic forces making growing numbers of people increasingly insecure easily can result in people turning against each other. On the cusp of the global financial meltdown of 2008, Kathleen Cleaver, the great Black Panther leader, lamented "the remarkable power of racism to perpetuate itself" in her introduction to a new edition of David Roediger's classic *Wages of Whiteness*. Cleaver noted "a resurgence of white supremacy to counter fears triggered by the spiraling crisis over globalization, downward mobility, and immigrant workers." Her words seem even more prescient and ominous in 2018, considering the controversial president of the United States (elected, at least in part, because some white Americans fear immigrants and people of color) and the recent resignation of a corrupt yet tenacious one in South Africa (who cynically played on fears of "white monopoly capitalism"). As racial capitalism, globally, sheds more of its weakest workers, more US, South African, and other workers become ever-more precarious and increasingly anxious. To put it another way, the work and life experiences of white US workers now more closely resembles what black and other peoples of color have experienced in South Africa, the United States, and elsewhere for much longer. Yet technological and other changes, in turn, create opportunities for resistance, to build new organizations and develop new tactics, as well as improve upon older ones, this book's third major theme.[8]

Dockworker Power documents and analyzes—also for the first time—San Francisco Bay Area and Durban dockworkers who boycotted ships and cargo in support of freedom struggles in nations other than their own. What motivated these bouts of transnational activism included beliefs in socialism, syndicalism, black internationalism, and Labor-Left Pan-Africanism. Bay Area longshoremen agitated for decades in solidarity with the struggle against apartheid and, more broadly, for the liberation of (black) people in southern Africa. In the 1950s and 1960s, the union repeatedly condemned white-minority rule in South Africa and highlighted the ironic similarities with Jim Crow segregation in the United States, rhetoric about equality notwithstanding. In the 1970s and 1980s, rank-and-file radicals in ILWU Local 10 formed the SALSC, which stood at the vanguard of working-class anti-apartheid activism in this era. The black and white members of the SALSC (and in Trotskyist groups) fought for the liberation of black people in South Africa, Mozambique, Rhodesia, and elsewhere in the best way they knew how—direct action on the job. To leftist and Pan-African dockworkers, the most logical way to attack apartheid and racial capitalism required flexing their economic muscle, that is, stopping work. Several times but most importantly for eleven days in 1984 (shortly after Reagan's landslide reelection), they boycotted South African cargo, growing the local and global struggle in the process. Similarly, members of the Durban branch of SATAWU boycotted a Chinese ship loaded with weapons intended for the Mugabe regime. They long have belonged to an African maritime workforce that fought in many a liberation movement. In 2008, they acted in solidarity with Zimbabwean workers leading the democratic opposition—simultaneously allying with the neighboring labor movement, supporting democracy against an autocratic ruler, and repaying a debt from the Zimbabweans' long support for the struggle against apartheid. In undertaking this boycott, Durban dockworkers returned to their militant roots and internationalist ways. These waterfront workers exerted the power they possessed for a political cause, one counter to their nation's stated foreign policy.

Chapter 6, thus, demonstrates how and why dockworkers in both the San Francisco Bay Area and Durban applied their commitments to working-class internationalism and racial solidarity. Dockworkers are more inclined than most to see their immediate, local struggles in larger, even global, contexts. For decades, workers in both ports used their power acquired on the job to advocate in solidarity with freedom movements globally. Although such notions might seem outdated in the twenty-first century, as unions have been in decline for decades, dockworkers grounded their ideals in the reality that they still occupy a central position in global trade and possessed the skills to shape—even stop—it. Thus, they combined leftist and antiracist ideological beliefs with a pragmatic understanding of their role in the global economy. Further, the spirit and ideals of Pan-Africanism continually shape black (and white) dockworkers in Oakland who have formal ties with black dockworkers in Durban by way of the International Transport Workers Federation and International Dockers Council.

Though this history matters, we risk forgetting it. Filmmakers Allan Sekula and Noël Burch offered a clarion call: "As the class character of the port cities changes, the memory of mutiny and rebellion, of intense class struggle by dockers, seafarers, fishermen, and shipyard workers—struggles that were fundamental to the formation of the institutions of social democracy and free-trade unionism—fades from public awareness." In her book *Port Cities and Global Legacies*, Alice Mah echoed the dangers facing today's port cities and workers: "They are 'precarious' cities existing within uncertain context of globalization and post-industrial change." The San Francisco waterfront, along the Embarcadero, has been either redeveloped as a tourist destination or an extension of the business district. No doubt it is appropriate that the Port of San Francisco's geographic center, the plaza in front of the Ferry Building, now is named for Harry Bridges (albeit without any marker to explain his significance) and Pier 27, the city's cruise ship hub, is dedicated to Jimmy Herman. Few, however, appreciate the importance—indeed centrality—of the ILWU and Local 10 to the city and metropolitan area. Similarly, in Durban the Point is fast being redeveloped into housing and hotels for wealthy, generally white, visitors and residents. There is no physical monument or landmark to the titanic struggles fought by dockworkers for more than half a century. Of course, these matters are of global relevance. In critiquing the redevelopment of France's great port city, Stuart Jeffries quoted Walter Benjamin's experience in the late 1920s: "Marseilles: the yellow studded maw of a seal with salt water running out between the teeth. When this gullet opens to catch the black and brown proletarian bodies thrown to it by ship's companies according to their timetables, it exhales a stink of oil, urine and printer's ink." Benjamin embraced the grittiness of port cities and its people. They represented life in all its gory, rough, vital glory. They were (and remain) the places at the forefront of global capitalism and resistance to it, much as in Durban, San Francisco, and Oakland.[9]

At least now, South African union activists know about San Francisco Bay Area ones and vice versa. In 2015, for instance, the National Union of Miners (NUMSA), a South African union committed to social-movement unionism, sent a letter to Local 10 praising its May Day "Stop Work" protest organized to protest racist police brutality: "We extend a message of solidarity to working people and poor communities who are at the receiving end of what clearly appears to be systematic police killings of unarmed black men in the US. As South Africans, we know the pain and the suffering that police brutality causes to working people and their communities. We also know how this brutality is meant to lead to fear and disorganization. . . . Your struggle is our struggle. Your pain is our pain!" Local 10 arranged for a stop-work meeting on the original workers' holiday, May 1, to protest a white police officer who shot and killed a black man while fleeing and then planted evidence to suggest the murder was in self-defense, only for a video to surface catching this policeman in his lie. Stacey Rodgers, a black woman, native Oaklander, and rank-and-file activist in Local 10, made the motion to create the "Labor against Police Terror" rally that resulted in the port shutting down for a rare daytime stop-work meeting. Although unions must defend workers on the job, this book argues that, to be truly effective, they also must participate in social movements. The sort of actions Rodgers helped organize drew several thousand people because it emerged out of and engaged with the community. Similarly, when thirty-four striking platinum miners in Marikana were killed by the South African police in 2012, the membership of Local 10, still majority black, condemned President Jacob Zuma of South Africa, who had risen to power in no small part by virtue of backing from the labor movement. At a subsequent meeting, Local 10 hosted Mazibuko Jara, representing the Marikana Miners Support Campaign, in support of this struggle. Dockworker unions continue to embrace the motto "an injury to one is an injury to all," promoting social justice and building transnational networks of (marine transport) workers.[10]

Nowadays, many people hold a melancholy view of dockworkers and their cities. Alice Mah, for instance, wrote, "Port cities harbour the collective inheritance of old global ages. Dockworkers unload sugar, tobacco, crude oil, and chicken around the world, carrying on the collective memory and traditions of past generations in a new global era of super-containers and weak trade unions." Not to entirely disagree with Mah, this book argues that dockworkers are far from weak. In fact, they conceivably possess more power than ever before. Dockworker power in Durban, the San Francisco Bay Area, and elsewhere derives from two distinct avenues— both rooted in the work process and still viable. Traditionally, dockworkers were relatively militant, strong, and willing to strike and unionize because the work cultivated solidarity; this reality has been demonstrated repeatedly across time and cultures. Containerization seriously threatened this tradition by transforming the work process and drastically reducing the number of workers who might not believe or act in solidarity with others. Enter the second key factor explaining dockworkers' enduring power, their strategic location in the global economy. Some may posit that containerization fatally wounded dock unions, but such a contention oversimplifies or, worse, distorts reality. Undeniably, the work changed and the number of workers plunged, yet dockworkers remain aware of their importance and demonstrate a willingness to deploy their power. Indeed, with the precision that computers and global positioning systems have wrought, shipping schedules are intractably planned, as is just-in-time production on the manufacturing side. And, with ever-larger ships,[11] larger amounts of more critically timed cargo can be held up, thereby sending shockwaves through global supply chains. If, that is, workers continue to prove willing to engage in their most tried-and-true tactic, what Clark Kerr and Lloyd Fisher in 1949 called the "quickie strike"—as everyone in the industry still knows:

> A ship in port is peculiarly vulnerable to a "quickie" strike. Port time is costly time. Charges pile up and no revenue is being earned. A quick turnaround is often the

necessary condition of a profitable operation. The tendency in the face of a "quickie" is to settle and get the ship moving. The men had a decided advantage in the short run. They might well win the "beef" under the circumstances; and if not, might at least earn extra overtime pay as the employer tried to make up for lost time. At worst, the work was still there to be done. The "quickies" penalized the employer heavily in higher costs and the prospects of lost business due to the uncertainty of maritime transportation. The "quickie" was a weapon almost cost-free in the eyes of the men but wickedly effective in the eyes of the employers.

As early as the 1930s, Harry Bridges was wary of pulling too many such actions, as he noted in 1979, shortly after his retirement, for "The ship is a moving warehouse. Every minute that ship is alongside that goddamned dock it's losing money. Big money. A ship is only making money when she's at sea with a belly-full of cargo." Thus, dockworker power rests—still—on their strategic location in the global economy. Moreover, as the work has been transformed from gangs of "unskilled" laborers into far fewer workers considered quite skilled and operating multimillion-dollar machinery, the potential of dockworkers to exert power arguably has increased.[12]

Not only do they possess power, many embrace ideals of equality and freedom as unionists and, for some, Pan-Africanism. These workers, now far fewer in number and highly skilled, could be considered craft unionists rather than industrial ones in that they do not represent all workers in (marine) transportation. True, the ILWU represents some other, if not most, logistics workers in the US West and SATAWU does represent many rail workers and truckers. Stereotypically, craft unions focus narrowly upon their economic self-interests at the expense of all other issues, unlike the large, social-movement-oriented industrial unions consisting of many types of workers in the same industry as defined in the United States by the early CIO or in South Africa by the metalworkers (now in the National Union of Metalworkers of South Africa). Yet neither the ILWU, an early member of and leader in the CIO, nor SATAWU acts in such a manner. Instead, these unions, which could be described using the old term "aristocracy of labor," do not act solely in their self-interest—as evidenced by their commitment to labor internationalism and other causes. Political scientists John S. Ahlquist and Margaret Levi convincingly proved that the ILWU opposed (and opposes) so-called free trade agreements, though increasing trade arguably benefits the material interests of its members; for instance, the ILWU contends the North American Free Trade Agreement and other free trade deals violate its Guiding Principles in that they hurt many US workers who lose jobs as companies move production to lower-wage locations. Thus, we might think of dockworkers as sharing the democratic spirit and militancy of the nineteenth-century iron puddlers, famously chronicled in David Montgomery's classic *Fall of the House of Labor*, who used their skills to control the production process and create more equitable, less harsh work conditions. Similarly, as David T. Wellman proved in his ethnography of Local 10 *The Union Makes Us Strong,* long after most CIO unions reverted to AFL-style business unionism, the ILWU and a handful of other unions continued to act militantly and on behalf of others.[13]

Although not the norm, Durban and San Francisco Bay Area dockworkers' actions, beliefs, and unions demand attention. In these great port cities, dockworkers collectively built powerful organizations and traditions of militancy over most of a century. At a basic level, they challenge the notion that workers are powerless to shape their lives and our world. We often turn to history to learn what went wrong, and there is plenty in both South African and US history that falls into that category. But it can also teach us of successes, providing inspirational examples when so-called ordinary people have stood up to oppression and spoken truth to power, denouncing bigotry and challenging powerful employers and the state. This book shows how people can combat racism, in their own workplaces and in other lands. Bay Area and Durban dockworkers fought racism when most others did not. In the never-ending struggle for freedom and justice, unions remain among the largest and most powerful groups of nonelites. Even today, with membership down dramatically from their twentieth-century highs, unions can play crucial roles in South Africa and the United States, helping their members earn living wages but also fighting for social justice.

NOTES

Introduction

1. Cooper, "Dockworkers and Labour History," 524; Starr, *Dream Endures*, 118; Hyslop, "Navigating Empire"; Sassen, *Global City*; Mah, *Port Cities and Global Legacies*, 8.

2. Sloterdijk, *In the World Interior of Capital*, 15; Linebaugh and Rediker, *Many-Headed Hydra*, 219; *OED*, "strike, v.," sense 17 and 24; Cowen, *Deadly Lives of Logistics*, 90; Rothenberg, "Ports Matter"; Killie Campbell Africana Library, Port Natal Affairs Administration Board [hereafter, PNAAB], "Accommodation: Stevedoring Labour, General Manager, Durban Stevedoring Labour Supply Company, 4 April 1975," 1, KCF 82, roll 64; Foucault, "Of Other Spaces," 27; Mah, *Port Cities and Global Legacies*, 1 (my emphasis); George, *Ninety Percent of Everything*.

3. Mah, *Port Cities and Global Legacies*, 2, 35 (Liverpool quote); Sekula and Burch, *Forgotten Space*.

4. Davies et al., *Dock Workers*, 3; Davis, *Waterfront Revolts*; Ibarz, "Recent Trends"; Hyslop, "Navigating Empire."

5. Tsing, "Supply Chains"; Nelson, *Workers on the Waterfront*, 10.

6. Levinson, *The Box* remains the best introduction to containerization.

7. Dubbeld, "Breaking the Buffalo," 97 (Marx quote from *Grundrisse*); Markoff, "Skilled Work."

8. Hobsbawm, "Machine Breakers," in *Labouring Men*; E. P. Thompson, *Making of the English Working Class*, 649; Conniff, "What the Luddites Really Fought Against"; Herod, *Labor Geographies*, 76.

9. Davies et al., *Dock Workers*; Broeze, *Globalisation of the Oceans*, esp. ch. 7; Wellman, *Union Makes Us Strong*; Herod, *Labor Geographies*, ch. 4–5. Unfortunately, in *Waterfront Revolts*, Davis

chose to stop before containerization. Dubbeld's thesis on containers in Durban, "Labour Management," remains a rare exception.

10. Coppersmith, "Comparative History" (all quotes). Levinson, an economist, does consider labor in several chapters of *The Box*. Wellman's *Union Makes Us Strong* explores some effects of containers.

11. Fredrickson, *White Supremacy*, xiv–xv.

12. Kennedy speech, University of Cape Town; Fredrickson, *White Supremacy*, 236.

13. Tyrrell, "What Is Transnational History?"; Stromquist, "Claiming Political Space," Fink, "Global Sea or National Backwater?" and other essays in *Workers across the Americas*; van der Linden, "Transnationalizing American Labor History," 1080–81; van der Linden, "Labour History," 170 (first quote, emphasis in original), 171 (second quote), 173 (third quote).

14. Legassick, "Past and Present of Marxist Historiography," 112; Wolpe, "Capitalism and Cheap Labour-Power"; Robinson, *Black Marxism, 2; Kelley, Race Capitalism Justice*, 7 (emphasis in original).

15. Beckert, *Empire of Cotton*; Lee, "Harvesting Cotton-Field Capitalism" (Baptist quote); Sugrue, *Origins of the Urban Crisis, 261–62*.

16. Roediger, *Wages of Whiteness*, 11; Lambert, "Political Unionism and Working Class Hegemony," 272; Blackburn, "Review."

17. Murray Schumach, "Martin Luther King Jr.: Leader of Millions in Nonviolent Drive for Racial Justice," *New York Times*, April 5, 1968.

Chapter 1. Context

1. French, "Another World History."

2. Koopman, "Post-Colonial Identity"; Mukherji, "Durban Largest 'Indian' City outside India"; T. Jones, "Port of Durban," 102.

3. SAHO, *Prehistory of the Durban Area*; L. Thompson, *History of South Africa*, ch. 1; Ross, *Concise History of South Africa*, ch. 1.

4. Horwood, *The Port of Durban*, 1–5 (quote on 2); SAHO, *Colonial History of Durban* and *Early Settlement at Bay of Natal*.

5. L. Thompson, *History of South Africa*, 80–87, 96–100; Ross, *Concise History*, 28–33, 43–44; Guy, *Theophilus Shepstone*. On the complicated history of Natal, including former President Jacob Zuma, see Dlamini, "Collaborators and the Riven Truth."

6. T. Jones, "Port of Durban"; Freund, *Insiders and Outsiders*; Halpern, "Solving the 'Labour Problem'"; Atkins, *The Moon Is Dead!*; Vahed, "Power and Resistance."

7. Callebert, "Livelihood Strategies," 33; Lumby and McLean, "Economy and the Development of the Port of Durban," 29; Hemson, "Eye of the Storm"; T. Jones, "Port of Durban," 69 (quote), 76–77.

8. Hemson, "Breaking the Impasse," 199; Horwood, *Port of Durban*, 16.

9. Johnston, *Durban Chronicle*, 205; Clark and Worger, *South Africa*, esp. ch. 2–3.

10. Killie Campbell Africana Library, Port Natal Affairs Administration Board [hereafter, PNAAB], "Accommodation," 1 (first quote), KCF 82, roll 64; Hindson, *Pass Controls*; Vahed, "Making of Indian Identity," 83; van Onselen, *Chibaro*, 157; Hemson, "Dock Work-

ers," 92 (quote); Hemson, "Breaking the Impasse," 199; Ross-Watt, "Housing," 15–18. See Callebert, "Livelihood Strategies," 21–25, for a depiction of a Durban docker's life, c. 1950.

11. Callebert, "Livelihood Strategies," 38, 61–63, 179; La Hause, "Drinking in the Cage," 65; Kiloh and Sibeko, *Fighting Union*, 20 (Nair quote); Hemson, "Dock Workers," *123;* van Onselen, *Chibaro*, 239; Mamdani, *Citizen and Subject*, ch. 7. On docker barracks from 1959 onward, see Ross-Watt, "Housing." Thanks to Brij Maharaj for help with Durban's geography.

12. Much of this book examines the Port of San Francisco, but, in the late 1960s, the Port of Oakland started to command an ever larger share of cargo. Today, nearly all cargo moves through Oakland, yet San Francisco remains the dominant, better-known city.

13. Sides, *Erotic City*, esp. ch. 1.

14. Golden Gate National Recreation Area, "Ohlones and Coast Miwoks"; Margolin, "The Ohlone Way"; Glass, "Native Americans in the Mission Economy."

15. Martin, "Captain John C. Frémont"; Golden Gate Bridge Highway and Transportation District, "What Is a Name—The Golden Gate?"; Seal of the City and County of San Francisco.

16. Virtual Museum of the City of San Francisco, "From the 1820s to the Gold Rush"; Seal of the City and County of San Francisco; Maldetto, "Why San Francisco?"; Brechin, *Imperial San Francisco*, esp. ch. 1 and 5.

17. Brechin, *Imperial San Francisco*; Greene, *Canal Builders*; Self, *American Babylon*, 153–55, 206–9; Cherny, "Longshoremen," 113–15.

18. Gibson, "Population of the Largest 100 Cities"; Kazin, *Barons of Labor*; Northern California Coalition for Immigrant Rights, "Immigration."

19. Saxton, *Indispensable Enemy*; Takaki, *Strangers*, esp. ch. 3 and 6; Pfaelzer, *Driven Out*.

20. Demographic data from U.S. Census, compiled by Bay Area Census; Kazin, *Barons of Labor*; Perry, "Historian Michael Kazin."

21. Gibson, "Population of the Largest 100 Cities"; Self, *American Babylon*; M. Johnson, *Second Gold Rush*; *Planning History of Oakland*, "Changing Face of Oakland."

22. San Francisco Bay Area Census; Miller, *Postwar Struggle for Civil Rights*, 1–3, 62; Moore, "Getting There, Being There," 106–12.

23. Broussard, *Black San Francisco*; Northern California Coalition on Immigrant Rights, "Japanese Internment"; Self, *American Babylon*, 211 (Cobb quote); *Planning History of Oakland*, "Changing Face of Oakland"; Murch, *Living for the City*, 20–25, 37–39.

24. Roger, "Liberal Journalist," 158–59; Cherny, "Longshore Workers," slides 23–24.

25. C. Barnes, *Longshoremen*, 3.

26. Sideris, *Sifuna Imali Yethu*, 4; Basinstreet.com, "Clarence Williams"; Williams, "Longshoreman's Blues"; Cole, *Wobblies on the Waterfront*, 12–19.

27. After the union emerged in the 1930s, San Francisco longshoremen's earnings and conditions improved dramatically, including a maximum limit on the weight of cargo per sling.

28. Sideris, *Sifuna Imali Yethu*, 1. Callebert, citing Mphiwa Buxton Mbatha in "Livelihood Strategies," noted that "Some, however, thought of the word *onyathi* as a derogatory term,

pointing to the fact that they were 'straight from the bush'" (171). Organizer Mike Morris wrote in 1986 that many dockworkers used the same term but considered themselves "shit bucket removers" (Morris, "Stevedoring and the General Workers Union," part 1, 99).

29. C. Barnes, *Longshoremen*, 133; Sideris, *Sifuna Imali Yethu*, 32; Theriault, *How to Tell*, 133–34.

30. Sideris, *Sifuna Imali Yethu*, 9–10 (Ngcobo), 23 (Khanye); Allen, *Port Chicago Mutiny*; Schwartz, *Solidarity Stories*, 12 (Bridges quote); Selvin, *Terrible Anger*, 41–42; C. Barnes, *Longshoremen*, 130–31 (last two quotes).

31. Sideris, *Sifuna Imali Yethu*, 19; Quin, *The Big Strike*, 31–32 (quote from "Maritime Crisis"); Selvin, *Terrible Anger*, 37; Weinhauer, "*Labour Market*."

32. Selvin, *Terrible Anger*, 34 (Foisie quote); L. Thompson, *History of South Africa*, 163–67; Hemson, "Dock Workers," 104–6.

33. C. Barnes, *Longshoremen*, 60–67; Selvin, *Terrible Anger*, 34–36 (quote on 34 from National Longshoremen's Board proceedings, held in San Francisco in July–August 1934); Schwartz, *Solidarity Stories*, 13–14.

34. PNAAB, "A Brief History of the Durban Municipal Department of Bantu Administration," file 1/12/6, n.d., but likely 1974, KCF 82, roll 64; Callebert, "Livelihood Strategies," 3, 33–34; Hemson, "Dock Workers," 120n108; Atkins, *Moon Is Dead*, 60, 100–114, esp. 109; Cooper, *On the African Waterfront*. Callebert defined *induna* as a "headman, both a position in the traditional political hierarchy and an African supervisor in the workplace," the plural being *izinduna*. Hemson, however, more sharply analyzed the position: "*Indunas* are African foremen; the language of tribalism has been incorporated into South African industrial relations. Management has embedded the concept of *induna* with its military and tribal associations into the supervision of labour at the place of work."

35. Sideris, *Sifuna Imali Yethu*, 14.

36. Roger, "Liberal Journalist," 280; Vrana interview; John Fern, "Good Man Gone," *ILWU Dispatcher*, December 1996, 11.

37. Hoffer, *Working and Thinking*; Linebaugh and Rediker, *Many-Headed Hydra*; van der Linden, "On the Importance of Crossing Boundaries"; Nelson, *Divided We Stand*, ch. 1–2. The Jamaican-born, Harlem-based leftist Claude McKay's novel, *Banjo* (1929), set on the waterfront in 1920s Marseilles, is an example of the cosmopolitan nature of maritime workers and the African diaspora, as is Ousmane Sembene's novel *Le Docker Noir* (1956).

38. Levinson, *Box*, 2 (first quote), 11 (second and third quotes); Fairley, *Facing Mechanization*; Dubbeld, "Breaking the Buffalo"; Cole, "Tip of the Spear."

39. "What's in a Name? For ILWU, It's Not 'Men,'" *Journal of Commerce*, May 4, 1997; Callebert, "Livelihood Strategies," 1–2; SATAWU, "Gender and HIV and AIDS"; Walsh, "Gender in the History," 545.

40. Alimahomed-Wilson, *Solidarity Forever?*, 127; Pilcher, *Portland Longshoremen*; Ayers, "Making of Men"; Barrett and Mesatywa interview; ILWU, "Women of the Waterfront"; Stanley, "When the 'Ladies' Took to Loading"; Letwin, "Interracial Unionism"; Roediger, *Wages of Whiteness*, 3–17.

41. Ringrose, *Natal Regional Survey*, 4: 7–8, 14; La Hause, "Drinking in the Cage," 64–65 (ellipses in Jameson quote); Sideris, *Sifuna Imali Yethu*, 5.

42. Callebert, "Livelihood Strategies"; Hemson, "Dock Workers," 109–10; Letwin, "Interracial Unionism"; Magubane, *Bernard Magubane*, 16.

43. Sideris, *Sifuna Imali Yethu*, 15; Cooper, *On the African Waterfront*.

44. Sideris, *Sifuna Imali Yethu*, 25–26; Ashby and Hawking, *Staley*.

45. Sideris, *Sifuna Imali Yethu*, 25–26; Callebert, "Cleaning the Wharves," 24–25 (quotes).

46. Maylam and Edwards, Preface to *People's City*, xi; Freund, "City Hall," 18, 36n16; La Hause, "Drinking in the Cage"; Magubane, *Bernard Magubane*, 20; Johnston, *Durban Chronicle*, 205–6, 242; Sideris, *Sifuna Imali Yethu*, 5; Callebert, "Livelihood Strategies," 85–94.

47. La Hausse, "Message of the Warriors"; Callebert, "Livelihood Strategies," 276–77; Edwards, "Recollections," 65–66; Vinson, *Americans Are Coming*, 72. After multiracial democracy emerged, downtown Durban's Alice Street was renamed for Nkosi and, nationally, the Day of the Covenant renamed Day of Reconciliation; SAHO, *Johannes Nkosi and December 16*.

48. Hemson, "Dock Workers," 91–92; Hyslop, "Navigating Empire"; Johnston, *Durban Chronicle*, 257; Horwood, *Port of Durban*, ch. 3.

49. Hemson, "Dock Workers," 91–102 (both quotes on 93); Cooper, "Race, Ideology, and the Perils," 1134; Ringrose, *Trade Unions in Natal*, 30; Callebert, "Livelihood Strategies," 102–3.

50. Hemson, "Dock Workers," 93–102 (first quote, 96; second, 97); Callebert, "Livelihood Strategies," 2 (*inyathi* quotes), 103–6, 285 (final quote); Edwards, "Recollections," 73–74; Kiloh and Sibeko, *Fighting Union*, 19. War Measure 145 remained law until 1953, meaning that striking remained illegal for African workers. In 1953, the Native Labour (Settlement of Disputes) Act of 1953 "again prohibited strikes by African workers": Horrell, *South African Trade Unionism*, 60.

51. Hemson, "Dock Workers," 104–15; Johnston, *Durban Chronicle*, 258; C. Ndlovu interview; Callebert, "Livelihood Strategies," 65 (Edwards's quote of Mthethwe); Vahed, "Making of Indian Identity," 258.

52. Vahed, "Making of Indian Identity," 233–40, 256–57; Callebert, "Livelihood Strategies," 108–12.

53. Toli, "Origins of the Durban Strikes," 127–29; Edwards, "Recollections," 71–72; Vahed, "Making of Indian Identity," 233–40, 256–57; Callebert, "Livelihood Strategies," 106. The CPSA was not the first organization to promote nonracialism, rather it was anarcho-syndicalists; see Cole and van der Walt, "Crossing the Color Lines"; van der Walt, "Anarchism and Syndicalism."

54. Vahed, "Making of Indian Identity," 257–62; C. Ndlovu interview; SADET, *Road to Democracy*, 1: 362 (final quote from C. Ndlovu).

55. SAIRR, "Durban Group Areas: Statement Submitted to the Land Tenure Advisory Board," September 30, 1952," folder 9, box 5, Hepple Papers; Hemson, "Dock Workers," 111–2; Vahed, "Making of Indian Identity," 261–68 (quote on 264); Vahed, "Segregation," 19–30; Sookrajh, "Plessislaer," 115.

56. Vahed, "Making of Indian Identity," 261–68 (quote on 268); Freund, "City Hall," 19; Maharaj, "Segregation"; Breckenridge, "Promiscuous Method," 43. Cato Manor was

designated white-only under the Group Areas Act of 1950. Despite massive resistance and suffering, by the late 1950s about eighty-one thousand Africans had been relocated to the KwaMashu and Umlazi townships and about seventy-five thousand Indians to Chatsworth and Phoenix.

57. Schwartz, *Solidarity Stories*, 36 (Kagel quote); Brecher, *Strike!* ch. 5; ILWU-PMA, 2017 Paid Holidays; correspondence with ILWU librarian Robin Walker; Quin, *Big Strike*.

58. Quin, *Big Strike*, 196–99, 231, 255–58; Freeman, "Organizing New York." If jobs remained to be filled after all union members seeking work had been dispatched, they were assigned to probationary unions members and, then, others not in the union. Sometimes, when other unions went on strike, longshore work was given to strikers.

59. Mills, "San Francisco Waterfront," part 1, 222–30 (quote on 230); Nelson, *Workers on the Waterfront*, esp. ch. 1; Kimeldorf, *Reds or Rackets*, 111–12; Cole and van der Walt, "Crossing the Color Lines."

60. Kagel interview, Schwartz, *Solidarity Stories*, 55–59. Thanks to Harvey Schwartz and Robert Cherny for discussions on arbitration.

61. Larrowe wrote the standard, if dated, biography, *Harry Bridges*, 5 (first quote); Cherny, "Making of a Labor Radical," 381 (second quote); and Cherny, "Longshoremen."

62. Broeze, "Militancy and Pragmatism"; Larrowe, *Harry Bridges*, ch. 3–8; Cherny, "Making of a Labor Radical," 383–88; Johns, "Winning for Losing," 4 (quote); Theriault, *Unmaking*, 30–34. I remain on the fence about whether Bridges belonged to the CPUSA, though many in his orbit definitely were members.

63. Schwartz, *March Inland*; Theriault, *Unmaking*, 5. On hip-pocket rules, see Larrowe, *Shape-Up and Hiring Hall*, 130–31, and C. Williams interview, August 16, 2014.

64. Jenkins, "Linking Up the Golden Gate," 274; Chester interview, 8–9; Schwartz, *Solidarity Stories*, 38–45 (Williams quote), 141 (Morrow quote).

65. David Hemson, "Class Consciousness"; Callebert, "Livelihood Strategies," 8–9; C. Williams interview, August 16, 2014; Robinson interview; Bagwell interview.

66. Luckhardt and Wall, *Organize or Starve*, 277.

Chapter 2. Fighting Racial Oppression in the 1940s and 1950s

1. Friedman, "Before and After," 4–12; Glaser, "Reflection on the Von Holdt–Plaut Debate"; Korstad, *Civil Rights Unionism*; Essa, "Opposition to Israeli Cargo at Durban's Dock."

2. Linebaugh and Rediker, *Many-Headed Hydra*, esp. ch. 5; Mah, *Port Cities*, 10.

3. Important histories of the postwar United States, especially the "long" 1960s, offer little on workers, unions, or working-class activism. See Gitlin, *The Sixties*; Chafe, *Unfinished Journey*; Isserman and Kazin, *America Divided*.

4. Maylam, introduction to Maylam and Edwards, *People's City*, 9.

5. Simons and Simons, *Class and Colour*, 611; Davidson, *No Fist Is Big Enough*, 16–17; Cooper, *On the African Waterfront*.

6. Edwards, "Recollections"; Lichtenstein, "Hope for White and Black?"; Johanningsmeier, "Communists and Black Freedom Movements"; Fredrickson, *Black Liberation*, 179–224 (quote on 179); Lodge, "Secret Party"; Magubane, *Bernard Magubane*, 41; Grant, *Winning*, 24.

7. Kiloh and Sibeko, *Fighting Union*, 19–20 (Nair quote). Grant's book was published just prior to this one, so I only could incorporate some of his book's insights into my own.

8. Simons and Simons, *Class and Colour*, 616; Sideris, *Sifuna Imali Yethu*, 5; Hepple, *African Worker*, 6 (Schoeman quote, ellipses in original).

9. Zulu Phungula, "Notice," n.d., Native Affairs Department, file 353/280, box 339/280–353/280, NTS 2206, National Archives of South Africa, Pretoria; SAHO, *Rowley Israel Arenstein*; Hemson, "Dock Workers," 113–17. Coincidentally, Alan Paton's famous novel *Cry, the Beloved Country* began "There is a lovely road which runs from Ixopo into the hills. These hills are grass covered and rolling, and they are lovely beyond any singing of it."

10. Hemson, "Dock Workers," 123; Sideris, *Sifuna Imali Yethu*, 13, 15; R. Watling, Acting Native Commissioner, Durban, to Chief Native Commissioner, Pietermaritzburg, "Labour Dispute: Dock Area," June 5, 1952, Native Affairs Department, file 353/280, box 339/280–353/280, NTS 2206. Callebert cited a 1948 incident when *togt* workers refused to elect a delegation to discuss conditions—but not during a strike; Callebert, "Livelihood Strategies," 288.

11. C. W. Slarke, Native Commissioner, Durban, to Chief Native Commissioner, Pietermaritzburg, "Dispute: Stevedores, Durban," July 9, 1954, and Central Native Labour Board, "Recommendation," July 8, 1954, in Native Affairs Department, file 353/280, box 339/280–353/280, NTS 2206; Hepple, *African Worker*, 25; Hemson, "Dock Workers," 88, 116–17 (Congress of Democrats quote); Callebert, "Livelihood Strategies," 290–93; Lichtenstein, "Making Apartheid Work"; "Stevedores' Pay Rate Explained," *Herald* [Port Elizabeth], March 23, 1957, n.p., and other clippings in box 1, folder 1, Hepple Papers, Melville J. Herskovits Library of African Studies. The Native Labour (Settlement of Disputes) Act of 1953 replaced War Measure 145. The minister of labour appointed the newly created CNLB "to represent the interests of African workers" though all its members were white and strikes by African workers and African unions remained illegal; see Alexander, *Workers*, 124.

12. Callebert, "Livelihood Strategies," 293–95 (Mentz quote, 294); Luckhardt and Wall, *Organize or Starve*, 277–79; Hemson, "Dock Workers," 116–17; Schwartz, *Solidarity Stories*, 12, 65.

13. Hemson, "Dock Workers," 117–18; Luckhardt and Wall, *Organize or Starve*, 279–81; *Natal Mercury*, March 6, 1958, 2.

14. Hemson, "Dock Workers," 117–19, 123; Horrell, *South African Trade Unionism*, 81; *Natal Mercury*, April 14, 1, April 19, 1958, 3 (quote), April 21, 1958, 1, April 22, 1958, 3, 13; Magubane, *Bernard Magubane*, 43; Lichtenstein, "Making Apartheid Work," 303–4; Sideris, *Sifuna Imali Yethu*, 15 ("overtime ban"); Baskin, *Striking Back*, 13–14; Callebert, "Livelihood Strategies," 299.

15. Lambert, "Political Unionism," 249 (quote); Baskin, *Striking Back*, 13 (SACTU quote); Hemson, "Dock Workers," 90; Freund, *Insiders and Outsiders*, 59; Lodge, "Secret Party," 440; Padayachee, Vawda, and Tichman, *Indian Workers*, 159–67.

16. C. Ndlovu interview; Curnick Ndlovu interview in SADET, *Road to Democracy*, 1: 363–69; SAHO, *Curnick Muzuvukile Ndlovu* (final quote); Lambert, "Political Unionism in South Africa," 481–82; Sambureni, "Working in the Apartheid City," 206; Lodge, "Secret Party," 455; Kiloh and Sibeko, *Fighting Union*; SAHO, *Sharpeville Massacre*.

17. Ndlovu in SADET, *Road to Democracy*, 1: 364–69 (quotes on 367–68); Horrell, *Racialism*, 13. Ndlovu's SADET interview, of course, provides far more depth than the one he gave in 1983 when shortly out of prison while the nation remained under apartheid. For more on the Durban MK, see Justice Mpanza and Eleanor Kasrils interviews in SADET, *Road to Democracy*, 1: 337–41 and 133–38. For a more critical view of Ndlovu's actions after arrested, see Fred Dube interview in same volume, 106.

18. SAHO, *SACTU and the Congress Alliance* (Nair quote); SAHO, *Kay Moonsamy*; SAHO, *Billy Nair*; Lambert, "Political Unionism in South Africa"; Sambureni, "'Listen, Whiteman.'"

19. *Natal Mercury*, February 25, 1959, 2, February 26, 1959, 1–2, February 27, 1959, 8; Horrell, *Racialism*, 13; Callebert, "Livelihood Strategies," 298–306 (quote on 304); Hemson, "Dock Workers," 120–22; Hughes, "African encounters," 361–62. The ILWU reported on this strike, by way of Australia's Waterside Worker Federation; see *Dispatcher*, August 5, 1959, 3.

20. Hemson, "Dock Workers," 89; Sideris, *Sifuna Imali Yethu*, 23–24; Labour History Group, *Durban Strikes*, 2.

21. Callebert, "Livelihood Strategies," 4 (first quote), 298n201 (Native Affairs quote); *Natal Mercury*, February 27, 1959, 8; Horrell, *South African Trade Unionism*.

22. Nelson, *Divided*, 89–90 (quotes), 95; Jenkins, "Linking Up the Golden Gate," 274; Miller, *Postwar Struggle*, 1–3, 26, 29; Dellums interview, 138–39.

23. Schmidt interview, 228–29; Chester interview, 6; Dellums interview, 139–40; Nelson, *Divided*, 96–97 (Bridges quote).

24. Schmidt interview, 228–29; Nelson, *Workers on the Waterfront*, 260 (Northrup quote); Mills, "San Francisco Waterfront," 3; Davis, "Shape or Fight," 146. In *Divided*, Nelson argued that the ILA was good in comparison with most US labor unions, if not the ILWU, on race matters (61).

25. Gregory, *Southern Diaspora*, preface; Kimeldorf, *Reds or Rackets*, 144–45; Record, "Willie Stokes"; McEntyre and Tranopol, "Postwar Status."

26. Williams interview, June 22, 2011; Chester interview, by Martin, 1–5.

27. Record, "Willie Stokes" (quote on 177); Schwartz, *Solidarity Stories*, 44–45; Broussard, *Black San Francisco*; Self, *American Babylon*, 54–56; Rhomberg, *No There*, 99–102; M. Johnson, *Second Gold Rush*, 80.

28. Oakland and San Francisco demographics from multiple pages at http://www.bayareacensus.ca.gov/; Williams in Schwartz, *Solidarity Stories*, 45–51 (quote on 51); Chester interview, by Martin, 6–12; Williams interview, June 22, 2011 (quote on rank and file); "Local 10 Probes Navy Officer's Storm-Trooper Discrimination against S. F. Negro Longshoreman," *Dispatcher*, April 23, 1943, 7; Bulcke interview, 60.

29. Williams in Schwartz, *Solidarity Stories*, 48 (Bridges quote); Ahlquist and Levi, *In the Interest*, 81–90, 100–101; Kimeldorf, *Reds or Rackets*, 144, 162–65 (quote on 144); Zieger, *CIO*; Halpern, *Down on the Killing Floor*. Johanningsmeier and van der Walt each argued that the IWW (and anarcho-syndicalism) influenced the CPUSA's and CPSA's antiracism: Johanningsmeier, "Communists and Black Freedom Movements," 159–60; van der Walt, "Bakunin's Heirs."

30. Roediger, *Towards the Abolition*, 139; Arnesen, *Waterfront Workers*; Woodrum, *"Everybody Was Black"*; Self, *American Babylon*, 53 (quote), 84.

31. Larrowe, *Harry Bridges*, ch. 5–7, 9–10; Larrowe, "Did the Old Left Get Due Process?" 41 (quote); Mills, "San Francisco Waterfront," addendum no. 4; ILWU, "Everlasting Bridges Case," 5 (Murphy quote) and 14 (criticizing Supreme Court quote); Seeger, "Ballad of Harry Bridges"; Schwartz, "Harry Bridges"; Lichtenstein, "Hope for White and Black,'" 133–36.

32. Chester, in Schwartz, *Solidarity Stories*, 6, 9–10, 26 (quote on 9–10); Kimeldorf, *Reds or Rackets*, 148 (Williams); Record, "Willie Stokes," 187–88 (quote on 188); Horne, *Black and Red*. On the instrumental role of the CPUSA in the southern civil-rights movement, see Gilmore, *Defying Dixie*.

33. Williams interview, June 22, 2011; Mills, "San Francisco Waterfront," 13; Watson interview, 32–36; Larrowe, *Harry Bridges*, ch. 5–7, 9. In addition to Bridges, the international's vice president, J. R. "Bob" Robertson, and coast committeeman Henry Schmidt were codefendants in a trial that ended with the Supreme Court absolving all three of guilt; see Bridges-Robertson-Schmidt Defense Committee, "The Real Target" in Mills's essay, addendum no. 4.

34. Nelson, *Divided*, 110–28 (Faustian quote, 124) and ch. 5–7; Alimahomed-Wilson, *Solidarity Forever*; Ahlquist and Levi, *In the Interest*, 95–97; Kimeldorf, *Reds or Rackets*, 145–46; Munk, "Francis Murnane"; Clarence Thomas, "ILWU Convention Denies Voice of Black Members," *Workers World*, June 26, 2006, http://www.workers.org/2006/us/ilwu-0706/; Davis, "Shape or Fight."

35. Chester, interview by Martin, 7–10 (quote on 8); C. Williams interview, June 22, 2011; Nelson, *Divided*, 89–141; Kimeldorf, *Reds or Rackets*, 144–47 (quote on 144); Arnesen, *Waterfront Workers*; Leo Robinson Memorial Service, ILWU Local 10.

36. Record, "Willie Stokes," 176; Williams, in Schwartz, *Solidarity Stories*, 47–48; Bulcke interview, 160, 213; Nelson, *Divided*, 113–22; Mills, "San Francisco Waterfront," 6; Alimahomed-Wilson, *Solidarity Forever*.

37. *Local 10 Longshore Bulletin*, February 19, 1948; Kerr and Fisher, "Conflict," 21–22; Nelson, *Divided*, 98–99; Kimeldorf, *Reds or Rackets*, 138, 148–51 (quote on 149); "Letter from Harry Bridges, International President, ILWU, to the Officers and Executive Board, Local 10, ILWU," n.d. [probably 1949], addendum no. 5, in Mills, "San Francisco Waterfront," 45–48; Alimahomed-Wilson, *Solidarity Forever*, 64 and ch. 3–4.

38. Mills, "San Francisco Waterfront," 1–12; Kimeldorf, *Reds or Rackets*, 149; Williams interview, August 16, 2014. My source for the standing vote was Williams. It seems curious that Bridges pushed for the standing vote after he had raised the issue (cutting Local 10 membership) in the first place and later highlighted this vote as an example of the members rejecting his advice. Bridges's motives only can be guessed at but he was a brilliant strategist.

39. Mills, "San Francisco Waterfront," 1–12 (quote on 12); US Congress, House of Representatives, *Study of Harbor Conditions*, 328–29 (Bridges's "Statement"); Williams interview, August 16, 2014; Nelson, *Divided*, 98–99; Ignatiev, "Treason to Whiteness."

40. Schwartz, *March Inland*, 6, 101, 169 (quotes on all three); "ILWU Vice-President Emeritus: Bill Chester Helped Lead ILWU during Tough Times," *Dispatcher*, November 12, 1985, 5; Rhomberg, *No There*, 47, 85–86, figure 11 (quote); Self, *American Babylon*, 69 (quote), 84.

41. Chester, interview by Martin, 27; Crowe, *Prophets*, 60; Audley L. Cole obituary, *SF Gate*, June 25, 2008, http://www.legacy.com/obituaries/sfgate/obituary.aspx?n=audley -l-cole&pid=112160802; Kelley, "*We Are Not*," 76 (quote); McGuire, *At the Dark End*, esp. ch. 3. Chester called him Audry but the obituary refers to him as Audley.

42. Chester, interview by Martin, 13–26 (quotes, in order, on 26, 29, 24 and 13); Crowe, *Prophets*, 60–61 (quote on 61).

43. Watson interview, 48–57 (quotes on 51, 56–57); Bagwell interview; *Dispatcher*, February 22, 1963, 1; Julian Guthrie, "Labor's Jimmy Herman Dies at 73," *SF Gate*, March 22, 1998, http://www.sfgate.com/bayarea/article/Labor-s-Jimmy-Herman-dies-at-73 -3099201.php.

44. Bagwell interview; Watson, in Schwartz, *Solidarity Stories*, 55–57; e-mail correspondence with Brian McWilliams (Local 34 member and a former international president), Gene Vrana, and Harvey Schwartz.

45. *Dispatcher*, June 14, 1963, 6, and January 6, 1967, 1; Chester, interview by Martin, 11–13 (quote 12–13); C. Williams interview, June 22, 2011; Kimeldorf, *Reds or Rackets*, 144–51; Self, *American Babylon*, 211 (Cobb quote).

46. Chester, interview by Martin, 31; Crowe, *Prophets*, 60; Self, *American Babylon*, 185; Jenkins, "Rivets and Rights."

47. Hemson, "Dock Workers," 117 (Congress of Democrats quote); Cooper, *On the African Waterfront*, 49, 278 (quote) and *Decolonization in African Society*.

48. Tomkins, "Profiles," 74.

Chapter 3. Fighting Racial Oppression in the 1960s and 1970s

1. Horwood, *Port of Durban*, 78; SADET, *Road to Democracy*, 2: xii; Turnbull, "Dock Strikes."

2. Lambert, "Eddie Webster," 27–28; Hemson, "Dock Workers," 120; Horwood, *Port of Durban*, 78; Brown, *Road to Soweto*; SAHO, *State of Emergency Declared*.

3. Ross-Watt, "Housing," 5; handwritten notes, in English, accompanying *Isisebenzi*, no. 1, n.d. [1971?], G.3.12 (iv), NUSAS Archive, University of Cape Town Special Collections, Cape Town; *Natal Mercury*, April 7, 1969, 1–2 (quotes), and "Durban Dock Labourers Average R68 a Month," April 9, 1969, n.p.; Hemson, "1973 Natal Strike Wave," 5.

4. *Natal Mercury*, April 7, 1969, 1 (first quote), April 8, 1969, 1 (rest of quotes), and April 9, 1969 (third quote); Hemson, "Dock Workers," 123; *Isisebenzi*, no. 1.

5. Ross-Watt, "Housing," 5; *Natal Mercury*, April 7, 1969, 1, April 8, 1969, 1, and "Durban Dock Labourers Average R68 a Month," April 9, 1969; Saul and Bond, *South Africa*, 59 (dumping ground quote); Dubbeld, "Labour Management," 7 (quote), 72; Horrell, *Survey: 1969*, 112.

6. Horrell, *Survey: 1968*, 112; Friedman, *Building Tomorrow Today*, 32, 37 (quote), 44.

7. Shaffer, "Competitive Position," 234; Baskin, *Striking Back*, 17; Freund, "Democracy and the Colonial Heritage," 107.

8. Saul and Bond, *South Africa*, 57 (golden age quote); Sideris, *Sifuna Imali Yethu*, 27; Hemson, "Eye of the Storm," 160; Hemson, Legassick, and Ulrich, "White Activists," in SADET, *Road to Democracy*, 2: 248 (Alexander quote), 2: 251–52; Hemson, "30 Anniversary" (final quote).

9. SAHO, *NUSAS Wages Commission Timeline 1971–1973*; *Natal Mercury*, January 20, 1970, 20; Horrell, *Survey: 1971*, 247 (quote on DSLSC manager); Dubbeld, "Breaking the Buffalo," 104; Davie, "Strength in Numbers," 413–14; Sithole and Ndlovu, "Revival," 191–92; Cronjé and Cronjé, *Workers of Namibia*, 77–89.

10. Hemson, "Eye of the Storm," 160.

11. Davie, "Strength in Numbers," 409–15 (Davis and final quote, 415); Cheadle interview; Ross, *Concise History*, 143; Friedman, *Building Tomorrow Today*, 46, 62. On the Wage Board, Davie writes, the South African "Department of Labour established the Wage Board to monitor working conditions and set wages for African labourers who had been excluded [because they were Africans] from the Industrial Conciliation Act" of 1924 (409).

12. Davie, "Strength in Numbers," 401–18; Cheadle interview; Lambert, "Eddie Webster," 29; Hemson, "30 Anniversary"; Hemson et al., "White Activists," 252–54.

13. Keniston, *Choosing*, 52, 84–86 (first quote on 84, Cheadle quote on 86); Webster, "Moral Decay," 1; Davie, "Strength in Numbers," 404–7; Macqueen, "Resonances."

14. Horrell et al., *Survey: 1972*, 325; Hemson, "Class Consciousness and Migrant Workers," 568–72; Friedman, *Building Tomorrow Today*, 62 (Bolton quote); Labour History Group, *Durban Strikes*, 6 (first Cheadle quote); Keniston, *Choosing*, 89 (second Cheadle quote); Keal, "Life's Work," 127–32; Sithole and Ndlovu, "Revival," 202–3; Cheadle interview; Davie, "Strength in Numbers," 413–18 (Ndlovu quotes on 418).

15. IIE, *The Durban Strikes*, 6; Maree, "Seeing Strikes in Perspective"; Hemson, "Eye of the Storm," 160 (quote); Hemson, "Trade Unionism," 22–23; Sithole and Ndlovu, "Revival," 211–20; Davie, "Strength in Numbers," 403n12; Ross-Watt, "Housing," 35.

16. SAHO, *Stephen J. C. Dlamini*; Hemson et al., "White Activists," 253 (Nxasana quote); Legassick, "Debating the Revival," 255–56; Keniston, *Choosing*, 128; Nxasana interviewed by Webster, *Cast in a Racial Mode*, 151n16; Badsha interview.

17. Badsha interview; Webster interview.

18. Sideris, *Sifuna Imali Yethu*, 19–22, 29 (quote on 29); *Natal Mercury*, October 24, 1972, 1–2, 11; Davie, "Strength in Numbers," 418; Hemson, "1973 Natal Strike Wave," 6 (quote). Fozia Fisher highlighted the class nature driving the hostility toward Buthelezi: "From the strikes and from conversations with workers it is possible to say that the workers are usually fairly hostile to any Africans, such as 'indunas' or personnel managers, who work for management. They see them in class terms, as part of management, rather than in race terms as fellow members of a group which is discriminated against." See "Class Consciousness," 218. Fisher was Turner's wife; though he was banned, he secretly contributed to her essays.

19. Lichtenstein, "Measure of Democracy," 118–19 (sleep quote); Dubbeld, "Labour Management," 59; Morris Ndlovu interview, in Killie Campbell Africana Library, University of KwaZulu-Natal [hereafter, Killie Campbell]; S. K. Ngubese interview, Umlazi, KCAV 185–185, Killie Campbell, 2; "Confidential to Members: The Current Bantu Labour Stoppages," Durban Chamber of Commerce, February 9, 1973, Port Natal Administration Board records, PNAAB, KCF 82, roll 64, Killie Campbell. Based upon Morris Ndlovu's and Curnick Ndlovu's interviews, they clearly were not related despite sharing a family name, one that happens to be quite common.

20. Horrell et al., *Survey: 1972*, 325; Morris Ndlovu interview; Sideris, *Sifuna Imali Yethu*, 28–29; Callebert, "Livelihood Strategies," 290–93.

21. Horrell et al., *Survey: 1972*, 327–28; Horrell and Horner, *Survey: 1973*, 261–62; Hemson, "Beyond the Frontier," 84–85; Labour History Group, *Durban Strikes*, 7; Toli, "Origins," 417.

22. IIE, *Durban Strikes*, 38; Toli, "Origins," abstract.

23. Toli, "Origins," 1, 13–14 (first quote), 210–13 (quote from *Daily News*, January 1, 1973); Hemson, "Eye of the Storm," 160–61; Morris Ndlovu interview; Friedman, *Building Tomorrow Today*, 62; Hemson, "1973 Natal Strike Wave," 5 (trucks quote), 14–15; Khwela, "1973 Strikes," 20–21 (report of Natal Worker History Project, including interviews with Coronation workers who refused to elect a committee); Sambureni, "Working in the apartheid city," 219–20, 228.

24. Sambureni, "Working in the Apartheid City," 235 (toilet quote); Hemson, "1973 Natal Strike Wave," 8–11; Morris, "Stevedoring," part 1, 103; Lichtenstein, "Making Apartheid Work" and "Measure of Democracy."

25. James Zurichm "Opening Address of President Bro. Jas. Zurich to the 42nd Conference of the Artisan Staff Association," *ASA Journal* 39, no. 4 (1973): 4, Utatu library, Johannesburg. Thanks to Jane Barrett, formerly of SATAWU, for helping me gain access to Utatu, a descendant of the ASA.

26. Toli, "Origins," 210–12; Kiloh and Sibeko, *Fighting Union*, 68–69; Morris, "Stevedoring," part 1, 90–95, 107–8; Labour History Group, *Durban Strikes*, 30 (quote); Hemson, "Class Consciousness and Migrant Workers," 719.

27. Hemson, "Beyond the Frontier," 84; Mamdani, *Citizen and Subject*, 233. Friedman's *Building Tomorrow Today* has "The 1970s began for South African employers early on the morning of January 9, 1973, when 2 000 workers at the Coronation Brick and Tile works on the outskirts of Durban gathered at a football field and demanded a pay raise" (37). Baskin's *Striking Back*, devotes one sentence to the dockers' 1972 strike (17) while Sithole and Ndlovu spend three sentences ("Revival," 191). In his abstract, Toli noted the Durban Strikes "have enjoyed very little scholarly analysis," and his statement remains as true today as in 1991 though Lichtenstein is researching this topic—his future book will be most welcome. Surveys of South African history give much shorter shrift to Durban, but the Durban Strikes universally are begun in January 1973 with Coronation. See Ross, *Concise History*, 152, 212; L. Thompson, *History of South Africa*, 212, 224.

28. Sparks, "Forces under the Surface," *Rand Daily Mail*, November 25, 1972, 9; Lichtenstein, "Measure of Democracy," 115–17.

29. Morphet, "Brushing History," 92; Toli, "Origins," Davie, "Strength in Numbers," 404–5; Keniston, *Choosing*, 88 (O'Meara quote); Macqueen, "Resonances"; Sithole and Ndlovu, "Revival," 201; Hadfield, "Christian Action"; SAHO, *Harold Bhekisisa Nxasana*; South Africa, *Truth and Reconciliation Commission Final Report*, vol. 2, ch. 3, subsection 16, paragraphs 148–59.

30. Hemson, "Eye of the Storm," 160; Sithole and Ndlovu, "Revival," 192; Fisher and Turner quote is in Keniston, *Choosing*, 180n28, but the original citation is F. Fisher, "Class Consciousness," 215–16; Freund, *African Worker*, 37–38.

31. Isserman and Kazin, *America Divided*, 49.

32. Miller, *Postwar Struggle*; Crowe, *Prophets of Rage*; Broussard, *Black San Francisco*; Isserman and Kazin, *America Divided*, 48–49. The first three books cited make up the entire monographic literature on civil rights for San Francisco and, together, offer but a handful of brief references to the ILWU.

33. Goldblatt interview, 281–90; Schwartz, "Union Combats Racism," 164 (Goldblatt quote).

34. Self, *American Babylon*, 4, 46, 53, 69, 77 (all otherwise unattributed quotes); *Dispatcher*, June 8, 1951, 8 (Chester quote), February 22, 1963, 7, February 22, 1963, 7, and April 3, 1964, 4; W. Jones, "Unknown Origins," 36.

35. *Dispatcher*, May 28, 1954, 2 (Bridges quotes), March 25, 1960, 2 (Sharpeville quote), and April 22, 1960, 1; Pach, *Dwight D. Eisenhower*.

36. Chester, interview by Martin, 22; Crowe, *Prophets of Rage*, 115. African Americans made up about 25 percent of Local 10 members but about 65 percent of those "screened," in other words, fired, during the Korean War.

37. US House Committee on Un-American Activities, *Communist Activities*, 1756; Marvin Howe, "Archie Brown, 79, Union Leader in Landmark Case on Communists," *New York Times*, November 25, 1990; Rorabaugh, *Berkeley*, ch. 1, esp. 15–16; Mills, "San Francisco Waterfront." Much more can be found in the *Dispatcher* and at "ILWU History. Un-American Activities Committee. U.S.," ILWU Library. The ILWU Library file discusses a 1953 HUAC hearing in San Francisco, in response to which Local 10 held a "stop work" meeting to protest the subpoenaing of ILWU officers; see "To the Membership of ILWU Local 10," December 3, 1953, and *Longshore Bulletin*, December 2, 1953.

38. Mills, "In Defense," 9–10 (quote); Mills interviews (1, 2, and 3).

39. Baldwin and Clark, "No Compromise," 27; Brahinsky, "Hush Puppies"; Goldblatt interview, 790–801; Cuénod, "Building," "The ILWU" and "Redevelopment A-1."

40. *Dispatcher*, May 31, 1963, 1, August 22, 1963, 7, September 6, 1963, 1–5, and November 12, 1985, 5; Miller, *Postwar Struggle*, 65–66 (makes no mention of Chester or the ILWU); Goldblatt interview, 844 (on the stop-work meeting, the only mention of this action).

41. Jo Freeman, *At Berkeley*, 94–100 (quote), 301; Miller, *Postwar Struggle*, 81; Leonard interview, 138–42. It is interesting that, "As the sixties moved along, it became apparent that for the first time in his life Bridges wasn't moving with the times. He had no sympathy for the student movement, nor apparently any understanding of it" (Larrowe, *Harry Bridges*, 376).

42. "Martin Luther King Speaks at Local 10 Hall," *Dispatcher*, September 29, 1967, 1, 8; Dispatcher, April 12, 1968, 1–2, 4–5, 12; C. Williams interview, June 22, 2011; King, "All Labor," 197–98. Ishmael Reed (*Blues City*, 142) cited David Hilliard about how the Black Panthers also played a key role in keeping Oakland peaceful after King's murder.

43. Ganz, *Why David*, 139–41 (quote on 140–41, ellipses in original); Watson interview, tape 5, side 10, 13–23 (quote on 13); Horne, *Fighting Paradise*.

44. Morris, *Alcatraz Indian Occupation Diary*, 21; *Dispatcher*, January 28, 1970, 5, March 11, 1970, 5, 7 (quote on 7), and March 19, 1971, 5; T. Johnson, *American Indian Occupation*, 79, 160–61, 168.

45. *Dispatcher*, January 6, 1967, 2; Self, *American Babylon*, 50 (second quote), 217 (first quote), 224, 293; Reed, *Blues City*, 84–85; Murch, *Living for the City*, 96; Seale, *Seize the Time*, 71.

46. C. Williams interview, June 22, 2011; Cobbs interview (Hilliard as Local 10 casual); Bagwell interview; Self, *American Babylon*, 50, 205–10, 217; Murch, *Living for the City*, 10, 20–25. Broussard, *Black San Francisco*, and Brahinsky, "Hush Puppies," both document the residential segregation suffered by blacks in San Francisco proper.

47. Black Panther Party Legacy and Alumni, "Jimmy Ward Biography" and "Panther Connection"; Meraji, "Seeking Oakland's Soul"; Murch, *Living for the City*, 20, 234–35.

48. C. Williams interview, June 22, 2011; Western States Golf Association, "Western States"; J. Williams interview; American Idle, "Cheesehead Rebellion"; Harry Bridges Project, "Captain Josh."

49. Rustin, *Down the Line*, 262; Dubow, *Apartheid*, ch. 4; Hemson, "Eye of the Storm," 155–59; Chisholm, "Waterfront Conflict"; Sambureni, "Working in the Apartheid City," 6.

50. Chester, interview by Martin, 22; Bussel, *Fighting*; Reed, *Blues City*, 170–71.

51. Webster, "Impact of Intellectuals"; Linebaugh and Rediker, *Many-Headed Hydra*.

Chapter 4. Decasualization and Containerization

1. A container is a large metal box of a standard design and size used for seamless multimodal transport; that is, the transportation of goods by road, rail, sea, or air.

2. National Museum of American History, "Transforming the Waterfront"; Matson, *History*, www.matson.com/corporate/about_us/history.html; Theriault, *Longshoring*, 3–4; Urbanus, "Rome's Imperial Port."

3. Levinson, *Box*, xi, 1–2; Mah, *Port Cities*, 1.

4. Weinhauer, "Power and Control," 582. The Port of New York City was America's largest and the first to experience containers. The ILA resisted their introduction, however, and so did not sign a contract on containers until later in the 1960s. See Levinson, *Box*; Herod, *Labor Geographies*.

5. Kimeldorf, *Reds or Rackets*, 29–37; Weinhauer, "Power and Control," 592–94. Of course, a worker always could decide whether to shape up and workers who belonged to "star gangs" (a favored group of longshoremen who regularly worked together) avoided shaping up.

6. Coast Education Project, "Hiring Hall"; ILWU Local 19, "Longshoremen's Strike of 1934"; Brecher, *Strike*, 150–80; Kennedy, *Freedom from Fear*. Gang bosses, also called walking bosses, later gained their own locals; see ILWU Local 94, "Walking Bosses and Foremen."

7. Kagel interview, California Historical Society; Weir, *Singlejack*, 256 (Plant quote); Goldblatt interview, 829; letter from Harry Bridges, International President, ILWU, to the Officers and Executive Board, Local 10, ILWU, n.d. [1949?] in Herb Mills, "San Francisco Waterfront," addendum 5, 45; Tomkins, "Profiles," 60–61; ILWU, "Ten Guiding Principles." Nelson cited ILWU Library Archives for Bridges's letter (*Divided*, 99) though I found in Mills.

8. Williams interview, 1; Robinson interview.

9. Mills, "San Francisco Waterfront, part 2, Modern Longshore Operations," 4 (first two quotes); Mills interviews, June 18, 2010, and June 15, 2011 (final quotes from 2011 interview).

10. Goldblatt interview, 830; Hoffer, *Working and Thinking*, 66, 76; Cole interview (Stacy Cole is no relation to this author and was a confidant of Hoffer for decades); Tomkins, "Profiles," 60–61; Parnaby, *Citizen Docker*, 89; Weinhauer, "Power and Control"; Keylor interview, August 12, 2014; Mills interview, June 18, 2010.

11. "Statement of Harry Bridges," U.S. Congress, *Study of Harbor Conditions* hearings, Oct. 21, 1955, 325; Kimeldorf, *Reds or Rackets*; Davis, *Waterfront Revolts*, 63–65; J. Fisher, *Irish Waterfront*; Weinhauer, "Power and Control," 580. Weinhauer claimed (583) that New York City and New Orleans proved harder to decasualize because of multiracial workforces, but he ignored the powerful incentives ILA leaders had to keep membership high in the form of more dues payers, resulting in higher salaries for leaders. ILA leaders maintained power despite repeated challenges by eliminating democracy and using strong-arm tactics; see Mello, *New York Longshoremen*.

12. Callebert, "Livelihood Strategies," 2; Weinhauer, "Power and Control," 580, 587; "Casual Labour," *Encyclopædia Britannica, 2006* (online).

13. Hemson, "Dock Workers"; T. Jones, *Port of Durban and the Durban Metropolitan Economy*, 14; Dubbeld, "Breaking the Buffalo," 101–3; Callebert, "Livelihood Strategies," 276–77, 305.

14. *Natal Mercury*, April 14, 1, April 15, 1958, 1–2, April 19, 1958, 3 (quotes), April 21, 1958, 1, April 22, 1958, 3, 13.

15. *Natal Mercury*, February 25, 1959, 2, February 26, 1959, 1–2, February 27, 1959, 8, March 26, 1959, 1 (quote), 18, March 27, 1959, 15, April 2, 1959, 16 (final quote), April 7, 1959, 1, 3; Horrell, *Racialism*, 13; handwritten notes, in English, accompanying *Isisebenzi* no. 1, n.d. [1971?], G.3.12 (iv), NUSAS Archive, University of Cape Town Special Collections; Callebert, "Livelihood Strategies," 296–300.

16. *Natal Mercury*, February 27, 1959, 8, March 27, 1959, 15; Morris, "Stevedoring," part 1, 101 (quote), 106; Callebert, "Livelihood Strategies," 296–300 (quote on 296).

17. Callebert, "Livelihood Strategies," 15, 170–79 (quote on 175), 296–301; *Natal Mercury*, April 7, 1959, 1; Morris, "Stevedoring," part 1, 101; Hemson, "Dock Workers," 98, 119–22 (worker quotes on 122); von Holdt, *Transition*.

18. *Natal Mercury*, March 6, 1958, 2 (quotes), April 24, 1958, 18; Callebert, "Livelihood Strategies," 296–97; Dubbeld, "Capital," 90.

19. Dubbeld, "Labour Management," 9; Posel, "Influx Control," 418; Sambureni, "Working in the Apartheid City," 42; Callebert, "Livelihood Strategies," 116 (quote), 296–308; Hemson, "30 Anniversary."

20. T. Jones, "Port of Durban," 72–73, 77, 90 (quote); Hemson, "Class Consciousness and Migrant Workers," 386, 412–16; Sambureni, "Working in the Apartheid City," 61–63 (quote on 62–63).

21. Cooper, *On the African Waterfront*, 49 (quote), 168; Kaijage, "*War of Clubs*"; Davis, *Waterfront Revolts*; Weinhauer, "Power and Control," 580–81 (quote on 580); Kimeldorf, *Reds or Rackets*, 29. Durban and Mombasa differed in that families were permitted to live with dockworkers in Mombasa but not in Durban, where they remained bachelor migrants in the city whose families remained in rural homes.

22. Davis, *Waterfront Revolts*, 79; Webster and Kuzwayo, "Research Note," 232–33 (second quote, 233, includes quote from F. A. Johnstone); Callebert, "Livelihood Strategies," 305–8; Dubbeld, "Breaking the Buffalo," 103.

23. Gorter and Hildebrand, *Pacific Coast Maritime Industry*, 2: 175 (first quote); Kerr and Fisher, "Conflict," 17; Larrowe, *Harry Bridges*, 291–99 (quote on 295); B. Glenn Ledbetter, "Who Said It's Simple: West coast stevedoring," *Pacific Maritime Magazine* in *Local 10 Bulletin*, March 15, 1985, 2 (Maritime Administration quote); Kimeldorf, *Reds or Rackets*, ch. 6.

24. Local 10, *Bulletin*, February 26, 1960, 2; Hoffer, "Automation," 48; Schumpeter, *Capitalism*, 81. The geographic impacts of containers on ports are important and fascinating but beyond this book's scope.

25. Livernash, "Review," 222; Bridges, "Up from Down Under: Fifty Years of Waterfront Unionism," January 16, 1978, 21, Bridges Papers, series 2, box 3, folder 13, Labor Archives and Research Center [hereafter, LARC], San Francisco State University; Fairley, *Facing Mechanization*, 1–4, 68 ("guerrilla" quote); Seligman, *Most Notorious*, 244–47 (quote on 245); Bridges-Robertson-Schmidt Defense Committee, "The Real Target"; Larrowe, *Harry Bridges*, 351–55 (quote on 352); ILWU, "Information and Union Comment on the 1960 Mechanization and Modernization Fund Agreement between the Longshoremen of the Pacific Coast and the Steamship and Stevedoring Employers," 3, ILRE (final two quotes). Bridges started but never finished a memoir with a professional writer; see Bridges Papers, series 2: Autobiography, LARC. His last wife, Nikki, conducted extensive interviews with her husband in 1978–79, shortly after his retirement. I only first discovered these tapes in August 2016, for the existence of this information is almost entirely unknown. Worse, these cassettes are neither indexed nor transcribed and seem to focus upon the pre-WWII era. Historian Robert Cherny, long at work on his needed biography of Bridges, was given the originals by Bridges's widow; the ILWU Library possesses the only other copy.

26. Sekula, *Fish Story*, 134; Gorter and Hildebrand, *Pacific Coast Maritime Industry*, 2: 211–12 (first quote), 2: 314 (second quote); Carrabino, *Engineering Analysis*, ii–iv; Levinson, *Box*, ch. 3–4, esp. 65; *Dispatcher*, October 24, 1958, 3.

27. Fairley, *Facing Mechanization*, 1, 3, 108–10; 253; Winter, "Thirty Years," 82–85; Kossoris, "Working Rules," 3; Larrowe, *Harry Bridges*, 352–55 (startled quote, 352); Wellman, *Union Makes Us Strong*, esp. 82–105; Ahlquist and Levi, *In the Interest*; ILWU, "About the Coast Longshore Division." Fairley noted that contract ratification votes in general, other than on first and second M&M, were more than 90 percent in favor.

28. ILWU-PMA, "Joint News Release," October 18, 1960, ILRE; Bridges, "Up from Down Under," 22, Bridges Papers, LARC; Goldblatt interview, 807–42, esp. 816–19 (quote on 818); Fairley, *Facing Mechanization*, 148–49 ("old-timer" quote), 228; *Dispatcher*, December 2, 1960, 8 ("guerrilla" quote) and January 13, 1961, 5; Bulcke, "Longshore Leader," 208–11; Williams interview 2; Seligman, *Most Notorious*, 245; Carrabino, *Engineering Analysis*, 24–25 (final quote).

29. Hagel and Goldblatt, *Men and Machines*, 3, 14.

30. Sidney Roger interview, 566; Fairley, *Facing Mechanization*, 193–221; Carrabino, *Engineering Analysis*, 23; Goldblatt interview, 814–16 (quote on 815); Larrowe, *Harry Bridges*,

356 (Hoffer quote); Weir, *Singlejack*, 303. Weir cited Local 10's *Longshore Bulletin*, February 8, 1962, for the accident rate.

31. Hartman, *Collective Bargaining*, 12; Fairley, *Facing Mechanization*, 69, 219–26, 305–22; Broeze, *Globalisation*, 237; Maritime Cargo Transportation Conference, *San Francisco Port Study*, 2.

32. Hagel and Goldblatt, *Men and Machines*, 33; Fairley, *Facing Mechanization*, 305–6 (quote), 320–22; Hartman, *Collective Bargaining*, 12; Bulcke interview, 209.

33. Rosenstein, "Rise," abstract (quote), 12, 85–88; Mayo and Nohria, "Truck Driver"; Fairley, *Facing Mechanization*, 69–70 (quote), 162, 221; Larrowe, *Harry Bridges*, 357–58.

34. Larrowe, *Harry Bridges*, 377–78; Vrana interview; J. Williams interview; Steve Murdock, "Labor for Peace: The Unions Find Consensus," *Nation*, July 10, 1972.

35. Dubbeld, "Capital," 89–91 (quote on 91); Haarhoff, "Cargo Handling," 19 (quote from Railways and Harbours general manager).

36. Weintraub, "Review of *Collective Bargaining*," 43 (first quote); "Labor," *Time*, December 27, 1963, 19–20 (subsequent quotes); King, Illinois AFL-CIO speech, October 7, 1965, Springfield, IL.

37. Theriault, *Unmaking*, 41–42; Hoffer, "Automation," 48–49, 150, 152 (quotes on 48–49); Levinson, *Box*, 3.

38. Glazier, "Automation," 61; Roger interview, 185–87 (quote on 187); Goldblatt interview, 814–15, 859 (quote); Schumpeter, *Capitalism*, 83.

39. Minott, *Harry Bridges*, Horvitz quote in part 3 (emphasis added); Goldblatt interview, 807–42 (quotes on 807, 821); Leonard interview, 177 (emphasis added); Kossoris, "1966," 1068–69; Larrowe, *Harry Bridges*, 355 (emphasis added).

40. First Fairley quote comes not from the published version of his book but a lengthier, earlier version with a confusing pagination system; thus, what was ch. 6 in the book was part 3, ch. 3, 14, in the draft manuscript: "Fairley notes on M&M," ILWU Library; Fairley, *Facing Mechanization*, 32–33 (final quote), 203, 253; Swados, "West Coast"; Goldblatt interview, 816; Glazier, "Automation," 58.

41. King, April 27, 1961, Detroit speech.

Chapter 5. Working Containers or Getting Worked by Them

1. Teitelman, "Don't Overuse."

2. Kossoris, "1966," 1075.

3. Fairley, *Facing Mechanization*, ch. 9, esp. 250 (second M&M), and ch. 10, esp. 255 (steady men); Mills interview 3; Mills, "San Francisco Waterfront," parts 1 and 2, esp. part 2, 21–22 (quote); Finlay, *Work*; ILWU Local No. 10 and PMA, 1967, 1–67, Re: dispatch hall mechanization, 10 (Kearney quote), Kagel Papers, LARC. Finlay argued that longshore workers in the container era possess many skills, though he largely focuses upon crane operators.

4. Mills, "An Expert's View of Port Problem," *San Francisco Examiner*, January 29, 30, and 31 (quote), 1979; Rosenstein, "Rise"; Little, *Port of San Francisco*; Levinson, "Container Shipping"; Levinson, *Box*, 74–79; Self, *American Babylon*, 149–55. In the 2010s, there is ongoing debate in Durban over shifting the main port about ten miles south of the city; see Bond, "Economic, Ecological and Social."

5. Fairley, *Facing Mechanization*, 318; ILWU, "ILWU Story"; "The Strike Demands and Statements of Local 10—San Francisco . . . and a Brief Addendum" (ellipses in original), Mills Collection, ILWU Library. Mills noted that, in 1969, 10,500 accidents among the fourteen thousand West Coast longshoremen occurred, with 2,080 being lost-time accidents. Mills described how other locals repeatedly reprinted his pamphlets; Mills interview, 3.

6. "The Strike Demands and Statements of Local 10," in "Strike Publications—1971," Box 2, Mills Collection, ILWU; Kossoris, "1966," 1075; Boyden, "Review."

7. Fairley, *Facing Mechanization*, 94–96, 148–49, 170–71, 276–77; Levinson, "Container Shipping," 65–68; Mello, *New York Longshoremen*; Boyden, "Why the 1971–72 Strike Failed"; Cole, "Behind."

8. Mills, "San Francisco Waterfront," 228; Robinson interview; Goldblatt interview, 827–29; Fairley, *Facing Mechanization*, 255–68; Minott, *Harry Bridges* (Bailey quote); Maritime Cargo Transportation Conference, *San Francisco*, 53.

9. Robinson interview; Rosenstein, "Rise," ch. 5, esp. 85–88; Vrana interview; Cowie, *Stayin' Alive*, esp. ch. 1; Windham, *Knocking*. Alas, if typically, neither Cowie and Windham discuss the ILWU or Local 10.

10. Fairley, *Facing Mechanization*, 255, 266; Vrana interview; Wright interview; J. Williams interview.

11. Larrowe, *Harry Bridges*, 378–82 (*Chronicle* quote, 378; second quote, 382); Goldblatt interview, 840 (St. Sure quote); Boyden, "Why the 1971–72 ILWU Strike Failed"; PMA, "Strike of 1971."

12. Larrowe, *Harry Bridges*, 382; C. Williams interview 2; Bagwell interview; Watson interview, 58–61 (quote on 61); "An Historic Moment . . . An Historic Strike!!!" (Goldblatt quote), "Strike Publications—1971," box 2, Mills Collection, ILWU.

13. ILWU, "ILWU Story"; "*USA v. ILWU*, filed October 20, 1971, a 'temporary restraining order' under Labor Management Relations Act, 1947," in "ILWU Int'l: Taft Hartley Injunction 1971 (Government Pleadings)," Box 68, ILWU, Coastwide Longshore Division, case files, Norman Leonard Papers, Labor Archives and Research Center (LARC), San Francisco State University; Larrowe, *Harry Bridges*, 382–84. The union's lack of a strike fund was an outgrowth of the many expensive legal trials of Bridges and others in the 1940s and 1950s. During that era, the government also attempted to seize some union assets, and so the Pacific Longshoremen's Memorial Association and Bay Area Longshoremen's Memorial Association, respectively, were established to take legal title of the international headquarters building and Local 10's hall.

14. Boyden, "Why the 1971–72 Strike Failed"; PMA, "Strike of 1971"; Mills interviews; Larrowe, *Harry Bridges*, 378–82; Fairley, *Facing Mechanization*, 296–97, 311–8, 332–33. During President George Meany's reign, there was little chance the AFL-CIO would have admitted the ILWU if it had applied for admission.

15. Larrowe, *Harry Bridges*, 384–88 (Bridges quote on 385); Watson interview, 61; PMA, "Strike of 1971"; Weir, *Singlejack*, 97 (paychecks quote).

16. *Dispatcher*, February 11, 1972, 1–8; Herod, *Labor Geographies*, esp. ch. 4; Larrowe, *Harry Bridges*, 386–87 (security quote), 388 (bluff quote; Larrowe did not name the per-

son); Boyden, "Why the 1971–72 Strike Failed"; Fairley, *Facing Mechanization*, 322 (quote), 333–38; C. Williams interview 2; Mills interview 1.

17. Kagel interview; PMA, "Strike of 1971"; Douglas Martin, "Sam Kagel, 98, Mediator of 1982 N.F.L. Strike, Is Dead," *New York Times*, May 31, 2007, http://www.nytimes.com/2007/05/31/sports/football/31kagel.html; Berkeley Law, "Sam Kagel, Famed Labor Mediator, Dies at 98," June 11, 2007, https://www.law.berkeley.edu/article/sam-kagel-famed-labor-mediator-dies-at-98/. Thanks to Cherny for sharing his interview notes.

18. Keylor 2014 interview; Goldblatt interview, 827; Weir, *Singlejack*, 97.

19. Fairley, *Facing Mechanization*, 69, 338; "Longshore Strike" (ellipses in original), "Strike Publications—1971," Box 2, Herb Mills Collection, ILWU Library, San Francisco; Rosenstein, "Rise," 55–56.

20. Baskin, *Striking Back*, 26–28; Friedman, *Building Tomorrow Today*.

21. Friedman, *Building Tomorrow Today*, 63; Haarhoff, "Cargo Handling," 16–20 (first quote on 16, second quote on 20).

22. *Natal Mercury*, January 23, 1970, 20 (quotes), January 20, 1970, 20; January 22, 1970, 26; *Rand Daily Mail*, November 1972, 4.

23. SARH, "Report of Committee of Investigation into Congestion in Durban Harbour," 1–3, 9–13 (quote on 12), Division Planning and Productivity, General Manager's Office, Johannesburg, March 1965, Transnet Heritage Library, Johannesburg, Gauteng [hereafter, Transnet]; W. F. J. Steenkamp, "Report of the Working Group Investigating New Cargo Handling and Packing Methods," 1970 (quotes on 19, 22, 36, 76), Transnet; "Railways Answer Container Critics: 'Stop Complaining,'" July 22, 1977, SARH newspaper clippings book, Transnet; Boucher, *Spes in Arduis*, 356; Kirby, "Containerization," 1, 8. Curiously, the pivotal Steenkamp Report has escaped all previous scholars of this topic.

24. Ross-Watt, "Housing," 13; Steenkamp, "Report," Transnet, 56; "Dr. Burger Looks at Containerization in the Transport Industry," *Railway Engineering*, November/December 1971, SARH clipping book, Transnet.

25. "S.A. Gears Up for Containers," *Natal Mercury*, March 2, 1975, SARH newspaper clippings book, Transnet; "Containerisation, a New Era for Shippers: Europe/Southern Africa" (Europe/South and South-East Africa Conference, Johannesburg, 1975?), Transnet.

26. Horwood, *Port of Durban*, 78; Cooper, *On the African Waterfront*, 278; M. J. Swales, Manager, Central District, Inspectorate Division, "Crime in Durban Point Area," November 5, 1974, and R. F. Drew, Labour Officer, Central District, to Manager, Central District, November 7, 1974, both in PNAAB, KCF 82, roll 64, Killie Campbell; "Dr. Burger Looks at Containerization."

27. Kirby, "Containerization," 50, 63; Govender, "Effects of Intermodal Transportation," 25; *Freight and Trading Weekly*, June 2002, 2, Transnet.

28. *Natal Mercury*, June 12, 1978, 4; Nixon, *Selling Apartheid*, 9; Nixon, "How apartheid" (Goebbels quote); "Minutes of a formal meeting that took place in the Board Room, 132 Ordnance Road, Durban, at 11.00 a.m. on the 20th November 1974, Re: Labour Problems: point and Harbour Areas," 2, PNAAB, KCF 82, roll 64, Killie Campbell; "Containerisation: How It Affects South Africa and South African Railways and Harbours," 1975–76 (?), 1–3, folder "Freight Containerisation," Transnet.

29. Morris, "Stevedoring," part 1, 93–95, 103; Dubbeld, "Breaking the Buffalo," 104–8; Hemson, "Beyond the Frontier," 90–92 (Stokeley quote on 91).

30. "Cynics believed it wouldn't work," *Freight and Trading Weekly*, June 2002, 14 (Williams quote; my emphasis), Transnet; "Containerisation," 5, Transnet; Dubbeld, "Labour Management," 49; Dubbeld, "Breaking the Buffalo," abstract (first quote), 97, 100–106, 117–18 (Stockley quote on 106); "Automation Will Continue," *Freight and Trading Weekly*, June 2002, 5, Transnet; Sideris, *Sifuna Imali Yethu*, 32–36 (Khanye quote on 33); Morris, "Stevedoring," part 1, 94–95.

31. Morris, "Stevedoring," part 1, 109 (quote); Morris, "Stevedoring," part 2, 106–7; Sideris, *Sifuna Imali Yethu*, 36–40 (quotes on 37); Lewis interview; Hemson, "Beyond the Frontier," 86–92 (quote on 88); Sithole and Ndlovu, "Revival," 208; Lichtenstein, "Measure of Democracy"; Kiloh and Sibeko, *Fighting Union*.

32. Morris, "Stevedoring," part 1, 108–12 (quote on 112).

33. Morris, "Stevedoring," part 1, 98–99; Hemson, "Beyond the Frontier," 83–95 (quote on 85; Morris quotes on 93).

34. Dubbeld, "Breaking the Buffalo," 98, 115–18; Hemson, "Beyond the Frontier," 96–111; Barchiesi, *Precarious Liberation*. On the National Dock Labour Scheme of the late 1990s, see Hemson, "Breaking the Impasse," 207–12, 217; Webster, "Trade Unions."

35. Hemson, "Beyond the Frontier," 96.

36. Sekula, *Fish Story*, 136; Sekula and Burch, *Forgotten Space* (quote); Coomber, "We're No Luddites," 14–16. On how containers affected seafarers or sailors, see Ruggunan, *Waves of Change*.

37. Hoffer, *Temper of Our Time*, 62. On the gender implications of containers, see Alimahomed-Wilson, *Solidarity Forever*, ch. 6–7, esp. 127–28.

38. Green, *Death in the Haymarket*; Zonderman, *Uneasy Allies*; Hunnicutt, *Kellogg's Six-Hour Day*; Schwartz, interview with Bridges; Minton and Stuart, *Men*, 175–77; ILWU Local 19, "Harry Bridges"; Jack Heyman, "Dockworkers Squeezed by Automation, Abandoned by Politicians," *SFGate*, July 20, 2017, http://www.sfgate.com/news/article/Dockworkers-squeezed-by-automation-abandoned-by-11303754.php.

39. Weir, *Singlejack*, 97.

40. *News and Letters*, November 1971, 3; Hemson, "Beyond the Frontier," 90.

41. Frank, "David Montgomery."

42. Herb Mills, Introductory Guide, 14 (quote, emphasis in original), and "San Francisco Waterfront: The Extension and Defense of the Community" (both in possession of author); Mills interviews 1, 2, and 3.

43. Theriault, *Unmaking*, vii–viii, 39–45 (quote on 41); Weir, *Singlejack*, 73–75, 91–106 (quotes on 73–75); Williams interview 2.

44. Weir, *Singlejack*, 93.

45. Montgomery, *Fall of the House of Labor*, 9; Will, "Faster Mousetrap" (Taylor quote); Fairley, *Facing Mechanization*, xii.

46. Fairley, *Facing Mechanization*, xii (second quote), 276 (first quote), 337, 342 (third quote); Theriault, *Unmaking*, 42; Mills, "An expert's view of Port Problem," *San Francisco Examiner*, January 30, 1979, 25; Hoffer, *In Our Time*, 25; Official Data, inflation calculator: http://www.in2013dollars.com/1970-dollars-in-1977.

47. Dubbeld, "Breaking the Buffalo," 97–98; Broeze, "Containerization."

48. Goldblatt interview, 844–45; Linda Charlton, "Bridges, Once a 'Troublemaker,' Takes Place of Honor in Capital," *New York Times*, January 18, 1978, 14 (Bridges quotes).

Chapter 6. "Striking" for Social Justice

1. "Rally at Pier in Protest of South African Apartheid," Associated Press, December 1, 1984; *International Labour Reports*, November–December 1984, 8–10; AAA, "Free South Africa Movement," http://africanactivist.msu.edu/organization.php?name=Free%20South%20Africa%20Movement (May 23, 2016).

2. "New Twist in Chinese Arms Shipment: Union Will Refuse to Handle Cargo" and "SA Government Says It Can't Interfere with China-Zim Shipment," in *Ports and Ships*, April 18, 2008, ports.co.za/news/article_2008_04_18_1308.html#one; Godwin, *Fear.* In media reports, the COSCO ship *An Yue Jiang* sometimes was spelled *Ai Yue Jiang.*

3. Van der Linden, *Workers of the World*, 259 (italics in original).

4. Grant, "Crossing the Black Atlantic"; Rickford, *We Are an African People*; Bhebe and Mazarire, "Paying the Ultimate Price."

5. Bonner, Hyslop, and van der Walt, "Rethinking Worlds of Labour," 147; Barrett, *History from the Bottom Up*, ch. 4; Hoffer, *Working and Thinking*, 99.

6. Linebaugh and Rediker, *Many-Headed Hydra*, ch. 5 (quotes on 144–45); Lewis, "International Transport Workers Federation," 24–25; Weiss, "International Seamen . . . and the 'Hands off Abyssinia' Campaign"; Hyslop, *Notorious Syndicalist*; Ahlquist and Levi, *In the Interest*, 13; "Around the World; Longshoremen Drop Ban on Handling Soviet Cargo," *New York Times*, June 4, 1981.

7. Wolf, "Introduction," 3; van der Linden, *Workers of the World*, 262–63 (quote), 272–73; Lewis, "International Transport Workers Federation," ch. 2; "Longshoremen Boycott Freighter," *San Francisco Chronicle*, September 30, 1997; Fox-Hodess, "(Re-)Locating."

8. Weiss, "International Seamen . . . and the 'Hands off Abyssinia' Campaign," 4; Gumbrell-McCormick, "South Africa," 397 (quote); Thorn, *Anti-apartheid*, 38 (glosses in the original).

9. Sjölander, "History Distorted"; Thorn, *Anti-apartheid*, 38; Cole and Limb, "Hooks Down"; Wenzl, "Memoir"; Woodrum, *"Everybody Was Black,"* ch. 6, esp. 197–200; Executive Committee Minutes, 1963–64, reel 5, 2/17; Steering Committee Minutes, 1963–64, reel 6; and "International Longshoremen's Association Boycott against Rhodesian Cargo," *Baltimore Sun*, March 29, 1973, reel 4, 2/1; Inter-Office Memorandums, Jan.–April, 1973—all in American Committee on Africa, Amistad Research Center, Tulane University, New Orleans.

10. Bolster, *Black Jacks*; Faussette, "Race, Migration, and Port-City Radicalism"; Linebaugh and Rediker, *Many-Headed Hydra*, 298–99 (Charleston quote), 319 (Haiti quote); Kelley, *Race Rebels*, ch. 6; Weiss, "International Seamen . . . and the 'Hands off Abyssinia' Campaign."

11. Korstad, *Civil Rights Unionism*; Woodard, "Amiri Baraka," 62.

12. Mills, "Dockers Stop Arms," 24 (quote); Mills, *Presente!*

13. Mills, "Dockers Stop Arms"; *Dispatcher*, October 5, 1984, 2; Goldblatt interview, 844; Bay Area Trade Union Conference, "Rally for Chile," 1975, item 201054183, and "Boycott

All Trade with the Chilean Junta: Restore Trade Union Rights," 1097, item 201054523, both in Oakland Museum of California.

14. Scipes, *AFL-CIO's Secret War;* Striffler, *Solidarity;* Minter et al., *No Easy Victories,* 12–14, 16 (quote), 24, 47.

15. "American Committee on Africa," African Activist Archive, Michigan State University Libraries Special Collections, East Lansing [hereafter, AAA]; Minter and Hill, "Anti-apartheid Solidarity," 766–67 (Luthuli quote); Nixon, *Selling Apartheid,* 46 (King quote); "Dock Caucus Urges South African Boycott," *Dispatcher,* April 22, 1960, 1.

16. *Dispatcher,* December 28, 1962, 3, March 8, 1963, 10, and February 25, 2005; ILWU Africa subject file, ILWU Library; "Mary-Louise Hooper," AAA; ACOA, "A Brief Review of Action Taken on and around Human Rights Day, December 10, in connection with the appeal for action against apartheid campaign," AAA; Bill Chester interview; correspondence between Hooper and Chester and "Mrs. Hooper Stops a South African Cargo," *Spark,* January 10, 1963, 6, in unnumbered folders in box 1, Hooper Papers, Michigan State University, East Lansing.

17. Friedman, "Before and After"; Glaser, "Reflection." In the late 1970s and '80s, one dockworker union was independent (GWU) and the other (TGWU) belonged to the workerist Federation of South African Trade Unions. Shortly after COSATU formed, in 1985, the GWU and TGWU merged and kept the TGWU name; Morris, "Stevedoring," part 1.

18. Weiss, "International Seamen . . . and the 'Hands off Abyssinia' Campaign"; Fronczak, "Local People's Global Politics"; Balachandran, "South Asian Seafarers"; Linebaugh, "All the Atlantic Mountains Shook," 119.

19. *Negro Worker* 5, no. 9 (1935): 3–6 (first quote on 3–4); Callebert, "Livelihood Strategies," 279–80.

20. Atkins, "Black Atlantic Communication Network," 23; Balachandran, "South Asian Seafarers"; Robert Trent Vinson, *Americans Are Coming;* Magubane, *Bernard Magubane,* 21–25.

21. Global Nonviolent Action Database, "Ovambo Migrant Workers"; Sithole and Ndlovu, "Revival," 191–92; Toli, "Origins," 210–12; Douwes Dekker et al., "Case Studies," 207.

22. Brown, *Road to Soweto,* ch. 6 (quote on 138); R. F. Drew, acting manager, Central District, Bantu Affairs, to all divisional heads, "Rumoured Strikes," file 1/12/9/1, 19 June 1975; and Port Natal Bantu Affairs Administration Board, "Minutes of the Special Meeting of the Sub-Committee on Labour and Transport held on 6th February, 1975 at 9.30 a.m.," both in PNAAB, KCF 82, roll 64, Killie Campbell; Saíde, "Mozambique's Solidarity," 746 (Machel quote).

23. Robinson interview; Nesbitt, *Race for Sanctions,* preface; Wright, "Internationalism on the Waterfront"; Magaziner, "Racial Nationalism."

24. Robinson interview; Wright interview; Keylor interview; Wright, "Internationalism on the Waterfront," 28; Minter et al., *No Easy Victories,* 182–83; Coalition of Black Trade Unionists, "About CBTU." Ingram, Jones, and Stewart all passed away well before I began my project.

25. "Exec Board Confers July 1–2," *Dispatcher* July 9, 1976, 1; Nelson, *Workers on the Waterfront,* ch. 1; Heyman and Keylor interview; Resolution at African Liberation Support

Committee of New Hampshire–Vermont, "Support the Boycott of White Supremacist Cargoes!" August 30, 1976, AAA, http://africanactivist.msu.edu/document_metadata .php?objectid=32–130–1074 (emphasis in original).

26. "South African Revolution: Black Unions the Key! Implement International Labor Boycott January 17!" *Workers Vanguard* 140, January 14, 1977, 1, 10; "Longshore-Warehouse Militant Leaflet: Implement Labor Boycott of South Africa!" *Workers Vanguard*, January 28, 1977, 5, 10, 12; "Pickets Block Unloading of South African Cargo," *New York Times*, April 11, 1977, 12; Robinson interview; Heyman and Keylor interview; *Longshore-Warehouse Militant*, October 28, 1977, 1, folder Local 10—Publications, Misc. "Militant" Bulletins, Local 10 Collection, ILWU Library. The *Dispatcher* did not report these boycotts, perhaps because invoking "health and safety" was risky or Bridges did not support the actions.

27. "It's Raining in Zimbabwe," *Dispatcher*, February 11, 1977, 1; "South Africa Freedom Fighters Thank ILWU," *Dispatcher*, October 21, 1977, 3; Wright interview; Robinson interview; Morrow et al., *Education in Exile*; Minter et al., *No Easy Victories*, 182–86 (Robinson and Nakana quotes).

28. Wellman, *Union Makes Us Strong*, 257 (ambush quote); Richard Austin, personal communications, December 8, 2013; Vrana interview. The term "cold decking," also used by poker players, originated among loggers when work in a lumberyard was delayed as opposed to when logs were milled quickly; K. Barnes, "Cold Deck."

29. Curling and Macfarlane, *Last Grave at Dimbaza*; Wright interview; Robinson interview; Parrott, "*Luta Continua.*"

30. Heyman phone interview; Keylor phone interview; Robinson interview; Howard and Isis Keylor, personal communications, 2014.

31. Details reconstructed from interviews, conversations, and e-mails with every activist still alive when I began my research: Bagwell, Heyman, Keylor, Proctor, Robinson, and Wright; Bagwell interview; Proctor e-mail to ILWU Yahoo Group, January 18, 2013 (quote, ellipses in original).

32. *Dispatcher*, December 11, 1984, 8; Wright phone interview; Proctor, personal correspondence, January 2013; Robinson interview; David Bacon, "Work a Day for Freedom." Robinson also recalled the black public school teachers who shamed longshoremen into action; Robinson interview.

33. Interviews with Bagwell, Heyman, Keylor, Robinson, and Wright; *Dispatcher*, December 11, 1984, 1, 8; Bacon, "Work a Day for Freedom"; ILWU, "Minutes of Meeting of the Coast Labor Relations Committee." Fortunately for the union and individuals fined, the judge who imposed the injunction did not force payment of these enormous fines. Technically, the injunction was not lifted.

34. Interviews with Bagwell, Heyman, Keylor, Robinson, and Wright; Robinson presentation; Tom Luther [Lupher] to James Herman, telegram, November 14, 1984, in "Boycott of South African Cargo, 1984, corres. from public, ILWU Attorneys, Int'l Officers", ILWU Library; Ganz, *Why David Sometimes Wins*, 140–41. Wright's sister worked at the international and had a sense of Herman's thinking. Harvey Schwartz helped with the union's tricky, not-written-down internal politics.

35. Bacon, "Work a Day for Freedom"; Bacon, "Leo Robinson"; interviews and discussions with Keylor and Heyman; Jack Heyman, e-mail to ILWU Yahoo Group, December 8, 2013; "Boycott of South African Cargo, 1984. corres. from public, ILWU Attorneys, Int'l Officers," ILWU Library.

36. "Statement of Policy on Apartheid," International Executive Board (IEB), 1985, and "Statement of Policy on South Africa," IEB, 1986, both in "ILWU History, Trade Union Relations, Foreign—Africa," ILWU Library; "No ILWU Funds for Apartheid!" *Dispatcher*, February 24, 1978, 1; "US Firms Bolster South Africa Regime," *Dispatcher*, February 24, 1978, 8; "Delegates Examine ILWU-PMA Pension Plan," *Dispatcher*, April 21, 1978, 4–5; "ILWU-PMA: Pension Trustees Implement Policy on South Africa," *Dispatcher*, April 11, 1983, 3; Bacon, "Work a Day for Freedom"; Bock, *Soweto to Berkeley*; Wright phone interview; Cyrus M. Musiker, "They Lost the Job: Divesting Oakland Council Dumps 'Tainted' B of A," *East Bay Express*, June 6, 1986, 3 (quote).

37. Wright, phone interview; Africa Fund, "Divestment," *Student Anti-Apartheid Newsletter*, Spring 1986, 1–2 (quote); Tom Price, "Longshore Union Honors Struggle against Apartheid, *Dispatcher*, February 25, 2005, http://www.peoplesworld.org/longshore-union -honors-struggle-against-apartheid/.

38. Nesbitt, *Race for Sanctions*, 91, 134–72; Dellums, *Lying Down with the Lions*; Bacon, "Work a Day for Freedom."

39. Magubane, *Bernard Magubane*, 337; "Nelson Mandela in Oakland," June 30, 1990, CV 004, Freedom Archives, San Francisco; Bacon, "Work a Day for Freedom"; Mandela, Foreword to Minter, Hovey, and Cobb, eds., *No Easy Victories*. Vukani Mawethu maintains a website at http://www.vukani.com/.

40. SAHO, *Congress of South African Trade* Unions; *South African Transportation and Allied Workers Union, Brief History*; Cole and van der Walt, "Crossing the Color Lines"; Bond and Desai, eds., "Foreign Policy Bottom Up."

41. Webster, "Trade Unions"; Barchiesi, "Informality and Casualization"; Barchiesi, *Precarious Liberation*. Webster's article included a section on Durban dockworkers but, curiously, ignored containers. The informal nature of many South Africans' jobs is less an issue in shipping because the technologies and commodities involve enormous capital and demand significant skill; in other words, dock work is less easily outsourced.

42. Human Rights Watch, "Zimbabwe"; Hamill and Hoffman, "'Quiet Diplomacy'"; Meersman, "Legacy of Thabo Mbeki"; Godwin, "Day of the Crocodile"; "A Grim Image of Politics in Zimbabwe Emerges," *New York Times*, June 27, 2008, http://www.nytimes.com/ 2008/06/27/world/africa/27zimbabwe.html.

43. Gumede and Dube interview; "Boycott: Durban Dockworkers Block Arms to Zimbabwe," *Maritime Workers' Journal* (Australia), July–August 2008, 32–33 (Dube and SATAWU quotes); "Chinese Ship Carrying Arms for Zimbabwe Refused Entry to Durban," *Ports and Ships*, April 17, 2008, ports.co.za/news/article_2008_04_17_5052.html#one; "Zimbabwe Arms Ship Quits S Africa," *BBC News*, April 19, 2008, http://news.bbc.co.uk/ go/pr/fr/-/2/hi/africa/7354428.stm (Masilela and Howard quotes).

44. Gumede and Dube interview; "Boycott," *Maritime Workers' Journal*, July/August 2008, 32 (Dube quote); Cole and van der Walt, "Crossing the Color Lines"; Douwes Dekker et al., "Case Studies," 212.

45. Hamill and Hoffman, "Quiet Diplomacy?" 379; Essa and Jansen, "'What Happens,'" 35 (Gasa and Shandu quotes).

46. "Zimbabwe Arms Ship Quits S Africa," *BBC News*, April 19, 2008; e-mails shared by Jane Barrett, who worked at SATAWU, May 2011; Howard, "SATAWU on Campaign"; Global Nonviolent Action Database, "Southern Africans Block Arms"; "A Bishop's Pursuit of Justice for South Africa's Shack Dwellers," *Christian Today*, June 3, 2010, http://www.christiantoday.com/article/a.bishops.pursuit.of.justice.for.south.africas.shack.dwellers/26028.htm. An alternative reading credited civil society (to which the author of the report and organization belonged) and the media for this boycott with but two references to dockworkers—who actually boycotted the ship—or unions; Fritz, "People Power."

47. Congress of South African Trade Unions, "COSATU Calls for International Boycott"; "COSATU Backs Indefinite Stay Away"; Essa, "Opposition to Israeli Cargo." These events foreshadowed the break of COSATU and the South African Communist Party from Mbeki at the 2007 ANC conference at Polokwane, which led to the rise of Jacob Zuma.

48. ITF, Forty-First Congress; "Boycott," *Maritime Workers' Journal*, July/August 2008, 32–33 (Cockcroft quote).

49. Mubangizi, "Constitutional Protection"; Constitution of the Republic of South Africa, 1996.

50. Wood et al., "Limits."

51. Dubbeld, "Breaking the Buffalo"; Webster, "Trade Unions"; Barchiesi, "Informality and Casualization" and *Precarious Liberation*; von Holdt, *Transition*.

52. "Swedish Dockworkers Block Israeli Goods in Boycott Action," *IMEMC News*, June 24, 2010, http://imemc.org/article/58994/; Labor for Palestine, "Turkish Dock Workers."

53. Essa, "Opposition to Israeli Cargo"; COSATU and Palestine Solidarity Committee, "Victory for Worker Solidarity"; Soske and Jacobs, *Apartheid Israel*, back cover (Kathrada quote).

54. Resolution R19-B, "Resolution on Israel, Palestine and U.S. Policy in the Middle East," ILWU International Convention, 1988; Resolution R-07, "Resolution on Palestine," ILWU International Convention, 1991; "Gaza-Israel Conflict: Is the Fighting Over?" *BBC News*, August 26, 2014, http://www.bbc.com/news/world-middle-east-28252155; Silver, "Bay Area Activists"; "Block the Boat"; Jack Heyman and Clarence Thomas, personal communications; "Picketlines Past and Present," *San Francisco Chronicle*, August 21, 2014, https://www.youtube.com/watch?v=Qk9ywbQcid0.

55. Erem and Durrenberger, *On the Global Waterfront*.

56. "Picketlines Past and Present," *San Francisco Chronicle*, August 21, 2014 (Keylor quote).

57. Essa, "Opposition to Israeli Cargo" (quotes); Korstad, *Civil Rights Unionism*; Friedman, "Before and After," 4.

58. Transport Workers Solidarity Committee, "SF Labor Council Resolution"; "ILWU Joins the Battle in Wisconsin for Workers' Rights," *Dispatcher*, March 2011, 1, 3; Cole, "Longshore Union Strikes," *Seattle Post-Intelligencer*, April 30, 2008; Villeggiante letter; Jara speech.

59. Grant, "Crossing the Black Atlantic"; McKay, *Banjo*.

60. Bonacich and Wilson, *Getting the Goods*.

Conclusion

1. Scipes, "Social Movement Unionism"; Bacon, "Legacy of Spain."

2. Smith, "Black Feminism and Intersectionality"; Mount, "When Slaves Go on Strike"; Rustin, "Blacks and the Unions," 338–39.

3. ILWU, "Information and Union Comment," 1–2 (emphasis in original), ILRE; Boyden, "Why the 1971–72 ILWU Strike Failed," 61.

4. Hoffer, "Automation," 48; Carson, "Motor Vessel," in *Waterfront Writers*, 196; Seligman, *Most Notorious*, ix; Freund, "Review: *Cast in a Racial Mould*"; Stewart, "Robot & Us"; *Amazon Warehouse Robots*; Ratner, "Here's When Machines."

5. Weinhauer, "Power and Control," 603; Theriault, *Unmaking*, 45.

6. Higbie, "Why Do Robots Rebel"; "Handwriting on the Wall," *Dispatcher*, April 22, 1960, 2.

7. Moberg, "Robots Are Coming"; Kolko, "Republican-Leaning Cities"; Harvey, *Seventeen Contradictions*, 155; Castells, *Rise of Network Society*, 1: 216; Rogers, "How Not to Argue"; Raphael, "Finland's Guaranteed Basic Income."

8. Cleaver, Introduction to Roediger, *Wages of Whiteness*, xxv.

9. Sekula and Burch, *Forgotten Space*; Mah, *Port Cities*, 12; Rubin, "Embarcadero Reborn"; "James R. Herman Memorial Sculpture Unveiled at San Francisco's Pier 27," *Dispatcher*, May 15, 2015, https://www.ilwu.org/james-r-herman-memorial-sculpture-unveiled-at-san-franciscos-pier-27/; Nce Mkhize, "Durban's Sought after Point Poised for New Wave of Development," *Business Day Live*, August 17, 2015; Jeffries, "In Praise of Dirty, Sexy Cities: The Urban World according to Walter Benjamin," *Guardian*, September 21, 2015, https://www.theguardian.com/cities/2015/sep/21/walter-benjamin-marseille-moscow-cities?CMP=share_btn_fb. Thanks to Laleh Khalili for the Benjamin piece.

10. Cloete letter; Cole "On May Day"; Villeggiante letter; Jara speech.

11. In 2016, the first ships carrying eighteen thousand containers docked in Oakland. As of 2018, the *Hong Kong*, operated by the Orient Overseas Container Line, is the world's largest ship, holding more twenty-one-thousand-containers.

12. Mah, *Port Cities*, 205; Mark Szakonyi, "Ocean Alliance to Deploy Up to 18,000-TEU Ships on Trans-Pacific," *Journal of Commerce*, July 19, 2016; "10 World's Biggest Container Ships in 2017," *Marine Insight*, June 14, 2017, http://www.marineinsight.com/know-more/10-worlds-biggest-container-ships-2017/; Kerr and Fisher, "Conflict," 18; Harry Bridges interview by Nikki Sawada Bridges, 1978–79, tape 10, side 21 (no transcript), ILWU Library.

13. Ahlquist and Levi, *In the Interest*, ch. 7; Montgomery, *Fall of the House of Labor*, 9–22; Wellman, *Union Makes Us Strong*, 6–7. One can argue that NAFTA would have hurt ILWU members if the PMA had built a container port in, say, Tijuana.

BIBLIOGRAPHY

Archival Collections

AFRICAN ACTIVIST ARCHIVE (AAA), MICHIGAN STATE UNIVERSITY LIBRARIES SPECIAL COLLECTIONS, EAST LANSING, MICHIGAN

Alan Zaslavsky Africa Collection

AMISTAD RESEARCH CENTER, TULANE UNIVERSITY, NEW ORLEANS, LOUISIANA

American Committee on Africa

BANCROFT LIBRARY, UNIVERSITY OF CALIFORNIA–BERKELEY

National Association for the Advancement of Colored People: Region I, Records, 1942–
    1986
H. K. (Hoh-Kun) Yuen Collection

KILLIE CAMPBELL AFRICANA LIBRARY, UNIVERSITY OF KWAZULU-NATAL, DURBAN

Durban City Council Records
Natal Chamber of Industries
Port Natal Affairs Administration Board (PNAAB), 1949–1987
Press cuttings (Native Affairs)
Richard Turner Collection

DURBAN ARCHIVES REPOSITORY, NATIONAL ARCHIVES OF SOUTH AFRICA, DURBAN, KWAZULU-NATAL

Port Natal Administration Board Records, 1976–84

MELVILLE J. HERSKOVITS LIBRARY OF AFRICAN STUDIES, NORTHWESTERN UNIVERSITY, EVANSTON, ILLINOIS

Africana Vertical Files
Alex Hepple Papers
Leo Kuper Papers

INTERNATIONAL LONGSHORE AND WAREHOUSE UNION (ILWU) LIBRARY, SAN FRANCISCO, CALIFORNIA

California and West Coast Labor and Industrial Relations
Harry Bridges
Lincoln Fairley, *Facing Mechanization* draft manuscript and notes
ILWU Africa subject file
ILWU History: Un-American Activities Committee
ILWU International Executive Board: Minutes
Local 10 Collection
Local 10 *Bulletin* and *Longshore Bulletin*
Longshore-Warehouse Militant (Local 6 and Local 10)
Herb Mills Collection

LABOR ARCHIVES AND RESEARCH CENTER, SAN FRANCISCO STATE UNIVERSITY

Harry R. Bridges Papers
Archie Brown Collection
ILWU, Longshore Division, Local 10
Sam Kagel Papers
Ruth Maguire Collection
Norman Leonard Papers
People's World Photograph Collection
David F. Selvin Collection
San Francisco Labor Council Collection
South Africa Collection

MICHIGAN STATE UNIVERSITY, AFRICANA COLLECTION, EAST LANSING

Mary-Louise Hooper Papers

NATIONAL ARCHIVES OF SOUTH AFRICA, PRETORIA, GAUTENG

Native Affairs Department
Central Native Labour Board

OAKLAND MUSEUM OF CALIFORNIA

OLD COURTHOUSE MUSEUM, DURBAN, KWAZULU-NATAL

Photo Collection, Durban Harbour and Wharves

SAN FRANCISCO PUBLIC LIBRARY

St. Francis Square Cooperative, Inc., Archives

TRANSNET HERITAGE LIBRARY, JOHANNESBURG, GAUTENG

Photographic Collection
South African Railways and Harbours newspaper clippings
SARH Division of Planning and Productivity
W. F. J. Steenkamp, "Report of the Working Group Investigating New Cargo Handling
    and Packing Methods," 1970

UNITED TRANSPORT AND ALLIED TRADE UNION LIBRARY, JOHANNESBURG, GAUTENG

UNIVERSITY OF CAPE TOWN SPECIAL COLLECTIONS, CAPE TOWN, WESTERN CAPE

David Goldblatt Photographic Collection
NUSAS Archive

UNIVERSITY OF WITWATERSRAND HISTORICAL PAPERS, JOHANNESBURG, GAUTENG

African Communist
Jane Barrett Papers
Jeremy Baskin Papers
Congress of South African Trade Unions (COSATU)
Federation of South African Trade Unions (FOSATU)
David Goldblatt Photographs

Speeches and Miscellaneous Other Primary Sources

"Block the Boat for Gaza." *Twitter*. https://twitter.com/BlockTheBoat.
Bridges-Robertson-Schmidt Defense Committee. "The Real Target: Hiring Halls, Wage
    Increases, No Speedup, No Discrimination, Job Conditions." San Francisco: n.p., pre-
    sumably ILWU, 1952?
Cloete, Karl. Deputy General-Secretary, NUMSA, to President Melvin Mackay, ILWU
    Local 10. April 29, 2015. In possession of author; courtesy of Jack Heyman.
Coalition of Black Trade Unionists. "About CBTU." http://www.cbtu.org/about.html.
Congress of South African Trade Unions (COSATU). "COSATU Backs Indefinite Stay
    Away." *Politicsweb*, April 15, 2008. http://www.politicsweb.co.za/politics/cosatu-backs
    -zimbabwean-stay-away.
———. "COSATU Calls for International Boycott of Zimbabwe Arms Ship," April 21, 2008.
    http://www.cosatu.org.za/show.php?ID=1492.
Congress of South African Trade Unions (COSATU) and Palestine Solidarity Commit-
    tee. "Victory for Worker Solidarity," February 6, 2009. http://www.cosatu.org.za/docs/
    pr/2009/pr0205c.htm.
Constitution of the Republic of South Africa, 1996. http://www.justice.gov.za/legislation/
    constitution/SAConstitution-web-eng.pdf.
Howard, Randall. "SATAWU on Campaign to Stop Weapons Reaching Zim." *Politicsweb*,
    April 22, 2008. http://www.politicsweb.co.za/politics/satawu-on-campaign-to-stop
    -weapons-reaching-zim.
Human Rights Watch. "Zimbabwe: No Justice for Rampant Killings, Torture," March 8, 2011.
    https://www.hrw.org/news/2011/03/08/zimbabwe-no-justice-rampant-killings-torture.

International Longshore and Warehouse Union (ILWU). "About the Coast Longshore Division." https://www.ilwu.org/ilwu-divisions/longshore/.

——. "Everlasting Bridges Case." San Francisco: ILWU, 1955.

——. "The ILWU Story." http://www.ilwu.org/history/the-ilwu-story/.

——. International conventions of 1988 and 1991.

——. "Minutes of Meeting of the Coast Labor Relations Committee," Meeting No. 22–84. San Francisco. November 27, 1984. In possession of author; courtesy of Howard and Isis Keylor.

——. "Ten Guiding Principles." www.ilwu.org/about/ten-guiding-principles/.

——. "The Women of the Waterfront," September 24, 2014. https://www.youtube.com/watch?v=8j9qRVFNKYg.

ILWU Local 19. "Harry Bridges: A Biography." http://www.ilwu19.com/history/biography.htm.

——. "Longshoremen's Strike of 1934." www.ilwu19.com/history/1934.htm.

ILWU Local 94. "The Walking Bosses and Foremen." http://www.ilwulocal94.org/files/The%20Walking%20Bosses%20and%20Foremen.pdf.

ILWU-PMA. 2017 Paid Holidays: Longshoremen, Clerks, Walking Bosses and Watchmen. http://www.oaklandseaport.com/files/PDF/PMA_Holiday_Calendar_2017.pdf.

International Transport Workers Federation (ITF). 41st Congress of International Transport Workers Federation. http://www.itfcongress2006.org/.

Kennedy, Robert F. "Day of Affirmation" speech. University of Cape Town, June 6, 1966. http://www.rfksafilm.org/html/speeches/unicape.php.

Jara, Mazibuko. Notes of speech to Local 10, San Francisco, January 17, 2013. In possession of author; courtesy of Jack Heyman.

Labor for Palestine. "Turkish Dock Workers Union Joins Boycott against Israel," June 25, 2010. http://laborforpalestine.net/2010/06/25/turkish-dock-workers-union-joins-boycott-against-israel/.

Matson. *History*. www.matson.com/corporate/about_us/history.html.

Morris, "Indian Joe." *Alcatraz Indian Occupation Diary, Also Early Life on Blackfeet Reservation*. Edited by Troy R. Johnson. San Francisco: ILWU Library, n.d.

Pacific Maritime Association (PMA). "Strike of 1971." http://apps.pmanet.org/?cmd=main.content&id_content=2142586624.

Robinson, Leo. Memorial service. ILWU Local 10, San Francisco, March 23, 2013.

——. *Anti-apartheid Struggle*. Local 10, San Francisco. September 20, 2010. DVD. In possession of author; courtesy of Local 10 member Marcus Holder.

San Francisco. "Seal of the City and County of San Francisco." https://web.archive.org/web/20090517005533/http://www.sfgov.org/site/visitor_index.asp?id=8082.

San Francisco Bay Area Census. www.bayareacensus.ca.gov.

San Francisco Labor Council. "SF Labor Council Resolution to Defend ILWU Local 10's April 4 Solidarity Action." April 11, 2011. http://sflaborcouncil.org/resources/resolutions/2011-resolutions/.

Seeger, Pete. "Ballad of Harry Bridges." http://unionsong.com/u130.html.

US Congress, House of Representatives, Committee on Merchant Marine and Fisheries. *Study of Harbor Conditions in Los Angeles and Long Beach*. Hearings, October 19–21, 1955. Washington, DC: Government Printing Office, 1955.

US Congress, House of Representatives, Committee on Un-American Activities. *Communist Activities among Seamen and on Waterfront Facilities*, Part 1, 86th Congress, 2nd sess., 1960. Washington, DC: US Government Printing Office, 1960.

Villeggiante, Mike. ILWU Local 10 letter to Jacob Zuma. October 2, 2012. In possession of author; courtesy of Jack Heyman.

Wenzl, Thurman. "Memoir of a Baltimore Longshoreman in 1970s." In possession of author.

Williams, Clarence. "Longshoreman's Blues." https://www.youtube.com/watch?v=71JfKBDrF9o.

Interviews

Badsha, Omar. Interview by Peter Cole, February 27, 2016, Cape Town.

Bagwell, Alex. Interview by Peter Cole, July 7, 2011, San Francisco.

Barrett, Jane, and Veronica Mesatywa. Interview by Peter Cole, July 21, 2009, Johannesburg.

Bridges, Harry. Interview by Harvey Schwartz, July 27, 2004. http://www.ilwu.org/oral-history-of-harry-bridges/.

Bulcke, Germain. "Longshore Leader and ILWU-Pacific Maritime Association Arbitrator," Interview by Estolv Ethan Ward. Regional Oral History Office, Bancroft Library, University of California–Berkeley, 1983.

Cheadle, Halton. Interview by Peter Cole, March 2, 2016, Cape Town.

Chester, Bill. "ILWU Civil Rights and Community Leader, 1938–1969." ILWU Oral History. Project, Volume 6, Part I. Introduction and interview by Harvey Schwartz. *Dispatcher* February 2003.

Chester, William. Interview by Robert E. Martin, July 23, 1969, Moorland-Spingarn Research Center, Howard University, Washington, DC. Copy at ILWU Library, San Francisco.

Cobbs, George. Interview by Peter Cole. June 28, 2011, San Francisco.

Cole, Stacy. Interview by Peter Cole. August 13, 2014, Fremont, CA.

Dellums, Cottrell Laurence. Interview by Joyce Henderson with an introduction by Tarea Hall Pittman. Earl Warren Oral History Project, 1970–73. Bancroft Library, University of California–Berkeley. http://content.cdlib.org/ark:/13030/hb938nb6fv/.

Goldblatt, Louis. "Working Class Leader in the ILWU, 1935–1977." Interview by Estolv Ward with an Introduction by Clark Kerr. 2 vols. Regional Oral History Office, Bancroft Library, University of California–Berkeley, 1978–1979.

Gumede, Bhekitemba Simon, and Joseph V. Dube. Interview by Peter Cole. July 29, 2010, Durban.

Kagel, Sam. Interview by Robert Cherny. 1986–87, San Francisco, CA.

——. Interview by Lucy Kendall. March 1980, San Francisco, CA. Hotel Strike Series Oral History Project California Historical Society, San Francisco.

Heyman, Jack. Phone interview by Peter Cole. April 8, 2011.

Heyman, Jack, and Howard Keylor. Interview by Peter Cole. August 3, 2011, Oakland.

Keylor, Howard. Interview by Peter Cole. August 12, 2014, Oakland.

——. Phone interview by Peter Cole. March 16, 2011.

Leonard, Norman. "Life of a Leftist Labor Lawyer." Interview by Estolv Ethan Ward with an Introduction by James R. Herman. Regional Oral History Office, Bancroft Library, University of California–Berkeley, 1985.

Lewis, David. Interview by Peter Cole. March 16, 2016, Johannesburg.

McWilliams, Brian. Interview by Peter Cole. August 2, 2012, San Francisco.

Mills, Herb. Interview by Peter Cole. June 18, 2010 (1), June 15, 2011 (2), July 29, 2012 (3), all in Berkeley, CA.

Ndlovu, Curnick. Interview by Jenni Duggan. October 26–27, 1983, Durban. KCAV 853. Killie Campbell Africana Library, University of KwaZulu-Natal, Durban.

Ndlovu, Morris. Interview by Deanne Collins and Andrew Manson. June 20, 1979, Durban. KCAV 183. Killie Campbell Africana Library, University of KwaZulu-Natal, Durban.

Ngubese, S. K. Interview by Deanne Collins and Andrew Manson. November 28, 1979, Umlazi. KCAV 185. Killie Campbell Africana Library, University of KwaZulu-Natal, Durban.

Robinson, Leo. Interview by Peter Cole. July 20, 2011, Raymond, CA.

Roger, Sidney. "A Liberal Journalist on the Air and on the Waterfront: Labor and Political Issues, 1932–1990." Interview by Julie Shearer in 1989 and 1990. Regional Oral History Office, Bancroft Library, University of California–Berkeley, 1998. http://bancroft.berkeley.edu/ROHO/collections/subjectarea/ics_movements/labor.html.

Schmidt, Henry. "Secondary Leadership in the *ILWU*, 1933–1966." Interview by Miriam F. Stein and Estolv Ethan Ward. Regional Oral History Office, Bancroft Library, University of California–Berkeley, 1983. http://bancroft.berkeley.edu/ROHO/collections/subjectarea/ics_movements/labor.html.

Vrana (Dennis), Eugene. Interview by Peter Cole. July 11, 2011, San Francisco.

Watson, Don. Interview by Harvey Schwartz, 1994, and revised by Don Watson in 2003. Labor Archives and Research Center Oral History Collection, San Francisco State University.

Webster, Eddie. Interview by Peter Cole. March 17, 2016, Johannesburg.

Williams, Cleophas. Interviews by Peter Cole. June 22, 2011, Emeryville, CA, and August 16, 2014, Oakland.

Williams, Josiah "Josh." Interview by Peter Cole. July 10, 2011, San Francisco.

Wright, Larry. Interview by Peter Cole. April 16, 2011 (telephone), and July 19, 2011, Oakland (in person).

Periodicals

Associated Press

Business Day Live (Johannesburg)

Christian Today
Crisis
Daily News (Durban)
Daily Vox (Rosebank, South Africa)
Dissent
Dispatcher (San Francisco)
Freighting/Containerising Weekly (South Africa)
The Guardian (London)
IMEMC News
Industrial Management
International Labour Reports (Manchester, England)
Isisebenzi
Journal of Commerce
LSM News (Liberation Support Movement)
Maritime Workers' Journal (Australia)
Natal Mercury (Durban)
The Nation
Negro Digest
The Negro Worker
New Politics
New York Times
News and Letters
Ports and Ships
Rand Daily Mail (Johannesburg)
San Francisco Chronicle
San Francisco Examiner
Seattle Post-Intelligencer
Time
Workers Vanguard
Workers World
The World Post

Secondary Sources

Ahlquist, John S., and Margaret Levi. *In the Interest of Others: Organizations and Social Activism*. Princeton, NJ: Princeton University Press, 2013.

Alexander, Peter. *Workers, War, and the Origins of Apartheid: Labour and Politics in South Africa, 1939–48*. Suffolk, UK: James Currey, 2000.

Alimahomed-Wilson, Jake. *Solidarity Forever? Race, Gender, and Unionism in the Ports of Southern California*. Lanham, MD: Lexington, 2016.

Allen, Robert L. *The Port Chicago Mutiny*. New York: Warner, 1989.

Amazon Warehouse Robots. Mind Blowing Videos. July 26, 2016. https://www.youtube.com/watch?v=cLVCGEmkJs0&feature=youtu.be.

American Idle. "Cheesehead Rebellion: California Dockworkers Shut Down Port, Hoist Wisconsin 'Distress' Flags in April 4 National 'Day of Action.'" April 5, 2011. http:// american-idle.newsvine.com/_news/2011/04/05/6412394-cheesehead-rebellion -california-dockworkers-shut-down-port-hoist-wisconsin-distress-flags-in-april -4-national-day-of-action.

Arnesen, Eric. *Waterfront Workers of New Orleans: Race, Class, and Politics, 1863–1923*. New York: Oxford University Press, 1991.

Ashby, Steven, and C. J. Hawking. *Staley: The Fight for a New American Labor Movement*. Urbana: University of Illinois Press, 2009.

Atkins, Keletso E. "The 'Black Atlantic Communication Network': African American Sailors and the Cape of Good Hope Connection." *Issue* 24, no. 2 (1996): 23–25.

———. *The Moon Is Dead! Give Us Our Money! The Cultural Origins of an African Work Ethic, Natal, South Africa, 1843–1900*. Portsmouth, NH: Heinemann, 1993.

Ayers, Pat. "The Making of Men: Masculinities in Interwar Liverpool." In *Working Out Gender: Perspectives from Labour History*, edited by Margaret Walsh, 66–83. Aldershot, Farnham, UK: Ashgate, 1999.

Bacon. David. "The Legacy of Spain and the Lincoln Brigade." *Stansbury Forum*. December 6, 2015. http://stansburyforum.com/the-legacy-of-spain-and-the-lincoln-brigade/.

———. "Leo Robinson: Soul of the Longshore." *In These Times*, January 19, 2013. http:// inthesetimes.com/working/entry/14448/leo_robinson_soul_of_the_longshore/.

———. "Work a Day for Freedom! A Short History of the Bay Area Free South Africa Labor Committee." *No Easy Victories*. http://www.noeasyvictories.org/research/bacon_bafsalc .php.

Balachandran, Gopalan. "South Asian Seafarers and Their Worlds, c. 1870–1930s." In *Seascapes: Maritime Histories, Littoral Cultures, and Transoceanic Exchanges*, edited by Jerry H. Bentley, Renate Bridenthal, and Kären Wigen, 186–204. Honolulu: University of Hawaii Press, 2007.

Baldwin, James, and Kenneth Clark, "There Is No Compromise: From the National Educational TV Symposium, 'The Negro and the American Promise,'" *Negro Digest* (October 1963): 25–31.

Baptist, Edward. *The Half Has Never Been Told: Slavery and the Making of American Capitalism*. New York: Basic Books, 2014.

Barchiesi, Franco. "Informality and Casualization as Challenges to South Africa's Industrial Unionism: Manufacturing Workers in the East Rand/Ekurhuleni Region in the 1990s." *African Studies Quarterly* 11 (Spring 2010): 67–85.

———. *Precarious Liberation: Workers, the State, and Contested Social Citizenship in Postapartheid South Africa*. Scottsville: University of KwaZulu-Natal Press, 2011.

Barnes, Charles B. *The Longshoremen*. New York: Survey Associates, 1915.

Barnes, Kim. "Cold Deck." *Home Ground: Language for an American Landscape*. http:// test.m.ourhomeground.com/entries/definition/cold_deck.

Barrett, James R. *History from the Bottom Up and the Inside Out: Ethnicity, Race, and Identity in Working-Class History*. Durham, NC: Duke University Press, 2017.

Basinstreet.com. "Clarence Williams." http://basinstreet.com/wp-content/uploads/ 2016/09/Clarence-Spencer-Williams.pdf.

Baskin, Jeremy. *Striking Back: A History of COSATU*. Johannesburg: Ravan, 1991.

Beckert, Sven. *Empire of Cotton: A Global History*. New York: Knopf, 2014.

Berkeley Law. "Sam Kagel, Famed Labor Mediator, Dies at 98." June 11, 2007. https://www
.law.berkeley.edu/article/sam-kagel-famed-labor-mediator-dies-at-98/.

Bhebe, Ngwabi M., and Gerald Chikozho Mazarire. "Paying the Ultimate Price: Zimbabwe
and the Liberation of South Africa, 1980 – 1994." In *The Road to Democracy in South Africa*.
Vol. 5, *African Solidarity*, edited by SADET. Part 1: Chapter 11. Pretoria: Unisa, 2013.

Blackburn, Robin. "Review: *The Many-Headed Hydra*, by Peter Linebaugh and Marcus
Rediker." *Boston Review*, February 1, 2001. http://bostonreview.net/books-ideas/robin
-blackburn-review-many-headed-hydra.

Black Panther Party Legacy and Alumni. "Jimmy Ward Biography" *It's about Time*. http://
www.itsabouttimebpp.com/Memorials/pdf/Jimmy_Ward_Bio.pdf.

——. "Panther Connection." *It's about Time*. http://www.itsabouttimebpp.com.

Bolster, W. Jeffrey. *Black Jacks: African American Seamen in the Age of Sail*. Cambridge, MA:
Harvard University Press, 1997.

Bonacich, Edna, and Jake Wilson. *Getting the Goods: Ports, Labor, and the Logistics Revolution*.
Ithaca, NY: Cornell University Press, 2008.

Bond, Patrick. "Economic, Ecological and Social Risks in Durban's Port-Petrochemical-
Coal Expansion." *Man in India* 94, no. 3 (2014): 471–500.

Bond, Patrick, and Ashwin Desai, eds. "Foreign Policy Bottom Up: South African Civil
Society and the Globalisation of Popular Solidarity." Durban: University of Kwa
Zulu-Natal, Centre for Civil Society, July 25, 2008. http://ccs.ukzn.ac.za/files/Bond_Desai
_Foreign_Policy_Bottom_Up_July_2008.pdf.

Bonner, Philip, Jonathan Hyslop, and Lucien van der Walt. "Rethinking Worlds of Labour: Southern African Labour History in International Context." *African Studies* 66
(2007): 137–68.

Boucher, Maurice. *Spes in Arduis: A History of the University of South Africa*. Pretoria: University of South Africa, 1973.

Boyden, Richard. "Review of Charles P. Larrowe's *Harry Bridges: The Rise and Fall of Radical
Labor in the U.S.*" *New Politics* 10, no. 3 (1973): 93–95.

——. "Why the 1971–72 ILWU Strike Failed." *New Politics* 10, no. 2 (1972): 61–69.

Brahinsky, Rachel. "'Hush Puppies,' Communalist Politics, and Demolition Governance: The
Rise and Fall of the Black Fillmore." In *Ten Years That Shook the City: San Francisco 1968–1978*,
edited by Chris Carlsson and LisaRuth Elliott, 141–53. San Francisco: City Light, 2011.

Brecher, Jeremy. *Strike!* San Francisco: Straight Arrow, 1972.

Brechin, Grey. *Imperial San Francisco: Urban Power, Earthly Ruin*. Berkeley: University of
California Press, 1999.

Breckenridge, Keith. "Promiscuous Method: The Historiographical Effects of the Search
for the Rural Origins of the Urban Working Class in South Africa." *International Labor
and Working-Class History* 65 (2004): 26–49.

Broeze, Frank. "Containerization and the Globalization of Liner Shipping." In *Global Markets: The Internationalization of the Sea Transport Industries since 1850*, edited by David J. Star-
key and Gelina Harlaftis, 385–423. St. John's, NL: International Maritime Economic
History Association, 1998.

——. *The Globalisation of the Oceans: Containerisation from the 1950s to the Present*. St. John's, NL: International Maritime Economic History Association, 2002.

——. "Militancy and Pragmatism: An International Perspective on Maritime Labour, 1870–1914." *International Review of Social History* 36 (1991): 165–200.

Broussard, Albert P. *Black San Francisco: The Struggle for Racial Equality in the West, 1900–1954*. Lawrence: University Press of Kansas, 1993.

Brown, Julian. *The Road to Soweto: Resistance and the Uprising of 16 June 1976*. Johannesburg: Jacana, 2016.

Bussel, Robert. *Fighting for Total Person Unionism: Harold Gibbons, Ernest Calloway, and Working-Class Citizenship*. Urbana: University of Illinois Press, 2015.

Callebert, Ralph Frans. "Cleaning the Wharves: Pilferage, Bribery and Social Connections on the Durban Docks in the 1950s." *Canadian Journal of African Studies/Revue canadienne des études africanes* 46, no. 1 (2012): 23–38.

——. "Livelihood Strategies of Dock Workers in Durban, c. 1900–1959." PhD diss., Queen's University, 2011.

Carrabino, Joseph D. "An Engineering Analysis of Cargo Handling—VI: Containerization: Determination of Optimum Sizes and Economic Feasibility of Shipping Containers." Report 57–56. Department of Engineering, University of California, Los Angeles, July 1957.

Carson, Robert. ed. *The Waterfront Writers: The Literature of Work*. San Francisco: Harper and Row, 1979.

Castells, Manuel. *The Rise of Network Society*, Vol. 1: *The Information Age: Economy, Society, and Culture*, 2nd ed. Oxford, UK: Blackwell-Wiley, 2010.

Chafe, William H. *The Unfinished Journey: America since World War II*, 7th ed. New York: Oxford University Press, 2010.

Cherny, Robert W. "Longshoremen of San Francisco Bay, 1849–1960." In *Dock Workers*, edited by Sam Davies, Colin J. Davis, David de Vries, Lex Heerma van Voss, Lidewij Hesselink, and Klaus Weinhauer, 1: 102–40.

——. "Longshore Workers on the Pacific Coast, 1848–1934." ILWU Longshore History and Traditions Conference, 2004. In possession of author.

——. "The Making of a Labor Radical: Harry Bridges, 1901–1934." *Pacific Historical Review* 64, no. 3 (1995): 363–88.

Chisholm, Jessie. "Waterfront Conflict: Dockers' Strategies and Collective Actions." In *Dock Workers*, edited by Sam Davies, Colin J. Davis, David de Vries, Lex Heerma van Voss, Lidewij Hesselink, and Klaus Weinhauer, 1: 141–59.

Clark, Nancy L., and William H. Worger, *South Africa: The Rise and Fall of Apartheid*, 2nd ed. New York: Routledge, 2011.

Coast Education Project. "The Hiring Hall—The Heart and Muscle of the ILWU." Seattle: ILWU, 1999. www.ilwu19.com/edu/hall.htm.

Cole, Peter. "Behind the Longshoremen's Strike Threat." *The Progressive*. December 29, 2012. http://www.progressive.org/behind-longshoremen-strike-threat.

——. "An Injury to One Is an Injury to All: San Francisco Longshore Workers and the Fight against Apartheid." *Journal of Civil and Human Rights* 1, no. 2 (2015): 158–81.

——. "On May Day, Longshore Workers Stop Work to Protest Police Brutality." *In These Times*, April 30, 2015. inthesetimes.com/working/entry/17894/may_day_police _brutality.

——. "No Justice, No Ships Get Loaded: Political Boycotts on the Durban and San Francisco Bay Waterfronts." *International Review of Social History* 58, no. 2 (2013): 185–217.

——. "The Tip of the Spear: How Longshore Workers in the San Francisco Bay Area Survived the Container Revolution." *Employee Responsibilities and Rights Journal* 25, no. 3 (2013): 201–16.

——. *Wobblies on the Waterfront: Interracial Unionism in Progressive-Era Philadelphia*. Urbana: University of Illinois Press, 2007.

Cole, Peter, and Peter Limb. "Hooks Down! Anti-Apartheid Activism and Solidarity among Maritime Unions in Australia and the United States." *Labor History* 58, no. 3 (2017): 303–26.

Cole, Peter, and Lucien van der Walt. "Crossing the Color Lines, Crossing the Continents: Comparing the Racial Politics of the IWW in South Africa and the United States, 1905–1925." *Safundi* 12, no. 1 (2011): 69–96.

Conniff, Richard. "What the Luddites Really Fought Against." *Smithsonian*, March 2011.

Coomber, Del. "'We're No Luddites,' Says Docker Leader." *Industrial Management* 77, no. 2 (February 1977): 14–16.

Cooper, Frederick. "Dockworkers and Labour History." In *Dock Workers*, edited by Sam Davies et al., 2: 523–41.

——. *Decolonization in African Society: The Labor Question in French and British Africa*. New York: Cambridge University Press, 1996.

——. *On the African Waterfront: Urban Disorder and the Transformation of Work in Colonial Mombasa*. New Haven, CT: Yale University Press, 1987.

——. "Race, Ideology, and the Perils of Comparative History." *American Historical Review* 101, no. 4 (1996): 1122–38.

Coppersmith, Jonathan. "Comparative History: Telling a Tale of Two Cities." *History News Network*, July 19, 2015: http://historynewsnetwork.org/blog/153650.

Cowen, Deborah. *The Deadly Lives of Logistics: Mapping Violence in Global Trade*. Minneapolis: University of Minnesota Press, 2014.

Cowie, Jefferson. *Stayin' Alive: The 1970s and the Last Days of the Working Class*. New York: New Press, 2010.

Cronjé, Gillian, and Suzanne Cronjé. *The Workers of Namibia*. London: International Defence and Aid Fund, 1979.

Crowe, Daniel. *Prophets of Rage: The Black Freedom Struggle in San Francisco, 1945–1969*. New York: Garland, 2000.

Cuénod, Carol. "Building the St. Francis Community." *FoundSF*. http://www.foundsf.org/ index.php?title=Building_the_St. Francis_Community.

——. "The ILWU and Western Addition Redevelopment A-2." *FoundSF*. http://www.foundsf .org/index.php?title=The_ILWU_and_Western_Addition_Redevelopment_A-2.

——. "Redevelopment A-1 and Origin of St. Francis Square." *FoundSF*. http://www.foundsf .org/index.php?title=Redevelopment_A-1_and_Origin_of_St. Francis_Square.

Curling, Chris, and Pascoe Macfarlane, directors. *Last Grave at Dimbaza*. London: Morena Films, 1974. DVD.

Davidson, Basil. *No Fist Is Big Enough to Hide the Sky: The Liberation of Guinea Bissau and Cape Verde: Aspects of an African Revolution*. London: Zed, 1981.

Davie, Grace. "Strength in Numbers: The Durban Student Wages Commission, Dockworkers and the Poverty Datum Line, 1971–1973." *Journal of Southern African Studies* 33, no. 2 (2007): 401–20.

Davies, Sam, Colin J. Davis, David de Vries, Lex Heerma van Voss, Lidewij Hesselink, and Klaus Weinhauer, eds. *Dock Workers: International Exploration in Comparative Labour History, 1790–1970*, 2 vols. Aldershot, Farnham, UK: Ashgate, 2000.

Davis, Colin. "'Shape or Fight?': New York's Black Longshoremen, 1945–1961." *International Labor and Working-Class History* 62 (2002): 143–63.

———. *Waterfront Revolts: New York and London Dockworkers, 1946–61*. Urbana: University of Illinois Press, 2003.

Dellums, Ronald. *Lying Down with the Lions: A Public Life from the Streets of Oakland to the Halls of Power*. Boston: Beacon, 2000.

Dlamini, Jacob. "Collaborators and the Riven Truth behind Zuma's Nklanda." *Business Day*, July 27, 2015. http://www.bdlive.co.za/opinion/2015/07/27/collaborators-and-the-riven-truth-behind-zumas-nkandla.

Douwes Dekker, Loet, D. Hemson, J. S. Kane-Berman, J. Lever, and L. Schlemmer, "Case Studies in African Labour Action in South Africa and Namibia (South West Africa)." In *The Development of an African Working Class*, edited by R. Sandbrook and R. Cohen, 205–38. London: Longman, 1975.

Dubbeld, Bernard. "Breaking the Buffalo: The Transformation of Stevedoring Work in Durban between 1970 and 1990." *International Review of Social History* 48 (2003), Supplement: 97–122.

———. "Capital and the Shifting Grounds of Emancipatory Politics: The Limits of Radical Unionism in Durban Harbor, 1974–85." *Critical Historical Studies* 2, no. 1 (2015): 85–112.

———. "Labour Management and Technological Change: A History of Stevedoring in Durban, 1959–90." MA thesis, University of KwaZulu-Natal, 2002.

Dubow, Saul. *Apartheid, 1948–1994*. New York: Oxford University Press, 2014.

Edwards, Iain. "Recollections: The Communist Party and Worker Militancy in Durban, Early 1940s." *South African Labour Bulletin* 11, no. 4 (1986): 65–84.

Erem, Suzan, and E. Paul Durrenberger. *On the Global Waterfront: The Fight to Free the Charleston 5*. New York: Monthly Review Press, 2008.

Essa, Azad. "Opposition to Israeli Cargo at Durban's Dock: The Significance of Dockworkers' Refusal to Offload Israeli Goods." *Pambazuka* 419 (February 12, 2009). pambazuka.org/en/category/comment/54031.

Essa, Azad, and Martin Jansen. "'What Happens in Zimbabwe Affects Us': Union Hounds Chinese Arms." *South African Labour Bulletin* 32, no. 3 (2008): 35–37.

Fairley, Lincoln. *Facing Mechanization: The West Coast Longshore Plan*. Los Angeles: University of California, Institute of Industrial Relations, 1979.

Faussette, Risa. "Race, Migration, and Port-City Radicalism: West Indian Longshoremen and the Politics of Empire, 1880–1920." In *Seascapes*, 169–85.

Fink, Leon. "Global Sea or National Backwater? The International Labor Organization and the Quixotic Quest for Maritime Standards, 1919–1945." In *Workers across the Americas: The Transnational Turn in Labor History*, edited by Leon Fink, 409–30. New York: Oxford University Press, 2011.

Finlay, William. *Work on the Waterfront: Worker Power and Technological Changes in a West Coast Port*. Philadelphia: Temple University Press, 1988.

Fisher, Fozia. "Class Consciousness among Colonized Workers in South Africa." In *Change, Reform and Economic Growth in South Africa*, edited by Lawrence Schlemmer and Eddie Webster, 197–223. Johannesburg: Ravan, 1978.

Fisher, James T. *On the Irish Waterfront: The Crusader, the Movie, and the Soul of the Port of New York*. Ithaca, NY: Cornell University Press, 2009.

Foucault, Michel. "Of Other Spaces." Translated by Jay Miskowiec. *Diacritics* 16 (Spring 1986): 22–27.

Fox-Hodess, Katy. "(Re-)Locating the Local and National in the Global: Multi-scalar Political Alignment in Transnational European Dockworker Union Campaigns." *British Journal of Industrial Relations* (2017): 1–22.

Frank, Dana. "David Montgomery: Grand Master Workman." *The Nation*, December 19, 2011.

Fredrickson, George M. *Black Liberation: A Comparative History of Black Ideologies in the United States and South Africa*. New York: Oxford University Press, 1995.

——. *White Supremacy: A Comparative Study of American and South African History*. New York: Oxford University Press, 1982.

Freeman, Jo. *At Berkeley in the Sixties: The Education of an Activist, 1961–1965*. Bloomington: Indiana University Press, 2004.

Freeman, Joshua. "Organizing New York." *Jacobin*, May 7, 2015: https://www.jacobinmag.com/2015/05/victor-gotbaum-dc-37-public-unions/.

French, John D. "Another World History Is Possible: Reflections on the Translocal, Transnational, and Global." In *Workers across the Americas*, 3–11.

Freund, Bill. *The African Worker*. Cambridge, UK: Cambridge University Press, 1988.

——. "City Hall and the Direction of Development: The Changing Role of the Local State as a Factor in Economic Planning and Development in Durban." In *(D)urban Vortex: South African City in Transition*, edited by Bill Freund and Vishnu Padayachee, 11–42. Pietermaritzburg, S. Afr.: University of Natal Press, 2002.

——. "Democracy and the Colonial Heritage in Africa: Revisiting Mamdani, *Citizen and Subject*." *Left History* 7, no. 1 (2000): 101–8.

——. *Insiders and Outsiders: The Indian Working Class of Durban 1910–1990*. Portsmouth, NH: Heinemann, 1995.

——. "Review: *Cast in a Racial Mould*." *South African Labour Bulletin* 11, no. 6 (1986): 116–18.

Freund, Bill, and Vishnu Padayachee, eds. *(D)urban Vortex: South African City in Transition*. Pietermaritzburg, S. Afr.: University of Natal Press, 2002.

Friedman, Steven. "Before and After: Reflections on Regime Change and Its Aftermath." *Transformation* 75 (2011): 4–12.

——. *Building Tomorrow Today: African Workers in Trade Unions, 1970–1984*. Johannesburg: Ravan, 1985.

Fritz, Nicole. "People Power: How Civil Society Blocked an Arms Shipment for Zimbabwe." SAIIA Governance and APRM Programme Occasional Paper 36. Johannesburg: South African Institute of International Affairs, 2009. http://www.saiia.org.za/images/ stories/pubs/occasional_papers/saia_sop_36_fritz_20090721_en.pdf.

Fronczak, Joseph. "Local People's Global Politics: A Transnational History of the Hands off Ethiopia Movement of 1935." *Diplomatic History* 39, no. 2 (2015): 245–74.

Ganz, Marshall. *Why David Sometimes Wins: Leadership, Organization, and Strategy in the California Farm Worker Movement.* New York: Oxford University Press, 2009.

George, Rose. *Ninety Percent of Everything: Inside Shipping, the Invisible Industry That Puts Clothes on Your Back, Gas in Your Car, and Food on Your Plate.* New York: Metropolitan, 2013.

Gibson, Campbell. "Population of the Largest 100 Cities and Other Urban Places in the United States: 1790–1990." Population Division Working Paper, no. 27. Washington, DC: U.S. Census Bureau, 1998. http://www.census.gov/population/www/documentation/ twps0027/twps0027.html.

Gilmore, Glenda Elizabeth. *Defying Dixie: The Radical Roots of Civil Rights, 1919–1950.* New York: W. W. Norton, 2008.

Gitlin, Todd. *The Sixties: Years of Hope, Days of Rage.* New York: Bantam, 1987.

Glaser, D. "A Reflection on the von Holdt–Plaut Debate." *Transformation* 7 (1988): 80–86.

Glass, Fred. "Native Americans in the Mission Economy," *Found SF.* http://www.foundsf .org/index.php?title=NATIVE_AMERICANS_in_the_MISSION_ECONOMY.

Glazier, William. "Automation and the Longshoremen: A West Coast Solution." *Atlantic,* December 1960, 57–61.

Global Nonviolent Action Database. "Ovambo Migrant Workers General Strike for Rights, Namibia, 1971–72." http://nvdatabase.swarthmore.edu/content/ovambo-migrant -workers-general-strike-rights-namibia-1971-72.

———. "Southern Africans Block Arms Shipment for Zimbabwe, 2008." https://nvdatabase .swarthmore.edu/content/southern-africans-block-arms-shipment-zimbabwe-2008.

Godwin, Peter. "Day of the Crocodile." *Vanity Fair,* September 2008. www.vanityfair.com/ politics/features/2008/09/zimbabwe200809.

———. *The Fear: Robert Mugabe and the Martyrdom of Zimbabwe.* New York: Little, Brown, 2011.

Golden Gate Bridge Highway and Transportation District. "What Is a Name—The Golden Gate?" http://goldengatebridge.org/research/Name.php.

Golden Gate National Recreation Area. "Ohlones and Coast Miwoks." http://www.nps .gov/goga/learn/historyculture/ohlones-and-coast-miwoks.htm.

Gorter, Wytze, and George H. Hildebrand. *The Pacific Coast Maritime Industry, 1930–1948.* Vol. 2, *An Analysis of Performance.* Berkeley: University of California Press, 1954.

Govender, Nerissa. "Effects of Intermodal Transportation Networks on Inbound and Outbound Durban Containerization." MA thesis, University of KwaZulu-Natal, 2014.

Grant, Nicholas. "Crossing the Black Atlantic: The Global Antiapartheid Movement and the Racial Politics of the Cold War." *Radical History Review* 119 (2014): 72–93.

———. *Winning Our Freedoms Together: African Americans and Apartheid, 1945–1960.* Chapel Hill: University of North Carolina Press, 2017.

Green, James. *Death in the Haymarket: A Story of Chicago, the First Labor Movement, and the Bombing That Divided Gilded Age America.* New York: Pantheon, 2006.

Greene, Julie. *The Canal Builders: Making America's Empire at the Panama Canal.* New York: Penguin, 2009.

Gregory, James N. *The Southern Diaspora: How the Great Migrations of Black and White Southerners Transformed America.* Chapel Hill: University of North Carolina Press, 2005.

Gumbrell-McCormick, Rebecca. "South Africa: The Fight for Freedom." In *The International Confederation of Free Trade Unions*, by Anthony Carew, Michel Dreyfus, and Geert van Goethem, 397–413, edited by Marcel van der Linden. Bern: Peter Lang, 2000.

Guy, Jeff. *Theophilus Shepstone and the Forging of Natal: African Autonomy and Settler Colonialism in the Making of Traditional Authority.* Pietermaritzburg, S. Afr.: University of KwaZulu-Natal Press, 2013.

Haarhoff, Errol. "Cargo Handling, Operations, and Amenity Centre: General Cargo Handling Facilities for the Point Habour, Durban." Baccalaureate thesis, University of Natal, 1970.

Hadfield, Leslie. "Christian Action and Black Consciousness Community Programmes in South Africa." *Journal for the Study of Religion* 23, nos. 1–2 (2010): 105–30.

Hagel, Otto, and Louis Goldblatt. *Men and Machines: A Photo Story of the Mechanization and Modernization Agreement between the International Longshoremen's and Warehousemen's Union and the Pacific Maritime Association Now in Operation in the Ports of California, Oregon and Washington.* San Francisco: ILWU and PMA, 1963.

Halpern, Rick. *Down on the Killing Floor: Black and White Workers in Chicago's Packinghouses, 1904–54.* Urbana: University of Illinois Press, 1997.

———. "Solving the 'Labour Problem': Race, Work and the State in the Sugar Industries of Louisiana and Natal, 1870–1910." *Journal of Southern African Studies* 30, no. 1 (2004): 19–40.

Hamill, James, and John Hoffman. "'Quiet Diplomacy' or Appeasement? South African Policy towards Zimbabwe." *The Round Table* 98, no. 402 (2009): 373–84.

"Harry Bridges." *Bill Moyers' Journal.* New York: WNET. January 29, 1974.

Harry Bridges Project. "Captain Josh and the Drill Team." http://theharrybridgesproject .org/Kagel.html.

Hartman, Paul T. *Collective Bargaining and Productivity.* Berkeley: University of California Press, 1969.

Harvey, David. *Seventeen Contradictions and the End of Capitalism.* London: Profile, 2014.

Hemson, David. "Beyond the Frontier of Control? Trade Unionism and the Labour Market in the Durban Docks." *Transformation* 30 (1996): 83–114.

———. "Breaking the Impasse, Beginning the Change: Labour Market, Unions and Social Initiative in Durban." In *(D)urban Vortex*, edited by Bill Freund and Vishnu Padayachee, 195–221.

———. "Class Consciousness and Migrant Workers: Dock Workers of Durban." PhD diss., University of Warwick, 1979.

———. "Dock Workers, Labour Circulation, and Class Struggles in Durban, 1940–59." *Journal of Southern African Studies* 4, no. 1 (1977): 88–124.

———. "In the Eye of the Storm: Dock-Workers in Durban." In *The People's City: African Life in Twentieth-Century Durban*, edited by Paul Maylam and Iain Edwards, 145–73. Pietermaritzburg, S. Afr.: University of Natal Press, 1996.

——. "The 1973 Natal Strike Wave: How We Rebuilt the Unions." *Congress Militant*, December 1990.

——. "30 Anniversary of Durban Strikes." Speech, Kwa Muhle Museum, Durban, KwaZulu-Natal, February 1, 2003. h-net.msu.edu/cgi-bin/logbrowse.pl?trx=vx&list=H-Africa&month=0302&week=a&msg=Pfi6DGvTaHMapocl9A2mIg&user=&pw=.

——. "Trade Unionism and the Struggle for Liberation in South Africa." *Capital and Class* 4–6 (1978): 3–41.

Hemson, David, Martin Legassick, and Nicole Ulrich. "White Activists and the Revival of the Workers' Movement." In *The Road to Democracy in South Africa*. Vol. 2, *1970–1980*, edited by SADET, 243–314.

Hepple, Alex. *The African Worker in South Africa: A Study of Trade Unionism*. London: Africa Bureau, 1957.

Herod, Andrew. *Labor Geographies: Workers and the Landscapes of Capitalism*. New York: Guilford, 2001.

Higbie, Tobias. "Why Do Robots Rebel? The Labor History of a Cultural Icon." *Labor: Studies in Working-Class History* 10, no. 1 (2013): 99–121.

Hindson, Doug. *Pass Controls and the Urban African Proletariat*. Johannesburg: Ravan, 1987.

Hobsbawm, Eric. *Labouring Men: Studies in the History of Labour*. London: Weidenfeld and Nicolson, 1964.

Hoffer, Eric. "Automation Is Here to Liberate Us." *New York Times Magazine*, October 14, 1965.

——. *In Our Time*. New York: Harper and Row, 1976.

——. *The Temper of Our Time*. New York: Harper and Row, 1967.

——. *Working and Thinking on the Waterfront: A Journal, June 1958–May 1959*. New York: Harper and Row, 1969.

Horne, Gerald. *Black and Red: W. E. B. Du Bois and the Afro-American Response to the Cold War, 1944–1963*. Albany: State University of New York Press, 1985.

——. *Fighting Paradise: Labor Unions, Racism, and Communists in the Making of Modern Hawai'i*. Honolulu: University of Hawaii Press, 2011.

Horrell, Muriel. *Racialism and the Trade Unions*. Johannesburg: South African Institute of Race Relations, 1959.

——. *South African Trade Unionism: A Study of a Divided Working Class*. Johannesburg: South African Institute of Race Relations, 1961.

——. *Survey of Race Relations in South Africa: 1968*. Johannesburg: South African Institute of Race Relations, 1969.

——. *Survey of Race Relations in South Africa: 1969*. Johannesburg: South African Institute of Race Relations, 1970.

——. *Survey of Race Relations in South Africa: 1971*. Johannesburg: South African Institute of Race Relations, 1972.

Horrell, Muriel, and Dudley Horner. *Survey of Race Relations in South Africa: 1973*. Johannesburg: South African Institute of Race Relations, 1974.

Horrell, Muriel, Dudley Horner, John Kane-Berman, and Robin Margo. *Survey of Race Relations in South Africa: 1972*. Johannesburg: South African Institute of Race Relations, 1973.

Horwood, O. P. F., ed. *The Port of Durban*. Natal Regional Survey, Vol. 15. Durban, KwaZulu-Natal: University of Natal, Department of Economics, 1969.

Hughes, Heather. "African Encounters with the Sea: Durban and Beyond," *Historia* 59, no. 2 (2014): 355–68.

Hunnicutt, Benjamin Kline. *Kellogg's Six-Hour Day*. Philadelphia: Temple University Press, 1996.

Hyslop, Jonathan. "Navigating Empire: Ports, Ships and Global History." Keynote Lecture, Social History Society, Portsmouth, England, April 1, 2015. In possession of author.

———. *The Notorious Syndicalist: J. T. Bain: A Scottish Rebel in Colonial South Africa*. Johannesburg: Jacana, 2004.

Ibarz, Jordi. "Recent Trends in Dock Workers' History." Paper delivered at the European Social Sciences History Conference, Valencia, Spain, April 1, 2016. In possession of author.

Ignatiev, Noel. "Treason to Whiteness Is Loyalty to Humanity." http://racetraitor.org/.

Institute for Industrial Education (IIE). *The Durban Strikes, 1973: "Human Beings with Souls."* Johannesburg: Ravan, 1974.

Isserman, Maurice, and Michael Kazin. *America Divided: The Civil War of the 1960s*, 5th ed. New York: Oxford University Press, 2015.

Jenkins, Robin Dearmon. "Linking Up the Golden Gate: Garveyism in the San Francisco Bay Area, 1919–1925." *Journal of Black Studies* 39, no. 2 (Nov. 2008): 266–80.

———. "Rivets and Rights: African-American Workers and Shipbuilding in the San Francisco Bay Area, 1890–1948." PhD diss., Carnegie Mellon University, 2004.

Johanningsmeier, Edward. "Communists and Black Freedom Movements in South Africa and the US, 1919–1950." *Journal of Southern African Studies* 30, no. 1 (2004): 155–80.

Johns, Michael. "Winning for Losing: A New Look at Harry Bridges and the 'Big Strike' of 1934." *American Communist History* 13, no. 1 (2014): 1–24.

Johnson, Marilyn S. *The Second Gold Rush: Oakland and the East Bay in World War II*. Berkeley: University of California Press, 1993.

Johnson, Troy R. *The American Indian Occupation of Alcatraz Island: Red Power and Self-Determination*. Lincoln: University of Nebraska Press, 2008.

Johnston, Peter. *The Durban Chronicle*. Durban, KwaZulu-Natal: Urban Strategy Department, 1995.

Jones, Trevor. "The Port of Durban: Lynchpin of the Local Economy?" In *(D)urban Vortex*, edited by Bill Freund and Vishnu Padayachee, 69–106.

———. *The Port of Durban and the Durban Metropolitan Economy*. Durban: University of Natal-Durban, Economic Research Unit, 1997.

Jones, William P. "The Unknown Origins of the March on Washington: Civil Rights Politics and the Black Working Class." *Labor: Studies in Working-Class History of the Americas* 7, no. 3 (2010): 33–52.

Kaijage, Frederick J. "The War of Clubs: Life, Labour and Struggles of the Tanga Dockworkers." In *Dock Workers*, edited by Sam Davies et al., 1: 290–318.

Kazin, Michael. *Barons of Labor: The San Francisco Building Trades and Union Power in the Progressive Era*. Urbana: University of Illinois Press, 1987.

Keal, Hannah. "A Life's Work: Harriet Bolton and Durban's Trade Unions, 1944–1974." MA thesis, University of KwaZulu-Natal, Durban, 2009.

Kelley, Robin D. G. *Race Capitalism Justice: Boston Review Forum I.* Edited by Walter Johnson and Robin D. G. Kelley. Cambridge, MA: Boston Review, 2017.

——. *Race Rebels: Culture, Politics, and the Black Working Class.* New York: Free Press, 1996.

——. "'We Are Not What We Seem': Rethinking Black Working-Class Opposition in the Jim Crow South." *Journal of American History* 80, no. 1 (1993): 75–112.

Keniston, Billy. *Choosing to Be Free: A Life Story of Rick Turner.* Johannesburg: Jacana, 2013.

Kennedy, David M. *Freedom from Fear: The American People in Depression and War, 1929–1945.* New York: Oxford University Press, 1999.

Kerr, Clark, and Lloyd Fisher. "Conflict on the Waterfront." *Atlantic*, September 1949: 17–23.

Khwela, S'bu. "1973 Strikes: Breaking the Silence." *South African Labour Bulletin* 17, no. 3 (1993): 20–23.

Kiloh, Margaret, and Archie Sibeko (Zola Zembe). *A Fighting Union: An Oral History of the South African Railway and Harbour Workers Union.* Johannesburg: Ravan, 2000.

Kimeldorf, Howard. *Reds or Rackets? The Making of Radical and Conservative Unions on the Waterfront.* Berkeley: University of California Press, 1985.

King, Martin Luther Jr. *"All Labor Has Dignity,"* edited and introduced by Michael K. Honey. Boston: Beacon, 2011.

Kirby, Robin Grafton. "Containerization: Its Implications for Land Use Planning and Effect on the Land Use Pattern of Durban." PhD diss., Town and Regional Planning University of Natal, S. Afr., 1978.

Kolko, Jed. "Republican-Leaning Cities Are at Greater Risk of Job Automation." *FiveThirtyEight*, February 17, 2016. http://fivethirtyeight.com/features/republican-leaning-cities-are-at-greater-risk-of-job-automation/.

Koopman, Adrian. "The Post-Colonial Identity of Durban." *Oslo Studies in Language* 4, no. 2 (2012): 133–59.

Korstad, Robert Rodgers. *Civil Rights Unionism: Tobacco Workers and the Struggle for Democracy in the Mid-Twentieth-Century South.* Chapel Hill: University of North Carolina Press, 2003.

Kossoris, Max D. "1966 West Coast Longshore Negotiations: An Observer's Critical Appraisal of the Parties' Decision to Recommit Themselves to Principles Established in the 1960 Contract." *Monthly Labor Review* 89, no. 10 (1966): 1067–75.

——. "Working Rules in West Coast Longshoring." *Monthly Labor Review* 84, no. 1 (1961): 1–10.

Labour History Group. *Durban Strikes.* Salt River, Cape Town, South Africa: Labour History Group, 1987.

La Hause, Paul. "Drinking in the Cage: The Durban System and the 1929 Beer Hall Riots." *Africa Perspective* 20 (1982): 63–75.

——. "The Message of the Warriors: The ICU, the Labouring Poor and the Making of a Popular Political Culture in Durban, 1925–1930." In *Holding Their Ground: Class, Locality and Culture in 19th and 20th Century South Africa*, edited by Philip Bonner, Isabel Hofemyr,

Deborah James, and Tom Lodge, 19–57. Johannesburg: Witwatersrand University Press, 1989.

Lambert, Robert. "Eddie Webster, the Durban Moment and New Labour Internationalism." *Transformation* 72/73 (2010): 26–47.

———. "Political Unionism and Working Class Hegemony: Perspectives on the South African Congress of Trade Unions, 1955–1965." *Labour, Capital and Society* 18, no. 2 (1985): 244–77.

———. "Political Unionism in South Africa: The South African Congress of Trade Unions, 1955–1965." PhD diss., University of the Witwatersrand, Johannesburg, 1988.

Larrowe, Charles P. "Did the Old Left Get Due Process? The Case of Harry Bridges." *California Law Review* 60, no. 1 (1972): 39–83.

———. *Harry Bridges: The Rise and Fall of Radical Labor in the United States*. New York: Lawrence Hill, 1972.

———. *Shape-Up and Hiring Hall: A Comparison of Methods and Labor Relations on the New York and Seattle Waterfronts*. Berkeley: University of California Press, 1955.

Ledbetter, B. Glenn. "Who Said It's Simple: West Coast Stevedoring." *Local 10 Bulletin*. March 15, 1985, 1–2.

Lee, Felicia R. "Harvesting Cotton-Field Capitalism: Edward Baptist's New Book Follows the Money on Slavery." *New York Times*, October 3, 2014. http://www.nytimes.com/2014/10/04/books/the-half-has-never-been-told-follows-the-money-of-slavery.html.

Legassick, Martin. "Debating the Revival of the Workers' Movement in the 1970s: The South African Democracy Education Trust and Post-Apartheid Patriotic History." *Kronos* 34, no. 1 (2008): 240–66.

———. "The Past and Present of Marxist Historiography in South Africa." Interview by Alex Lichtenstein. *Radical History Review* 82 (2002): 111–30.

Letwin, Daniel. "Interracial Unionism, Gender, and 'Social Equality' in the Alabama Coalfields." *Journal of Southern History* 61, no. 3 (1995): 519–54.

Levinson, Marc. *The Box: How the Shipping Container Made the World Smaller and the World Economy Bigger*. Princeton, NJ: Princeton University Press, 2006.

———. "Container Shipping and the Decline of New York, 1955–1975." *Business History Review* 80, no. 1 (2006): 49–80.

Lewis, Harold. "The International Transport Workers Federation (ITF) 1945–1965: An Organizational and Political Anatomy." PhD diss., University of Warwick, Warwick, UK, 2003.

Lichtenstein, Alex. "'The Hope for White and Black'? Race, Labour and the State in South Africa and the United States, 1924–1956." *Journal of Southern African Studies* 30, no. 1 (2004): 133–53.

———. "Making Apartheid Work: African Trade Unions and the 1953 Native Labour (Settlement of Disputes) Act in South Africa." *Journal of African History* 46 (2005): 293–314.

———. "'A Measure of Democracy': Works Committees, Black Workers, and Industrial Citizenship in South Africa, 1973–1979." *South African Historical Journal* 67, no. 2 (April 2015): 113–38.

Linebaugh, Peter. "All the Atlantic Mountains Shook." *Labour/Le travail* 10 (Autumn 1982): 87–121.

Linebaugh, Peter, and Marcus Rediker. *The Many-Headed Hydra: Sailors, Slaves, Commoners, and the Hidden History of the Revolutionary Atlantic*. Boston: Beacon, 2000.

Little, Arthur D. *The Port of San Francisco: An In-Depth Study of Its Impact on the City, Its Economic Future, the Potential of Its Northern Waterfront*. San Francisco: San Francisco Port Authority, 1966.

Livernash, E. R. "Review of Paul T. Hartman, *Collective Bargaining and Productivity*." *Journal of Business* 44, no. 2 (1971): 222–23.

Lodge, Tom. "Secret Party: South African Communists between 1950 and 1960." *South African Historical Journal* 67, no. 4 (2015): 433–64.

Luckhardt, Ken, and Brenda Wall. *Organize or Starve! The History of the South African Congress of Trade Unions*. New York City: International, 1980.

Lumby, Anthony, and Ian McLean. "The Economy and the Development of the Port of Durban." In *Receded Tides of Empire: Aspects of the Economic and Social History of Natal and Zululand since 1910*, edited by Bill Guest and John M. Sellers, 25–49. Pietermaritzburg, S. Afr.: University of Natal Press, 1994.

Macqueen, Ian. "Resonances of Youth and Tensions of Race: Liberal Student Politics, White Radicals and Black Consciousness, 1968–1973." *Southern African Historical Journal* 65, no. 3 (2013): 365–82.

Magaziner, Dan. "Racial Nationalism and the Political Imagination." *Africa Is a Country*. May 24, 2016. http://africasacountry.com/2016/05/racial-nationalism-and-the-political -imagination/.

Magubane, Bernard Makhosezwe, with Mbuelo Vizikhungo Mzamane. *Bernard Magubane: My Life and Times*. Scottsville: University of KwaZulu-Natal Press, 2010.

Mah, Alice. *Port Cities and Global Legacies: Urban Identity, Waterfront Work, and Radicalism*. New York: Palgrave Macmillan, 2014.

Maharaj, Brij. "Segregation, Desegregation and De-Racialisation: Racial Politics and the City of Durban." In *(D)urban Vortex*, edited by Bill Freund and Vishnu Padayachee, 171–93.

Maldetto, K. "Why San Francisco??? City Origins: 1835–1849." *Found SF*. http://www.foundsf .org/index.php?title=WHY_SAN_FRANCISCO%3F%3F%3F_CITY_ORIGINS :_1835–1849.

Mamdani, Mahmood. *Citizen and Subject: Contemporary Africa and the Legacy of Late Colonialism*. Princeton, NJ: Princeton University Press, 1996.

Maree, Johann. "Seeing Strikes in Perspective: *Review of the Durban Strikes 1973*, by Institute for Industrial Education." *South African Labour Bulletin* 2, no. 9–10 (1976): 107–8.

Margolin, Malcolm. "The Ohlone Way." *Found SF*. http://www.foundsf.org/index. php?title=THE_OHLONE_WAY.

Maritime Cargo Transportation Conference. *San Francisco Port Study*. Vol. 2: *Tests of Modified Cargo-Loading and the Port as a System*. Washington, DC: National Academy of Sciences, National Research Council, 1964.

Markoff, John. "Skilled Work, without the Worker." *New York Times*, August 18, 2012.

Martin, Ginny, director. "Captain John C. Frémont." *U.S.-Mexican War, 1846–1848*. KERA, 1998. http://www.pbs.org/kera/usmexicanwar/biographies/john_fremont.html.

Marx, Karl. *Grundrisse: Foundations of the Critique of Political Economy*. New York: Penguin, 1973.

Maylam, Paul, and Iain Edwards, eds. *The People's City: African Life in Twentieth-Century Durban*. Pietermaritzburg, S. Afr.: University of Natal Press, 1996.

Mayo, Anthony J., and Nitin Nohria. "The Truck Driver Who Reinvented Shipping." *Working Knowledge*, October 3, 2005. http://hbswk.hbs.edu/item/5026.html.

McEntyre, Davis, and Julia R. Tranopol. "Postwar Status of Negro Workers in the San Francisco Area." *Monthly Labor Review* 70 (June 1950): 612–17.

McGuire, Danielle L. *At the Dark End of the Street: Black Women, Rape, and Resistance—A New History of the Civil Rights from Rosa Parks to the Rise of Black Power*. New York: Knopf, 2010.

McKay, Claude. *Banjo*. New York: Harper and Brothers, 1929.

Meersman, Brent. "The Legacy of Thabo Mbeki." *Safundi* 13, no. 3–4 (2012): 425–32.

Mello, William J. *New York Longshoremen: Class and Power on the Docks*. Gainesville: University Press of Florida, 2010.

Meraji, Shereen Marisonl. "Seeking Oakland's Soul in the 'New Oakland.'" National Public Radio, April 17, 2013. http://www.npr.org/sections/codeswitch/2013/04/17/177513003/seeking-oaklands-soul-in-the-new-oakland.

Miller, Paul T. *The Postwar Struggle for Civil Rights: African Americans in San Francisco, 1945–1975*. New York: Routledge, 2010.

Mills, Herb. "Dockers Stop Arms to Pinochet: The West Coast Longshore Union's 1978 Refusal to Load U.S. Military Aid to Chile's Dictator, Augusto Pinochet." *Social Policy* 35, no. 4 (2005): 24–28.

——. "In Defense of the Student Movement." *New University Thought* 2, no. 1 (1961): 8–13.

——. *Presente!* c. 2008. Manuscript in possession of author.

——. "The San Francisco Waterfront: The Extension and Defense of the Community." Manuscript in possession of author, 2006.

——. "The San Francisco Waterfront: The Social Consequences of Industrial Modernization. Part One, 'The Good Old Days.'" *Urban Life* 5, no. 2 (July 1976): 222–49.

——. "The San Francisco Waterfront: The Social Consequences of Industrial Modernization. Part Two, 'The Modern Longshore Operations.'" *Urban Life* 6, no. 1 (April 1977): 3–32.

Minott, Berry, director. *Harry Bridges: A Man and His Union*. San Francisco: KQED, 1992. VHS.

Minter, William, and Sylvia Hill, "Anti-apartheid Solidarity in United States–South Africa Relations." In *The Road to Democracy in South Africa*. Vol. 3, *International Solidarity*, edited by SADET. Part 2: 745–822. Pretoria: Unisa, 2008.

Minter, William, Gail Hovey, and Charles Cobb Jr., eds. *No Easy Victories: African Liberation and American Activists over a Half Century, 1950–2000*. Trenton, NJ: Africa World, 2008.

Minton, Bruce, and John Stuart. *Men Who Lead Labor*. New York: Modern Age, 1937.

Moberg, David. "The Robots Are Coming: Whether They'll Be Job Terminators or Job Transformers Is Up to Us." *In These Times*, November 27, 2015: http://inthesetimes.com/article/18578/dont-fear-the-robot-revolution.

Montgomery, David. *Fall of the House of Labor: The Workplace, the State, and American Labor Activism, 1865–1925*. New York: Cambridge University Press, 1989.

Moore, Shirley Ann. "Getting There, Being There: African-American Migration to Richmond, California, 1910–1945." In *The Great Migration in Historical Perspective: New Dimensions of Race, Class, and Gender*, edited by Joe William Trotter Jr., 106–26. Bloomington: Indiana University Press, 1991.

Morphet, Tony. "Brushing History against the Grain: Oppositional Discourse in South Africa." *Theoria* 76 (1990): 89–99.

Morris, Mike. "Stevedoring and the General Workers Union." Part 1, "The Stevedoring Industry and the GWU's Impact." *South African Labour Bulletin* 11, no. 3 (1986): 90–114.

———. "The Stevedoring Industry and the General Workers Union." Part 2, "The Impact of the Stevedores on the GWU." *South African Labour Bulletin* 11, no. 4 (1986): 100–118.

Morrow, Sean, Brown Maaba, and Loyiso Pulumani. *Education in Exile: SOMAFCO, the ANC School in Tanzania, 1978 to 1992*. Cape Town, S. Afr.: HSRC, 2004.

Mount, Guy Emerson. "When Slaves Go on Strike: W. E. B. Du Bois's Black Reconstruction 80 Years Later." Pittsburgh, PA: African American Intellectual History Society, December 28, 2015. http://www.aaihs.org/when-slaves-go-on-strike/.

Mubangizi, John Cantius. "The Constitutional Protection of Socio-economic Rights in Selected African Countries: A Comparative Evaluation." *African Journal of Legal Studies* 2, no. 1 (2006): 1–19.

Mukherjil, Anahita. "Durban Largest 'Indian' City outside India." *Times of India*. July 23, 2011. http://timesofindia.indiatimes.com/city/mumbai/Durban-largest-Indian-city-outside-India/articleshow/9328227.cms.

Munk, Michael. "Francis Murnane and Racism in ILWU Portland Local 8." September 2014. In possession of author.

Murch, Donna. *Living for the City: Migration, Education, and the Rise of the Black Panther Party in Oakland, California*. Chapel Hill: University of North Carolina Press, 2010.

National Museum of American History. "American on the Move." amhistory.si.edu/onthemove/exhibition/exhibition_17_2.html.

Nelson, Bruce. *Divided We Stand: American Workers and the Struggle for Black Equality*. Princeton, NJ: Princeton University Press, 2001.

———. *Workers on the Waterfront: Seamen, Longshoremen, and Unionism in the 1930s*. Urbana: University of Illinois Press, 1990.

Nesbitt, Francis Njubi. *Race for Sanctions: African Americans against Apartheid, 1946–1994*. Bloomington: Indiana University Press, 2004.

Nixon, Ron. "How Apartheid Sold Its Racism." *The Star*, June 25, 2015. https://www.iol.co.za/the-star/how-apartheid-sold-its-racism-1876547.

———. *Selling Apartheid: South Africa's Global Propaganda War*. Johannesburg: Jacana, 2015.

Northern California Coalition for Immigrant Rights. "Immigration." *Found SF*. http://www.foundsf.org/index.php?title=Immigration.

———. "Japanese Internment." *Found SF*. http://www.foundsf.org/index.php?title=Japanese_Internment.

Pach, Chester J. *Dwight D. Eisenhower: Domestic Affairs*. Charlottesville: University of Virginia, Miller Center of Public Affairs. http://millercenter.org/president/biography/eisenhower-domestic-affairs.

Padayachee, Vishnu, Shahid Vawda, and Paul Tichman. *Indian Workers and Trade Unions in Durban, 1930—1950*. Durban, KwaZulu-Natal: Institute for Social and Economic Research, 1985.

Parnaby, Andrew. *Citizen Docker: Making a New Deal on the Vancouver Waterfront, 1919–1939*. Toronto: University of Toronto Press, 2008.

Parrott, R. Joseph. "*A Luta Continua*: Radical Filmmaking, Pan-African Liberation and Communal Empowerment." *Race and Class* 57, no. 1 (2015): 20–38.

Paton, Alan. *Cry, the Beloved Country*. New York: Scribner, 1948.

Perry, Doug. "Historian Michael Kazin: Labor and the 1906 Quake." *Indybay*, July 18, 2005. http://www.indybay.org/newsitems/2006/03/13/18076051.php.

Pfaelzer, Jean. *Driven Out: The Forgotten War against Chinese Americans*. New York: Random House, 2007.

Pilcher, William W. *Portland Longshoremen: A Dispersed Urban Community*. New York: Holt, Rinehart and Winston, 1972.

Planning History of Oakland, CA. "The Changing Face of Oakland, 1945–1990." http://oakland planninghistory.weebly.com/the-changing-face-of-oakland.html.

Posel, Deborah. "Influx Control and Urban Labour Markets." In *Apartheid's Genesis, 1935—1962*, edited by Philip Bonner, Peter Delius, and Deborah Posel, 411–30. Johannesburg: Ravan, 1993.

Quin, Mike. *The Big Strike*. Olema, CA: Olema, 1949.

Raphael, T. J. "Finland's Guaranteed Basic Income Is Working to Tackle Poverty." *The Takeaway*, May 6, 2017. https://www.pri.org/stories/2017-05-06/finlands-guaranteed-basic -income-working-tackle-poverty.

Ratner, Paul. "Here's When Machines Will Take Your Job, as Predicted by AI Gurus." *Big Think*. June 4, 2017. http://bigthink.com/paul-ratner/heres-when-machines-will-take-your -job-predict-ai-gurus.

Record, Cy W. "Willie Stokes at the Golden Gate," *Crisis* 56 (1949): 175–79, 187–88.

Reed, Ishmael. *Blues City: A Walk in Oakland*. New York: Crown Journeys, 2003.

Rhomberg, Chris. *No There There: Race, Class, and Political Community in Oakland*. Berkeley: University of California Press, 2005.

Rickford, Russell. *We Are an African People: Independent Education, Black Power, and the Radical Imagination*. New York: Oxford University Press, 2016.

Ringrose, H. G. *Trade Unions in Natal*. Natal Regional Survey, vol. 4. Cape Town, S. Afr.: Oxford University Press, 1951.

Robinson, Cedric J. *Black Marxism: The Making of the Black Radical Tradition*. Chapel Hill: University of North Carolina Press, 1983.

Roediger, David R. *Towards the Abolition of Whiteness: Essays on Race, Politics, and Working Class History*. London: Verso, 1994.

———. *Wages of Whiteness: Race and the Making of the American Working Class*, 3rd ed. Introduction by Kathleen Cleaver. London: Verso, 2007.

Rogers, Brishen. "How Not to Argue Basic Income." *Boston Review*, October 31, 2016. http:// bostonreview.net/politics/brishen-rogers-universal-basic-income.

Rorabaugh, W. J. *Berkeley at War: The 1960s*. New York: Oxford University Press, 1990.

Rosenstein, Mark. "The Rise of Maritime Containerization in the Port of Oakland: 1950 to 1970." MA thesis, New York University, 2000.

Ross, Robert. *A Concise History of South Africa*, 2nd ed. New York: Cambridge University Press, 2008.

Ross-Watt, D. M. "Housing for Bantu Stevedores." Baccalaureate thesis, University of Natal, S. Afr., 1970.

Rothenberg, Janell. "Ports Matter: Supply Chain Logics and the Sociocultural Context of Infrastructure in Port Studies." *Mobility in History* 8 (2017): 115–22.

Rubin, Jasper. "The Embarcadero Reborn." *FoundSF*. http://www.foundsf.org/index.php ?title=The_Embarcadero_Reborn.

Ruggunan, Shaun. *Waves of Change: Globalisation and Seafaring Labour* Markets. Cape Town, S. Afr.: HSRC, 2016.

Rustin, Bayard. "The Blacks and the Unions." *Harper's Magazine*, May 1971.

———. *Down the Line: The Collected Writings of Bayard Rustin*. Introduction by C. Vann Woodward. Chicago: Quadrangle, 1971.

Saíde, Alda Romão Saúte. "Mozambique's Solidarity with the National Liberation Struggle in South Africa." In *The Road to Democracy in South Africa*. Vol. 5, *African Solidarity*, edited by SADET. Part 2: 729–808. Pretoria: Unisa, 2014.

Sambureni, Nelson Tozivaripi. "'Listen, Whiteman, You Have Launched a War You Cannot Win': Forced Removals and the Outbreak of Riots in Natal, 1959–1963." *Contree* 38 (1995): 23–29.

———. "Working in the Apartheid City: Worker Struggles in Durban, 1960–1979." MA thesis, University of Natal–Durban, 1994.

Sassen, Saskia. *The Global City: New York, London, Tokyo*. Princeton, NJ: Princeton University Press, 1991.

Saul, John S., and Patrick Bond. *South Africa—The Present as History: From Mrs Ples to Mandela and Marikana*. Johannesburg: Jacana, 2014.

Saxton, Alexander. *The Indispensable Enemy: Labor and the Anti-Chinese Movement in California*. Berkeley: University of California Press, 1971.

Schumpeter, Joseph. *Capitalism, Socialism, and Democracy*. New York: Routledge, 2003.

Schwartz, Harvey. "Harry Bridges and the Scholars: Looking at History's Verdict." *California History* 59, no. 1 (1980): 66–79.

———. *The March Inland: Origins of the ILWU Warehouse Division, 1934–1938*. Los Angeles: UCLA, Institute of Industrial Relations, 1978.

———. *Solidarity Stories: An Oral History of the ILWU*. Seattle: University of Washington Press, 2009.

———. "A Union Combats Racism: The ILWU's Japanese-American 'Stockton Incident' of 1945." *Southern California Quarterly* 62, no. 2 (1980): 161–76.

Scipes, Kim. *AFL-CIO's Secret War against Developing Country Workers: Solidarity or Sabotage?* Lanham, MD: Lexington, 2010.

———. "Social Movement Unionism or Social Justice Unionism? Disentangling Theoretical Confusion within the Global Labor Movement." *Class, Race and Corporate Power* 2, no. 3 (2014). http://digitalcommons.fiu.edu/classracecorporatepower/vol2/iss3/9/.

Seale, Bobby. *Seize the Time: The Story of the Black Panther Party and Huey Newton*. New York: Black Classic, 1991.

Sekula, Allan. *Fish Story*, 2nd ed. Dusseldorf: Richter, 2002.

Sekula, Allan, and Noël Burch, directors. *The Forgotten Space*. Doc.Eye Film, 2010. http://www.icarusfilms.com/new2012/fs.html.

Self, Robert O. *American Babylon: Race and the Struggle for Postwar Oakland*. Princeton, NJ: Princeton University Press, 2003.

Seligman, Ben B. *Most Notorious Victory: Man in an Age of Automation*. New York: Free Press, 1966.

Selvin, David F. *A Terrible Anger: The 1934 Waterfront and General Strikes in San Francisco*. Detroit, MI: Wayne State University Press, 1996.

Sembene, Ousmane. *Le Docker Noir*. Translated by Ros Schwartz. Portsmouth, NH: Heinemann Educational, 1988.

Shaffer, N. Mandred. "The Competitive Position of the Port of Durban." Studies in Geography No. 8. Evanston, IL: Department of Geography, Northwestern University, 1965.

Sideris, Tina, ed. *Sifuna Imali Yethu: The Life and Struggles of Durban Dock Workers 1940–1981*. Johannesburg: South African Institute of Race Relations, 1983.

Sides, Josh. *Erotic City: Sexual Revolutions and the Making of Modern San Francisco*. New York: Oxford University Press, 2009.

Silver, Charlotte. "Bay Area Activists Declare Victory after Israeli Carrier Cancels All Ships." *Electronic Intifada*, October 31, 2014. https://electronicintifada.net/blogs/charlotte-silver/bay-area-activists-declare-victory-after-israeli-carrier-cancels-all-ships.

Simons, H. J., and R. E. Simons. *Class and Colour in South Africa, 1850–1950*. Baltimore, MD: Penguin, 1969.

Sithole, Jabulani, and Sifiso Ndlovu, "The Revival of the Labour Movement, 1970–1980." In *The Road to Democracy in South Africa*, edited by SADET. Vol. 2: *1970–1980*, 187–241.

Sjölander, Jonas. "History Distorted: Anti-Apartheid Movement and Swedish Union Solidarity." *South African Labour Bulletin* 34, no. 5 (2010–11): 55–58.

Sloterdijk, Peter. *In the World Interior of Capital: Towards a Philosophical Theory of Globalization*. Translated by Wieland Hoban. Cambridge, UK: Polity, 2013.

Smith, Sharon. "Black Feminism and Intersectionality." *International Socialist Review* 91 (2013–14). http://isreview.org/issue/91/black-feminism-and-intersectionality.

Sookrajh, Reshma. "Plessislaer, Cato Manor, Shallcross: A Personal Narrative." In *Chatsworth*, edited by Ashwin Desai and Goolam Vahed, 112–22. Pietermaritzburg, S. Afr.: University of KwaZulu-Natal Press, 2013.

Soske, Jon, and Sean Jacobs, eds. *Apartheid Israel: The Politics of an Analogy*. Chicago: Haymarket, 2015.

South Africa. Truth and Reconciliation Commission. *Final Report*. Cape Town: Truth and Reconciliation Commission, 1999. http://sabctrc.saha.org.za/reports.htm.

South African Democracy Education Trust (SADET). *The Road to Democracy: South Africans Telling Their Stories*, Vol. 1, *1950–1970*. Pretoria: Unisa, 2008.

———. *The Road to Democracy in South Africa*, Vol. 2, *1970–1980*. Pretoria: Unisa, 2004.

South African History Online (SAHO). *Billy Nair*. http://www.sahistory.org.za/people/billy-nair.

——. *Colonial History of Durban*. http://www.sahistory.org.za/durban/colonial-history -durban.

——. *Congress of South African Trade Unions (COSATU)*. http://www.sahistory.org.za/topic/ congress-south-african-trade-unions-cosatu.

——. *Curnick Muzuvukile Ndlovu*. http://www.sahistory.org.za/people/curnick-muzuvukile -ndlovu.

——. *December 16, the Reflection of a Changing South African Heritage*. http://www.sahistory .org.za/article/december-16-reflection-changing-south-african-heritage.

——. *Early Settlement at Bay of Natal*. http://www.sahistory.org.za/early-settlement-bay -natal.

——. *Harold Bhekisisa Nxasana*. http://www.sahistory.org.za/people/bhekisisa-harold -nxasana.

——. *Johannes Nkosi*. http://www.sahistory.org.za/people/johannes-nkosi.

——. *Kay Moonsamy*. http://www.sahistory.org.za/people/kesval-kay-moonsamy.

——. *NUSAS Wages Commission Timeline 1971–1973*. http://www.sahistory.org.za/topic/ nusas-wages-commission-timeline-1971-1973.

——. *Prehistory of the Durban Area*. http://www.sahistory.org.za/durban/prehistory-durban -area.

——. *Rowley Israel Arenstein*. http://www.sahistory.org.za/people/rowley-israel-arenstein.

——. *SACTU and the Congress Alliance*. http://www.sahistory.org.za/archive/sactu-and -congress-alliance.

——. *Sharpeville Massacre, 21 March 1960*. http://www.sahistory.org.za/topic/sharpeville -massacre-21-march-1960.

——. *State of Emergency Declared after Sharpeville Massacre*. http://www.sahistory.org.za/ dated-event/state-emergency-declared-after-sharpeville-massacre.

——. *Stephen J. C. Dlamini*. http://www.sahistory.org.za/people/stephen-j-c-dlamini.

South African Transport and Allied Workers Union (SATAWU). *A Brief History*. http:// www.satawu.org.za/aboutUsHistory.php.

——. *Gender and HIV and AIDS*. http://www.satawu.org.za/genderHIVAndAIDS.php.

Stanley, Jo. "When the 'Ladies' Took to Loading: A Preliminary Survey of Gendered Ste- vedoring Practices in History." Turin, Italy: European Labour History Network, 2015. In possession of author.

Starr, Kevin. *The Dream Endures: California Enters the 1940s*. New York: Oxford University Press, 2002.

Stewart, Jack. "Robot and Us: Self-driving Trucks Coming to Save Lives and Kill Jobs." *Wired*, May 5, 2017. https://www.wired.com/2017/05/robot-us-self-driving-trucks -coming-save-lives-kill-jobs/.

Striffler, Steve. *Solidarity: Latin America and the US Left in the Era of Human Rights and Global- ization*. London: Pluto, 2018.

Stromquist, Shelton. "Claiming Political Space: Workers, Municipal Socialism, and the Reconstruction of Local Democracy in Transnational Perspectives." In *Workers across the Americas: The Transnational Turn in Labor History*. Edited by Leon Fink, 303–28. New York: Oxford University Press, 2011.

Sugrue, Thomas J. *The Origins of the Urban Crisis: Race and Inequality in Postwar Detroit*. Princeton, NJ: Princeton University Press, 1996.

Swados, Henry. "The West Coast Waterfront: The End of an Era," *Dissent*, August 1961. 448–60.

Takaki, Ronald. *Strangers from a Different Shore: A History of Asian Americans*, rev. ed. Boston: Little, Brown, 1998.

Teitelman, Robert. "Don't Overuse the Word 'Revolution,'" *Huffington Post*, February 21, 2011, http://www.huffingtonpost.com/robert-teitelman/transactions-feb-21-2011_b _825214.html.

Theriault, Reg. *How to Tell When You're Tired: A Brief Examination of Work*. New York: W. W. Norton, 1995.

———. *Longshoring on the San Francisco Waterfront*. San Pedro, CA: Singlejack, 1978.

———. *The Unmaking of the American Working Class*. New York: New Press, 2002.

Thompson, E. P. *The Making of the English Working Class*. London: Victor Gollancz, 1963.

Thompson, Leonard. *A History of South Africa*, 4th ed. Revised by Lynn Berat. New Haven, CT: Yale University Press, 2000.

Thorn, Hakan. *Anti-apartheid and the Emergence of a Global Civil Society*. New York: Palgrave Macmillan, 2006.

Toli, Robinduth. "The Origins of the Durban Strikes, 1973." MA thesis, University of Durban-Westville, 1991.

Tomkins, Calvin. "Profiles: The Creative Situation." *New Yorker*, January 7, 1967, 34.

Tsing, Anna. "Supply Chains and the Human Condition." *Rethinking Marxism* 21, no. 2 (2009): 148–76.

Turnbull, Peter. "Dock Strikes and the Demise of the Dockers' 'Occupational Culture.'" *Sociological Review* 40, no. 2 (1992): 294–318.

Tyrrell, Ian. "What Is Transnational History?" École des Hautes Études en Sciences Sociale, Paris, January 2007. https://iantyrrell.wordpress.com/what-is-transnational -history/.

Urbanus, Jason. "Rome's Imperial Port." *Archaeology*, February 10, 2015. www.archaeology .org/issues/168–1503/features/2971-rome-portus-rise-of-empire.

Vahed, Goolam H. "The Making of Indian Identity in Durban, 1914–1949." PhD diss., Indiana University, 1995.

———. "Power and Resistance: Indentured Labour in Colonial Natal, 1860–1911." *Man in India* 92, no. 2 (2012): 299–317.

———. "Segregation, Group Areas and the Creation of Chatsworth." In *Chatsworth*, edited by Ashwin Desai and Goolam Vahed, 19–30. Pietermaritzburg, S. Afr.: University of KwaZulu-Natal Press, 2013.

Van der Linden, Marcel. "Labour History: The Old, the New and the Global." *African Studies* 66, nos. 2–3 (2007): 169–80.

———. "On the Importance of Crossing Boundaries." *Labor History* 40, no. 3 (1999): 362–65.

———. "Transnationalizing American Labor History." *Journal of American History* 86, no. 3 (1999): 1078–92.

———. *Workers of the World: Essays toward a Global Labor History*. Leiden, Neth.: Brill, 2008.

Van der Walt, Lucien. "Anarchism and Syndicalism in an African Port City: The Revolutionary Traditions of Cape Town's Multiracial Working Class, 1904–1931." *Labor History* 52, no. 2 (2011): 137–71.

———. "Bakunin's Heirs in South Africa: Race and Revolutionary Syndicalism from the IWW to the International Socialist League, 1910—21." *Politikon* 31, no. 1 (2004): 67–89.

Van Onselen, Charles. *Chibaro: African Mine Labour in Southern Rhodesia, 1900–1933*. London: Pluto, 1976.

Vinson, Robert Trent. *The Americans Are Coming! Dreams of African American Liberation in Segregationist South Africa*. Athens: Ohio University Press, 2012.

Virtual Museum of the City of San Francisco. "From the 1820s to the Gold Rush." http://www.sfmuseum.org/hist1/early.html.

Von Holdt, Karl. *Transition from Below: Forging Trade Unionism and Workplace Change in South Africa*. Scottsville: University of KwaZulu-Natal Press, 2003.

Walsh, Margaret. "Gender in the History of Transportation Services: A Historiographical Perspective." *Business History Review* 81 (2007): 545–62.

Webster, Eddie. *Cast in a Racial Mode: Labour Process and Trade Unionism in the Foundries*. Johannesburg: Ravan, 1985.

———. The Impact of Intellectuals on the Labour Movement." *Transformation* 18 (1992): 88–92.

———. "Moral Decay and Social Reconstruction: Richard Turner and Radical Reform." *Theoria* 81/82 (October 1993): 1–13.

———. "Trade Unions and the Challenge of the Informalisation of Work." In *Trade Unions and Democracy: COSATU Workers' Political Attitudes in South Africa*, edited by Sakhela Buhlungu, 21–43. Pretoria: HSRC, 2006.

Webster, Eddie, and Judson Kuzwayo. "A Research Note on Consciousness and the Problem of Organization." In *Change, Reform and Economic Growth in South Africa*, edited by Lawrence Schlemmer and Eddie Webster, 224–38. Johannesburg: Ravan, 1977.

Weinhauer, Klaus. "Labour Market, Work Mentality and Syndicalism: Dock Labour in the United States and Hamburg, 1900–1950s." *International Review of Social History* 42, no. 2 (1997): 219–52.

———. "Power and Control on the Waterfront: Employment, Work and Industrial Relations in International Perspective." In *Dock Workers*, edited by Sam Davies et al., 2: 580–603.

Weintraub, Hyman. "Review of *Collective Bargaining and Productivity*, by Paul T. Hartman." *Pacific Northwest Quarterly* 62, no. 1 (1971): 43.

Weir, Stan. *Singlejack Solidarity*. Edited by George Lipsitz. Minneapolis: University of Minnesota Press, 2004.

Weiss, Holger. "International of Seamen and Harbour Workers and the 'Hands off Abyssinia' Campaign." European Social Science History Conference, Valencia, Spain, 2016. In possession of author.

———. "The International of Seamen and Harbour Workers—A Radical Global Labour Union of the Waterfront or a Subversive World-Wide Web?" In *International Communism and Transnational Solidarity: Radical Networks, Mass Movements and Global Politics, 1919–1939*, edited by Holger Weiss, 256–317. Leiden, Neth.: Brill, 2017.

Wellman, David T. *The Union Makes Us Strong: Radical Unionism on the San Francisco Waterfront.* New York: Cambridge University Press, 1995.

Western States Golf Association. "Western States Golf Association—57 Years Strong!" http://profileengine.com/groups/profile/430199328/western-states-golf-association -57-years-strong.

Will, George F. "A Faster Mousetrap: Review of *The One Best Way: Frederick Winslow Taylor and the Enigma of Efficiency,* by Robert Kanigel." *New York Times,* June 15, 1997.

Winter, Jennifer Marie. "Thirty Years of Collective Bargaining: Joseph Paul St. Sure, 1902–1966." MA thesis, California State University, Sacramento, 1991.

Wolf, Johanna. "Introduction: The State of the Art on Transnational Actors in Trade Union Movements." European Social Science History Conference, Valencia, Spain, 2016. In possession of author.

Wolpe, Harold. "Capitalism and Cheap Labour-Power: From Segregation to Apartheid." *Economy and Society* 1, no. 4 (1972): 425–56.

Wood, Geoffrey, Pauline Dibben, and Gilton Klerck. "The Limits of Transnational Solidarity: The Congress of South African Trade Unions and the Swaziland and Zimbabwean Crises." *Labor History* 54, no. 5 (2013): 527–39.

Woodard, Komozi. "Amiri Baraka, the Congress of African People, and Black Power Politics from the 1961 United Nations Protests to the 1972 Gary Convention." In *The Black Power Movement: Rethinking the Civil Rights–Black Power Era,* edited by Peniel Joseph, 55–77. New York: Routledge, 2006.

Woodrum, Robert. *"Everybody Was Black Down There": Race and Industrial Change in the Alabama Coalfields.* Athens: University of Georgia Press, 2007.

Wright, Larry. "Internationalism on the Waterfront." *LSM News* 14 (Fall 1977): 28–36.

Zieger, Robert. *The CIO, 1935–1955.* Chapel Hill: University of North Carolina Press, 1995.

Zonderman, David A. *Uneasy Allies: Working for Labor Reform in Nineteenth-Century Boston.* Amherst: University of Massachusetts Press, 2011.

INDEX

African Americans. *See* black international-ism; civil rights; civil-rights unionism; Great Migration; Pan-Africanism

African National Congress (ANC), 42, 44, 59, 88, 185. *See also* South African Congress of Trade Unions (SACTU)

American Committee on Africa (ACOA), 188–90

American Federation of Labor–Congress of Industrial Organizations (AFL-CIO): Cold War, 188; conflict with ILWU, 240n14; history of, 46, 221; race, 101, 195; Vietnam, 141

American Indians, 111

Angola, 55, 192, 205

anti-apartheid movement: ANC, 42, 44, 59, 88, 185; antipass law protests, 40–41; civil disobedience in DC, 181; divestment, 185–86, 199; global labor solidarity, 185; ILWU and, 105, 194; Local 10 actions, 189–200; Mozambique, 193; San Francisco Bay Area, 198–200; South Africa, 167, 190; tactics, 185–86; Zimbabwe, 183, 201. *See also* South African Congress of Trade Unions (SACTU)

anticommunism: Harry Bridges, 72–73, 105, 124; Archie Brown, 105; Local 10, protest-ing, 235n36; NAACP, 105; others in ILWU, 231n33; PMA, 124, 135; South Africa, 56–57, 64; inside US labor movement, 72–73

antipass law protests, 40–41

An Yue Jiang (ship), 182, 203, 205, 243n2

apartheid: Central Native Labour Board, 59–60; influx control, 57–58, 129–30; labor legislation, 86, 98, 129, 229n11; laws, 33, 41, 130; "quiet decade," 65, 85–88, 101, 115, 166. *See also* Bantu Labour Act; Group Areas Act

arbitration, 47–48

Arenstein, Rowley Israel, 58, 62

automation, 133, 136–40, 143–47, 158, 213–16. *See also* containerization; Mechanization and Modernization Agreement (M&M); technology

Badsha, Omar, 94

Bagwell, Alex: 1971–72 strike, 157; anti-apartheid movement, 197, 200; integrating Local 34, 80

Baldwin, James, 107

Bantu Labour Act (South Africa), 86, 129

Berkeley, CA, 24, 28–29, 198–99. *See also* Oakland; University of California, Berkeley

PETER COLE is a professor of history at Western Illinois University. He is the author of *Wobblies on the Waterfront: Interracial Unionism in Progressive-Era Philadelphia*.

THE WORKING CLASS IN AMERICAN HISTORY

The University of Illinois Press
is a founding member of the
Association of American University Presses.

Composed in 10.25/13 Marat Pro
with DIN Condensed and Gill Sans displays
by Lisa Connery
at the University of Illinois Press
Cover designed by Dustin J. Hubbart
Cover illustration: Durban dockworkers, ca. 1950. Photograph by
David Goldblatt. University of Witwatersrand Historical Papers,
Johannesburg. Image used with permission of David Goldblatt.

University of Illinois Press
1325 South Oak Street
Champaign, IL 61820-6903
www.press.uillinois.edu